INDIGENT OFFICERS

INDIGENT OFFICERS

Civil War Officers Rewarded by Charles II

The 1663 'Indigent Officers' List
Transcribed and Indexed

Edited by S.F. Jones

Tyger's Head Books

Published by Tyger's Head Books

Copyright ©Tyger's Head Books, 2015

All rights reserved. No part of this publication may be reproduced, stored in a retrieval system or transmitted in any form or by any means whatsoever without the prior written permission of Tyger's Head Books.

Typeset in Adobe Caslon Pro
Typesetting and cover design by Tyger's Head Books
Printed by Lightning Source UK Ltd
ISBN 978-1-909596-04-7

The publisher is not responsible for third-party URLs referenced in this book, and can make no guarantees in respect of their accuracy or continued availability.

Tyger's Head Books welcomes notice of errors in this volume.
See the website for information about our 'Bounty' system.

www.tygersheadbooks.co.uk
info@tygersheadbooks.co.uk

Contents

Editor's Note 2015	5
Preface 1663	7
Indigent Officers (layout as per 1663)	
Senior officers requesting inclusion	9
Officers by regiment	13
Stray officers (Horse)	157
Stray officers (Foot & Dragoons)	163
Sea captains	167
Auxiliary staff	169
Appendix I – Changes of regimental command	175
Appendix II – Brief statistics	181
Bibliography	183
Index	185

Editor's Note 2015

By an Act of 1662 King Charles II offered financial relief to former military officers and personnel who had fought for the Royalist side during the English Civil Wars. In 1663 the claimant names submitted, over 5,000 of them, were printed in pamphlet form: *A List of Officers Claiming to the Sixty Thousand Pounds, &c. Granted by His Sacred Majesty for the Relief of His Truly-Loyal and Indigent Party*. The pamphlet, generally known by historians as 'Indigent Officers', or 'I.O.', formed the basis of Stuart Reid's invaluable five volume *Officers and Regiments of the Royalist Army*, published in 1985. Reid rearranged the raw data, ironing out errors in the original and supplementing it with biographical information from other sources.

Unfortunately Reid's work has not been reprinted, and nowadays a full set of these fragile card and paper booklets is not easy to come by. Furthermore I.O. itself has never been reprinted in its raw state for modern researchers. This Tyger's Head Books edition aims to combine the best features of both: offering a straight transcription of I.O. as the data appears in the original, to allow researchers to see the raw data in a modern book, without any modern analysis or supposition imposed on it; and then to include a full index and some biographical data, in the manner of Reid. Unlike Reid's work, however, the focus of this edition is purely on I.O. and does not attempt to begin collating a wider Royalist army list: therefore it includes no names gathered beyond the original list.

This edition also takes a different approach to indexing the officers' names. Reid does not seem to have had a copy of the original document's index; when compiling his own, he indexed individuals in sections, according to their rank, but that method does not account for officers being mentioned more than once but with different ranks, by subordinates who fought under them at different times; therefore one officer could be mistakenly recorded as two individuals. Neither does it allow a clear understanding of the scale of involvement of larger families such as the Byrons, Erringtons, and Fenwicks, who supplied many members to the King's cause. This edition contains only one alphabetic index, which immediately indicates where an officer has been mentioned several times, clarifying the course of his career, and indicates a family's military presence. It also makes evident potential duplicates and errors in the original text. As the purpose of the original document was only to show which men had claimed relief, its index did not include officers mentioned by their subordinates but who had not claimed themselves. All 'mentioned' officers are now indexed in this edition. Furthermore, this edition includes the names of the many men with auxiliary positions such as commissaries, engineers, scoutmasters etc. who were included in 1663 but omitted by Reid for lack of space, and those whose names were submitted late to the printer and were only included in a section at the end of the pamphlet. The original document contained an extensive list of errata, which have also been actioned here.

Senior officers in the list at the beginning of the pamphlet were evidently still alive in 1662-1663, as they specifically applied to be included; conversely, as noted, in the body of the list many men are mentioned by a claimant but did not claim themselves. This does not mean they were deceased: many were provably still living at the time. Whilst some with existing incomes did not qualify for relief (see Appendix II), others may have chosen not to claim or did not hear about the scheme in time, or in the case of colonels had perhaps held a regiment in name only, delegating field command to someone else.

To provide the raw data part of this edition, the information has been transcribed directly from a copy of the original document. To avoid making unresearched assumptions about identity, spellings are left strictly 'as is' unless there is an obvious printing error or the index reveals the correct name. Punctuation has been corrected and modernised. Abbreviated names have been lengthened (e.g. 'Thos.' to Thomas), unless the first name is unclear (e.g. 'Edw.' could be Edward or Edwin; 'Jo.' could be John, Joseph, Josiah; 'Matth.' could be Matthew or Matthias, etc.). The only deliberate omission is the original index, which of course is only relevant to the pagination of the original document, and is replaced by the index relating specifically to this republication.

Notation

As the original document explains (see 'Advertisement' in the original preface below), it used particular formatting, fonts and symbols to alert the reader to particular information. To present the data as originally intended, and to keep something of the feel of the original, these conventions have been preserved.

- **A dagger** † denotes that the individual gave no company/troop/regiment. However, the original document often applies this incorrectly.
- **The county** inserted on the left is where the man registered for his bounty.
- **Men bracketed together** claimed from the same troop or company.
- **L. & W.** means the officer claimed from 'London & Westminster'.
- **(In this edition) square brackets around a space [   ]** indicate that the regiment's arm was omitted for all officers in both the original list, and the original index. Where an officers' arm is revealed in the index, but not in the main list, that information is used to correct the entries for his entire regiment.
- **(In this edition) [Information in square brackets]** is supplied by other sources.

The original displays some ranks in 𝔅𝔩𝔞𝔠𝔨𝔩𝔢𝔱𝔱𝔢𝔯, to denote 'The first of Every Degree, or Quality of Command'; however it applies this inconsistently in places, so it is not clear whether 'first' refers to those literally placed first in the list, or those highest in rank within a company/troop. However, as the aim of this edition is to offer the data 'as is', Blackletter has been applied as in the original, with a flag of caution raised to readers.

It appears that I.O.'s index was compiled separately to the main text, as it uses different spellings. Where spellings vary, the modern index gives the name as it appears in the original list body, followed by the version in the original index, e.g. Barret/Barrett.

This edition adds one final convention. Many regiments changed their commanders, and thus 1663 claimants originating in the same regiment frequently claimed under different men. Whilst Reid grouped all claimants of a regiment together, regardless of commander, this edition lists everyone as per the original document. However where regimental commanders changed, a star * next to their names indicates that the reader should refer to the list of changes of regimental command in Appendix I, to seek out other men in the same regiment.

Preface 1663

Whereas in consideration of many Worthy persons brought into great Distress for their fidelity to the Crown; and at the Request of the Lords Spiritual and Temporal, and Commons assembled in Parliament, His sacred Majesty has been graciously pleased to Enact the Summe of Threescore thousand Pounds, together with the product of a Tax upon Offices, to be distributed amongst Such Truly Loyal and Indigent Officers who have had Real Command of Soldiers according to their Several Commissions, and who have never Deserted His Majesty nor his Blessed fathers Service During the late times of Rebellion and Usurpation, and who have not a sufficient Livelyhood of their own: nor have since His Majesties Return obtained any Reward, Office or Imployment sufficient for a Livelyhood by such Wayes, Means and Propositions as in the Act before mentioned are Directed and Appointed.

And for as much as the Honorable the Commissioners appointed by Act of Parliament for Distribution of the said Moneys, are upon good Grounds perswaded to believe, that many Certificates have been unduly Introduc'd, whereby not only every mans Share will be lessened, through the Multitude of Pretenders; but without a Strict and Accurate Inspection, a great part of the Moneys will fall into wrong hands.

Upon Consideration hereof, and to the End that all possible Right be done, as well to the Pious and Bountiful Intentions of His Sacred Majesty, as to the honourable wants of His Loyal Servants, the Commissioners aforesaid have resolv'd upon a Printed List of the Persons Certif'd, as the most apt Expedient for the Discovery of any Fraud, or Imposture. Persuant to which Resolve, is This Publication; wherein, to render the Inspection more Obvious, and Easie, Every Officer is Exhibited in his proper Regiment, Quality and County (so far at least as may be gathered from his Certificate) In which Proceeding, as the Commissioners themselves have done Their part, to the Utmost of their Skill and Industry, So they doubt not but all other persons of Justice, Honour, and Loyalty will Contribute their Aid likewise, to so Pious and Publique a Work. With Caution, that a Singular Regard be had to all Circumstances of Order, Modesty, and Prudence, befitting the Dignity of the Matter in question.

To which purpose, and for prevention of those Inconveniences which commonly Attend the Unbounded Motions of Prejudice, Passion, and Clamour, the Commissioners aforesaid have thought fit to Publish This Advertisement; that (with respect to all other ways of Fair and Undeniable proof) the Manner which is most Agreeable to their Opinions and Desires, will be This, that all Informations may be first Delivered in to some Commissioners Residing in the County, where such Informations arise, who may be Desired to transmit them to some Other Commissioner of the same Body, and serving for the same County, then Resident in London, by him to be Recommended to the Consideration of the Commissioners sitting in the Star-chamber, &c. Who shall thereupon proceed according to the Strictest Rules of Equity and Tenderness: For They do further Declare, that it is not their Aim, to pinch upon Niceties, to the Disadvantage of any Worthy person; But to doe His Majesty a Service, in the Detection of palpable Confederacies; to doe the Truly Loyal and Indigent Party, Justice, in Distributing among Them alone, that which the King has Intended only to them; And finally, to doe Themselves a Right, in Manifesting to the World that they have done their Duty.

ADVERTISEMENT

For the better Effect of this following List of Officers, some Light should be properly given Concerning the Order of it: Let it be therefore Observ'd, that

The Persons Certifi'd, are Printed in a Small Letter, Close to the Rule, with their Surnames foremost; and the Place or County whence they are Certifi'd, in the Margin, (where Note, that L&W stand for London and Westminster) The Officers, under whose Command or Regiment They enter themselves, are Express'd in a Larger Character, and in the Middle of the Columne, over the Heads of Them: Which Chief Officers are Placed Alphabetically, and Dispos'd (together with Such as Claim under them) in their several Inclosures. To the first Officer of every Distinct Denomination (unless it be the Printers fault) is Joyn'd in Capitals either HORSE, FOOT, or DRAGOONS according to his Command; and that Mark serves for all Inferiour Officers till another Distinction. The first of Every Degree, or Quality of Command, is Noted with an English Letter; as **Cap. Lieut. Ens.** &c.[1] and so far as the Certificates will bear it, Every man is set down in his proper Regiment, and Troop or Company: but where any Officer, under the Degree of a Captain, Mentions the Regiment he Serv'd in, without saying in which particular Troop or Company, That Defect is signifi'd by a Cross, or Dagger added to his Name;[2] and so likewise, where a Captain Renders himself Only under the Command of some General Officer, without Naming the Regiment. Where Two, or Three, or More Officers are link'd together (with a Brace, as they call it) Those Officers are understood to Claim to the same Troop or Company.

Touching the Different and Ill-spelling of several Names, It can only be said, that the Clerks that Drew the Certificates were none of the best Heralds; and save in Case of Manifest Errour, the Transcriber durst not vary from his Copy.

In a Work of this Nature Many Slips are to be born with and expected; but in Truth not altogether so many, as the Printer (of the first Half Especially) has Committed, (unless the Confusion and Disorder of his Copy may serve him for an Excuse) And therein to help him, It must be Confess'd that the last Resolve of Printing only such Field-Officers Names as should Desire it, left him a very Hazzardous Copy. For in the first Draught, all Field-Officers as well as Others were Ranged in their proper Places; and the Removal of those Officers had an Influence upon the Coherence of All the Rest (Contingently subjecting the Business both to Delay and Mistake.)

The Errata are placed at the End of the Book; and it is left to the Reader to distinguish betwixt the Errors of the Method, and Those of the Press. So many of the Field-Officers (as being within distance of giving timely notice) have enter'd their desires to be inserted; are (according to direction) dispos'd of in the Front of the Book; and their Names, and Qualityes, are as follows.

---

[1] As per the foregoing Editor's Note, the original document applies this font use inconsistently: readers should exercise caution.
[2] This notation is also applied inconsistently.

Senior officers requesting inclusion

Collonels
Ashby, Godfrey Coll. H.
Burgesse, Francis Coll. F.
Cardiffe, Thomas Coll. F.
Cary, Sir Henry Coll. H. & F.
Cary, Sir Horatio Coll. H.
Cary, Theodore Coll. F.
Chamberlayn, William Coll. H.
Chapman, Edmund Coll. H.
Chester, Henry Coll. H. & F.
Collins, Degory Coll. F.
Crofts, Robert Coll. F.
Crow, Henry Coll. Dr.
Dymock, Cressy Coll. H.
Egerton, Richard Coll. H. & F.
Gerard, Edward Coll. F.
Hay, James Coll. Dr.
Holtby, Marmaduke Coll. H. & F.
Le Hunt, Sir John Coll. F.
Lucas, Sir Gervase Coll. H. & F.
Napier, Thomas Coll. F.
Prestwich, Sir Thomas Coll. H. & F.
St. Leger, Sir Anthony Coll. H.
Stuart, William Coll. Dr.
Trafford, Francis Coll. H.
Walsh, Sir Robert Coll. H.
Wintour, William Coll. F.

Lieut. Collonels
Bardsey, James L. Coll. F.
Collins, Thomas L. Coll. F.
Conyngsby, Thomas L. Coll. F.
Day, Philip L. Coll. Dr.
Deane, William L. Coll. H
Egerton, Thomas L. Coll. H.
Eyton, Edward L. Coll. H
Forbes, Alexander L. Coll. F.
Gerard, Edw. Coll. F.
Gibson, Thomas L. Coll. Dr.
Gordon, James L. Coll. Dr.
Gwillim, George L. Coll. F.

Gwinn, George L. Coll. F.
Heveningham, Simon L. Coll. F.
Leigh, Urian L. Coll. F.
Leighton, Sir William L. Coll. F.
Lowe, Hercules L. Coll. H.
Luntly, John L. Coll. H
Mackmoyler, Richard L. Coll. H.
Marks, Robert L. Coll. H.
Merydale, Richard L. Coll. F.
Meautys, John L. Coll. F.
Musgrave, Henry L. Coll. H.
Parry, Owen L. Coll. F.
Pell, Sir Bartholomew L. Coll. F.
Pilkington, Henry L. Coll. Dr.
Robinson, Daniel L. Coll. F.
Roe, Francis L. Coll. F.
Ross, William L. Coll. F.
St. Clare, William L. Coll. F.
Salkield, George L. Coll. F.
Sandys, Dudly L. Coll. H.
Smith, Paul L. Coll. H.
Stradling, Thomas L. Coll. F.
Wigmore, Richard L. Coll. F.
Wigmore, Robert L. Coll. H.

Majors
Bermingham, John M. H.
Beversham, John M. H.
Bradbury, Henry M. F.
Bufkin, Lewin M. F.
Bywaters, Thomas M. F.
Constable, Ralph M. H.
Conyers, Thomas M. Dr.
Cornwallis, Francis M. H.
Cromwell, Gregory M. H. & Adjut. Gen.
Dennis, Godfrey M. H.
Dewit, Cornelius M. H.
Downing, Thomas M. F.
Fines, Norris M. H.
Floyd, Matthias M. F.
Floyd, William M. F.
Gordon, James M. F.
Green, Edmund M. F.

Senior Officers Requesting Inclusion

Grey, Andrew M. H.
Hacker, Rowland M. H.
Haslewood, John M. H.
Haswel, James M. H.
Huddleston, Edward M. F.
Hughes, John M. F.
Jones, Richard M. F.
Kirk, Charles M. F.
Le Neve, Thomas M. F.
Lorymer, Roger M. F.
Lyne, Aeneas M. F.
Mason, Michael M. Dr.
Mason, Thomas M. H.
Molineux, Prestland M. H.
Moore, Daniel M. F.
Norwood, Charles M. F.
Prestwich, Thomas M. H.
Price, Morgan M. F.
Price, Richard M. F.
Pudsay, Peter M. H.
Raynger, Francis M. F.
Roche, Adam M. F.
Rossiter, John M. F.
Rustat, Robert M. F.
Salway, Thomas M. F.
Skirrow, Robert M. F.
Trevillian, Peter M. F.
Walters, Edmund M. F.
Woodward, Richard M. F.
Worsopp, Walter M. F.

Officers by regiment

Ackland, Sir John [Prince Charles's regiment]
Sussex	White, Thomas **Lieut**. HORSE, to Maj. Thomas Cary
Devon	Chanon, William **Capt**. FOOT
	Blewet, William Capt.
	Shobrooke, John **Lieut**. to Capt. William Reeves
Somerset	Rottenbury, John Lieut. to Capt. Simon Weekes
Cornwall	Roberts, John Lieut. †
	Blake, William Lieut. †
	Gage, John **Ens**. †
Devon	Upton, John **Quart**.

Ancthill, William
Somerset	Harrison, Lionel **Cor**. HORSE, to Ca. Ancthill

Anderson, Sir Francis*
Durham	Tayler, John **Capt**. ⎫
	Tayler, Ralph Lieut. ⎬ HORSE
	Preston, John Cor. ⎭
	Jackson, Thomas Capt.
York	Leighton, Robert **Lieut**. ⎫ To Lt. Col. George Tonge
Durham	Dobson, Robert Quart. ⎭
	Machell, Marmaduke Lieut. ⎫ To Maj. Sam Davison
	Teasdel, Robert. Quart. ⎭
Westmo.	Sandford, Edmund Lieut. to Capt. Kirkbride
Durham	Trollop, William. **Cor**.
	Johnson, Thomas Cor. to Capt. Richard Cole
Newcastle	Hodgeson, Leonard Cor. †
Essex	Haggerston, George Cor. †
Northumb.	Spoore, Anthony **Quart**. to Capt. Francis Read
Durham	Unthank, John Quart. †

Appleyard, Sir Matthew*
L. & W.	Tirwhytt, John **Capt**. FOOT
	Thomson, James **Lieut**. to M. Palmer

Apsley, Sir Allen*
L. & W.	Walker, Thomas **Capt**. FOOT
	Nokes, Richard Capt.
	Oneale, Hugh Capt.

	Phillips, Rice Capt.
Middlesex	Hambden, John Capt.
Oxon	Aston, James Capt.
Cornwall	Sheeres, George Capt.
Devon	Richards, Richard Capt.
	Rowcliffe, Roger Capt.
	Ivat, Thomas Capt.
Somerset	Hobbs, William **Capt. Lieut.**
Devon	Poyntz, Edward Lieut. to Capt. Francis Morley
L. & W.	Foster, Thomas Lieut.
Cornwall	Meager, Gilbert Lieut. †
Dorset	Chetmell, Arthur Lieut. †
Devon	Shapcote Philip **Ens**. to Capt. Henry Southcot
	Stukely John Ens. †
Wilts	Langford, Thomas **Quart.**
Devon	March, Nicholas Quart. HORSE, to Maj. St. Leger

Apsley, James

Carmarth.	Farmer, William **Lieut.** FOOT to Capt. Henry Chichester
Devon	Bayly, Thomas Lieut. †
	Leay, John **Quart.** HORSE †

Apsley, John

Sussex	Booker, Richard **Capt. Lieut.** HORSE

Arundell, John[3]

Devon	Hernaman, Richard **Lieut.** HORSE †
Cornwall	Allen, Leonard Lieut. †
	Courtenay, William Lieut. †
	Hawes, Reynold **Cor**. †
	Dinham, John **Quart.** †
	Huddy, John Quart. †
Cornwall	Blewitt, Richard **Capt.** FOOT
	Kempson, George Capt.
	Courtenay, Reskemmer Capt.
	Courtenay, Peter Capt.
	Zacherly, Sampson Capt.
	Collings, George Capt.
	Lyne, Richard **Lieut.** †
	Whare, Samuel Lieut. †
	Jewell, Joseph Lieut. †

---

[3] Reid notes that two colonels are involved here: Colonel John 'Jack' Arundell commanded the foot, which formed Pendennis garrison; the horse belonged to his son, another Colonel John, killed at Plymouth in 1644.

Simons, Thomas Lieut. †
Hittson, John Lieut. †
Nance, William Lieut. †
Twiggs, Francis Lieut. †
Hallamore, John Lieut. †
Pierce, John Ens. to Lieut. Col. Robinson
Bawden, William Ens. †
Chegwin, Thomas Ens. †
Edwards, Edward Ens. †
Sands, Richard Ens. †
Sands, John Ens. †
Maine, William Ens. †
Treglawne, Matthew Ens. †

Arundell, Richard
Cornwall

Gully, Francis Capt. FOOT
Blight, John Capt.
Courtenay, Peter Capt.
Keat, Ralph Lieut. †
Wyat, Thomas Lieut. †
Petegrew, Nicholas Lieut. †
Cooke, Nathaniel Lieut. †
Polsue, Peter Lieut. †
Kestell, Thomas Lieut. †
Carne, Thomas Ens. †
Pierce, Richard Ens. †
Williams, George Ens. †
Dunkin, William Ens. †
Tucker, Joseph Ens. †

Arundell, William
Cornwall Spry, John Lieut. FOOT, to Maj. Phil. Dart
Devon Ford, Gilbert Ens. to Maj. John Spry

Ashburnham, William
L. & W.

Richardson, John Capt. FOOT
Tart, Christopher Lieut. to Capt. James Hussy

Somerset Keymor, Lionell Lieut. †
Dorset Hoskins, James Lieut. †
Christopher, Thomas Lieut. †
French, Giles Ens. to Capt. John Richardson
Hill, William Quart. † HORSE

Ashly-Cooper, Lord
Somerset   Weston, Cornelius Lieut. FOOT
Dorset   Hodder, Fabian Lieut. to Capt. James Geare
            Hodder, John Ens. to Capt. John Cade

Astley, Lord [Sir Jacob Astley]*
Hereford   Coningsby, Thomas Lieut. Col. ⎫ FOOT
            Coningsby, Fitzwilliam Lieut. ⎭

L. & W.   Gore, Matthew Capt. ⎫
            Bowles, Francis Lieut. ⎭

Surrey   Bray, Edward Capt. ⎫
L. & W.   Fawkett, George Lieut. ⎭
Warwick   Parker, Edmund Capt. †
            Loveday, John Lieut. †

Somerset   Keymor, John Ens. †
Stafford   Hickin, Samuel Ens. †

Berks   Whitehead, Francis Capt. HORSE

Astley, Sir Bernard
L. & W.   Chapman, Richard Capt. FOOT
Sussex   Wivall, Duke Capt.
Somerset   Bridges, Edward Capt.
            Hart, Thomas Lieut. to Capt. William Pearsons
            Fry, Thomas Ens. to Maj. Thomas Simmons
            Bull, Robert Ens. to Capt. Thomas Pitman

Aston, Sir Arthur*
Oxon   Hildsly, William Lieut. HORSE, to Maj. Bunkly
L. & W.   Byrd, Theophilus Lieut. †
Stafford   Hinton, Roger Cor. to Capt. Richard Egerton
L. & W.   Deschato, John Cor. to Sir Tho. Hooper

Berks   Stamp, John Capt. FOOT
Hertford   Thomas, John Lieut. to Capt. Ralph Clark
Middlesex   Baldwyn, Thomas Lieut. ⎫
L. & W.   Fox, John Ens. ⎭ To Maj. Bagnall

            Prichard, Robert Lieut. ⎫
Bucks   Tyrringham, Oliver Ens. ⎬ To Capt. William Allen
L. & W.   Baston, John Ens. ⎭
Bucks   Goodridge, Arthur Lieut. ⎫
            Dowset, John Ens. ⎭ To Capt. Scot
L. & W.   Dangerfield, Fulk Lieut. †
Surrey   Stevens, Robert Ens. to Capt. George Tettershall
L. & W.   Wall, James Ens. to Capt. Robert Hunt

Aston, Lord [Walter Aston, Lord Aston of Forfar]
Stafford	Collier, Francis **Capt. Lieut.** ⎱ HORSE
	Jefferyes, Thomas Cor. ⎰
	Gaywood, Laurence **Lieut.** to Capt. T. Gaywood
Worcester	Marshal, Walter **Cor.** to Lieut. Col. Peters
Gloucester	Coster, John **Quart.**

Aston, Sir Thomas
Lancaster	Haulgh, Robert **Lieut.** HORSE ⎱ To Sir William Ratcliffe
L. & W.	Hanslop, Thomas. Cor. ⎰
Wilts	Anne, Thomas Lieut. to Lieut. Col. Egerton
York	Wright, Robert Lieut.
Kent	Short, Thomas Lieut. †
L. & W.	Starky, Edw. Lieut. †
Chester	Wright, Robert Lieut. †
Lancaster	Mason, Robert **Cor.**
Chester	French, Hugh **Quart.** to Capt. Flemming
	Grosvenor William Quart.
Montgom.	Thomas, John Quart. to Lieut. Col. Bridgeman
L. & W.	Mason, Michael **Maj.** ⎱ DRAGOONS
	White, George Lieut. ⎰
	Newland, Thomas **Capt.**
Chester	Starky, Thomas Capt. †
L. & W.	Eldridge, John **Lieut.** to Capt. Thomas Salway

Aston, Ralph
L. & W.	Spencer, John **Capt.** HORSE
Derby	Alsop, Thomas **Quart.** to Capt. Wiltshire

Atkins, Jonathan
L. & W.	Wincheppe, Roger **Capt.** FOOT
	Mottershed, Thomas **Lieut.** to Maj. John Errington

Ayliffe, William
L. & W.	Skirrow, Robert **Maj.** FOOT
Essex	Rules, Robert **Ens.**

Bagott, Harvey*
Stafford	Startin, Timothy **Capt. Lieut.** FOOT
L. & W.	Wadeson, Thomas **Lieut.** †
York	Byrd, James **Ens.**
Salop	Buckeridge, Ralph Ens. to Capt. Francis Collier
Stafford	Wilks, John Quart.
	Horsman, Thomas Quart.

Bagott, Sir Richard*
L. & W.	Underhill, Thomas **Lieut**. HORSE, to Capt. Rugely †
	Million, Lewis Lieut. †
Derby	Roade, John Lieut. †
Stafford	Beardmore, Walter Lieut. †
L. & W.	Scudamore, Vincent **Cor**. to Capt. W. Gibbons
Warwick	Chiles, Edw. Cor. †
Stafford	Wilcox, Robert **Quart**. ⎫
Salop	Keene, John Quart. ⎬ To Maj. William Warner
Stafford	Barlow, Thomas Quart. †
	Haddock, Walter Quart. †
L. & W.	Bodeley, William **Capt**. FOOT
Stafford	East, Michael **Lieut**. to Capt. Hugh Henne
	Blenkhorne, Robert Lieut. to Capt. Anthony Dyott
	Walmsly, Richard Lieut. †
	Bakewell, Zach. **Ens**. to Capt. Zach. Turnpenny
	Petty, Walter Ens. †
Berks	Eaman, Timothy **Cor**. DRAGOONS

Baker, Francis
L. & W.	Beck, Thomas **Capt**. FOOT & DRAGOONS
Salop	Compton, John **Quart**. FOOT

Bale, William
Leicester	Musson, William **Cor**. HORSE
	Pippin, Matthew **Quart**.

Bampfield, Joseph
L. & W.	James, William **Capt**. FOOT
Somerset	Walsh, Thomas Capt.
	Bonvill, John Capt.
Wilts	Bayly, William Capt.
Devon	Green, Humphrey **Ens**. to Capt. Richard Carr
Somerset	Danyell, John Ens. †
	Body, George Ens. †

Bampfield
Warwick	Waad, John **Cor**. HORSE to. Maj. Peter Hagedot

Bard, Lord
Northumb.	Lawson, John **Capt. Lieut**. FOOT
Durham	Richardson, Henry **Ens**. to Capt. John Errington

Barlow, John
Carmarth.	Thomas, William **Cor**. HORSE
Pembroke	Rossant, Francis Cor. to Capt. Addys

Barnard, John
L. & W.	Pickering John **Capt. Lieut**. HORSE
L. & W.	Brisco, John **Capt**. FOOT
Worcester	Harris, Thomas **Quart**. to Maj. Thomas Jennings

Barnes, George
L. & W.	Bardsey, James **Lieut. Col**. FOOT
Dorset	Williams, Henry **Capt**.
Wilts	Pope, Jeffery **Lieut**. to Capt. Thomas Pierce
Dorset	Morton, Henry Lieut. †
Cornwall	Guy, Charles Lieut. †
L. & W.	Bush, Nicholas **Ens**.

Basset, Sir Arthur
L. & W.	Baker, Robert **Lieut**. FOOT, to Maj. George Berridge
York	Corpes, Edward Lieut. to Capt. William Pennyman
Cornwall	Barnes, Nicholas Lieut. †
	Bray, Joseph Lieut. †
Durham	Hedworth, William **Ens**. to Capt. Ralph Selby
Devon	Whitfield, David **Quart**.

Basset, Sir Thomas*
Cornwall	Hawk, Josias **Capt**. HORSE
	Hawk, Nicholas Lieut.
	Good, Walter Quart.
	Whare, John Capt.
	Knight, William Lieut.
	Martin, James Cor.
	Mill, Richard Quart.
	Hawes, Nicholas Capt.
	Noy, William Capt.
Somerset	Byam, Laurence **Lieut**. †
Cornwall	Barrett, Lewis Lieut. †
	Hawes, Thomas Lieut. †
	Hearle, Francis Lieut. †
	Robins, William **Cor**. †
	Richards, Robert Cor. †
	Saul, Richard Cor. †
L. & W.	Jewel, John **Quart**. to Lieut. Col. Arundell
Cornwall	Lawlyn, Bartholomew Quart. to Maj. Polwheele

	Smith, William Quart. †
	Spry, Richard Quart. †
Kent	Fairbrother, Anthony Quart.
L. & W.	Rossiter, John 𝔐aj. ⎫ FOOT
	Rossiter, William Lieut. ⎭
Cornwall	Tregone, Reignald **Capt**.
	Bond, William Capt.
	Jenkin, Patrick Capt.
Durham	Stuart, Alexander **Capt. Lieut**.
Cornwall	Giddy, William Lieut. †
Essex	Hele, Philip **Ens**. to Capt. Henry Bidlake
Cornwall	Bawden, Tobias Ens. †
	Rawling, John Quart. †
Cornwall	Penfound, Arthur Capt. DRAGOONS

Bath, Earl of [Sir John Grenville]*

Dorset	Hore, John **Capt**. FOOT
Cornwall	Greenvile, Chammon Capt.
	Plumly, John Capt. ⎫
	Elliot, John Ens. ⎭
	Matthew, John **Lieut**. to Lieut. Col. Rosecarrock
	Hugh, Thomas Lieut. to Lieut. Col. Pomeroy
Devon	Bissett, Tristram Lieut. †
Cornwall	Bissett, Tristram Lieut.
	Tucker, Mark Lieut. †
	Leatherden Hugh Lieut. †
	Winslade, James Lieut. †
	Lower, Thomas Lieut. †
	Tyack, Wilden Lieut. †
L. & W.	Reardan, Aeneas Lieut.
Cornwall	Hoskins, Thomas **Ens**. †
	Clark, John Ens. †
	Hodge, Peter Ens. †
	Eedy, John Ens. †
	Pethick, John Ens. †
	Heddon, Edmund Ens. †
	Olyvy, Richard **Quart**.

Bawds, Maurice

Lincoln	Rickitt, George **Lieut**. † HORSE
	Wattson, John **Cor**.

Baynes, John [1651]
L. & W.	Baynes, John **Capt**. HORSE
	Pooly, William **Cor**. to Lieut. Col. Baynes
Oxon	Wise, Edw. **Lieut**. FOOT to Capt. Charnock

Beard, Richard*
L. & W.	Porter, Andrew **Capt**. ⎫ FOOT
	West, William Lieut. ⎬
	Long, Richard Ens. ⎭
	Rainsford, Francis Capt.
	Hicks, John Capt.
Monmouth	Morgan, Thomas **Capt. Lieut**.
Norfolk	King, Thomas **Lieut**. ⎫ To Lt. Col. Bagaley
L. & W.	Kelly, John **Ens**. ⎭
	Badger, Thomas Ens. to Capt. James Huddleston
	Cox, Richard Ens.
	Smith, William Ens. to Maj. Timothy Blencow
	Mand, George **Quart**.

Beaumont, Sir John*
Stafford	Fleetwood, Robert **Capt**. FOOT
	Dormer, Anthony Capt.

Beddingfield, Thomas
Lincoln	Hardy, John **Lieut**. FOOT ⎫ To Capt. H. Bradbury
Middlesex	Yarmouth, Edmund **Ens**. ⎭
L. & W.	Cocker, Edward. Ens. to Capt. Edw. Styles
Norfolk	Okelly, Daniel Ens. †
L. & W.	Blundell, Edmund **Quart**. HORSE

Beeton
L. & W.	Hawley, William **Lieut. Col**. FOOT
	Lowick, Thomas Lieut. to Capt. Thomas Eyre

Belassis, Lord*
L. & W.	Standen, Griffith **Capt**. HORSE
York	Thompson, Michael Capt. ⎫
	Pearson, John Lieut. ⎬
Nottingh.	Cade, John Quart. ⎭
York	Wise, Metcalf Capt. ⎫
	Syley, Robert Lieut. ⎭
Durham	Cholmeley, Richard Capt.

L. & W.	Lasenby, Edw. Capt. ⎫
York	Thornton, William Lieut. ⎬
	Tayler, William **Capt. Lieut.**
L. & W.	Thornly, Richard **Cor**.
	Rockly, Toby Cor. to Capt. John Crossland
Durham	Ily, Thomas Cor.
York	Dawson, Anthony Cor. to Capt. George Dawson
	Scafe, Peter **Quart**.
Lincoln	Hughes, Richard Quart. to Capt. John Coot †
L. & W.	Monck, Thomas **Capt**. FOOT
	Woolverston, John Capt.
York	Trueman, William Capt.
	Gower, Doyly Capt.
Lincoln	Booth, Thomas Capt. †
York	Milner, John **Lieut**. ⎫ To Lt. Col. Henry Darcy
	Harrison, Michael Ens. ⎬
	Nodding, John Lieut. to Capt. David Gore
	Fosse, James Lieut. ⎫ To Capt. Alphonso Thwing
	Dickenson, Robert Ens. ⎬
	Orrey, John Lieut. to Capt. Robert Gale
L. & W.	Swale, Thomas **Ens**. to Maj. John Hillyard
Essex	Sawkins, Richard Ens. †
York	Geldart, William Ens. to Capt. John Pollock
	Chambers, John Ens. to Maj. William Booth

Bellingham, Sir Henry

L. & W.	Bagaley, Humphrey **Capt**. ⎫ FOOT
	Bagaley, Simon Lieut. ⎬
Westmo.	Prissoe, Richard Capt.
	Guy, William Capt.
Norfolk	Thurston, Hamon Capt.
Westmo.	Preston, Anthony **Lieut**. ⎫ To Capt. Orbel
	Briggs, Edward Ens. ⎬
	Bayly, Giles Lieut. †
	Tayler, Bryan Lieut. †
Cumberl.	Churnel, Francis Lieut.
L. & W.	Anderson, Peregrine Lieut. to Capt. Giles
Stafford	Sharp, John **Ens**. to Maj. Thomas Glasier
Westmo.	Hunter, Francis Ens. †
	Beck, John Ens. to Capt. Peter Shepheard
	Rose, Gerard Ens. to Capt. Prissoe

Bennet, Sir Humphrey

Southam.	Love, Robert **Capt.** HORSE
	Allwin, John Capt.
	Munday, William Capt.
Berks	Young, William **Lieut.** to Lieut. Col. Daniel
L. & W.	Hunt, Edw. Lieut. †
Bucks	Aris, Nicholas **Cor.** to Capt. Allen
Southam.	Whistler, John Cor. †
	Drewit, John **Quart.**
Wilts	Mallory, Robert Quart. to Maj. Hunt
Southam.	Knight, Francis **Capt.** FOOT
Middlesex	Knipe, Francis Capt.
Southam.	South, Edw. Capt.
	Manwaring, John Capt. ⎫
	Atthow, William Ens. ⎭
Durham	Tayler, Christopher **Lieut.** to Capt. John Knight
Southam.	Mew, John **Ens.** †

Berkly, Sir Edward

Somerset	Reynolds, Peter **Ens.** FOOT to Capt. Norton
	Owen, Thomas **Quart.**

Berkly, Lord John

L. & W.	Paganuzzi, Daniel **Capt.** HORSE
Wilts	Gouldsborough, Robert Capt.
Devon	County, Peter Capt.
Somerset	Court, Edw. Capt. ⎫
Devon	Eveleigh, Miles Quart. ⎭
	Fulford, William Capt. ⎫
	Battyn, Christopher Lieut. ⎬
	Mawditt, John Cor. ⎭
	Chamberlayn, Joshua Capt. †
	Awbry, Thomas Capt. †
Cornwall	Burrel, Benjamin Capt.
	Wills, John **Lieut.** to Capt. Sampson Manaton
Devon	Isaac, Erasmus Lieut. to Capt. William Ellesden
	Earl, Henry Lieut. to Maj. Henry Little
Somerset	Court, Henry Lieut. †
Cornwall	Tudor, William Lieut. †
Devon	Cake, Roger Lieut. †
Somerset	Alford, William **Cor.** ⎫ To Capt. Gregory Alford
	Serry, Mark Quart. ⎭
Devon	Jenkins, Thomas Cor. ⎫ To Capt. William Ash
	Sweet, Nathaniel Quart. ⎭

Somerset	Lasenby, Edw. Quart. to Capt. Edw. Berkly	
Devon	Farrant, Nathaniel Quart. to Capt. William Cokayn	
Cornwall	Lobb, Nathan Quart. to Capt. John Wills	
Somerset	Hambridge, Henry Quart. to Capt. Compton	

L. & W.   Yeo, Robert **Capt.**   } FOOT
Devon   Gorford, Richard Ens. }
Kent   Beales, Francis Capt.
Devon   Powell, David Capt.
               Robinson, Nicholas Capt. }
                 Palmer, Richard Ens. }
               Burt, Edward Capt.
               Prym, Thomas Capt.
               Browning, Mark Capt. }
                 Carter, Robert Lieut. }
               Eveleigh, John Capt.
               Eveleigh, George Capt.
               Webber, Robert Capt.
               Box, Thomas Capt. †
Norfolk   Skottow, Robert **Lieut.** }
Cornwall   Glover, Robert Lieut. } To Maj. J. Fletcher
L. & W.   Viguers, John Lieut. to Capt. Hoddenot
Devon   Vile, John Lieut.
               Maddock, John Lieut. } To Capt. William Webb
               Varley, William Ens. }
               Blechenden, Robert Lieut. to Capt. Phil. Shapcote
               Jordan, Samuel Lieut. to Capt. William Billet
               Greenvile, John Lieut. to Capt. Richard Newman
               Westcot, Robert Lieut. to Capt. Thomas Scott
               Read, John Lieut. to Sir John Coryton
Southam. Cave, William Lieut. †
Cornwall   Vigors, Stephen Lieut. †
L. & W.   Morton, Richard Lieut. †
Wilts   Andrews, Thomas **Ens.** to Capt. Thomas Piercy
Devon   Salter, Thomas Ens. to Capt. David Powell
               Comings, Peter Ens. to Capt. John Bluckmore
Cornwall   Badcock, Henry Ens. †
               Martin, William Ens.
               Bond, Ezekiel Ens. †
Somerset   Sowtrell, Isaac **Quart.** †

Berty, Sir Peregrine
Lincoln   Spooner, William **Lieut.** † HORSE
               Ely, William **Cor.** †
Rutland   Wingfield, John Cor. †

Lincoln	King, Roger Cor. to Capt. Richard King
Northam.	Catesby, John Quart. †
L. & W.	Sprecklow, William Quart. ⎫ To Capt. Christopher Wilson
Lincoln	Wheat, John Quart. ⎭
	Jackson, Thomas Quart. to Capt. Edw. Whitchcott
	Odling, Richard Quart. to Sir Charles Bolles
	Searles, William Quart. to Lieut. Col. Skipwith
	Davison, Benjamin Quart. to Capt. Markham
Lincoln	Brocklesby, Thomas Ens. [ ] to Capt. Edw. Berty

Billingsly, Francis

Warwick	Billingsly, George Capt. FOOT
Salop	Healing, Edward Lieut.
Hereford	Tayler, Henry Ens. to Maj. Billingsly

Bishop, Sir Edward

L. & W.	Busbridge, Joseph Capt. DRAGOONS

Bisse, Edward

Somerset	Boys, John Capt. HORSE
Somerset	Bingham, George Lieut. FOOT to Capt. Davies

Blackwell, Sir Thomas

L. & W.	Meridel, Richard Lieut. Col. ⎫ FOOT
	Martin, Charles Ens. ⎭
	Buttman, Thomas Lieut.
Nottingh.	Babington, Ferdinando Ens.

Blague, Thomas

Suffolk	Barber, Edmund Capt. HORSE
Oxon	Moulins, Charles Cor. ⎫ To Capt. Wharton
York	Hardy, Nicholas Quart. ⎭
Suffolk	Snelling, John Capt. FOOT
Berks	West, Cromwell Capt.
Suffolk	Barber, John Capt.
York	Dinsdale, Ralph Lieut. to Capt. Dun
L. & W.	Anderkin, Philip Lieut. to Capt. Wharton
	Demaret, John Lieut. to Lieut. Col. Sir William Lower
Suffolk	Brydon, Jasper Lieut. to Capt. Thomas Clark
	Welham, John Lieut. to Capt. Bernard de Gomme
	Loudell, Thomas Lieut. to Capt. Thomas Bayly
L. & W.	Lugge, Peter Lieut. †
	Naylor, Thomas Ens. †
Berks	Freeman, Richard Ens. †

Blakeston, Sir William [of Archdeacon Newton]
York	Kirk, Michael **Lieut.** HORSE	} To Capt. Douglass
	Garbutt, Christopher Quart.	
Durham	Eden, John **Cor.**	} To Capt. Gascoygne Eden
	Walton, George Quart.	

York	Atkinson, William **Quart.**	} BRIGADE
	Reed, Thomas Quart.	
	Deighton, Francis Quart. to Lieut. Col. Thornton	
Cambridge	Sweat, John Quart. to Lieut. Col. William Blakeston	
Durham	Shadforth, George Quart. to Capt. William Lambton	

Blayney, John [Sir Francis Mackworth's regiment]
Montgom.   Glynne, Edmund **Capt.** DRAGOONS
           Williams, Edw. **Cor.** †

Blunt, John
Durham   Crawhall, John. **Lieut.** HORSE, to Maj. Haslewood

Bodenham, Sir Wingfield
Leicester Marshall, William **Capt. Lieut.** HORSE
Huntingd. Scot, Henry **Cor.**

Bolles, Richard*
L. & W.   Pocklington, Thomas **Capt.** FOOT
           Heron, William **Lieut.** to Maj. Bevis Floyd
Lincoln   Hunt, John **Ens.**
Stafford   Littleton, James Ens. †

Bolles, Sir Charles [Sir Peregrine Bertie's regiment]
Lincoln   Bradley, Thomas **Lieut.** † HORSE

Borlace, Nicholas
Somerset   Mayo, John **Capt. Lieut.** HORSE
Devon   Came, Thomas **Lieut.**
Cornwall   Borlace, James Lieut. †
Devon   Comer, John **Cor.** to Maj. Thomas Curtys

Bosa, Samuel
Durham   Colvell, Adam **Capt. Lieut.** DRAGOONS

Bovill, Jordan
Suffolk   Davis, William **Capt.** HORSE
Southam.   Hunt, John **Cor.** †
           Pile, Will. **Quart.**

Boynton, Sir Matthew [1651?]
York	Sollet, Francis **Lieut**. FOOT, to Capt. Tompson
	Dutton, Thomas Lieut. †
York	Lakin, Nicholas **Cor**. HORSE

Boys, Sir John
Denbigh	Jefferies, Edw. **Capt**. FOOT
Gloucester	Lambe, William **Lieut**. to Maj. Henry Bennet
L. & W.	Done, Valentine Lieut. to Capt. Edmund Done
	Alexander, Paul Lieut. †
	Theaker, William Lieut. †
Oxon	Skingsly, John **Ens**. †
Kent	Oxenbridge, Thomas **Quart**.
L. & W.	Smith, John **Lieut**. HORSE
	Tooly, Robert **Cor**. †
	Tooly, Thomas Cor.

Bradshaw, Sir William
Lancaster	Tildsly, Edw. **Capt**. } HORSE
	Duhurst, John Lieut. }
	Brockhills, Thomas Capt.
York	Neale, John **Lieut**. to Capt. Dunhill
	Foster, John **Cor**. }
Lancaster	Walmsly, John **Quart**. } To Maj. Thomas Vavasor
York	Michell, William Quart.
	Tomlinson, William Quart.

Brandling, Charles
Northumb.	Collingwood, John **Capt**. FOOT
	Carre, Ralph **Lieut**. †
	Fenwick, William Lieut. †
	Rutherford, Thomas Lieut. †
Durham	Davison, George Lieut. to Lieut. Col. Robert Brandling
Northumb.	Errington, Ralph **Ens**. to Capt. Robert Brandling
Durham	Goodrick, Philip **Quart**.
Northumb.	Harwood, John Quart.

Brandling, Robert
Northumb.	Lewins, Thomas **Capt**. HORSE
	Lewins, Thomas **Capt**. **Lieut**.
York	Parving, John **Cor**. }
Durham	Pallester, James Quart. } To Sir George Bowes
York	Pinckney, Henry Cor. to Capt. William Tonstall

Northumb.	Forster, John 𝕼uart.	⎫
Durham	Harrison, Stephen Quart.	⎬ To Maj. Ralph Brandling
Northumb.	Charlton, Richard Quart.	⎪
Durham	Farrow, Gerard Quart.	⎭

Bridges, Sir Thomas

Somerset	Byam, John 𝕷ieut.	⎫ HORSE
	Wickham, Thomas 𝕮or.	⎬ To Lt. Col. Ryslye
	Hodges, Henry 𝕼uart.	⎭
L. & W.	Hall, William 𝕮apt. FOOT	
Somerset	Chapman, Henry Capt.	
	Palmer, John Capt.	
	Bridges, George Capt.	⎫
	Cox, Francis Lieut.	⎬
	Massey, John Ens.	⎭
	Combe, Henry 𝕷ieut.	⎫ To Capt. Richard Bull
	Combe, John Ens.	⎭
	Smith, John 𝕰ns. to Capt. Henry Bull	
	Parfet, William Ens. to Lieut. Col. Rislye	
	Taunton, Robert Ens. †	
	Creech, Henry Ens. †	
L. & W.	Fox, Edward Ens. to Capt. Peter Gleane	
	Meeres, Anthony Ens. to Capt. William Morgan	
Dorset	Cox, John 𝕼uart.	

Bridges, Sir William [Sir Wm. Pennyman's / Sir R. Page's regiment]
Stafford	Robinson, Daniel 𝕷ieut. 𝕮ol. FOOT

Bristol, Earl of [George Digby]
L. & W.	Graham, John 𝕮apt. HORSE
Somerset	Ivy, Ferdinando 𝕮or. to Capt. John Gifford
Montgom.	Scarlett, Silvanus Cor. to Col. Richard Herbert
Salop	Bromhall, John Cor.
L. & W.	Clayton, Richard 𝕼uart. to Sir Kenelme Digby
Stafford	Granger, Hugh Quart. to Col. John Lane

Broughton, Sir Edward*
L. & W.	Beverly, Lenox 𝕰ns. [ ] to Timothy Blencow

Broughton, Robert
Carmarth.	Morgan, John 𝕮apt. FOOT
Cambridge	Mallory, Edward Capt.
Denbigh	Wynne, Cadwallader 𝕷ieut. †
L. & W.	Pritchard, Thomas Ens. to Major Lill

	Johnson, Thomas Ens. to Capt. Freestone
Anglesey	Parry, David Ens. †

Browne, Sir Adam
Surrey Leigh, Miles **Cor**. † HORSE

Buckingham, Duke of [1648]
Glamorg. Penry, Henry **Capt**. † HORSE

Buck, Brutus
Southam. Lewyn, Edw. **Capt**. FOOT

Buckly [Bulkeley], Richard
Denbigh Price, Robert **Capt**. HORSE
Flint Griffith, Thomas **Lieut**. †

Buller, John
Worcester Nanfan, Giles **Capt**. ⎫ FOOT
　　　　　Morris, Walter **Lieut**. ⎭

Bunkly, Sir George*
Northumb. Morton, Henry **Capt**. HORSE
Lincoln Gromett, Samuel **Lieut**. to Capt. William Skipwith
Durham Newton, Thomas Lieut. ⎫ To Lieut. Col. Michael Trollop
　　　　Cummin, Edward. Quart. ⎭
Lincoln Jackson, William **Cor**. ⎫
York Binns, John Cor. ⎬ To Capt. Coxhead
Lincoln Quinsey, Thomas Quart. ⎭
Durham Knaggs, John **Quart**. †
　　　　Goston, John Quart. to Capt. Sebastian Bunkly

Bunkly, Sebastian*
Surrey Smart, Collet **Capt**. HORSE

Burgesse, Francis
L. & W. Goswel, George **Capt**. FOOT
　　　　George, Henry **Ens**.

Burgesse, Roger*
Northam. May, Edmund **Capt**. FOOT

Butler, John
Carmarth. Fisher, Robert **Lieut**. FOOT to Capt. Walter Fl___
　　　　　Howel, Benjamin **Ens**. to Capt. William Sheales

Butler, Thomas
Carmarth.	Donne, Daniel Ens. [ ] to Capt. Arnold Butler
Pembroke	Merrick, John Ens.

Butler, Sir William
Oxon	Wood, Basil Capt. HORSE
L. & W.	Parker, Alexander Capt.
	Peak, Gregory Cor.
	Mallory, Richard Quart.
	Paris, John Quart.
Stafford	Broome, John Cor.
L. & W.	Hamlett, John Quart. to Capt. John Bis___
	Champion, John Quart. to Capt. John He___
Bucks	Howard, Alexander Quart. to Capt. Hacket

Byerly, Anthony
L. & W.	Gaines, Francis Capt. Lieut. } FOOT
Durham	Bouck, Hercules Capt. Lieut. }
York	Grange, Ralph Lieut. to Maj. Thomas Hall
Durham	Oswold, Richard Ens.
	Blackwell, Marmaduke Quart.

Byron, Lord John
L. & W.	Berkenhead, Roger Capt. HORSE
Cumberl.	Carleton, Thomas Capt. }
	Carleton, John Cor. }
	Hetherington, William Quart. }
Flint	Dymock, William Capt.
L. & W.	Dean, Edward Capt. †
	Cory, Degory Lieut. to Capt. John Saye
Westmo.	Bacon, George Lieut. to Maj. William Byron
Denbigh	Jones, Evan Lieut. to Lieut. Col. William Walton
L. & W.	Littlefare, William Lieut. †
	Conyers, Henry Cor. to Capt. Jer. Fry___
Chester	Fryer, John Cor. to Capt. John Greenho___ [4]
Salop	Pey, John Cor. to Capt. William Dymock
Carmarth.	Francklin, Walter Cor. }
	Johnson, George Quart. } To Lt. Col. Gilbert Byron
L. & W.	Scot, Thomas Quart. }
	Powel, David Cor.
Chester	Hodgekin, Ralph Quart. to Capt. Bavand
Nottingh.	Pasmuch, John Quart. †

---

[4] The edge of the original document has been lost, along with the ends of several men's names. Despite being mentioned by colleagues these men did not claim bounty themselves, so are not included in the original document's index and cannot be cross-referenced.

Lancaster	Brotherton, John Quart. †
L. & W.	Napier, Thomas **Col**. FOOT
Cumberl.	Porter, Anthony **Capt**.
Chester	Brereton, Richard Capt. ⎫
L. & W.	Hughes, William Lieut. ⎬
Salop	Jones, Edw. Ens. ⎭
	Delaval, John Capt.
Denbigh	Sutton, Ellis Capt. ⎫
	Powell, William Lieut. ⎭
	Baker, Thomas Capt.
	Manly, Roger Capt. ⎫
L. & W.	Fowler, Bartholomew Lieut. ⎭
Flint	Phillips, Edw. Capt.
L. & W.	Willmot, John **Lieut**. to Capt. Norris
Chester	Weston, Richard Lieut. to Capt. Norton
Derby	Sale, John **Quart**. †

Byron, Sir Nicholas
Berks	Burchall, John Lieut. to Maj. William Cole
Salop	Jones, William **Ens**. to Capt. Phil. Ellis

Byron, Sir Philip
L. & W.	Cresheld, Arthur **Lieut**. FOOT to Capt. Webb
	Ward, John Lieut. to Capt. Hercules Lowe
Middlesex	Bretton, Robert Lieut. †
York	Dillingham, Roger **Quart**.

Byron, Lord Richard
Nottingh.	Cartwright, Francis **Capt**. **Lieut**. HORSE
	Harrison, William Lieut. to Capt. Kirton
L. & W.	Riches, John **Cor**.
Norfolk	Beddingfield, Henry Cor. †
Nottingh.	Brightman, Richard **Capt**. FOOT

Byron, Sir Robert*
Lancaster	Haughton, Thomas **Capt**. HORSE
	Halsall, Thomas **Lieut**. to Lieut. Col. Walton
	Parker, John Lieut. ⎫ To Capt. George Talbot
	Barker, Thomas Cor. ⎭
	Gradell, William Lieut. to Maj. John Lowyck
	Massey, Hamlet **Cor**. †
	Tickle, Robert **Quart**.

| L. & W. | Trapps, Henry **Capt**. FOOT |
| Chester | Malpas, Richard **Ens**. to Capt. Harlow |

Calender, Earl of
| Cumberl. | Lyndsey, Thomas **Capt**. HORSE |

Cambden [Campden], Lord
Essex	Swan, John **Capt**. HORSE
Rutland	Sheffield, George Capt.
Middlesex	Forrest, John **Lieut**. to Capt. John. Caywood
Rutland	Martin, William Lieut.
Northam.	Chattris, William **Cor**. ⎫ To Capt. Walter Kirkham
	Tampian, William **Quart**. ⎭
Middlesex	Uffington, John Quart.
Lincoln	Clark, Roger Quart. to Capt. John Brudenell
Rutland	Foster, Robert Quart. to Capt. Manwaring

Rutland	Moody, Richard **Capt**. FOOT
Lincoln	Andrews, Richard Capt.
Rutland	Mowbrey, John. **Lieut**. ⎫ To Capt. Thomas Sheffield
Northam.	Blaxly, Lancelot **Ens**. ⎭

Campian, Sir William
Bucks	Darell, Peter **Capt**. HORSE
L. & W.	Knowles, Thomas Capt.
Oxon	Mildmay, Thomas **Cor**. †

Cansfield, Sir John [Queen's regiment]
L. & W.	Powell, Richard **Lieut**. HORSE, to Capt. Meade
	Dodson, Miles **Quart**. **Gen**. in Oxon
Derby	Lancaster, Thomas Quart. to Sir Thomas Smith

Lord Capell
L. & W.	Chapman, Edmund **Col**. HORSE
Norfolk	Lynne, John Capt.
Devon	Seymore, John Capt.
	Stuckey, Thomas Capt.
Merion.	Nanny, Robert **Capt**. **Lieut**.
Warwick	Halyburton, William Lieut. to Sir Henry Newton
Montgom.	Bowen, John **Cor**. to Capt. Edw. Floyd
L. & W.	Hanes, Thomas **Quart**. to Sir. Anthony St. Leger
Middlesex	Grover, James Quart. to Capt. Kingsly
Salop	Hartshorne, Maurice Quart. to Capt. Laurence Benthall
L. & W.	Dacres, John Quart. †

L. & W.	Crow, Henry Col. DRAGOONS	
Cornwall	Hughes, David **Capt**. FOOT	
	Collins, Edward **Ens**. †	

Carbery, Earl of

L. & W.	Cotterell John **Capt**. FOOT
Cardigan	Lewis, George Capt.
Carmarth.	Bradshaw, John Capt.
L. & W.	Methwold, Thomas Capt. †
	Bradshaw, Edmund Lieut. †
Pembroke	Phillips, John Capt. } †
	Elliott, John Lieut. } †
Carmarth.	Rees, David **Ens**. to Capt. Charles Hughes
	Jones, David Ens. to Capt. Rowland Gwynne
Pembroke	Phillips, John Ens. to Capt. John Butler †
Carmarth.	Awbry, John **Quart. Gen**.
Carmarth.	Awbry, Richard **Cor**. HORSE
Pembroke	Howell, John **Quart**.
Carmarth.	Delahay, Thomas Quart. to Sir Francis Floyd

Cardiffe, Thomas

Monmouth	Vaughan, Roger **Capt**. FOOT
L. & W.	Cardiffe, Lancelot Capt.
Hereford	Mynors, Richard **Lieut**. †

Carleton, Sir William [1648]

Cumberl.	Walker, Lancelot **Capt**. FOOT
	Stevenson, John Capt.
Durham	Carre, John Capt. }
	Rountree, Thomas Lieut. }
L. & W.	Hetherington, George **Lieut**. to William Chamberlane
Cumberl.	Rumny, Thomas **Ens**. to Thomas Whelpdale
	Carleton, Nicholas Quart.

Carlos, William

Stafford	Brunly, Francis **Capt**. HORSE
Leicester	Watts, Richard **Lieut**. †
L. & W.	Astly, Wootton **Cor**. †
Hereford	Astly, Thomas **Quart**. †
L. & W.	Pyott, Simon **Lieut**. † FOOT

Carlisle, Earl of
Essex   Wood, Tobias **Capt**. HORSE

Carnaby, Francis
Northumb.	Carnaby, Ralph **Capt**. HORSE
	Fenwick, Thomas Capt.
	Carnaby, Richard Capt.
L. & W.	Sampson, John Capt.
Northumb.	Newton, William **Lieut**. †
	Bell Edw. **Cor**. to Maj. Thomas Carnaby
Durham	Eubanke, Tobias Cor. } To Capt. Henry Eubanke
	Hodgson, Matthew Cor.
York	Wilson, Jeremy Cor. } To Capt. Thomas Carleton
Durham	Gantley, Cutbert Quart.
Northumb.	Addison, Richard **Quart**. to Lieut. Col. Reignald Carnaby
	Dawson, John Quart. to Maj. Tristram Fenwick
Northumb.	Bell, Albany **Capt. Lieut**. DRAGOONS
	Fenwick, Thomas **Cor**.

Carnaby, Ralph
Northumb.	Fenwick, Robert **Capt**. HORSE
	Surtys, William **Cor**. to Capt. Francis Ord
	Bell, Thomas **Quart**.

Carnarvon, Earl of *
Bucks	Badghot, Thomas **Capt**. † HORSE
	Bridges, Richard Capt. †
L. & W.	Preston, Simon Capt.
York	Daniel, James Cor.
	Sherborne, Robert **Lieut**.
Lancaster	Standish, Laurence Quart.
	Worthington, Thomas Quart. } To Lieut. Col. Standish
Wilts	Barton, Roger Quart.
Dorset	Hoddy, Henry Quart.
Lancaster	Grimshaw, Robert Lieut. to Capt. Brent
Northam.	Monk, George Lieut.
Bucks	Bridges, Henry **Cor**. to Capt. Richard Parsly
	Bury, Richard Cor.

Carne, Edward
Glamorg.	Cradock, Richard **Capt**. FOOT
	Gammage, Thomas Capt.

Carre, Robert

Northumb.	Elrington, Francis **Capt**. HORSE	
	Widdrington, Francis **Cor**. to Capt. Widdrington	
	Stocko, Francis Cor. } To Maj. Errington	
L. & W.	Errington, Ralph Cor. }	
Northumb.	Carre, Andrew Cor. †	
	Forster, Matthew Cor.	

Carteret, Sir George

L. & W.   Blake, William **Lieut**. HORSE

L. & W.   Canham, Simon **Capt**. FOOT
            Johnson, Robert Capt.
            Coates, John **Lieut**.
Cornwall   Collins, John **Ens**. to Maj. Gen. Collins

Cary, Edmond

Derby   Gilberthorp, Francis **Ens**. [   ] to Capt. Coningsby

Cary, Sir Henry

Devon   Standen, Nicholas **Lieut**. } HORSE
            Gifford, John Cor.   } To Maj. Belfore
Somerset   Harman, Francis Lieut. †
Devon   Hamlyn, William **Cor**.   } To Capt. Peter Boone
            Stawell, Humphrey Quart.   }
L. & W.   Browne, Francis **Quart**.   } To Sir Ames Meredith
Devon   Hayne, Zachary Quart.   }
            Ward, Christopher Quart. to Capt. Church

L. & W.   Parry, Owen **Lieut. Col**. } FOOT
            Parry, William Lieut.   }
Hereford   Parry, James Ens.   }
Devon   Bennet, Nicholas **Capt**.
            Jordan, Richard Capt.
            Lyde, Edw. Capt.
            Drake, John Capt.   }
            Horne, William Ens.   }
Devon   Bagge, George Capt.   }
            Merson, Ralph Ens.   }
            Hulland, Lewis **Lieut**. to Capt. Nicholas Newman
            Cary, Edward Lieut. to Maj. John Jacob
            Prouse, Robert Lieut.   } To Capt. Edw. Cary
            Luccombe, Thomas Ens.   }
            Hooper, Henry Lieut. to Lieut. Col. Prouse

L. & W.	Elliot, John Lieut.	} To Maj. Coppleston
	Gates, Christopher Ens.	
Devon	Buckland, William **Ens**. to Capt. John Waltham	
	Carpenter, Edward Ens.	} To Maj. Walters
	Cockram, Roger Ens.	
	Hele, John Ens. to Capt. Gideon Waldron	
	Pierce, Thomas Ens. †	

Cary, Sir Horatio*

L. & W.	Chauke, Jacob **Capt**.	} HORSE
	Overfield, Christopher **Cor**.	
Cornwall	Yeo, Humphry Capt.	
Gloucester	Horner, Joseph Capt. **Lieut**.	
L. & W.	Brook, Henry Lieut.	} To Lieut. Col. William Rumball
	Woolscot, Thomas Cor.	
	Clark, Henry Lieut. to Maj. Debee	
Somerset	Champnes, John **Cor**. to Capt. John Debee	
L. & W.	Julian, James Cor. to Capt. Agmondisham Pickhay	
	Boad, Nathaniel Cor. to Capt. Whelland	
	Nicholson, Richard **Quart**. to Capt. Edw. Zouch	

Cary, Theodore

Cornwall	Ackland, Hugh **Capt**. FOOT
L. & W.	Cary, George **Ens**.

Cavendish, Charles*

Northam.	Browne, Sir Robert **Capt**. HORSE
York	Reasby, Leonard **Cor**. to Maj. Tuke
Nottingh.	Smith, William **Quart**. to Lieut. Col. Markham

Cavendish, Lord Henry

York	Stanhope, George **Capt**.	} HORSE
	Wilson, Richard Cor.	
	Banks, John Capt.	
	Lakin, Robert Capt.	
	Markenfield, Thomas Capt.	
	Pullen, John Lieut.	
	Hardcastle, Edward Cor.	}
Westmo.	Chambers, Robert Cor.	
York	Sympson, Christopher Quart.	
	Naylor, Thomas Capt.	
Warwick	Latham, John **Lieut**. to Capt. Bilby	
L. & W.	Sturdy, Peter **Cor**. to Maj. Anthony Skinner	
Lincoln	Cawdron, Anthony Cor. to Capt. Poyntz	
Durham	Greenwell, Samuel Cor. to Lieut. Col. Skrimshaw	

Champernon, Philip*
Devon	Hutchins, Thomas **Capt**. FOOT
	Fortescue, Nicholas Capt.
	Hutchins, William **Lieut**. to Maj. Robert Warren
	Mostyn, Henry **Ens**. to Capt. John Richardson
L. & W.	Ryder, Roger Ens. to Capt. Anthony Strut
Devon	Campian, Josias Ens.

Chandois, Lord
Salop	Winnington, Francis **Capt**. HORSE
Berks	Cave, Robert **Lieut**. to Capt. Sawyer
Gloucester	Gynnet, Richard Lieut. to Capt. Ralph Freeman
	Harwood, Thomas **Cor**. to Capt. John Batts
Northam.	Littlepage, John Cor. to Lieut. Col. Sawyer
Gloucester	Robbins, Thomas **Capt**. FOOT
L. & W.	Robbins, Thomas Capt.

Charles, Prince*
Oxon	Blunt, William **Capt**. ⎫ HORSE
Berks	Curtys, John Cor. ⎭
L. & W.	Fitzgerald, Edward Capt.
Worcester	Clark, John Capt. **Lieut**.
L. & W.	Jackson, John Lieut. to Maj. John Jackson
Somerset	Nevill, Thomas Lieut. to Capt. Henry Nevill †
York	Harland, Christopher **Cor**. ⎫
Westmo.	Webb, William Cor. ⎬ To Maj. Fame
Huntingd.	Rowden, Edmund Quart. ⎭
L. & W.	Foxton, John Cor. ⎫ To the Duke of York
York	Arnold, Stephen, Quart. ⎭
L. & W.	Crisp, Thomas Cor. ⎫ To Capt. Samuel Pinder
	Irish, James Quart. ⎭
Durham	Hutton, John **Quart**. to His Highness' Guards
L. & W.	Gregory, William Quart. to Capt. Leapenny
L. & W.	Egerton, William **Capt**. FOOT
	Price, John **Lieut**. to Capt. John Bishoppe
Cornwall	Stevens, Nicholas Lieut. †
Devon	Wilston, Henry Lieut. to Capt. Thomas Warren
Cornwall	Stevens, Ezekiel **Ens**. †

Cheator, Henry
L. & W.	Pawlet, John **Capt**. FOOT
	Wharton, William Capt.
Cumberl.	Walker, Lancelot Capt.
Durham	Willy, Ralph Capt.

Chesterfield, Earl of
Derby	Browne, Edward **Capt**. FOOT

Chisnall, Edward
L. & W.	Mort, George Capt. HORSE
Hereford	Banister, John Lieut. to Capt. Dixon
Lancaster	Ashton, Henry **Capt**. ⎫
	Ashton, John Lieut. ⎬ FOOT
	Holme, Thomas Ens. ⎭
	Goodwin, William **Lieut**. to Capt. Thomas Rigby
	Mandsly, John Lieut. to Maj. Farmer
	Hunter, Thomas **Ens**. to Capt. Robert Heskith
	Twisse, Laurence **Quart**.

Cholmly, Sir Hugh*
York	Lakin, Robert **Capt**. HORSE
	Welborne, Robert **Lieut**. ⎫
	Young, William Cor. ⎬ To Capt. Wharton
	Reed, Robert Quart. ⎭
Durham	Brabant, Ralph Lieut. to Capt. Robert Thomas
L. & W.	Gero, Abraham Lieut.
	Bambridge, Francis Lieut. to Maj. Jenkins
York	White, Jonathan **Cor**.
	Michaell, Robert Cor. to Capt. George Elrington
	Skipton, Nicholas Cor. to Capt. Toby Jenkins
	Huntrayds, William **Quart**.
Northumb.	Denton, James **Capt**. FOOT
Durham	Cholmly, James Capt.
	Wright, Cholmly Capt.
L. & W.	Legerd, Richard Capt. ⎫
York	Collingson, John Lieut. ⎭
	Farside, William **Lieut**. to Lieut. Col. William Blakiston
	Banks, John Lieut. to Capt. Sheafe
	Cliffe, Daniel **Ens**. to Capt. John Garrett
	Graham, Arthur **Quart**.

Cholmondly, Lord [Robert, 1st Viscount]*
Chester   Horton, Robert Capt. HORSE

Cholmly, Sir Richard*
Devon   Hoskins, Henry Capt. FOOT
L. & W.   Harris, Thomas Capt.
Somerset   Bale, John Lieut.

Chudleigh [Sir George or James]*
Devon   Knill, Anthony Ens. [   ] to Capt. John Dynham

Chute, George
Kent   Lovelace, Dudley Capt. HORSE
               Bateman, James Lieut. to Capt. Richard Hulse

Clavering, Sir Robert*
L. & W.   Kere, Nicholas Capt. HORSE
York   Messenger, Henry Capt.
               Beckwith, Thomas Lieut. to Capt. William Fenwick
               Bishop, Thomas Lieut. to Capt. John Sayer
Durham   Hunter, George Lieut. to Capt. John Danby
L. & W.   Merryman, Michael Lieut. to Capt. Francis Ord
York   Hawkins, Peter Lieut.
               Lotherington, Thomas Quart. to Capt. Thomas Craythorn
Northumb.   Strother, Arthur Quart. to Capt. Thomas Clavering

Westmo.   Whitfield, John Capt. FOOT
Northumb.   Davison, Robert Capt.
               Moore, Robert Capt.
               Gayre, Thomas Capt.
               Lawson, Richard Capt.
               Scott, John Capt.
York   Dabbs, Daniel Capt.
Durham   Heighington, Robert Capt.   ⎫
                 Steevenson Humphry Ens. ⎬
               Curtys, Richard Capt.
Northumb.   Swinhoe, William Lieut. to Capt. James Swinhoe
Durham   Rountree, Thomas Lieut. to Capt. John Carre
York   Crome, Henry Lieut.
Northumb.   Satterthwaite, Richard Ens. to Capt. Robert Matthews
               Reed, Lancelot Ens. to William Reed
L. & W.   Lyddal, John Ens.
Northumb.   Maine Edw. Ens. to Capt. Thomas Ord

Durham	Gargrave, Anthony **Lieut**. DRAGOONS to Capt. Wilkinson
Northumb.	Barletson, Thomas **Quart**. to Maj. Armorer

Clayton, Henry
York	Metcalf, Edw. **Lieut**. † FOOT
	Steele, John **Ens**. to Capt. Thomas Bedborough

Clerk, Sir Francis [1648]
Kent	Penry, Henry **Ens**. † FOOT
	Moore, John **Ens**. †

Cleveland, Earl of*
L. & W.	Hill, Robert **Capt**. ⎫ HORSE
	Linch, Theophilus Quart. ⎭
	Cox, Griffith Capt.
	Cownly, William Capt. †
Nottingh.	Reresby, Thomas **Capt. Lieut**.
Somerset	Mildmay, Humphry Capt. Lieut.
L. & W.	Bell, Phillip Capt. Lieut.
Worcester	Dangerfield, George Lieut. to Capt. Vernon
Bedford	Wells, Samuel **Cor**.
Wilts	Smith, William Cor. ⎫ To Capt. Barber
Somerset	Newman, John Quart. ⎭
Southam.	Wandsford, Francis Cor. to Capt. Atkinson
L. & W.	Cave, Henry Cor. to Capt. Richard Atkins
York	North, Thomas **Quart**. †
Devon	Hornabrook, Henry Quart. †
Somerset	Gilbert, William Quart. ⎫
Dorset	Clark, Thomas Quart. ⎬ To Maj. Clark
L. & W.	Button, Abell Quart. ⎭
	Nicholls, Thomas Quart.
Somerset	Gibson, John Quart. †
Worcester	Mascal, John Ens. to Capt. John Mozyn

Clifton, Cuthbert
Lancaster	Bordman, John **Ens**. [ ] to Maj. William Westby
Lancaster	Cooban, William **Quart**. HORSE

Cobb, Sir Francis
York	Plaxton, William **Capt. Lieut**. [ ]

Coker, Sir Henry
Wilts	Cooke, Henry **Capt. Lieut**. HORSE
Dorset	Moore, Charles **Cor**. †

Wilts	Hayward, Robert Cor. †
	Muckleston, Edw. **Quart**. †
Somerset	Ford, Robert Quart. †
	Moulton, Adam Quart. to Capt. Humphry Cooke

Cole, Sir Nicholas
York	Metcalfe, Henry **Lieut**. HORSE to Capt. Fenwick
Durham	Carmigall, Thomas **Cor**. to Capt. Richard Cole
	Manger, Henry **Quart**.
	Wilson, William Quart. to Sir Francis Liddell
	Stobbs, Thomas Quart.

Collins, Degory
L. & W.	Collins, Thomas **Lieut**. **Col**. FOOT
	Burgesse, John **Capt**.

Colt, Henry
Gloucester	Long, Henry **Lieut**. HORSE, to Capt. Adway

Colepepper, Thomas*
Southam.	Peachy, Gregory **Capt**. HORSE
Dorset	Winter, William Capt. ⎫
	Furmidge, William Lieut. ⎭
Essex	Brampston, John Capt.
Surrey	Hatcher, Nicholas Capt.
	Bromfield, Edward Capt.
L. & W.	Sandys, Edwin Capt. ⎫
	Hinckly, Edward Cor. ⎭
	Sayer, George **Lieut**. to Lieut. Col. William Gage
	Carew, John Lieut. to Capt. Poole
Kent	Hall, Thomas Lieut. †
Huntingd.	Edwards, Humphry Lieut. †
Surrey	Shelly, William Lieut. †
Oxon	Bond, Robert **Cor**.
York	Littleboys, George Cor.
Kent	Welch, Thomas **Quart**. to Lieut. Col. Gamlyn
	Jones, John Quart.
L. & W.	Lane, Rich Quart. to Maj. Boswell
Kent	Horsmanden, Warham Capt. FOOT
	Symmonds, Caleb Lieut.

Comberford
Stafford	Weston, Ralph **Capt**. HORSE
	Kempson, Edw. **Cor**. to Capt. Treswell

Compton, Sir William [1648]
L. & W.	Wright, John **Capt**. FOOT
	Dussing, John Capt. ⎫
	Griffin, Thomas Ens. ⎭
Rutland	Cannyng, Endymion Capt.
Oxon	Leighton, Henry **Capt**. **Lieut**.
Suffolk	Andrewes, John Lieut. to Capt. John Birssing
	Neale, William **Ens**. to Capt. Snellgrove
Northam.	Adams, Richard Ens.
Kent	Pike, George Ens. †

Coningsby, Fitzwilliam
Dorset	Oldis, John **Capt**. HORSE
Worcester	Russell, Francis **Lieut**. ⎫ To Maj. Roberts
Gloucester	Lugg, Jasper Quart. ⎭
L. & W.	Cornwallis, Thomas Lieut. ⎫ To Capt. Francis Cornwallis
Middlesex	Cornwallis, John **Cor**. ⎭
Hereford	Smith, John Cor.
	Harding, John **Quart**. to Lieut. Col. Coningsby
	Smith, Thomas Quart.
L. & W.	Wiggmore, Richard **Lieut**. **Col**. FOOT
Hereford	Booth, John **Capt**. ⎫
L. & W.	Dausy, de Labere Lieut. ⎭
Hereford	Booth, Charles Capt. ⎫
	Brace, James Lieut. ⎭
Salop	Booth, Coningsby Capt. ⎫
Hereford	Hill, Anthony Lieut. ⎭
Carmarth.	Caethmayde, Thomas **Lieut**. to Capt. Thomas Cardiffe
L. & W.	Baker, William Lieut. to Capt. Arthur Burghill
Hereford	Howarth, Humphry **Ens**. to Capt. Baskeville
Carmarth.	Garland, John Ens. to Capt. William Dancy
Worcester	Stacy, Ralph Ens. to Capt. Barrell
Hereford	Garnons, Thomas Ens. †

Connock, John
L. & W.	Hawkes, John **Lieut**. FOOT, to Lieut. Col. Huskyn

Conquest, Richard
Bedford	Ironmonger, William **Quart**. HORSE

Conyers, Cuthbert
Durham	Woodhouse, John **Capt**. ⎫ FOOT
	Harrison, Cutbert **Ens**. ⎭

Sheraton, William Capt. ⎫
Hett, John Ens. ⎭
Smith, Christopher Lieut. to Capt. John Killinghall
Pearne, John Lieut. to Capt. Abraham Clark

Cook Francis
L. & W.	Goldsmith, Thomas Capt. HORSE
Somerset	Yngs, Richard Cor.
L. & W.	Walker, Marmion Capt. FOOT
Wilts	Penruddock, Edw. Capt.

Corbett, John
Leicester Hawley, Christopher Capt. FOOT

Corbett, Sir Vincent
Salop	Young, John Capt. HORSE
Salop	Oakly, Anthony Lieut. DRAGOONS, to Capt. Pigott
	Pen, Humphry Cor. to Capt. Edw. Baldwin
	Sandford, Arthur Cor. to Capt. Robert Sandford
	Pigeon, Ambrose Cor.

Coryton, John
Cornwall Smally, John Capt. Lieut. FOOT

Coryton, William
Cornwall	Smyth, Robert Capt. FOOT
Devon	Haughton, William Lieut. to Capt. Ambrose Manning
Cornwall	Adams, John Lieut. †
	Moore, Goyen Lieut. †
	Geddy, Nicholas Ens. to Capt. Nevill Blight
	Haughton, John Ens. †
	Piper, Arthur Ens. to Capt. Arthur Piper

Courtenay, Sir Peter
Devon	Tallant, Roger Capt. FOOT
Cornwall	Lavers, John Capt.
	Vigors, John Lieut. †
	Penwarden, John Ens. †

Courtenay, Sir William [of Powderham]
Dorset	Sturton, Philip Capt. HORSE
Berks	Peniall, Matthew Capt.
Wilts	White, John Capt.

L. & W.	Bates, Thomas Capt.	⎫
Somerset	Fanning, James Lieut.	⎬
L. & W.	Tayler, Robert Cor.	⎭
Southam.	Phillpott, George Capt.	
Middlesex	Fursdon, Philip Capt. Lieut.	
Southam.	Bale, William Lieut. ⎫ To Maj. Gardiner	
	Rudsby, Philip Cor. ⎭	
Somerset	Esmond, Thomas Lieut. ⎫ To Capt. John Gardiner	
Kent	Fisher, William Lieut. ⎭	
Wilts	Courtenay, James Quart. †	
Dorset	Norman, Edw. Quart. to Capt. Henry Wells	
	Lillington, Francis Quart.	
L. & W.	Athrelpho John Quart. to Maj. Addison	
Devon	Hanse, Thomas Capt. FOOT	
	Dart, Charles Capt.	
L. & W.	Cooly, Anthony Lieut. to Capt. Rob. Amery	
Cornwall	Penny, William Lieut. †	
	Colmer, Edward Lieut. †	
Middlesex	Chowles, John Lieut. to Capt. Thomas Latymer	

Covely, Sir Hugh
Chester	Okelly, Robert Quart. † HORSE

Coventry, John
Oxon	Potter, Samuel Capt. FOOT
Somerset	Cannon, James Capt. Lieut.
	Slape, Thomas Lieut.

Covert, John
Glamorg.	Gadford, Thomas Cor. HORSE

Crane, Sir Richard [Prince Rupert's Lifeguard of Horse]*
Stafford	Coyney, Thomas Lieut. HORSE to Capt. Richard Fox
Brecon	Williams, Thomas Cor. to Maj. Edw. Williams
Hereford	Exton, Anth. Quart. to Capt. William Rumball
Salop	Robinson, Edw. Quart. to Maj. Richard Fox
	Burton, Roger Quart.

Crawford, Earl of
L. & W.	Pool, Benjamin Capt. HORSE
	Rychaut, James Capt.
Durham	Unthank, William Capt.
L. & W.	Coningsby, Robert Lieut. to Capt. John Vangarish
Bucks	Floyd, Thomas Cor. to Capt. Richard Harrison

Somerset	Dowthwaite, Nicholas Cor. †
L. & W.	Graham, George Regt. Quart.
Oxon	Paslew, William Quart. to Capt. Humphry Hyde
York	Finister, Christopher Quart. to Capt. John Ridpith
Surrey	Ramsy, Simon Quart. to Lieut. Col. Latymer
L. & W.	Gibson, Thomas Lieut. Col. ⎱ DRAGOONS
	Michell, Hugh Lieut. ⎰
Worcester	Harrison, William Lieut. to Capt. Charles Frederick Seabish
Dorset	Corbyne, Robert Cor. ⎱ To Lieut. Col. Humes
	Pouncy, Roger Quart. ⎰
Middlesex	Scott, Andrew Cor. to Capt. Alexander Charter
Wilts	Getly, Richard Quart. to Capt. Meacham

Crisp, Sir Nicholas

Middlesex	Grigger, Nicholas Capt. HORSE
	Capell, John Capt.
	Bradshaw, Robert Capt. ⎱
Somerset	Cox, Philip Cor. ⎰
Surrey	Flower, Thomas Lieut. ⎱
L. & W.	Cobb, James Cor. ⎬ To Lieut. Col. J. Luntly
Surrey	Briggstock, Edward Quart. ⎰
L. & W.	Wicks, Thomas Lieut. to Capt. William Bushel
Middlesex	Butcher, John Lieut. †
L. & W.	Turner, Thomas Lieut. †
Lincoln	Tilson, Samuel Cor. to Capt. Richard Hackett
Gloucester	Laight, John Cor. to Maj. Slingsby
Cornwall	Willy, Theophilus Cor. †
Somerset	More, Philip Cor. †
Dorset	Joyliffe, John Cor. to Capt. Gregory
Somerset	Harding, Giles Quart. †

Crofts, Robert*

Gloucester	Hughes, William Capt. ⎱ FOOT
Hereford	Matthews, William Ens. ⎰
Worcester	Owens, Evan Lieut. to Capt. Lambert Saul
Hereford	Wall, Bartholomew Lieut. ⎱ To Capt. Gregory Wall
L. & W.	Hughes, Charles Ens. ⎰
Hereford	Tayler, William Lieut. to Capt. John Morgan
	Tyler, William Lieut. †

Crofts, Sir William

Hereford	Blunt, Francis Capt. ⎱ FOOT
	Pitt, Henry Ens. ⎰
Salop	Buckly, Benjamin Lieut. to Capt. Francis Walker
Hereford	Brace, Francis Ens. to Capt. Humphry Cornwall

Croker, Gerard
Oxon   Wharton, Robert Capt. **Lieut.** HORSE
L. & W.   Hathaway, Thomas **Cor.** } To Lieut. Col. Harris
                Whitly, William Quart. }
Oxon   Digger, R. **Quart.** to Capt. Peter Flower
                Prescot, Richard Quart.

Cromwell, Henry
Norfolk   Cromwell, Gregory **Maj.** HORSE & **Adjut. Gen.**
Lincoln   Bradshaw, Richard **Capt.**
Cambridge   Moore, Maurice **Cor.** to Capt. Lieut. John Heron

Cromwell, James*
Northumb.   Muschamp, Edw. **Lieut. Col.** } HORSE
                Rutherford, Ralph. Lieut. }
L. & W.   Wright, Hustthwayte **Maj.** }
Lincoln   Blenkhorn, John **Lieut.** }
York   Nelson, Robert Lieut. }
L. & W.   Hill, James **Quart.** }

Crooke, John
Dorset   Scudamore, George **Ens.** FOOT
Wilts   Barnes, Robert **Quart.**

Crosland, Sir Jordan
York   Raggett, John **Lieut.** HORSE to Maj. Potts
Cumberl.   Catherick, Robert **Quart.**
York   Kirk, William Quart.
Westmo.   Law, Thomas Quart. to Capt. Douglas

Crow, Henry
Salop   Shepheard, Vincent **Capt.** } FOOT
                Beynon, John Lieut. }
Hereford   Edwards, William Capt.

L. & W.   Fisher, John **Capt.** DRAGOONES

Cumberland, Earl of
Durham   Ward, Joseph **Capt.** FOOT (in York)

Curwen, Sir Patricius
Cumberl.   Towerson, Erasmus **Capt.** HORSE
                Patrickson, Thomas **Lieut.** to Capt. Jos. Patrickson
                Semple, William Lieut. †
                Skelton, Thomas **Cor.** †

Cumberl.	Tickell, Thomas **Capt.** FOOT	
	Highmore, Robert Capt.	
	Patrickson, Richard **Lieut.** †	
	Southgate, Edw. Lieut. †	
	Troutbeck, William Lieut. to Capt. John Whelpdale	
	Sibson, Anthony **Ens.** †	
	Rawling, Henry **Quart.**	

Dacres, Sir Richard

York	Freeman, Gabriel **Capt.**	} HORSE
Cumberl.	Sanderson, John Cor.	
York	Steele, Francis Capt.	}
	Rowel, Robert Lieut.	
	Wood, Thomas Capt.	
Durham	Selby, Thomas Capt.	
Wilts	Nevinson, Roger Capt.	}
York	Rooksby, John Cor.	
Northumb.	Errington, Ralph **Capt. Lieut.**	
York	Turner, John Lieut. to Sir Henry Fetherston	
Durham	Mills, Stephen Lieut.	} To Capt. John Shaftoe
Newcastle	Shaftoe, Robert Cor.	
York	Dixon, Nicholas **Cor.** to Lieut. Col. Francis Carre	
	Suttle, William **Quart.** to Capt. Thomas Wood	
Westmo.	Bell, Christopher Quart.	

Dacres, Sir Thomas

Cumberl.	Skelton, George **Capt.** HORSE
	Winder, Peter **Cor.** †
	Milburne, John Cor. †
	Nicholson, John Cor. †

Dallison, Sir Charles

Lincoln	Quadring, William **Capt.**	} HORSE
	Quadring, Richard Cor.	
	Newstead, Robert Capt.	}
	Smith, Anthony Lieut.	
York	Holm, Henry Capt.	
Lincoln	Sherborne, Robert **Cor.** to Capt. John Chappel	
Nottingh.	Fenton, Charles Cor. to Maj. Chappel	
Lincoln	Ealand, Robert **Quart.**	

Dallison, Sir Robert

Lincoln	King, William **Capt.**	⎫ HORSE
	Sutton, Richard Lieut.	⎬
	Southern, William Quart.	⎭
	Thorpe, Thomas Lieut.	
L. & W.	Chippingdale, John. Capt.	
	Brown, Valentine Capt.	
	Brown, John Capt.	⎫
	Emotson, Thomas Cor.	⎬
	Jackson, Andrew Quart.	⎭
	Cracroft, John **Capt. Lieut.**	
Rutland	Heron, Richard Lieut.	⎫ To Maj. Thomas Heron
L. & W.	Russel, Thomas Quart.	⎭
York	Hall, William Lieut. to Lieut. Col. Valentine Browne	
Nottingh.	Thornton, Hamm Lieut.	⎫
Leicester	Gheast, William Lieut.	⎬ To Capt. Richard King
L. & W.	Hodgson, Andrew Quart.	⎭
Lincoln	Parker, Richard Lieut.	⎫
	Lanham, William Quart.	⎬ To Capt. Cressy
	Hutchinson, Joseph Quart.	⎭
	Southern, William **Quart.** to Captain William King[5]	
	Sibsey, John Quart.	

Dallison, Sir Thomas*

L. & W.	Eden, Henry **Capt.**	⎫ HORSE
	Knight, William Lieut.	⎭
Carmarth.	Page, John **Regt. Quart.**	
Hereford	Launder, John Quart.	

Dalston, Sir William [1648]*

Westmo.	Routledge, John **Capt.** HORSE
Cumberl.	Ellis, Philip **Capt. Lieut.**
	Warwick, Guy **Cor.** to Lieut. Col. Warwick
Cumberl.	Wilson, Thomas **Lieut.** FOOT to Capt. Henry Gent___[6]
	Lowther, George Lieut. to Lieut. Col. George Denton
	Hodgson, Alexander Lieut. †
	Blaymyre, Robert **Quart.**

Dalton, Thomas*

Lancaster	Dickenson, Hugh **Quart.** HORSE, to Lieut. Col. Haughton

---

[5] A duplication: Southern and his captain are also mentioned at the top of the list.
[6] The name is abbreviated or cut off in the original. Reid gives it as 'Gentle', but offers no source.

Danby
York   Booth, Beeston **Capt**. HORSE

Danby, Sir Thomas
Lancaster   Booth, Beeston **Cor**. HORSE

Dangell
Somerset   Lewis, Thomas **Capt**. FOOT

Daniel, Sir Thomas [Prince Charles's regiment]
Essex   Knap, Christopher **Lieut**. HORSE to Capt. Metham

Darcy
York   Atkinson, Ralph **Capt**. FOOT
                Crofts, Christopher Capt.
                Jaques, Francis **Lieut**. to Maj. Darcy
                Conyers, Thomas Lieut. } To Lieut. Col. Dalton
                Wright, John **Ens**.

Darcy, Lord Conyers
York   Robinson, John **Lieut**. } FOOT
                Pybus, Christopher Ens. } To Capt. Beverly
                Thompson, Luke **Ens**. to Capt. Thomas Darcy
                Bearperk, William Ens. to Capt. Thomas Metcalf

Davaleere, John
Salop   Bishop, Edward **Capt**. } HORSE
                Bayton, Edw. Cor. }

Davis, Thomas
Flint   Floyd, Edward **Capt**. FOOT

Dean, William
Wilts   Cox, Thomas **Lieut**. HORSE to Capt. John Doddington
Dorset   Burt, James Lieut.

Somerset   Furber, Henry **Lieut**. DRAGOONS to Capt. John Chilcot

Deeyell
L. & W.   Smith, John **Capt**. FOOT

Denton, George [1648]*
Cumberl.   Addison, Thomas **Lieut**. FOOT to Capt. Laurence Walker
                Eglesfield, John **Ens**.
Westmo.   Hindmer, William Ens. †

Derby, Earl of

Anglesey	Davis, Owen **Lieut**. HORSE, to Col. Standish
L. & W.	Brockden, Henry **Capt**. FOOT
	Smith, William Capt.
Lancaster	Zouch, James Capt. †
	Molineux James Capt. †
	Steevenson, Nicholas Capt. †
	Bower, William Capt. †
	Haughton, John **Lieut**.

Digby, John [son of the 1st Earl of Bristol]*

Somerset	Holmes, Thomas **Capt**. ⎫ HORSE
	Talbot, William Quart. ⎭
Dorset	Wallcot, Edward **Capt. Lieut**.
Somerset	Hutchins, Thomas Lieut. to Capt. Simon Cottrell
Devon	Whitechurch, William Lieut. to Capt. William Easton
Middlesex	Crane, William Lieut. †
Cornwall	Duncalf, William Lieut. †
Dorset	Ward, Thomas **Cor**.
Somerset	Collins, Edward Cor. ⎫
	Buffing, John Quart. ⎭ To Capt. Arthur Upton
Cornwall	Williams, William Cor. †
Devon	Whichalls, Robert Cor. †
Dorset	Churchhill, Matthew Cor. †
Devon	Hartford, Anthony **Quart**. to Capt. R. Downe
Denbigh	Lewis, Hugh Quart. to Capt. John Hanmer
L. & W.	Coleman, Henry Quart.
Cornwall	Hutchins, Abraham Quart. †
Cornwall	Battersby, John **Capt**. FOOT
Devon	Bishop, John Capt.
Dorset	Hammond, Robert Capt.
Cornwall	Marshall, John Capt.
	Smith, Nicholas **Capt. Lieut**.
	Abraham, Richard Lieut. †
Devon	Bennett, Richard Lieut. †
Cornwall	Marten, Roger **Ens**. to Maj. John Coswarth
	Howell, Nicholas Ens. †
	Stacy, Reignold Ens. †
	Couch, Richard Ens. †
	Davy, Ralph Ens. †
Cornwall	Gill, John **Capt**. DRAGOONS

Digby, Sir John [of Gayhurst]
L. & W.	Grove, William **Capt.**	} HORSE
	Sheen, Thomas Cor.	
Middlesex	Holt, Thomas **Cor.** †	
Bucks	Collingridge, Richard **Quart. Gen.** BRIGADE	
Wilts	Pruett, William Quart. to Capt. William Grove	
L. & W.	Taylor, John Quart. to Capt. Clark	

Digby, Sir John [of Mansfield Woodhouse]*
Nottingh.	Thompson, Joseph **Capt.** FOOT
	Styles, William Capt.
	Holder, Henry Capt.
	Wray, Jonathan **Lieut.** } To Capt. John Cooper
	Cooper, Michael Ens.
	Garlick, John Lieut. } To Capt. Edm. Pate
	Poole, Robert Ens.
	Worsdall, Richard **Ens.**
Kent	Cranbury, William Ens.
Derby	Wilkinson, John Ens.

Dives, Sir Lewis
Dorset	Willoughby, Christopher **Capt. Lieut.** HORSE
Somerset	White, George **Lieut.**
	Fry, Stephen **Cor.** to Captain Robert Fry
	Toogood, Edw. **Quart.** to Maj. Fitzherbert
Dorset	Harris, John Quart. to Capt. Bludd
L. & W.	Salway, Thomas **Maj.** † FOOT
Middlesex	Norris, Edw. **Capt.**
L. & W.	Napier, Robert Capt.
Dorset	Speed, Walter Capt. }
Somerset	Plucknet, Robert Lieut.
Dorset	Pyne, Lionell Capt.
Somerset	Alford, Robert Capt.
Dorset	Rogers, William **Lieut.** to Capt. Hadonett
York	Wastnesse, John Lieut.
L. & W.	Townesend, Robert Lieut. to Capt. John Moulins
Sussex	Levett, Thomas Lieut. †
L. & W.	Jennings, John Lieut. to Capt. Bright
	Griffin, Thomas **Ens.** to Sir Thomas Sherley
Dorset	Collins, Barnaby Ens. to Capt. Cresswell
Bedford	Gale, Richard Ens. †
Somerset	Moulins, Adrian Ens. †
	Warcopp, Gervase **Regt. Quart.**
Bedford	Paly, Thomas Quart.

Doddington, Sir Francis
Middlesex	Paddon, Robert **Capt**. HORSE
Somerset	Hamme, Richard **Cor**.

Donnell, Richard
Glamorg.	Evans, Leyson **Capt**. FOOT
	Morgan, John Capt.
Carmarth.	Barrett, Bonaventure **Lieut**.
Monmouth	Williams, William Lieut.
	Morgan, Charles **Ens**. to Capt. Morgan
Glamorg.	Watkin, Hopkin Ens. †

Dover, Earl of
L. & W.	Bradshaw, James **Capt**. FOOT
	Read, Thomas Capt.
Southam.	Reniger, Samuel Capt.
L. & W.	Heskith, Richard **Lieut**. to Capt. Partridge
Oxon	Ball, William Lieut. †
L. & W.	Colcott, Arthur Ens. to Capt. James Bradshaw

Drury, Edward*
L. & W.	Pilkington, Henry **Lieut**. **Col**. DRAGOONS

Dudley, Sir Gamaliel
L. & W.	Strong, John **Capt**. HORSE
	Frothingham, Michael **Lieut**. to Capt. Robinson
	Stanton, John Cor. to **Maj**. Richard Sherborne
L. & W.	Leech, Jeremy **Capt**. DRAGOONS

Duncomb, Sir Edward
L. & W.	Mackmoyler, Richard **Lieut**. **Col**. HORSE
York	Vincent, Richard **Capt**. ⎫
Durham	Rackett, William Lieut. ⎭
L. & W.	Thurnham, Thomas **Cor**. to Capt. Duncombe
York	Smyth, Henry **Quart**. to Capt. James Ranson
	Man, Thomas Quart. to Capt. Conyers
York	Duncombe, William **Capt**. DRAGOONS
	Thompson, Robert **Cor**.

Dutton, Sir Ralph*
L. & W.	Dymock, Cressy **Col**. HORSE
Oxon	Pollard, Anthony **Capt**.

Gloucester	Coxwell, John Capt.	
	Whittorn, George **Capt. Lieut.**	
Lincoln	Cardinall, Thomas **Capt.** FOOT	
L. & W.	Hull, Thomas Capt.	
Berks	Hull, Samuel Lieut.	
Kent	Grimes, George Capt.	
Worcester	Rixon, John **Lieut.** to Capt. Charles Morris	
Hereford	Herbert, John **Ens.** to Maj. Degory Collins	
Gloucester	Brown, Thomas Ens. to Capt. Hoskins	
L. & W.	Carter, Thomas **Quart.**	

Dyer, Edward
Somerset
King, Henry **Capt.** } HORSE
Grabham, Hector, Cor. }
Dibble, Richard **Lieut.** } To Capt. Stephen Dyer
Dibble, Henry Quart. }
Bunter, Thomas Lieut. to Capt. Edw. Watts
Bray, John **Quart.**
Fry, Robert Quart.
Morse, John Quart. to Maj. John Wilde

Dyer, Sir Lodowick
Lincoln   Greaves, John Lieut. HORSE, to Capt. Barnard

Dymock
L. & W.   Rawson, Thomas **Capt.** HORSE

Earnly, Sir Michael
Wilts   Ranger, Evan **Maj.** } FOOT
Salop   Cole, Thomas Ens.   }
L. & W.   Long, William **Capt.**
             Kirk, John **Lieut.** to Capt. Pagenham
Wilts   Ady, Thomas Lieut. to Capt. Cary

Eden, John
Durham
Parkin, Timothy **Capt.**   } FOOT
Pilkington, Thomas Lieut.   }
Appleby, Cutbert Capt.   }
Batmanson, John Lieut.   }
Green, Alexander Ens.   }
Allenson, John Capt.
Bowbank, George **Lieut.**   } To Capt. John Steevenson
Ward, Christopher Ens.   }
Morlye, John Lieut. to Col. Nicholas Cheator

Armstrong, William Lieut. to Maj. James Bolt

Cradock, William **Cor**. HORSE
Martingdall, Percivall **Quart**. †

Edgecumbe, Pierce
Cornwall   Bond, Christopher **Capt**. HORSE
           Norris, Henry **Lieut**. †
           Edwards, Robert **Cor**. †
           Beare, John Cor. †
           Emmett, John Cor.
           Billing, Robert **Quart**. †
           Wallis, Richard Quart. †

Cornwall   Scawen, John **Capt**. FOOT
           Scawen, Thomas Capt.
           Grills, William Capt.   ⎫
              Poppleston, Lyney Lieut. ⎭
           Arundell, John **Lieut**. †
           Burrell, James Lieut. †
           Killyow, William Lieut. †
           Cudlip, Richard Lieut. †
           Hore, Matthew **Ens**. to Maj. Edgecumbe
           Pope, John Ens. †
           Poppleston, Ferdinando Ens. †
           Curbyn, John Ens. †
           Grills, Hanniball Ens. †
           Moon, Alexander Ens. †
           Skelton, Thomas Ens. †
           Lavers, Paul Ens. †
           Pope, John Ens. †

Egerton, Randolph
Worcester   Awbry, Edw. **Capt**. HORSE
Pembroke   Davis, Thomas Capt.   ⎫
               Davis, Chauncy Lieut. ⎬
               Davis, John Cor.   ⎭
Stafford   Manwaring, Peter Capt.
            Dod, Thomas **Lieut**. ⎫ To Capt. Edw. Locket
Carmarth.   Lewis Rees, Cor.   ⎭
            Farmer, John Lieut. to Lieut. Col. Edw. Price
            Floyd, Walter Lieut.   ⎫ To Capt. Jonathan Floyd
            Richards, John Quart.   ⎭
            Floyd, David Lieut. to Capt. John Barlow

Monmouth	Morgan, Edmund Lieut. to Capt. Thomas Rudde
Chester	Oldham, Edw. Lieut.
L. & W.	Beverly, John **Cor**. to Capt. Thomas Beverly
	Fulke, Gerard Cor.
Derby	Purdee, John Cor.
Lancaster	Billing, Richard **Quart**.
L. & W.	Twydall, Arthur Quart. to Maj. Edmund Broad

Egerton, Richard
Chester   Nicholls, Robert **Lieut**. † HORSE

Ellis, Robert
Denbigh	Powell, Thomas **Capt**. FOOT
	Edwards, John Capt.
Merion.	Morgan, John Capt.
Salop	Gregory, John **Lieut**.
Merion.	Edwards, Rice Lieut. to Maj. Morgan
Carmarth.	Bowen, Griffith Lieut. to Maj. Floyd
Denbigh	Lewis, David Lieut. to Capt. Dalben
	Blodwell, Richard **Ens**. to Maj. Gillmore
	Edwards, David Ens. to Capt. George Hosyer

Ennys
Cambridge   Deane, Edward **Lieut**. HORSE, to Capt. Petts

Errington, John
Durham	Errington, John **Capt**. HORSE
York	Middleton, Thomas Capt. Lieut. ⎫
	Wardell, Richard Cor. ⎭
	Middleton, John Lieut. to Capt. Francis Ashly
Durham	Leadham, Samuel Lieut. to Capt. Thomas Turner
York	Tayler, Michael **Quart**.
Durham	Emerson, Robert Quart.
	Ingledew, John Quart.
York	Ashly, Craithorne **Capt**. **Lieut**. DRAGOONS
	Garbut, William **Cor**.
Northumb.	Bartram, John **Quart**.

Eure, Matthew
Nottingh.   West, John **Quart**. HORSE, to Capt. Molineux

Eure, Ralph

L. & W.	Carlisle, Francis **Capt**. HORSE
Lincoln	Chippingdale, Francis Capt. ⎫
L. & W.	Hawksly, Gregory Quart. ⎬
Nottingh.	Pole, German Capt.
Lincoln	Dolby, James **Lieut**. to Capt. John Dawson
Nottingh.	Molineux, Francis Lieut. to Capt. Molineux
L. & W.	Lambe, Nicholas **Cor**. to Capt. John Chippingdale
Nottingh.	Molineux, Edmund Cor.
L. & W.	Charlesworth, Thomas **Quart**. ⎫ To Capt. Mansford
Lincoln	Fletcher, John Quart. ⎬
	Dolby, Thomas Quart.
L. & W.	Harber, William Quart. to Lieut. Col. Rolleston

Eure, William

Middlesex	Stevenson, William **Capt**. HORSE
York	Fleming, Nicholas Capt.
L. & W.	Smith, William **Lieut**. to Maj. Robert Busbridge
York	Anne, John Lieut. to Philip Dolman
	Hardcastle, Christopher **Cor**.
Durham	Chambers, Matthew Cor. to Capt. Wellfoot
	Swinburne, Thomas Cor. to Maj. Thomas Eure
	Swinburne, John Cor. to Lieut. Col. Busbridge
	Sayer, Thomas Cor. ⎫
York	Smith, James **Quart**. ⎬ To Capt. Laurence Sayer
	Steele, Thomas Quart. ⎭
	Brown, William Quart. to Capt. William Dolman
L. & W.	Leyborn, Ralph Quart.
York	Metcalfe, William **Capt**. FOOT
	Pullen, Henry Capt.
	Ascough, Thomas **Lieut**. to Maj. Emmanuel Gilby
	Richardson, John **Ens**.
	Lightfoot, William Ens. to Capt. Thomas Barner
	Pullen, Robert Ens.
	Benson, Robert Ens. to Capt. John Plimpton

Eyre, Anthony*

Nottingh.	Love, Hastings **Capt**. † HORSE
Suffolk	Taylor, Thomas Capt.
L. & W.	Skelton, Robert **Lieut**. to Capt. Thomas Muckly
Lincoln	Phillips, Henry Lieut. to Capt. Whitchcote
Nottingh.	Lassells, George Lieut.
Lincoln	Johnson, Robert Lieut.
	Standish, William Lieut.

Cambridge	Tassell, John **Quart.**
Durham	Richardson, John Quart. to Lieut. Col. Ralph Pudsey
York	Kerchwall, Roger Quart. to Capt. Thomas Moughly

Eyre, Sir Gervase*
Nottingh. Hall, Edmund **Quart.** HORSE

Eyre, Rowland
Derby Brock, Howard **Capt.** ⎫ HORSE
          Steeple, John Quart. ⎭

          Barker, Matthew **Cor.** ⎫
          Hayward, Henry Quart. ⎭ To Lieut. Col. Eyre

          Furnis, Rowland Cor. †
          Bowyer, Thomas **Quart.**

Nottingh. Bold, John **Lieut.** FOOT, to Capt. Allen
Derby Bradbury, John Lieut.
          Francis, Rowland Lieut.

Derby Tunstead, James **Capt.** DRAGOONS

Fane, Sir Francis*
Gloucester Briggs, Richard **Capt.** FOOT
York Purday, William Capt.
          Kirk, John Capt.
L. & W. Moore, Thomas **Lieut.** to Lieut. Col. Forbes
          Eliot, John Lieut. to Maj. Redmain Burrell
Derby Wainwright, John Lieut. to Maj. George Rogers
York Shaw, William Lieut. to Capt. Balgy
Lincoln Naylor, James **Ens.** to Capt. Robert Sandford
          Barraclough, Richard Ens. to Capt. Halton
          Spencer, Thomas **Quart.**

Lincoln Ranes, Edward **Capt.** HORSE

Farmer, Sir William
Stafford Hall, Richard Cor. HORSE
Northam. Hunt, Valentine Quart. †

Farr, Henry
Essex Jennings, Richard **Capt.** ⎫ FOOT
          Sergeant, Humphry Lieut. ⎭
          Stevens, Matthew Capt.
            White, James Lieut.
          Tilford, William Capt.

Indigent Officers

          Ulting, Thomas Capt.
          Hedge, Matthew Ens.
          Piggott, Thomas Ens. to Lieut. Col. Stephen Smith
          Wakefield, Giles Ens. †
          Hoyden, Thomas Ens.

Fawcett, Samuel
York   Horne, Thomas Quart. [   ]

Fenwick, John
Northumb.   Fenwick, George Capt. ⎫ HORSE
              Shield, Francis Lieut. ⎬
York   Oliver, John Cor.   ⎬
Northumb.   Shield, Ralph Quart. ⎭
            Fenwick, Ralph Capt. Lieut.
York   Tayler, James Lieut. to Capt. Nathaniel Crosland
Northumb.   Carre, Ephraim Lieut. †
York   Haynes, Edward Cor. to Lieut. Col. Bellasis
Northumb.   Greenwell, William Cor.
            Soulby, Christopher Quart.
            Forster, Peter Quart.

Newcastle   Watson, Robert Lieut. DRAGOONS, to Capt. Fenwick

Fetherston, Sir Henry
Cumberl.   Brathwayt, Geo. Quart. HORSE

Durham   Dawson, Lancelot Ens. FOOT

Fetherston, John
Durham   Gaynes, John Lieut. ⎫ FOOT
Newcastle   Foster, Robert Ens. ⎭ To Maj. Charles West
Durham   Buston, William Lieut. to Lieut. Col. Ambrose Maxton
            Johnson, Oswald Lieut. to Capt. John Martindall

Fetherston, Sir Timothy
York   Giles, Lawrence Capt. ⎫ FOOT
            Banks, Francis Lieut. ⎬
            Hally, George Ens.   ⎭
            Bradly, Edward Capt.
Lancaster   Heskith, Thomas Capt.
Durham   Anderson, Edward Lieut. ⎫
York   Potter, Ralph Ens.   ⎬ To Capt. Cuthbert Best
Cumberl.   Hutchinson, Nicholas Ens.
            Lancake, Thomas Quart.

Fielding, Richard*
L. & W.	Norwood, Charles **Maj.** FOOT
Bedford	Halley, John **Ens.** to Capt. Peter Walthall

Finch, Charles
Somerset	Hodges, William **Capt.** HORSE
Devon	England, George Capt. ⎫ Lenthall, Peter Cor. ⎭
Kent	Hyde, Anthony Capt. ⎫
L. & W.	Green, Francis Quart. ⎭
Berks	Woodington, Henry Capt. ⎫
Southam.	Cook, Robert Lieut. ⎬
Somerset	Hodges, John Cor. ⎭
Devon	Raymond, Thomas **Capt. Lieut.**
L. & W.	Francis, Matthew Lieut. ⎫ To Capt. Henry Manning
Salop	Adams, Edward Quart. ⎭
Surrey	Gardiner, Timothy Lieut. ⎫ To Lieut. Col. Clark
Hertford	Newport, William Cor. ⎭
Wilts	Larguise, Walter Lieut. to Capt. Earle
	Goldston, Philip Lieut. ⎫ To Capt. Combes
	Best, Matthew Cor. ⎭
Oxon	Sturton, Robert **Cor.**
Wilts	Tattershall, John Cor. to Maj. Webbe
York	Smith, Richard Cor.
Cornwall	Tolley, Stephen **Quart.** to Capt. Browne
Surrey	Fetherston, John **Quart.** BRIGADE

Fitton, Sir Edward*
L. & W.	Leigh, Urian **Lieut. Col.** FOOT
Chester	Green, Thomas **Capt.**
	Littler, William **Lieut.** to Capt. William Davenport

Fitzherbert, Sir John
Derby	Low, Arthur **Capt.** ⎫ HORSE
	Low, Ferdinando Lieut. ⎬
	Sanderson, Thomas Quart. ⎭
	Barnsly, Charles Capt. ⎫
	Topples, Ralph Quart. ⎭
	Bennet, Anthony Capt.
	Fitzrandolph, George Capt.
	Eyre, John Capt. ⎫
	Eyre, George Cor. ⎭
Surrey	Moore, Robert Capt. HORSE & FOOT
York	Eyre, Reynold **Lieut.**

Derby	Statham, John Lieut. to Capt. John Lingly
	Dixwell, Thomas **Cor.** ⎫
	Brewine, Thomas Quart. ⎬ To Capt. William Fitzherbert
Stafford	Hodgson, Thomas Cor.
Notting.	Wyld, Richard Cor. ⎫
Derby	Allen, Edw. **Quart.** ⎬ To Capt. Edw. Fitzrandolph
Stafford	Cotton, Thomas Quart.
L. & W.	Heveningham Simon **Lieut. Col.** FOOT
Nottingh.	Royston, Thomas **Capt.**
Lancaster	Cawsey, John Capt.
Derby	Lancaster, John **Quart.**

Fleetwood, Dutton*
Bedford	Batt, Henry Capt. ⎫ HORSE
	Colling, Samuel Lieut. ⎭

Fleetwood, Sir Richard
Stafford	Sherborne, John **Capt.** FOOT
	Ball, Thomas **Lieut.** †

Fletcher, Sir Henry
Cumberl.	Brisby, Richard **Lieut.** FOOT to Lieut. Col. Carleton
	Stavely, John **Ens.** to Maj. Will Flemin

Flower, William
Monmouth	Flower, Thomas **Capt. Lieut.** FOOT

Floyd, Sir Evan
Denbigh	Jones, Richard **Maj.** FOOT
	Yale, Thomas **Capt.**
	Vaughan, John Capt.

Floyd, Godfry
Lancaster	Mort, Seth **Capt.** FOOT
York	Wettinghall, Christopher Capt.
	Gayle, Matthew **Lieut.** to Lieut. Col. Duhurst
	Calvert, John Lieut. to Capt. Crow
	Clough, Francis **Ens.** to Lieut. Col. Jackson
	Turner, Edward **Quart.**

Floyd
York	Best, Thomas **Capt.** FOOT

Floyd, Sir Charles*
Salop	Williams, Roger **Capt**. FOOT
L. & W.	Williams, Francis Capt.
Denbigh	Pris, Ellis Capt.
	Vaughan, John **Lieut**. to Capt. Robert Challoner
Montgom.	Jones, Robert **Ens**. to Capt. Hugh Jones
L. & W.	Pugh, Thomas Ens. to Capt. Sarraway
	Thorold, John Ens. to Lieut. Col. Edw. Tyrwhyt
	Challoner, Anthony Ens. †
	Garaway, William Ens. †
Durham	Rickaby, James **Lieut**. HORSE to Capt. Stephen Dawson

Floyd, Sir Richard
Salop	Cavely, John **Capt**. DRAGOONS
Merion.	Floyd, David Capt. ⎫
Salop	Evans, Edward **Lieut**. ⎬ To Capt. Edw. Floyd
Merion.	Floyd, Hugh Cor.
Denbigh	Hughes, Robert **Lieut**. to Capt. William Broughton
	Ledsam, Edw. Lieut.
Chester	Barrow, William **Ens**. †
Flint	Jones, Thomas **Lieut**. HORSE
Denbigh	Vaux, Gilbert **Quart**.
Chester	Dawson, John Quart.

Floyd, Thomas
Carmarth.	Williams, Thomas **Ens**. [ ]

Forcer, John*
York	Bartram, Francis **Capt**. ⎫ HORSE
	Aslaby, Bartholomew Lieut. ⎭
Durham	Metcalf, John Capt. ⎫
York	Blakeston, Francis Lieut. ⎬
Durham	Wood, Thomas Quart. ⎭
	Clavering, Thomas Capt. ⎫
Northumb.	Forster, Clement Lieut. ⎬
Newcastle	Westgarth, Anthony Cor. ⎬
Durham	Morton, James Quart. ⎭
York	Metcalf, Anthony **Capt**. **Lieut**.
	Rymer, Simon Lieut. ⎫
Northumb.	Collingwood, John Cor. ⎬ To Maj. Craithorne
York	Ambler, John Quart. ⎭
	Metcalf, Christopher Lieut. to Lieut. Col. John Sayer

Durham	Pearson, John Lieut.	⎫
	Rose, Thomas Cor.	⎬ To Capt. Henry Messenger
	Stones, Richard Quart.	⎭
Newcastle	Bell, John Lieut. to Capt. Musgrave	
Northumb.	Hunter, Andrew **Cor**.	
York	Colston, Thomas Cor.	⎫ To Capt. Wilkinson
	Shaw, Alexander Quart.	⎭
Durham	Hodgeson, Francis Cor.	
	Forcer, Thomas **Quart**. to Capt. Peter Forcer	
Northumb.	Hall, John Quart.	

Ford, Sir Edward

Southam.	Ford, William **Capt. Lieut.**	⎫ HORSE
L. & W.	Roane, John Capt. Lieut.	⎭
Surrey	Crosse, Henry Lieut.	
Sussex	Malbrank, Francis Lieut.	⎫ To Maj. Malbrank
Southam.	Westbrook, John Cor.	⎭
Surrey	Smith, John **Cor**.	
Sussex	Napper, Matthew **Quart**.	
	Hartford, John Quart.	
	Odham, John Quart. to Capt. Gage	
L. & W.	Colles, Thomas Quart.	
Leicester	Ironmonger, Nicholas Quart.	

Forster, Thomas

Northumb.	Ord, John **Capt**. FOOT
	Forster, John Capt.
	Forster, George **Lieut**.
	Forster, Matthew **Ens**.
	Forster, Thomas Ens.
Newcastle	Forster, Thomas Ens. to Lieut. Col. John Forster

Forrester, Lord James

L. & W.	Finelay, James **Capt**. HORSE

Fortescue, Sir Edmund

Devon	Reynell, William **Capt**. FOOT
Dorset	Strode, John Capt.
	Fitzgerald, John **Capt. Lieut**.
Bucks	Edmonds, Henry Lieut. to Capt. John Blewet
Devon	Palfry, Thomas Lieut. to Capt. Peter Fortescue
Somerset	Drue, George Lieut. †
Devon	Mole, Thomas Lieut. †
Dorset	White, Edw. **Ens**. to Lieut. Col. John Somerset

Cornwall	Roscruge, Henry Ens. †	
Devon	Vennor, John **Lieut.** † HORSE	

Fortescue, Faithfull
L. & W.	Tirry, Roger **Regt. Quart.** HORSE

Fox, Somerset
Worcester	Bentall, Sampson **Capt.** FOOT
Gloucester	Horton, William Capt.
	Morris, Somerset Capt.
Hereford	Garnons, Roger Capt.
Salop	James, William **Ens.** to Capt. Thomas Fox
	Grosvenor, Richard **Quart.**

Frechevile, John
L. & W.	Beversham, John **Maj.** HORSE
	Alsop, Richard **Capt.**
Derby	Fletcher, William **Lieut.** to Capt. John Low
	Eyre, Thomas Lieut. } To Capt. John Eyre
	Eyre, Thomas Quart. }
	Poole, Ignatius Lieut. } To Capt. Gervase Poole
	Harris, John Quart. }
	Rodes, Clifton **Cor.** to Capt. Edw. Nicholls
	Scorer, Hugh **Quart.** to Sir Henry Hunlock
Nottingh.	Bullock, Robert Quart.
Nottingh.	Bates, William **Capt.** FOOT

Frowd, Philip
Surrey	Howard, Thomas **Lieut.** HORSE
L. & W.	Miller, William **Quart.**
L. & W.	Shepheard, Sylvester **Lieut.** FOOT, to Maj. Rychaut

Fulks
Northam.	Crane, Henry **Lieut.** † HORSE

Gallop, Thomas
Dorset	Hayne, George **Ens.** † FOOT

Gamage
Glamorg.	Walters, Edmond **Maj.** FOOT

Gamul, Sir Francis
Chester Barnston, Richard **Capt**. **Lieut**. FOOT
Janines, Richard Lieut. ⎫
Littler, Richard Ens. ⎭ To Capt. Daniel Bavand
Hodgekin, Michael Lieut. to Capt. Edw. Morgan
Langly, John Lieut. to Capt. David Humphreys
Wright, Richard Lieut. †
Broster, Charles **Ens**. to Capt. James Hudleston
Minshall, Randall Ens. to Capt. Henry Brereton

Gainsford, John
Hereford Morgan, John **Capt**. ⎫
 Morgan, Charles **Ens**. ⎭ FOOT
Morgan Thomas Ens. †

Gerard, Lord [Colonel Charles Gerard]
L. & W. Doubleday, Francis **Capt**. HORSE
Brecon Herbert, Walter Capt.
L. & W. Butler, Hugh Capt. †
 Gaughegan, John Capt. †
 St. George, _____ **Lieut**. to Capt. Windsor
Carmarth. Leney, Nicholas Lieut. ⎫
L. & W. Browne, John Quart. ⎭ To Sir Gilbert Gerard
Glamorg. Basset, Charles Lieut. †
Lancaster Wainehouse, John Lieut. †
L. & W. Smith, Francis Lieut. †
 Smallwood, John Lieut. ⎫
Monmouth Pritchard, John Cor. ⎭ To Maj. William Blayne
L. & W. Heap, Thomas Lieut. †
 Norris, William Lieut. † to Capt. Lane
 Basset, Charles **Cor**. ⎫
York Fisher, Thomas Quart. ⎭ To Lieut. Col. Russel
Gloucester Master, Robert Cor. to Maj. Gen. David Walter
Carmarth. Harris, Humphry Cor. †
L. & W. Blaney, Edward Cor. to Lieut. Col. Price
Merion. Humphreys, Richard **Quart**.
Carmarth. Williams, Richard Quart. to Capt. Martin
Wilts Hargett, Francis Quart. to Sir Timothy Tyrrell
L. & W. Dod, Thomas Quart. to Capt. Russell
 Randall, Richard, Quart. to Capt. Croker
 Perkinson, William Quart.
 Le Geyt, Noah Quart. †

L. & W. Gerard, Edw. **Col**. FOOT
Hereford Ross, William **Lieut**. **Col**.

Gerard

L. & W.	Young, John **Capt**.
	Hill, George Capt.
	Beynon, Henry Capt.
	Peere, Benjamin Capt.
	Hinton, Daniel Capt.
Denbigh	Vaughan, Richard Capt. ⎫
	Floyd, Richard Lieut. ⎭
Cambridge	Bourne, Anthony Capt.
	Harris, Edmund Capt.
Essex	Fitch, Thomas Capt.
Glamorg.	Basset, William Capt.
Carmarth.	Sanders, William Capt. † ⎫
	Palmer, Henry Lieut. ⎭
	Williams, Griffith Capt. †
Pembroke	Bowen, Owen Capt. †
	Owen, William Capt. †
Carmarth.	Phillips, Thomas Capt.
L. & W.	Pollard, Lewis **Lieut**. ⎫ To Capt. Trevillyan
	Pollard, Charles Ens. ⎭
Oxon	Raynsford, John Lieut. to Capt. Deane
Chester	Chantrell, Robert Lieut. to Maj. Halsall
Stafford	Boughey, John Lieut. to Capt. Leigh
Pembroke	Williams, Richard Lieut. to Capt. David Howell
Montgom.	Morgan, Ellis Lieut. ⎫ To Capt. Cotterell
	Ellis, John Ens. ⎭
Glamorg.	Basset, James Lieut. †
Carmarth	Jeanes, George Lieut. †
L. & W.	Worrall, George Lieut. †
	Fox, Henry Lieut. †
Monmouth	Proger, Charles Lieut. †
Merion.	Floyd, Lewis **Ens**. to Capt. Bladwell
L. & W.	Stamp, Simon Ens.
	Aubin, Germain Ens. to Sir Charles Cotterell
	Harrison, Ralph Ens. to Capt. Robert Earnly
	Moor, Hugh Ens. to Major Leigh
Norfolk	Sluer, Edw. Ens. †
Middlesex	M. Donnough, Kelley O Katlou Ens.[7] ⎫
Denbigh	Floyd, Robert Ens. ⎬ To Capt. Soames
Pembroke	Williams, Richard Ens. ⎭

---

[7] The name is reproduced here as it appears in the original document, although in the index to the same it is rendered as 'Mac-Donough O Kelly'. Almost certainly it has suffered a printer's error, or a misunderstanding of the officer's claim certificate. Conceivably 'O Katlou' could be a mistake for 'Of Carlow'.

Gerard, Edward
L. & W.	Parham, William **Capt**. FOOT
Carmarth.	Wynne, William Capt.
	Thomas, Philip **Lieut**. to Capt. Plackledge
	Floyd, Walter Lieut. ⎫ To Capt. Edw. Floyd
	Floyd, Phee. Ens. ⎭
Glamorg.	Lucas Thomas Lieut. †
L. & W.	Kelly, Dennis Lieut. †
	Hopton, William **Ens**. †
	Pretheretch, William Ens. †

Gerard, Sir Gilbert*
Huntingd.	Walwyn, Thomas **Capt**. HORSE
L. & W.	Cupper, Henry Capt.
	James, Robert **Quart**.

Worcester	Mozey, John **Capt**. FOOT
Surrey	Young, Gabriel Capt.
Nottingh.	Warberton, William Capt.
Middlesex	Stanly, William Capt. ⎫
Warwick	Dormer, Francis Ens. ⎭
Worcester	Pilkington, Thomas **Lieut**. to Capt. John Byram
L. & W.	Waldron, William Lieut. to Capt. John Potters
Lancaster	Powell, William Lieut. †
Wilts	Whittingham Henry Lieut. †
Lancaster	Holt, Robert **Ens**. to Capt. William Young

Gerard, Ratcliffe*
Carmarth.	Floyd, Hugh **Capt**. ⎫ FOOT
	Floyd, Rowland Lieut. ⎬
	Floyd, Maurice Ens. ⎭

Gerard, Richard [Queen's Lifeguard of Foot]
L. & W.	Hughes, John **Maj**. FOOT
	Hazard, Thomas **Ens**. to Capt. John Tallowcarne
Dorset	Fitzjames, John Ens. †

Gerard
Somerset	Bently, William **Lieut**. [ ] to Capt. Gerard Croker

Gibbons
Kent	Hart, Thomas **Cor**. HORSE

Gibson, Sir John [Sir Edward Osborne's regiment]
Bucks   Simpson, Edmund Quart. HORSE

Gibson, Richard
L. & W.   Kynnaston, Richard Capt. FOOT
Somerset   Sydenham, William Capt.
Chester   Ward, Arthur Capt.
Norfolk   Mallome, Thomas Capt. ⎫
L. & W.   Overley, William Ens. ⎭
             Jones, John Ens.

Gifford, John
Devon   Rawleigh, Joseph Lieut. FOOT, to Maj. Newcourt
             Venner, Roger Ens. to Capt. George Broughton

Gilborne, Henry
Surrey   Evans, Randolph Capt. HORSE

Gilby, Anthony*
Lincoln   Wharton, Abraham Capt. FOOT
York   Marshall, Benjamin Capt.
Nottingh.   Tye, John Capt. Lieut.
             Grundy, William Lieut. to Capt. Pate
             Royston, Ralph Lieut. to Capt. Womtwell
             Broadhead, William Lieut. to Capt. Patrick Cox
York   Wray, Jonathan Lieut. †
Lincoln   Howson, William Ens. to Capt. John Barker

Derby   Tye, John Quart. † HORSE

Gilby, Sir Theophilus*
L. & W.   Pell, Sir Bartholomew Lieut. Col. FOOT
Sussex   Marsh, William Capt.
Lincoln   Frobisher, Martin Capt. ⎫
York   Forster, Stephen Lieut. ⎭
             Askew, Charles Lieut. to Maj. John Beverly
L. & W.   Rythe, James Lieut. to Capt. Matthew Francis
York   Kay, William Ens.

Girling, William
Norfolk   Morse, John Capt. FOOT

Girlington, Sir John

Merion.	Floyd, Hugh **Capt.**	⎫ HORSE
York	Read, John Lieut.	⎭
Lincoln	Sherborne, Alexander **Lieut.** to Lieut. Col. Middleton	
York	Harwood, Laurence Lieut. †	
	Burton, Ralph **Cor.**	⎫ To Maj. John Watson
	Driffield, Symon Quart.	⎭
Lancaster	Atkinson, Miles **Quart.** †	
Lancaster	Greene, Thomas **Capt.** FOOT	
	Burton, Bryan **Ens.**	

Glendore, Lord

L. & W.　　Twisleton, John **Capt.** FOOT

Glenham, Sir Thomas

L. & W.	Whittington, Mark **Capt.**	⎫ HORSE
Derby	Adamson, William Lieut.	⎭
L. & W.	Richardson, William Capt.	
	Whittington, Luke Capt.	⎫
	Paty, Andrew Lieut.	⎪
York	Bilton, Ralph Cor.	⎬
	Calverly, Robert Quart.	⎭
Kent	Tayler, William Capt.	⎫
L. & W.	Napier, William Lieut.	⎭
Kent	Silson, John Capt.	
York	Gomersal, John Capt.	
L. & W.	Casy, John Capt. in Oxon	
York	Laurence, Thomas **Lieut.** to Capt. Crompton	
	Sunderland, Abraham Lieut. to Maj. Portington	
Durham	Cassada, Patrick Lieut.	
	Wilkinson, Ralph Cor.	
York	Constable, George **Cor.**	
	Appleton, Robert Cor. †	
York	Thornton, William Capt. FOOT	
Northumb.	Hodgson, William Capt.	
	Stokeld, William Capt.	
	Swinburne, Thomas Capt. †	
	Fenwick, William Lieut. to Capt. Thomas Swinburne	
Newcastle	Blenkensoppe, Jacob Capt.	
Middlesex	Parr, Thomas Lieut.	
York	Darcy, Lewis Capt.	
	Wilson, James Lieut.	
	Girdler, Christopher Ens.	

L. & W.	Pickering, John **Lieut**. to Capt. George Loope
York	Chaderton, Francis Lieut. to Capt. Robert Gosnold
Northumb.	Hutchinson Hugh Lieut. to Capt. Darly Mackerly
Durham	Taylor, Robert **Ens**. to Capt. William Hodgson
L. & W.	Barlow George Ens. to Maj. Lewins
York	Rudd, Thomas Ens. †

Gloucester, Duke of*

L. & W.	Thorold, Robert **Capt**. } HORSE
York	Skelton, Henry Cor. }
Middlesex	Walker, Henry Capt.
Nottingh.	Wood, Robert Lieut.
	James, Richard Cor.
	Gregge, Robert Quart.
	Widdrington, Francis **Lieut**. to Lieut. Col. Stanhoppe
Lincoln	Smith, William Lieut. to Maj. Charles Wilson
L. & W.	Scott, John **Cor**. to Maj. John Scott
Lincoln	Langly, Joseph **Quart**. to Capt. John Cole

Godfrey, John*

L. & W.	Tyrringham, Francis **Capt**. FOOT
	Gwatkin, Thomas **Capt. Lieut**.
	Ennis, Thomas **Ens**. to Capt. Gilbert Thomas

Godolphin, Sir William

Cornwall	Jenkin, Petherick **Capt**. FOOT
	Gunne, John **Capt. Lieut**.
	Marshall, Richard Lieut. †

Godolphin, William

Cornwall	Keliow, Henry **Capt**. FOOT
	Robinson, Francis Capt.
	Orchard, William Capt.
Devon	Hutchins, Francis Capt. }
L. & W.	Teige, Cornelius Lieut. }
Cornwall	Reskilly, Anthony **Capt. Lieut**.
	Hayme, John Lieut. †
	Tomkins, Edw. Lieut. †
	Harris, Thomas Lieut. †
	Trenwith, Thomas Lieut. †
	Painter, John Lieut. †
	Job, Richard Lieut. †
	Penlease, William **Ens**. †
	Luke, John Ens. †

	Gregory, Thomas Ens. †
	Trenhick, Michael Ens. †
	Clyes, Ralph Ens. †
	Torack, William Ens. †
	Bray, Anthony Ens. †
Devon	Tomkins, John **Quart. Gen.**
Cornwall	Flemin, Thomas Quart.

Goring, Lord Charles [1648]

Sussex	Smith, William **Lieut.** † HORSE
L. & W.	Wynne, Francis **Cor.** to Capt. Thomas Bowen
Sussex	Bransden, John Cor. to Maj. William Smith
	Smith, Benjamin **Quart.**
York	Kidny, William Quart. to Sir Bernard Gascoyne
L. & W.	Gargrave, John Quart.

Goring, Lord George

Southam.	Burleigh, Bernard **Capt.** † HORSE
Hereford	Harpur, John Capt. †
Southam.	Peachy, Thomas **Lieut.** to Capt. William Smith
Devon	Beckalack, William Lieut. to Sir Thomas Aston
York	Spink, John Lieut. †
L. & W.	Duteil, John Baptista **Cor.**
Glamorg.	Thomas, Henry Cor. to Sir James Bridgman
Surrey	Kennet, Jordan **Quart.** to Maj. Leicester †
Worcester	Pitt, Richard **Lieut.** H. & **Quart. Gen.**
Bucks	Digby, Kenelm **Gen. Ordnance**
Newcastle	Wright, Thomas &c.

Gower, Sir Thomas*

York	Browne, Christopher **Capt.** HORSE
Lincoln	Swale, James Capt.
York	Kendall, Philip **Quart.**
L. & W.	York, Edw. Quart.
York	Stockdale, Thomas **Ens.** FOOT
	Sympson, John **Quart.**
Durham	Frickly, Samuel **Lieut.** DRAGOONS to Capt. Andrews
York	Odby, John **Cor.** to Capt. Edm. Gower
	Leppington, Thomas Cor.
	Saltmarsh, Philip **Quart.**

Grady, Henry
L. & W.	Wiggmore, Robert **Lieut. Col.** HORSE
	Grady, John **Capt.**
Monmouth	Conell, Jeffery Capt.
	Gerard, John **Lieut.** †
Gloucester	Nanfan, Richard **Cor.**
Salop	Swain, George Quart. } To Maj. Thomas Nanfan
Montgom.	Cooper, William Quart.
Kent.	Tonney, Barnard Cor. †
L. & W.	Mageon, Edmund **Quart.** to Capt. Coningsby

Graham, Sir Richard
Cumberl.   Grimston, Stephen **Capt.** HORSE

Grandison, Lord
L. & W.   Roe, Francis **Lieut. Col.** FOOT

Montgom.   Floyd, Meredith **Cor.** HORSE, to Maj. Willy

Greenvile, Sir Bevile
Cornwall	Cory, Andrew **Capt.** FOOT
Devon	Harwell, George **Lieut.** to Capt. John Taverner
Cornwall	Crabbe, John Lieut. to Sir Peter Courtenay
	Holman, John Lieut. to Capt. Greenvile
	Butt, William Lieut. }
	Hay, John Ens.
	Murfill, William Lieut. to Capt. Richard Porter
	Berry, Nicholas Lieut. †
	Hutchins, Thomas Lieut. †
	Ferris, John Lieut. †
	Sharsell, Philip **Ens.** to Maj. Degory Tremayne
	Canne, William Ens. †
	Row, Henry Ens. †
	Spour, Henry Ens. †
	Roberts, Henry Ens. †
Devon	Kendall, Zachary Ens. †

Greenvile, Sir Richard
Devon   Cary, Sir Henry **Col.** HORSE & FOOT

L. & W.	Chamberlain, William **Col.** HORSE
Somerset	Matthew, Francis **Capt.**
Devon	Vivian, Richard Capt.
Cornwall	Gully, William Capt.

Indigent Officers

	Ellery, Anthony Capt. ⎫
	Tresahar, Henry Cor. ⎭
L. & W.	Rosecarrock, Humphry **Lieut**. to Capt. Shuckborough
	Adams, Thomas Lieut. ⎫
Devon	Seagar, William Cor. ⎬ To Maj. Edw. Rosecarrock
Norfolk	Harmer, Thomas Lieut.
Cornwall	Matthews, Richard Lieut.
Devon	Austin, Peter Lieut. to Capt. Reynold Mohun
	Seager, Hugh **Cor**. to Capt. William Wallcot
	Sheere, Joseph Cor. †
Cornwall	Lisle, Anthony **Quart**. †
	Geich, John Quart. †
	Hodge, Walter Quart.
L. & W.	Cary, Theodore **Col**. FOOT
Cornwall	Gilbert, Francis **Capt**.
	Thomas, Peter Capt.
	Coyesgarne, William Capt.
L. & W.	Sturton, Thomas Capt.
Devon	Greenwood, Edward Capt.
Cornwall	Taprell, John **Lieut**. ⎫
	Hawke, Nevill Ens. ⎭ To Capt. Charles Hawke
	Weeks, William Lieut. to Maj. John Carnock
L. & W.	Evans, Thomas Lieut. to Maj. George Collins
Cornwall	Hawkins, Edward Lieut. †
	Wayte, John Lieut. †
	Ford, Christopher Lieut. †
Devon	Beare, Simon **Ens**. to Capt. Richard Weeks
	Holdich, Philip Ens. to Capt. Henry Ellis †
Cornwall	Sheere, William Ens. †
	Cock, John Ens. †
	Jenkin, John Ens. †
	Dewen, Thomas Ens. †
L. & W.	Matthew, William Ens. †
Devon	Easton, William **Capt**. DRAGOONS

Grey, Edward

?	Carre, Francis **Lieut. Col**. HORSE
L. & W.	Smith, Malcomb **Capt**.
Northumb.	Carre, William Capt. ⎫
	Rydley, Musgrave Lieut. ⎭
Durham	Fawcet, James Capt. ⎫
Northumb.	Murrin, Edw. Cor. ⎭
	Brandling, Francis Capt.

Westmo.	Sargison, George **Capt. Lieut.**	
York	Wright, Alexander Cor.	
Northumb.	Richardson, Thomas Quart.	
Durham	Thorpe, Robert Lieut.	To Lieut. Col. Francis Carre
	Whitfield, Arthur Quart.	
Northumb.	Richardson, William Lieut. to Maj. Peter Palmer	
	Salkeild, Henry Lieut.	To Lieut. Col. John Salkeild
	Nichollson, Cutbert, Quart.	
York	Wright, Henry Lieut. to Maj. Jackson	
L. & W.	Buchannon, Walter **Cor.**	
Durham	Pinckney, Christopher Cor. to Capt. Foster	
Northumb.	Selby, Alexander Cor. to Capt. Thomas Selby	
	Wilkinson, Oswald Cor.	
	Dawson, Thomas Quart.	
L. & W.	Carre, Ralph Quart.	To Capt. Ralph Grey
Northumb.	Grey, Robert Cor.	
	Grey, Ralph Cor. †	
	Foster, Matthew Cor.	
	Ramsy, Robert **Quart.** †	
York	Gibson, John Quart. †	
	Brinch Thomas Quart. †	

L. & W.	Huddleston, Edward **Maj.** FOOT
Northumb.	Craister, George **Capt.**
	Thompson, Thomas **Lieut.** †
L. & W.	Fenwick, William **Ens.** to Capt. Ralph Carre

Northumb.	Fenwick, John **Capt.** DRAGOONS
	Roddam, Edmund **Lieut.**
Salop	White, George **Cor.** to Capt. Woodhall
Durham	Hutton, Ralph **Quart.** to Capt. Lancelot Holtby

Griffen
Wilts	Cutler, Benjamin **Cor.** HORSE to Capt. Gardiner

Griffin, Conyers
L. & W.	Filks, Edward **Capt.** FOOT
Wilts	Wilson, Abraham **Ens.** to Maj. Edmund Uvedale

Griffith, Sir Henry
L. & W.	Robinson, Stephen **Quart.** HORSE to Capt. Gaughegan
York	Anderson, John **Ens.** FOOT to Capt. Robert Ellis

Gunter, George
Sussex   Crossfield, Thomas **Quart**. HORSE
L. & W.   Bonny, George Quart.

Gwynne
L. & W.   Harman, James **Lieut**. FOOT, to Capt. Floyd

Haggerston, Sir Thomas
Northumb.   Haggerston, Ralph **Capt**. FOOT
                 Smith, John Ens.
L. & W.   Fenwick, Henry Capt.

Hales, Sir Edward
Kent   Maplesden, Edw. **Capt**. HORSE
        Fowle, John Capt.
Lincoln   Denham, George Capt.

Hamilton, Sir James*
Worcester   Norgrove, John **Lieut**. HORSE to Capt. Walsh
Stafford   Tayler, William **Cor**. to Capt. John Blunt
Dorset   Bamfield, James Cor. †
Oxon   Walter, John **Quart**. to Lieut. Col. Carre
Worcester   Smith, John Quart. to Lieut. Col. Profitt

York   Harland, Michael **Capt**. DRAGOONS
        Bullock, Robert Capt.
Worcester   Moses, Richard Capt.
        Collyer, John **Lieut**. to Capt. David Musset
Somerset   Ridly, Thomas **Quart**. to Capt. Dennis

Hamilton, James
L. & W.   Rey, Arthur **Capt**. HORSE
        Johnson, Archibald Capt.
        Leigh, Francis Capt.
Wilts   Leonard, John Capt.   ⎫
        Leonard, William Cor. ⎭
L. & W.   Lawson, William **Capt. Lieut**. ⎫
        Burton, Richard Quart.   ⎬
        Hamilton, John Cor.   ⎭
        May, John Lieut. to Capt. James Rychaut
        Hamilton, Patrick Lieut. to Maj. John Ridpeth
Hereford   Mynors, Roger **Cor**. to Sir Anthony St. Leger
Berks   Angel, Richard Cor. to Capt. Robert Lyndsy
Leicester   Scarborow, Robert **Quart**. to Capt. John Tayler

L. & W.	Wood, Robert **Capt.** DRAGOONS	

Hamilton, John
Bucks   Hall Alexander **Ens.** [   ] to Capt. M. Hamilton

Hammond, Edward
L. & W.	Richardson, Thomas **Lieut.** ⎫ HORSE
	Newman, Robert Cor. ⎭ To Maj. Edw. Rosecarrock
Kent	Stokes, John **Capt.** FOOT [1648]
	Parker, Thomas **Lieut.** †
	Burre, Thomas Lieut. †
Suffolk	Brydon, John **Ens.** to Capt. Thomas Busby
Kent	Elgar, Henry Ens.

Harpur, Sir John
Lincoln	Alsop, Durand **Capt.** HORSE
L. & W.	Alsop, Durand Capt. H. & F. ⎫
	Alsop, Thomas Cor. ⎬
	Ogle, William Lieut. ⎭
Derby	Whinyates, John **Capt. Lieut.**
	Scriven, Andrew Lieut. ⎫
	Smith, William Lieut. ⎬ To Capt. William Bullock
	Whinyates, Richard Cor. ⎪
	Smith, William Quart. ⎭
Worcester	Jellico, John Lieut. ⎫ To Capt. Anthony Mozine
Nottingh.	Mozine, Francis Cor. ⎭
Rutland	Willcocks, William **Cor.** to Capt. Syke
Nottingh.	Wright, Thomas Cor. to Capt. Kniveton
Derby	Mason, Richard Cor. ⎫ To Capt. John Low
	Valence, Luke Quart. ⎭
Salop	Corbett, Richard **Capt.** ⎫ DRAGOONS
	Cook, Andrew Lieut. ⎬
	Pitchford, Andrew Cor. ⎭

Harris, Robert
Dorset	Plucknett, Thomas **Capt.** HORSE
	Hyde, Mandevile **Lieut.** ⎫ To Maj. Belfore
Devon	Ewins, Edward Cor. ⎭
L. & W.	Mussell, Nicholas Lieut. to Capt. Henry Jarvis
Devon	Lugger, Nicholas Lieut. †

Hart, Sir William [1651]
Worcester	Mackafrey, Spencer **Capt**. FOOT
	Farly, John Capt.
	Best, Samuel **Lieut**. }
	Mince, William Ens. }

Hastings, Sir Richard
Dorset	Knapper, Shelton **Capt**. HORSE
	Davis, John **Quart**.
Somerset	Bridle, Francis Quart.

Hatton, Robert
L. & W.	Pyard, Godfrey **Lieut**. HORSE to Capt. Merryweather
	Baker, John Cor.

Hawkins, Sir Stephen*
L. & W.	Kirke, Charles **Maj**. } FOOT
	Jordan, Edw. Ens. }
	Hack, Fane **Capt**.
Lincoln	Humphrevile, William Capt.
Radnor	Jauncy, John **Capt. Lieut**.
L. & W.	Atkins, Thomas Capt. Lieut.
Surrey	Browne, William **Ens**.

Hawly, Lord
L. & W.	Fowler, Thomas **Capt**. HORSE
Middlesex	O Brian, Morrough Capt.
L. & W.	Hutton, William **Lieut**. to Lieut. Col. Blunt
	Partridge, Oliver **Cor**. to Capt. William Jones
Salop	Dovy, Richard Cor. †
Somerset	Hier, William **Quart**. to Capt. Francis Paulet
L. & W.	Barry, Miles **Capt**. FOOT
	Dillon, Christopher Capt. }
Gloucester	Jones, Howel Lieut. }
L. & W.	Bishop, John Capt.
	Worly, Thomas Capt.
Surrey	Ward, Richard Capt.
L. & W.	Worly, Thomas **Lieut**. to Capt. John Hasset
Somerset	Atkinson, Robert Lieut. } To Capt. William Lewis
	Jones, Lewis Ens. }
L. & W.	Lone, Highgate Lieut. to Capt. Vokliere

Heath, Francis
Berks	Dormer, William **Capt. Lieut**. FOOT

Heath, John
Kent   Amhurst, Giles **Ens**. [   ]

Hebburn, Ralph
Newcastle	Forster, Richard **Capt**. ⎫ FOOT
	Nichollson, Thomas Ens. ⎭
Northumb.	Dryden, George **Lieut**. ⎫ To Capt. Richardson
	Smith, Robert Ens. ⎭
Newcastle	Nicholson, George Lieut. to Capt. Martin Errington
Durham	Shaftoe, William Lieut. to Lieut. Col. Roddam

Hele, Sir John
Dorset	Clarke, William **Capt**. ⎫ HORSE
	Thornton, William Lieut. ⎭
Wilts	Rawley, Walter Capt.
Dorset	Bird, John **Cor**. to Capt. William Norton
Middlesex	Oliver, George **Quart**. to Sir Courtney Poole
Dorset	Cleves, Henry Quart. to Capt. Henry Hastings
Middlesex	Barnard, Laurence **Capt**. FOOT
Dorset	Napper, Andrew **Lieut**. to Capt. John Burges
	Thornton, Jacob **Ens**. to Capt. John Boys
	Thornton, Samuel Ens. to Capt. John Dolling

Hele, Sir Thomas
L. & W.	Molineux, Prestland **Maj**. ⎫ HORSE
	Browne, George Lieut. ⎭
Cornwall	Parsons, Matthew Capt.
	Arundell, John Capt.
	Oliver, Thomas Capt. ⎫
	Tregascus, John Quart. ⎭
Devon	Hele, Lewis Capt.
	Hill, Robert Capt.
	Newton, William Capt.
	Brooking, John Capt.
L. & W.	Wawfer, William **Lieut**. to Sir Ames Meredith
Somerset	Parker, Austin Lieut. to Capt. Jonas Westwood
Devon	Jackson, John Lieut. to Capt. Thomas Rich
	Ackland, Arthur Lieut. ⎫
	Gifford, Thomas Cor. ⎬ To Capt. John Gifford
	Darracot, William Quart. ⎭
	Yeabsley, John Lieut. to Capt. Thomas Drake
	Larkworthy, Anthony Lieut. HORSE & Capt. FOOT
	Marwood, William Lieut. †
	Stripling, John Lieut. †

Cornwall	Newsham, Edw. **Cor.**	} To Capt. Pomeroy
	Lugger, Peter Quart.	
Devon	Sheere, Isaac Cor. †	
	Turges, Thomas Cor. †	
	Ham, Henry Cor. †	
	Somerset, John Cor. †	
Cornwall	Blight, John Cor. †	
Devon	Campian, Arthur Cor. †	
L. & W.	Byrd, John Cor. †	
Devon	Webber, Samuel **Quart.**	
	Shepheard, Thomas Quart.	
	Ching, George Quart. †	
Cornwall	Burrow, Reynold Quart. †	
	Patchcote, William Quart. †	

Helyer, William
Devon	Morey, Simon **Quart.** † HORSE
Somerset	Masters, John Quart.
	Phelps, Giles Quart. †

Henderson
Lincoln	Anthony, John **Quart.** HORSE to Lieut. Col. Richard Nevill

Herbert, Charles Proger
Monmouth	Jones, William **Lieut.** FOOT, to Capt. Poyntz

Herbert, [Edward] Lord Cherbury*
Denbigh	Price, Edw. **Capt.** FOOT
Montgom.	Blayny, Andrew Capt.
Monmouth	Williams, Thomas **Lieut.** to Capt. Edmund Rogers
Montgom.	Jones, Richard Lieut. to Capt. John Pierce
	Blodwell, Nathaniel **Ens.** to Capt. John Blodwell
	Lewis, Rees Ens.

Herbert, Edward
L. & W.	Leighton, Edward **Capt.** FOOT

Herbert, Lord Richard
Salop	Price, Edw. **Capt.** FOOT
	Evans, Thomas **Quart.**

Herbert, Richard
L. & W.	Floyd, David **Capt.** FOOT
Lincoln	Cardiffe, Edmund **Lieut.** †
L. & W.	Jervis, John **Ens.** to Capt. Peter Newton

Herlackenden, Thomas [1648]
Kent   Francis, John **Lieut**. FOOT

Heron, George*
Northumb.   Delavall, Henry **Lieut**. HORSE to Sir George Bowes
York   Place, Robert **Cor**. to Capt. George Tonge
Lincoln   Berisford, William **Cor**. to Capt. Hassellwood
Durham   Conyers, John Cor.
Northumb.   Salkield, John **Quart**. to Capt. Gardiner

Heron, John
Cambridge   Hardy, Richard **Lieut**. HORSE to Capt. Thomas Saul
Hertford   Carter, William **Quart**. to Capt. John Hussy

Hertford, Marquess
Middlesex   Cotton, Charles **Lieut**. ⎫ HORSE
L. & W.   Winter, Thomas **Cor**. ⎭ To Capt. Sir Francis Chock
Somerset   Cutbert, Edward Lieut. ⎫
                 Williams, John Lieut. ⎬ To Sir Henry Coker
                 Reeves, John Cor. ⎭
                 Mercer, Thomas Lieut. to Capt. Lock †
Wilts   Fauston, Robert **Cor**. to Capt. Richard Davy
                 Harwood Richard, Cor. to Capt. Yarborow
Dorset   Gibbons, Owen **Quart**. to Capt. Heymor
Somerset   Cook, Anthony Quart. to Capt. John Gifford

Somerset   Brown, Robert **Capt**. FOOT
Dorset   Cantloe, John Capt.
                 Ivy, William Capt.
Hereford   Guy, William **Lieut**. to Capt. John Anguish
Oxon   Huckwell, Edward Lieut. to Capt. Hampson

Heveningham, Nathaniel
Norfolk   Hobart, George **Cor**. † HORSE
                 Grimes, John **Quart**. to Capt. Bozoun

Heymor, Richard
Wilts   Cook, John **Quart**. HORSE to Capt. Henry Greys
                 Friend, George Quart. to Capt. Robert Raddon
Cornwall   Shatford, William Quart. †

Somerset   Wintle, Samuel **Lieut**. ⎫ FOOT
Gloucester   Hemmings, John Ens. ⎭ To Maj. Anthony Harding

Hillyard, Henry
York   Tayler, John Capt. FOOT

Hilton, John
Durham Richardson, John **Capt**. FOOT
     Follenssby, Robert **Capt. Lieut.** ⎫
      Garret, Cutbert Ens.   ⎬
     Grigson, John Lieut. ⎫
     Chipchase, Thomas Ens. ⎬ To Maj. Robert Eden
     Pearson, Thomas Lieut. ⎫
     Stobbart, John Ens. ⎬ To Capt. John Hilton
     Cutbert, John Lieut. ⎫
     Gascoyne, Francis Ens. ⎬ To Capt. Robert Carre
     Harper, Roger **Ens**.
     Todd, Thomas Ens. ⎫
     Leaver, William Ens. ⎬ To Lieut. Col. Lyndly Wren
     Hackworth, James Ens. to Capt. Martin Forster
     Crispe, Arthur **Quart**.

York   Frickly, Samuel **Lieut**. ⎫ DRAGOONS
Durham Bambrigge, Arthur **Cor**. ⎬ To Capt. Jackson

Holland, Earl of [1648]
L. & W. Gwynne, John **Capt**. † FOOT

Holland
York   Hodginson, George **Lieut**. HORSE to Capt. Cowsly

Hollis, Gervase
Lincoln Callcroft, Robert **Capt**. FOOT
L. & W. Gardiner, Thomas Capt.
Lincoln Lacon, William **Ens**. to Capt. William Hollis
York   Hindmarsh, James Ens.

Hollyland
L. & W. Druel, George **Lieut**. FOOT to Capt. Fotherby

Holtby, Marmaduke
York   Lindly, John **Quart**. † HORSE
     Whitehead, William Quart. †

Norfolk Beddingfield, Edmund **Capt**. FOOT

Hooper, Sir Thomas*
L. & W. Read, Robert **Capt**. DRAGOONS

	Rentham, John Capt.
	Piercy, Thomas **Lieut.** to Maj. Cornwallis
	Conner, Charles Lieut. ⎱ To Capt. Nugent
	Keirnane, Terence Cor. ⎰
Gloucester	Wilson, John Lieut. to Capt. James Mateland
Durham	Awde, John Lieut. to Capt. John Ford
L. & W.	Innes, Alexander **Cor.** to Maj. Sinclare
	Smith, Richard Cor. †
Middlesex	Lisle, Richard **Reg. Quart.**

Hopton, Sir Edward*

Pembroke	Whittorn, Christopher **Capt. Lieut.** FOOT
L. & W.	Kneebone, Gilbert Lieut. †
Hereford	Rees, John Lieut. to Capt. Walker
L. & W.	Greene, Arthur **Quart.**

Hopton, Lord

Kent	St. Leger, Sir Anthony **Col.** HORSE
L. & W.	Deane, William **Lieut. Col.** ⎱
Gloucester	Windle, Jasper Lieut. ⎰
L. & W.	Buxton, William **Capt.**
	Leigh, Patrick Capt.
Wilts	Parsons, John Capt.
Somerset	Hall, William Capt.
	Butts, William Capt. ⎱
Wilts	Butts, Joseph Cor. ⎰
Somerset	Gifford, John Capt. ⎱
Dorset	Burt, Thomas Quart. ⎰
Durham	Ward, Marmaduke Capt.
Devon	Reynell, Nicholas Capt.
Cornwall	Blewit, Valentine Capt.
	Penhallow, Emmanuel Capt.
Dorset	Gower, William Capt. †
Somerset	Fry, Hugh Capt. †
Denbigh	Floyd, John Capt. †
York	Moncton, Edmund **Capt. Lieut.**
Gloucester	Fowler, Henry Lieut.
Surrey	Pollatsy, Percivall Lieut. to Maj. Pomeroy
Kent	Smith, William Lieut. to Capt. Thomas Roberts
Southam.	Hillyard, Ralph Lieut. to Capt. Langley
Wilts	Wilcocks, William Lieut. to Capt. Edw. Eyre
Somerset	Harbyn, William Lieut. ⎱ To Capt. John Harbyn
	Harbyn, Robert Cor. ⎰
	Gully, Thomas Lieut. to Lieut. Col. Hopton
	Newshaw, George Lieut. to Maj. Hasselwood

Devon	Moore, Ames Lieut. to Capt. George Moore	
Monmouth	Williams, Walter Lieut. to Capt. Herbert Vaughan	
Dorset	Barnes, Walter Lieut. † White, Thomas Cor.	} To Capt. Sturges
Somerset	Gibbs, Thomas Lieut. † Gibbs, Walter Cor. †	} To Capt. Arthur Hobbs
Devon	Arscott, Richard Lieut. †	
	Colverly, Peter Lieut.	
Cornwall	Keat, Ralph Lieut. †	
	Blewitt, Samuel Lieut. †	
L. & W.	Tirry, Christopher Lieut. †	
Suffolk	Brook, John Lieut. to Capt. John Lusher †	
L. & W.	May, Thomas Cor. to Maj. Thomas Lusher	
Somerset	Griffith, Edw. Cor. to Capt. Thomas Gay	
	Beaumont, John Cor. to Capt. John Stocker	
Cornwall	Thorne, Martin Cor. †	
	Gully, John Cor. †	
Somerset	Barker, Leonard Cor. †	
Dorset	Young, Robert Quart. to Capt. John Pearson	
	Laurence John Quart. Capt. Robert Ford	
Wilts	Filldowne, Henry Quart. to Capt. Edw. Eyres	
	Sweatman, William Quart. to Capt. Thomas Poulton	
	Helme, Richard Quart. to Capt. Thomas Woodcock	
Cornwall	May, Robert Quart. to Sir James Colebrand	
Southam.	Farrock, John Quart. †	
Cornwall	Lamerton, Richard Quart. †	
	Masters, Charles Quart. †	
	Sweet, John Quart. †	
	Langhorne, John Quart. †	
L. & W.	Burgess, Francis Col. FOOT	
	Collins, Degory Col.	

	Smithwick, Francis Capt.
	    Minshall, Peter Lieut.
	    Durant, John Lieut.
		}

Huntingd.		
Somerset	Waldron, John Capt.	

	Shepheard, John Capt.
	    Wiltsheere, John Lieut.
	    Shepheard, David Ens.
		}

	Fleshier, William Capt.	
Devon	Ford, William Capt.	
Glamorg.	Matthew, Miles Capt.	
Somerset	Salter, George Capt. †	
	Blake, George Capt. †	
Cornwall	Heaten, Samuel Capt. †	

L. & W.	Pitt, John **Lieut.** to Capt. Richard Yeomans
	Jones, Richard Lieut. to Maj. Garnier
Somerset	Walter, Thomas Lieut. to Capt. Phil. Culme
	Carver, Walter Lieut. to Capt. Robert Marks
	Tomlinson, Thomas Lieut. to Capt. Randall
	Seavyer, Thomas Lieut. to Capt. Thomas Gallopp
Dorset	Newman, John Lieut. to Capt. Tristram Turges †
Somerset	Rogers, John Lieut. to Capt. Thomas Milward
	Wrentmore, John Lieut. to Capt. Morgan
	Hopton, Joseph Lieut. to Capt. John Philpot
	Cox, Nicholas Lieut. to Capt. Edw. Poulton
	Burt, John Lieut. to Maj. Hawley
	Barnard, John Lieut. to Lieut. Col. Phil. Day
Monmouth	Young, Evan Lieut. to Capt. Thomas Rogers †
Cornwall	Sanders, John Lieut. †
Northam.	Williams, Henry Lieut. †
	Fisher, John Lieut. †
L. & W.	Cox, Thomas Lieut. to Capt. William Poulton
Hereford	Sayes, Richard **Ens.** to Capt. Richard Hall
Dorset	Simms, John Ens. to Capt. Pope
Somerset	Mason, Thomas Ens. to Captain William Swanton
	Hartgill, Arthur Ens. to Capt. John Knowles
Glamorg.	Freame, David Ens. to Capt. William Button
Devon	Ford, Henry Ens. †
Glamorg.	Gwynne Richard Ens. †
Somerset	Hammond, Anthony **Regt. Quart.**

Somerset	Day, Philip **Lieut. Col.** DRAGOONS
Wilts	Duke, George **Capt.**
	Stone, William Capt.
Cornwall	Wallys, Richard Capt.
Southam.	Odber, John Capt.
Somerset	Keymor, Henry Capt. †
Wilts	Kent, William **Lieut.** ⎫ To Capt. Robert Duke
Southam.	Blashford, Richard Cor. ⎭
Cambridge	Carpenter Walter Lieut. to Capt. William Buxton
Wilts	Deverell, Francis Lieut. †
L. & W.	Penrose, William Lieut. †
Wilts	Matthew, William **Cor.** to Capt. Sharpe †
Somerset	Green, Richard Cor. †
	Warham, John **Quart.** to Capt. Gallop
Devon	Holman, Andrew **Regt. Quart.**

Hopton, William
L. & W.	Robinson, Michael **Capt**. FOOT
	Dod, Thomas **Lieut**. to Maj. William Powel
Hereford	Waldron, Thomas Lieut. to Capt. John Waldron

Houghton, Sir Gilbert
Cumberl.	Seahouse, Joseph **Lieut**. DRAGOONS to Capt. Kirby

Howard, Sir Francis*
Northumb.	Lockey, James **Quart**. HORSE to Maj. Reevly
Durham	Merryman, Robert **Quart**. DRAGOONS to Maj. Thomas Ewer

Howard, Sir Robert*
L. & W.	Tayler, Henry **Capt**. HORSE
Salop	Stanly, Thomas **Lieut**. to Lieut. Col. Marmaduke Holtby
Worcester	Lurcock, John **Lieut**. FOOT, to Maj. Winnington
Salop	Atkinson, William Lieut. †
Warwick	Catesby, Richard **Capt**. DRAGOONS
Salop	Corbet, William **Lieut**. to Capt. Lewkenor
Montgom.	Floyd, Charles **Quart**. †

Howard, Thomas* [8]
L. & W.	Button, Martin **Capt**. HORSE
Cornwall	Clark, John Capt.
Northumb.	Reed, Thomas **Lieut**. to Maj. William Reevely
Devon	Holdich, Nicholas Lieut. ⎫
Southam.	Hobbs, Peter Quart. ⎬ To Maj. George Lower
Monmouth	Richmond, Peter **Cor**. ⎫
L. & W.	Alden, Richard Quart. ⎬ To Capt. John Webb
	Anton, James Cor. to Capt. Harrison
Cumberl.	West, Henry Cor. †
L. & W.	Chamberlaine, John Cor. †
York	Wood, Phineas Quart. Brigade
L. & W.	Webbe, Francis **Lieut**. FOOT, to Capt. Howard
	Cooke, Edward Lieut. †
Wilts	Bates, Robert **Ens**. †

---

[8] It seems some of these men were claiming under Thomas Howard, who ran dragoons in the north; some under his nephew Thomas Howard, a northern cavalry commander; and some under a Thomas Howard, brother of Viscount Andover, who fought in the West Country. By virtue of their claiming in the north, Reid has reasonably assumed that Lieut. Reed and Cornet West served under Thomas Howard jr., and dragoon officer Brown under Thomas Howard snr.; the rest of the cavalry serving under Andover's brother in the south. He places the foot officers as serving under Henry Howard, another brother of Andover's, as garrison of Malmesbury.

Northumb.	Walter, Robert **Quart**. †
	Brown, Henry **Cor**. DRAGOONS to Capt. Danby

Huddleston, Sir William
L. & W.	Bedborrow, Thomas **Capt**. HORSE
	Fetherston, Ralph Capt.
Cumberl.	Huddleston, Joseph Capt.
	Carter, Joseph **Cor**. †
	Irton, Christopher Cor. †
	Kirkbank, John Cor.
Durham	Morton, William **Quart**.
York	Hanby, Christopher **Capt**. FOOT
Cumberl.	Studdurt, Richard Capt. ⎫
	Bow, John Lieut. ⎬
	Hunter, Anthony Capt.
	Irton, Roger Capt.
Northumb.	Rames, Roger **Lieut**. to Capt. John Punchion
Cumberl.	Latus, William Lieut. to Capt. Ingoldby Huddleston
	Ascough, Hugh Lieut. †
Westmo.	Bradly, Hillary **Ens**. to Capt. Jos. Huddleston
Durham	Bland, Christopher Ens. to Maj. Edw. Huddleston
	Bincks, Ambrose Ens. to Capt. William Punchion
Cumberl.	Fox, Jeffery Ens.
	Leech, William **Quart**.

Hudson, Michael
Surrey	Dalton, Thomas **Cor**. HORSE, to Maj. Greene
Cambridge	Greene, Edmund **Maj**. FOOT

Hungate, Francis*
York	Thorpe, John **Capt**. ⎫ HORSE
	Garnet, John Cor. ⎬
Lancaster	Calvert, Richard **Cor**. †
York	Dolman, John Cor. †
	Eratt, William **Quart**. to Lieut. Col. John Vavasor
L. & W.	Watson, Robert Quart. to Capt. William Dolman
Lancaster	Eyves, Thomas Quart.

Hungerford, John [Earl of Marlborough's regiment]
Wilts	Norborne, William **Capt**. FOOT

Hunks, Sir Fulk
Salop	Nash, Richard **Lieut**. HORSE to Lieut. Col. Gerard Fulk

Surrey	Dring, Lewis **Capt**. FOOT
Montgom.	Roberts, Lewis **Ens**. to Maj. Theodore Morris

Hurter, John Phillip
Monmouth	Walter, William **Lieut**. HORSE to Capt. John Walter
L. & W.	Dowle, Theophilus **Cor**. to Capt. Fines
Warwick	Littleton, John Cor.

Hutton, Sir Richard
York	Dearelove, Thomas **Capt**. FOOT
	Massy, Peter Capt.
	Banister, Ralph Capt. ⎫
	Staining, Nicholas Ens. ⎭
L. & W.	Skeldain, John Capt. ⎫
York	Cowling, Robert Ens. ⎭
	Dickenson, Thomas **Ens**. to Capt. Harrison
	Sheldon, Edw. Ens. to Maj. Sir Richard Tankard
	Hare, William **Quart**.
	Robinson, Thomas Quart.

Jenkins, Tobias*
Northumb.	Morton, Barra. **Lieut**. FOOT

Jennings, Charles
Cornwall	Blake, John **Capt**. FOOT
L. & W.	Blake, John Capt.
Devon	Newton, Gilbert **Ens**. †
Cornwall	Willoughby, Andrew **Quart**.

Johnson
Middlesex	Fountaine, William **Lieut**. HORSE, to Capt. Brown

Kanett
L. & W.	Cary, John **Lieut**. HORSE, to Capt. Loanes

Kay, Sir John
York	Hanson, Edward **Capt**. ⎫ HORSE
	Beaumont, William Cor. ⎭
	Fullwood, Thomas **Lieut**. †
	Wood, Thomas **Cor**. †
	Hare, Richard **Quart**.

Kelly, Earl of [1651?]
Kent	Platt, William **Capt**. FOOT, at Worcester, and formerly **Maj**. to the Marquess Montrose

Kemys, Sir Charles

Glamorg.	Sayes, Edw. **Capt.** FOOT
	Morris, Edmund Capt.
	Thomas, John Capt.
	Morris, Edw. Capt.
	Thomas, Gabriel Capt.
	Stacy, Henry **Capt. Lieut.**
	Griffith, Evan Lieut. to Lieut. Col. Miles Button
Monmouth	Williams, William Lieut. ⎫ To Capt. William Powell
	Macklen, Adam Ens. ⎭
Glamorg.	Matthews, Lewis Lieut. †
	Jones, Henry **Ens.** †
	Brigges, Edward Ens.
Pembroke	Williams, Edw. Ens. †
Monmouth	Wills, John **Quart.**

Kemys, Sir Nicholas [1648][9]

Hereford	Scudamore, Rowland **Capt.** HORSE, to Lieut. Col. Thomas Lewis
Monmouth	Crump, Edward **Capt. Lieut.** FOOT
	Leech, Lewis Lieut. to Capt. Thomas Walter
	Hughes, Walter **Ens.** to Maj. Richard Lewis
	Mason, Robert Ens. to Capt. John Dewxtell

King, Lord General [James King, Lord Eythin]

York	Mountain, James **Capt.** ⎫ HORSE
	Wade, Thomas Lieut. ⎬
	Medd, Christopher Quart. ⎭
L. & W.	Hume, James Capt.
Northumb.	Richardson, James Capt.
Durham	Vasey, Thomas **Lieut.** ⎫
York	Stafford, Edward Cor. ⎬ To Maj. Edw. Gower
	Holland, Peter Quart. ⎭
L. & W.	Wake, Christopher Lieut. ⎫ To Capt. Ord
York	Wake, Thomas Quart. ⎭
	Packington, Thomas **Cor.** to Capt. Lyndsey
Durham	Pease, Stephen Cor. to Capt. Richard Cole
Northumb.	Urwin, Robert Cor. to Maj. Claudius Hamilton
Derby	Royston, Ralph Cor. ⎫
York	Ramsden, Thomas Quart. ⎬ To Capt. Sack. Glenham
	Harland, George Quart. ⎭
L. & W.	Fairely, William Cor. ⎫ To Sir Robert Carre
	Thompson, Patrick Cor. ⎭

---

[9] Originally a Parliamentarian unit; changed sides in 1648.

York	West, Marmaduke **Quart.** to Sir Arthur Cayley
Northumb.	Murton, Thomas Quart. to Capt. George Cooke
L. & W.	Gordon, James **Maj.** FOOT
	Brown, William **Capt.**
York	Smith, William Capt.
	Redman, Thomas Capt.
Durham	Frizell, William Capt. ⎫
	Davison, William Ens. ⎭
York	Hoginson, George Lieut. to Capt. King
Newcastle	Anderson, Francis Lieut. to Capt. Thomas Cliberon
Nottingh.	Wilson, Robert Lieut. to Capt. Peters
L. & W.	Phillips, Charles Lieut. †
Westmo.	Machell, John **Quart.**
York	Hinchcliffe, Thomas Quart.
York	Hory, Robert **Capt.** DRAGOONS

Kingsmill, William
L. & W.	Street, Thomas **Ens.** [ ] to Capt. James Oldfield

Kingston, Earl of
Lincoln	Dighton, Gervase **Ens.** [ ] to Maj. Richard Cony

Kirke, Sir Lewis
L. & W.	Maylord, Edward **Capt.** † FOOT
	Villequier, Isaac **Lieut.** to Maj. Billingsly
	Cleaver, John Lieut. to Lieut. Col. Wine
Salop	Lem, John **Sen. Ens.** to Capt. Richard Singe
L. & W.	Allman, Richard **Quart.** †

Kirkebride, Richard
L. & W.	Salkield, George **Lieut. Col.** ⎫ FOOT
	Ryly, Edmund Lieut. ⎭
Cumberl.	Huddleston, William **Capt.**
L. & W.	White, Henry **Capt. Lieut.**
Leicester	Brisby, Edw. Lieut. ⎫
Cumberl.	Brisby, Edw. Lieut. ⎬ To Maj. Milford
Wilts	Edwards, Thomas Ens. ⎭
Westmo.	Humphryston, Edw. **Ens.** to Capt. Uriall
Durham	Kenion, George **Quart.**

Kirkby
Lancaster	Stanton, Edw. **Capt.** FOOT

Knottsford, Sir John*
Warwick	Knottsford, Francis **Capt.** HORSE
Northam.	Manly, John **Capt. Lieut.**
Chester	Oldham, William **Cor.** to Capt. Thomas Westly
Worcester	Knottsford, Richard Cor.
Warwick	Haynes, John **Quart.**
Warwick	Gibbons, Charles **Capt. Lieut.** FOOT
	Edwards, John **Quart.**

Knyveton, Sir Andrew
Stafford	Brough, Thomas **Capt.** HORSE
L. & W.	Dudly, Henry **Capt. Lieut.**
	Knyveton, Thomas **Cor.**
	Doddington, William Cor.
Derby	Fletcher, Roger Cor. †
	Allestry, Richard Cor. } To Lieut. Col. Peter Knyveton
Stafford	Ilsley, George Quart. }

Lambton, Sir William
York	Nicholson, Thomas **Capt.** FOOT
Northumb.	Lesley, Talbot Capt.
Durham	Lisle, Talbot Capt.
	Richardson, Richard **Lieut.** to Capt. Benson
	Watson, John Lieut. to Capt. John Pemberton
	Williamson, Thomas **Ens.** to Capt. Williamson
	Lambton, Robert Ens.

Lamplaw, John
Cumberl.	Lamplaw, Edw. **Capt.** HORSE
	Briscoe, George Capt.
	Wyber, Thomas **Cor.** †
York	Busfield, Thomas **Capt.** } FOOT
L. & W.	Wright, Christopher Ens. }
Cumberl.	Dickenson, William **Capt. Lieut.**

Lane, John
Derby	Lassells, John **Capt.** HORSE
L. & W.	Fairely, Richard **Lieut.** †

Langdale, Lord [Sir Marmaduke Langdale]

York	Constable, Ralph Maj.	⎫ HORSE
	Jackson, John Lieut.	⎬
	Hodgson, Ralph Cor.	⎪
	Escrick, John Quart.	⎭
	Langley, Richard **Capt.**	⎫
	Constable, Peter Lieut.	⎬
	Smith, Stephen Cor.	⎪
	Forster, Thomas Quart.	⎭
Cumberl.	Porter, William Capt.	
Lincoln	Hyde, Richard Capt.	
L. & W.	Constable, Edward Capt. & Advoc. Gen.	
Oxon	Harriman, Francis Capt. †	
York	Dale, Thomas Capt. †	
Westmo.	Wharton, William Capt. †	
York	Wilkinson, Edw. **Lieut.** to Maj. Brandling	
	Hope, John Lieut.	⎫
Westmo.	Bradly, William Lieut.	⎬ To Capt. Thompson
York	Harwood, James Cor.	⎭
L. & W.	Macvicar, Archibald Lieut. to Capt. Keightly	
York	Flesher, George **Cor.**	⎫ To Capt. William Dunnell
	Parker, John Quart.	⎭
	Gibson, Thomas Cor.	⎫ To Capt. Langdale Sunderland
	Richardson, John Quart.	⎭
	Tomlin, Thomas Cor.	⎫ To Sir Robert Hillyard
	Renthall, Robert Quart.	⎭
	Durham, Anthony Cor. to Capt. Killinghall	
Lincoln	Hallford, Matthew Cor. to Maj. Bale	
Nottingh.	Edlington, Edmund **Quart.** to Capt. Cooke	
	Hyde, Martin Quart.	⎫ To Capt. Haxby
York	Pallester, Cutbert Quart.	⎭
	Hall, Basill Quart. to Capt. Anderson	
	Allen, Thomas Quart. to Capt. Yeord	
	Walker, James Quart.	
	Smith, Francis Quart.	
	Sclater, William Quart. †	
	Salvin, Thorp Quart.	
	Worker, William Quart.	
L. & W.	Peele, John Quart. to Capt. John Tomlinson †	
	Pattison, Richard Quart. †	
	Forcer, Barnaby Quart. †	
York	Squire, Robert **Capt.** FOOT	

	Banks, James **Lieut**. to Capt. Monckton	
	Wright, Richard Lieut. to Capt. Skelton	
Leicester	Thornborrow, Henry **Ens**. to Capt. Rogers	

Berks	Moody, William **Capt**. }	DRAGOONS
York	Penser, Henry Lieut. }	
	Harrison, William Quart. }	
	Wardropper, John **Lieut**. }	To Capt. Gower
	Barker, George Cor. }	

La Plane
Dorset	Ancthill, Nicholas **Cor**. }	HORSE
L. & W.	Channyn, Mich. Quart. }	To Lieut. Col. Barree
Dorset	Babbidge, Greg. Cor. to Capt. Peter County	
L. & W.	Morpaigne, John Cor. to Capt. John Gaultier	
	Morphey, Daniel Cor. to Capt. Pouch	
	Cary, Peter Cor. †	

Laughorne, Rowland [1648]¹⁰
Carmarth.	Powell, William **Capt**. }	HORSE
Pembroke	Adams, John Lieut. † }	
	Williams, George **Lieut**. †	

Cardigan	Shales, William **Capt**. FOOT
Pembroke	Bowen, Phillip Capt. †
Radnor	Betty, William **Lieut**. to Capt. Pitcher
Pembroke	Mab, John **Ens**. to Capt. John Butler †

Laurence, Robert
Somerset	Brett, Henry **Lieut**. HORSE †
Dorset	Miller, Abraham **Cor**.
Somerset	Horsey, John **Quart**.

Lawdy, Sir Richard*
Glamorg.	Turbervile, Francis **Cor**. HORSE to Capt. John Miller

Layland
L. & W.	Carew, John **Lieut**. HORSE †

Leake, Charles
Lincoln	Maycock, John **Cor**. H. to Capt. Daniell

---

¹⁰ Laughorne, Parliament's commander in South Wales, had defected to the Royalists in 1648.

Lee
Kent	Paul, Robert **Lieut.** FOOT †
	Hadds, Christopher **Ens.** †

Legge, William*
Bedford	Warner, Henry **Capt.** HORSE
L. & W.	Crafford, John **Lieut.** FOOT to Lieut. Col. Smith

Le Hunt, Sir John
L. & W.	Peachell, Richard **Capt.** FOOT
	Macgill, Bryan Capt.
Northumb.	Potts, Reynold **Quart.**

Leigh, Sir Ferdinando
York
    Lassells, Francis **Capt.** ⎫ HORSE
    Lister, John Lieut. ⎭
    Consett, John Capt. ⎫
    Dunnell, Nicholas Quart. ⎭
    Hutchinson, Robert **Lieut.** to Maj. Robert Watson
    Cooper, John Lieut. ⎫
    Dixon, George Cor. ⎬ To Capt. Robert Dixon
    Dixon, Joseph Quart. ⎭
    Swillivant, Anthony Lieut. †
    Nailor, Joseph **Cor.**
    Lister, Nathaniel **Quart.** to Capt. John Leigh

Leigh, Thomas
Middlesex	Warcoppe, Samuel **Capt.** FOOT
Chester	Beverly, Thomas Capt.
	Newton William **Ens.** to Maj. Berminsham
	Aldersey, John Ens.

Leighton, Sir William [King's Lifeguard of Foot]
Oxon   Englefield, Thomas **Capt.** FOOT
L. & W.   Green, William Capt.
Worcester   Savage, John **Lieut.** ⎫
    Barnsly, Henry **Ens.** ⎭ To Capt. William Sheldon

Leveson, Sir Richard
Salop	Revell, Edw. **Capt.** HORSE
Worcester	Middlemore, Thomas **Lieut.** †
Salop	Pierce, Gabriel **Cor.** to Capt. Henry Bostock
	Bradbury, Thomas **Quart.** †

Leveson, Thomas
Stafford	Potts, John **Capt.**	} HORSE
	Caney, Richard Lieut.	
	Birch, John **Capt. Lieut.**	
	Collier, Richard Lieut.	} To Lieut. Col. Walter Gifford
L. & W.	Freeman, Thomas Quart.	
Warwick	Fortescue, Francis Lieut.	
Worcester	Osborn, Thomas Quart.	} To Maj. Christopher Heveningham
Bucks	Elliot, William Quart.	
Stafford	Shenton, Richard Quart.	
Stafford	Gifford, Thomas **Capt.**	} FOOT
Salop	Sandford, Walter Ens.	
Stafford	Colles, Francis Capt.	}
L. & W.	Rumny, Thomas Ens.	
	Colles, Charles **Capt. Lieut.**	
Salop	Harris, Robert Ens.	} To Lieut. Col. J. Beaumont
L. & W.	Draycott, Phillip Ens.	
Stafford	Hickmans, William Ens. to Maj. Simon Heveningham	
	Capplewood, William Ens.	

Lewkenor, Anthony
Bucks	Eyton, Edward **Lieut. Col.** HORSE
Kent	Gaultier, William **Capt.**

Lewkenor, Sir Christopher
Warwick	Phipps, Benjamin **Capt.** HORSE	
Sussex	Lyndsey, Richard Capt.	
Hereford	Winwood, Arthur **Lieut.**	} To Capt. Winwood
	Winwood, Ralph **Quart.**	
Southam.	Lorimer, Roger **Maj.** FOOT	

Liddel, Sir Francis
Northumb.	Watson, John **Capt.** HORSE
	Ord, Ralph **Cor.**
	Douglasse, Thomas Cor.

Lindore, Lord
Warwick	Meautys, John **Lieut. Col.**	} FOOT
L. & W.	Rycroft, Thomas Ens.	
York	Scroop, Thomas **Capt.**	
Northumb.	Dixon, Andrew **Capt. Lieut.**	
L. & W.	Dowglasse, Ferdinando **Ens.** to Capt. Lowdon	

Lingen, Sir Henry

Hereford	Enett, Richard **Capt**. HORSE
L. & W.	Acton, Samuel **Lieut**. †
Hereford	Hill, John **Cor**. †
	Snead, John Cor. †
	Cook, Richard Cor. †
Middlesex	Prist, John **Quart**. to Capt. Streat

Hereford	Cornwall Humprey **Capt**. ⎫ FOOT
	Molineux William Lieut. ⎬
	Ward, John Ens. ⎭

Hill, Thomas Capt.
Coningsby, Fitzwilliam Capt.
Bradford, Barnaby Capt.
Beal, Roger Capt. †
Seaborne, Edw. **Lieut**.

Radnor	Knill, Thomas Lieut.
Hereford	Cox, Roger **Ens**. to Maj. Anthony Awbry
	Jansey, Lewis Ens. †
Monmouth	Carthy, Richard Ens. †

| L. & W. | Mayley, Alpheus **Cor**. DRAGOONS to Capt. Sevidall |

Lisle, Sir George

Stafford	Littleton, Rugely **Capt**. FOOT
Essex	Whitgrave, Humphrey Capt.
York	Norbury, Edw. **Lieut**. to Maj. Skirrow
L. & W.	Robinson, James Lieut. to Capt. Thomas Smith
Worcester	Holman, Henry Lieut. to Capt. John Tichborne
	Hill, Richard Lieut. to Capt. Thomas Corbett
Carmarth.	Matthews, Edw. **Ens**. to Capt. John Tayler
Cumberl.	Graham, William Ens. †
Salop	Cresswell, Richard **Quart**.
Essex	Moore, Robert **Capt**. HORSE

Litchfield, Earl of [Lord Bernard Stewart; King's L'guard of Horse]

Kent	Aldridge, Rowland **Capt**. HORSE
Warwick	Sheldon, Thomas Maj. to His Majesties own troop

Littleton, Lord Keeper

L. & W.	Warner, Peter **Ens**. [ ] to Capt. Walter Vernon

Long, James

Wilts	Cusse, William **Capt**. HORSE
	Gouldsborough, George Capt.
	Townsend, Ralph Capt.
Southamp.	Lisle, George Capt.
Somerset	Chapman, Simon Capt.
L. & W.	Maxwell, Thomas Capt.
Wilts	Massham, William **Lieut**. †
Somerset	Smith, William Lieut. to Capt. Thomas Gowen
Surrey	Hart, John Lieut. †
Wilts	Poulton, Thomas Lieut. †
	Long, Walter **Cor**. ⎫
Chester	Freath, Charles Quart. ⎬ To Capt. Thomas Long
Wilts	Bridges, Edward Quart. ⎭
Montgom.	Jones, Edw. Cor. †
Dorset	Chamberlain, William Cor. ⎫
Wilts	Tenham, John Quart. ⎬ To Lieut. Col. Bolles
	Adams, William Quart. ⎭
Southamp.	Simms, Ralph Quart. to Capt. Bartholomew Barnes
Wilts	Wilson, William Quart. to Capt. Richard Staples
	Done, Henry Quart.

Loughborough, Lord [Colonel-General Henry Hastings]

L. & W.	Lucas, Sir Gervase **Col**. HORSE & FOOT
Lincoln	Hacker, Rowland **Maj**. ⎫ HORSE
Nottingh.	White, Robert Lieut. ⎭
Essex	Ruddings, William **Capt**.
Nottingh.	Robinson, George Capt. ⎫
L. & W.	Dixon, John Lieut. ⎭
Stafford	Fleetwood, William Capt.
Leicester	Dudly, Richard Capt. ⎫
	Dudly, Henry Lieut. ⎬
Warwick	Hall, John Quart. ⎭
Leicester	Squire, William Capt. †
	Mawson, Thomas Capt. †
	Trimnell, William Capt. †
	Duport, James Capt. †
Stafford	Fleetwood, Henry Capt. †
L. & W.	Wharton, John Capt. †
Warwick	Cooke, Jonathan Capt. †
L. & W.	Caesar, John **Capt**. **Lieut**.

96   Indigent Officers

Middlesex	Duncombe, Nathaniel Lieut.	} To Maj. Bale
Leicester	Roberts, Wolston Cor.	
	Everard, John Lieut. to Capt. Walter Hastings	
Stafford	Mathar, John Lieut.	} To Capt. Milward
	Milward, Thomas Cor.	
Nottingh.	Bend, Henry Lieut. to Capt. Archer	
Stafford	Grey, Ambrose Lieut. †	
L. & W.	Barnwell, John Lieut. †	
York	Hobman, William Lieut. to Capt. Rooksby	
Leicester	Gilbert, Thomas Lieut. to Capt. Gregory	
L. & W.	Monck, Henry Lieut. to Lieut. Col. William Bale	
Northam.	Gibbs, Roger Cor. †	
Surrey	Brown, William Cor. to Capt. Smith	
Leicester	Waldron, Henry Cor.	} To Capt. Wright
	Harrington, James Cor.	
	Mowsley, Thomas Cor.	
	Durant, John Quart.	
	Dudly, William Quart.	
	Eaton, John Quart. to Capt. George Stanly	
Stafford	Hunt, William Quart. to Lieut. Col. Standford	
L. & W.	Batts, James Quart. to Capt. Phillip Stanhop	
Salop	Fletcher, Simon Quart. to Capt. Sir Richard Astly	
Wilts	Hitchcock, George Capt. FOOT	
Leicester	Bayly, Thomas Capt.	
L. & W.	Benchkin, Samuel Capt.	
Cambridge	Loosmore, George Lieut.	}
L. & W.	Fisher, Lawrence Ens.	
	Hare, James Capt.	
	Holden, John Capt. †	
	Kelton, William Lieut. to Capt. Robinson	
Leicester	Robinson, Daniel Ens. to Capt. George Robinson	
Nottingh.	Wakefield, John Ens.	
Leicester	Daniel, Robert Capt. DRAGOONS	

Lovelace, Francis

Glamorg.	Andrews, Thomas Capt. Lieut. FOOT
Carmarth.	Williams, Thomas Lieut. to Capt. Thomas Lee
	Phillips, Owen Lieut. to Maj. Henry Furnivall
Surrey	Askew, George Ens. to Capt. Buckly
L. & W.	Baxter, Richard Quart.

Lowther, Sir Christopher

Cumberl.	Briscoe, George Capt. HORSE

Lowther, Gerard
York	Hodgson, Thomas **Lieut**. HORSE
	Hodgson, Lawrence **Quart**.
York	Vavasor, Robert **Capt**. FOOT
Lincoln	Chapman, John **Ens**. to Capt. Banister
Glamorg	Williams, Arnold Ens. †

Lowther, John
Westmo.	Richardson, John Cor. HORSE

Lucas, Sir Charles*
L. & W.	Grey, Barnard **Capt**. HORSE
	Aylet, John Capt.
	Bacon, Robert Capt.
Norfolk	Casson, Edward Capt.
L. & W.	Coke, Edward **Lieut**. ⎫ To Capt. Anthony Mennell
Durham	Sedgwick, John Cor. ⎭
L. & W.	Trapps, Edward **Cor**. to Capt. John Grey
	Hancock, Jonathan Cor. to Sir Simon Fanshaw
York	Frankland, William Cor. ⎫ To Lieut. Col. Maxy
	Womersly, John Quart. ⎭
Lincoln	Wiggemore, Daniel Cor. to Capt. Colster
York	Tayler, Robert Cor. †
Hertford	Tufnell, Edw. Capt. †
Nottingh.	Alcock, William **Quart**.
L. & W.	Worsop, Walter **Maj**. FOOT [1648]
	Hicks, William **Capt**.
	Derby, Michael Capt. ⎫
Suffolk	Dewes, Roger Lieut. ⎬
L. & W.	Elliot, Thomas Ens. ⎭
Essex	Mason, Solomon Lieut. ⎫ To Capt. Barker
	Bond, John Ens. ⎭
Dorset	Wats, Robert **Lieut**. †
Middlesex	Russell, George Lieut. †
L. & W.	Crowder, William Lieut. †
	Edwards, James **Ens**. to Capt. Rosecarrock
Bucks	Bullmer, William Capt. DRAGOONS

Lucas, Sir Gervase
Stafford	Nedham, Peter **Capt**. ⎫ HORSE
Lincoln	Rawson, William Cor. ⎬
L. & W.	Hall, Armelius Quart. ⎭

Rutland	Colby, William Capt.
York	Wright, Anthony **Lieut.** †
Northam.	Barton, Edw. **Cor.** to Capt. Barton †
	Rogers, Thomas **Quart.** to Capt. Harding
L. & W.	Johnson, Laurence Quart.
L. & W.	Brellisford, George **Capt.** FOOT
Lincoln	Steevens, John Capt.
	Broome, Andrew Capt.
Essex	Loker, Joseph **Lieut.**
Leicester	Page, Henry Lieut.

Lucas, Lord
York	Cotes, William Capt. Lieut. HORSE
Essex	Herris, Christopher Lieut. ⎫ To Capt. John Aylet
Middlesex	Mowbray, William Cor. ⎭

Lunsford, Sir Herbert [Lord General's regiment]
L. & W.	Albion, Philologus **Lieut.** FOOT
	Francklin, Robert **Ens.** to Capt. Roger Bendish
	Goffe, Clement Ens. to Capt. Dormer

Lunsford, Sir Thomas*
Stafford	Popham, Andrew **Capt.** HORSE
Denbigh	Hill, John **Ens.** [ ] to Capt. Pine

Lyndsy, Andrew
L. & W.	Haswell, James **Maj.** ⎫ HORSE
	Montgomery, Ezekiel Lieut. ⎭

Lyndsy, Earl of [King's Lifeguard of Foot]
L. & W.	Leighton, Sir William **Lieut. Col.** FOOT
Berks	Beeton, John **Capt.**
L. & W.	Berty, Nicholas Capt. ⎫
Gloucester	Fordred, William Lieut. ⎭
L. & W.	Stevenson, Charles Capt.
	Fox, Charles Capt. ⎫
	Berkenhead, William Ens. ⎭
	Cordwayne, Thomas **Lieut.** to Capt. Thomas Draper
	Havercamp, Robert Lieut. †
Warwick	Mowshall, Peter **Ens.** to Capt. Robert Levens
L. & W.	Hubberstay, Robert Ens. †
Somerset	Ball, John Ens. to Capt. Stuart
L. & W.	Chamberlain, Robert Ens. †

Lincoln	Stacy, Montagu **Quart.** HORSE †	
York	Challoner, Frederick **Capt.** DRAGOONS	

Mackworth, Sir Francis
L. & W.	Haslewood, John **Maj.** HORSE
Lincoln	Coxhead, William **Capt.**
L. & W.	Coxhead, Thomas Lieut.
	Hodenot, Peter **Quart.** to Capt. Francis Bradgstow

?	Carre, George **Maj.** FOOT.
York	Loope, George **Capt.**
Norfolk	Cory, Thomas Capt.
Lincoln	Wright, Edw. Capt. †

Malham, Francis
York	Tatham, Edmund **Capt.** HORSE
Lancaster	Banister, John **Cor.** †
York	Gudgeon, Henry Quart. †

Mallory, Sir John
York	Catterell, Edward **Capt.** HORSE
	Catterell, Arthur Lieut.
	Dixon, Richard Lieut.
	Broome, Hugh **Cor.** †
	Fish, John **Quart.**
	Walsh, Stephen Quart. †

York	Stavely, Thomas **Capt. Lieut.** FOOT

York	Hardcastle, William **Capt.** DRAGOONS
	Storzaker, John **Lieut.**
Durham	Cutbert, Robert Quart. } To Lieut. Col. Norton
York	Duffield, Thomas Lieut.
	Linton, John Quart. } To Capt. John Lister
Lincoln	Waad, Samuel Lieut. †
York	Wise, John Lieut.
	Richardson, Thomas **Cor.** to Capt. Thomas Stavely
	Steele, William Cor. to Capt. John Leicester
	Beck, Anthony **Quart.** to Capt. George Dawson

Manly
Glamorg.	Williams, William **Ens.** [ ] †

Manning, [Richard]
Surrey	Woodman, Charles **Lieut**. HORSE to Maj. Clark
L. & W.	Fishborn, George **Cor**. to Lieut. Col. Scott

Mansfield, Lord
York	Tomlinson, John **Capt**. HORSE
Kent	Justice, Richard Capt.
	Mittford, Henry Lieut. ⎫
	Underwood, Thorp Quart. ⎬ To Capt. Bealby
	Campanet, Gilbert Quart. ⎭
	Perkins, Thomas Lieut. ⎫
	Lewyns, Lucian Lieut. ⎬ To Capt. W. Harebread
	Pollard, Gowen Cor. ⎭
L. & W.	Webb, Edward **Cor**. to Capt. Anthony Nevill
Nottingh.	Tong, William Cor. to Capt. John Cooke
York	Watson, Robert Cor.
	Holland, John Cor. to Capt. White
	Jefferson, William **Quart**. to Capt. George Stanhop
Salop	Hall, John **Capt**. FOOT
Durham	Theobalds, William Capt.
Derby	Greaves, George Capt. ⎫
	Holme, John Ens. ⎭
York	Withes, John **Lieut**. to Capt. Thomas Craw

Marlay, Sir John
Newcastle	Metcalfe, Charles **Capt**. HORSE
	Bowes, Ralph Capt. HORSE & FOOT
	Bowes, Henry **Cor**. to Capt. Thomas Jackson
Newcastle	Forbes, Alexander **Lieut**. **Col**. FOOT
	Errington, George **Capt**. ⎫
	Robinson, William Lieut. ⎭
Northumb.	Archibald, Henry **Lieut**. ⎫
Newcastle	Archibald, Robert Ens. ⎭ To Capt. Ninian Shafto
L. & W.	Read, Francis Lieut. to Capt. Eleazer Hodgson
Durham	Surtys, Edw. Lieut. to Capt. Thomas Wright
Newcastle	Wright, Thomas Lieut. to Capt. John Lake
	Anderson, Bartram Sen. Lieut. to Capt. Robert White
	Heron, Ralph Lieut. to Capt. John Marlay
	Rutter, Robert **Ens**. to Capt. Joseph Davison
	Rickaby, George Ens. to Capt. Thomas Swinburne
Newcastle	Randal, Thomas **Lieut**. DRAGOONS to Capt. Thomas Jackson

Marlborough, Earl of*
Devon	Morse, Adam **Capt.** FOOT †
Cornwall	Vincent, John **Lieut.** to Capt. Abraham Carteret
Dorset	Tommes, Richard Lieut. to Capt. Thomas Gower
L. & W.	Cox, Alexander Lieut. to Lieut. Col. John Hungerford
Wilts	Striker, Nicholas Lieut. †
Somerset	Strode, Richard **Capt.** HORSE
	Lister, Edw. **Cor.**

Marrow, John*
Chester	Weld, Alexander **Lieut.** HORSE to Capt. Walthall
	Bancks, Robert **Cor.** to the Lord Cholmondly
	Weaver, Hatton **Quart.** to Capt. Dod
	Wickstead, Charles Quart. to Capt. James Thornton
	Stringer, Peter Quart. to Maj. Werden
	Kell, Randolph Quart. †
Chester	Church, Thomas **Ens.** [ ] to Capt. Phil. Prichard

Mason, Sir William
L. & W.	Mason, Thomas **Maj.** } HORSE
	Mason, Thomas Lieut.
York	Clayton, John **Cor.** } To Lieut. Col. Jo. Galliard
	Roe, Clinton Quart.
L. & W.	Pindar, John Cor. †
Surrey	Paddison, James Cor. †
Cumberl.	Bartram, William **Quart.** †
York	Sharpe, Isaac Quart.

Massey, Sir Edward [1651][11]
L. & W.	Reghamorter, John **Capt.** HORSE
Cumberl.	Bell, Robert **Cor.** †
Westmo.	Harrison, Robert **Quart.** †

Matthews, Humphry
Monmouth	Morgan, Rees **Capt.** FOOT

Maurice, Prince*
L. & W.	Roberts, Thomas **Capt.** HORSE
	Ford, William Capt.
Denbigh	Salisbury, John Capt.

---

[11] Massey was a Parliamentarian during the first and second civil wars, changing sides shortly afterwards. He did not actually fight at Worcester in 1651, having been injured beforehand.

Gloucester	Horton, William **Lieut.**	} To Capt. Freake
Warwick	Mason, William Cor.	
L. & W.	Arscott, William Lieut. †	
Gloucester	Morse, Robert Lieut. †	
L. & W.	Elliot, Richard Lieut. to Capt. James Elliot	
Gloucester	Guise, George Lieut.	
L. & W.	Sill, Wellsborne Cor.	} To Capt. W. Sheldon
Worcester	Sheldon, John Cor.	
Lancaster	Lyon, Henry **Cor.** to Capt. Roger Renekers	
L. & W.	Smith, Stephen Cor. to Capt. Robert Snead	
Cornwall	Grills, William Cor. †	
L. & W.	Watts, John **Quart.** to the Lifeguard	
York	Hebden, Edward Quart.	
Cornwall	Nation, George Quart.	

L. & W.	Trevillyan, Peter **Maj.** FOOT
Dorset	Bramble, Samuel **Capt.** †
Somerset	Bragge, John Capt. †
L. & W.	Waddam, George Capt. †
Dorset	Freak, William **Ens.** to Capt. John Hawes

Dorset	Summers, William **Capt.** DRAGOONS

Maxwell, George
L. & W.	Davison, Robert **Ens.** [ ] †

Mayne, Sir John
York	Cooling, Bartholomew **Capt.**	} HORSE
Nottingh.	Cooling, George Quart.	
York	Davill, Thomas Capt.	}
	Worsly, John Cor.	
Kent	Rychaut, Andrew Capt.	
	Hewit, Thomas Capt.	
L. & W.	Smith, Erasmus Capt.	
	Bright, William Capt.	
	Fitzjames, John **Lieut.** to Sir N. Fortescue	
	Cooling, Godfrey Lieut. †	
York	Hedly, Martin Lieut. †	
	Surdevile, George **Cor.**	} To Maj. W. Beckwith
Norfolk	Hichmough, Thomas Quart.	
York	Dolman, Thomas Quart.	
	Garnet, Henry Cor. to Capt. Miles Stanhop	
	Aspenwell, Matthew **Quart.**	
Kent	Cooper, George **Ens.** [ ]	
	Sell, Daniel **Regt. Quart.**	

Middlemore, Edward
Lincoln   Bennet, Thomas **Ens**. [   ] †

Middleton, Sir Francis
L. & W.   Stamford, James **Capt**. HORSE ⎫
                Pilkington, Ralph Cor.   ⎭
York   Asmall, Thomas Capt.
Middlesex   Bateson, Henry **Cor**. to Capt. William Foxcroft
Lancaster   Middleton, Jeffery Cor. †
                Thornborough, John Cor. †

Middleton, Sir George
York   Nelson, Abraham **Capt**. H.
Westmo.   Layburne, Thomas **Lieut**. to Capt. Thomas Kidson
                Duckett, Charles L. to Capt. Layburne
Lancaster   Harris, Christopher Lieut. to Lieut. Col. Carvis
                Danby, Christopher **Cor**. to Capt. Carnes
                Charley, Walter **Quart**. to Capt. Thomas Carts

Middleton, William
York   Burgoyn, Peter **Capt**. FOOT
L. & W.   Middleton, Thomas **Lieut**.
York   Steele, Francis Quart.

Mill, Sir John
Southam.   Lewin, John **Lieut**. HORSE
                Ryves, Cosme **Quart**. †
                Fitchett, Edward Quart. to Capt. George Rodney

Southam.   Mill, Lewkenor **Capt**. FOOT
L. & W.   Combe, Matthew **Ens**. to Maj. W. Abarrow

Millward, John
Derby   Ellis, David **Capt**. FOOT
Bedford   Bruce, Francis Capt.
Derby   Pott, Thomas **Lieut**. †
                Cotterell, Francis **Ens**.

Lincoln   Todd, John **Capt**. DRAGOONS

Mohun, Lord*
Cornwall   Maynard, Henry **Capt**.   ⎫
                Maynard, John Lieut.   ⎬ FOOT
                Sleepe, John Ens.   ⎭
                Mannaton, Sampson Capt.

	Vashmond, John Lieut. †
	Gilbert, Nicholas Lieut. †
	Typper, Nicholas Ens. to Capt. Arthur Bassett
	Vosper, Thomas Ens. †
	Jay, Stephen Ens. †
	Collier, Christopher Ens. †
L. & W.	Adams, Thomas Regt. Quart.

Moldsworth, Guy [Prince Maurice's regiment]
L. & W.	Turner, John Cor. HORSE

Molineux, Lord
L. & W.	Gerard, Thomas Capt. HORSE
Flint	Salisbury, Thomas Capt.
Chester	Bavand, Daniel Capt.
Lancaster	Middleton, Robert Capt.
	Sherborn, Thomas Capt. ⎫
	Latham, Edw. Cor. ⎭
Southam.	Rishton, Ralph Cor. to Capt. Edw. Standish
Lancaster	Clifton, Gervase Cor. ⎫ To Capt. Francis Clifton
	Clifton, Thomas Quart. ⎭
Bedford	Field, Abell Cor. ⎫ To Capt. William Fazacarle
Lancaster	Molineux, Edmund Cor. ⎭
	Gore Edward Quart.
Lancaster	Latham, Richard Capt. FOOT
	Turner, William Ens. to Capt. Henry Byron

Molineux, Roger
L. & W.	Fines, Norris Maj. ⎫ HORSE
Lincoln	Mowbray, William Quart. ⎭
L. & W.	Wilkinson, Anthony Capt.
Derby	Evans, Richard Lieut. †
Lincoln	Wilkinson, John Cor.
Derby	Belson, John Cor.
Nottingh.	Holland, Edward Quart.
L. & W.	Smith, Hezekias Quart. †
Nottingh.	Statham, Henry Quart. FOOT

Monck, Thomas
Devon	Tattershall, John Capt. Lieut. ⎫ HORSE
Dorset	Tattershall, John Cor. ⎭
Middlesex	Stukely, Hugh Lieut.

Montgomery, Robert
Essex — Blaume, Robert **Quart**. HORSE †

Morgan, Anthony
Glamorg. — Price, John **Capt**. FOOT
Brecon — Games, William Capt.
Carmarth. — Floyd, David **Lieut**. to Lieut. Col. Vaughan

Morgan, Sir Edward
Salop — Frankland, Richard **Capt**. FOOT
Monmouth — Pryor, Michael **Ens**. †

Morgan, James
Carmarth. — Bevan, Thomas David **Capt**. ⎫ FOOT
           David, Evan Ens.   ⎭
Monmouth — Bevan, Thomas Capt. ⎫
Carmarth. — Jones, Thomas Lieut. ⎭
Monmouth — Stubbs, Thomas Capt.
Brecon — Morgan, Matthew Capt.
L. & W. — Parry, James Capt.
           Coles, Laurence **Lieut**. †
           James, Richard **Ens**. to Capt. Michael Morgan
           Proger, Wroth Ens. to Capt. Sir John Herbert

Morgan, Thomas
L. & W. — Fermor, Edmund **Cor**. HORSE †

Morley, Lord
York — Miller, Marmaduke **Cor**. HORSE to Lieut. Col. Baines

Morris [1648?]
Somerset — Levingston, John **Capt**. FOOT
York — Atkinson, Francis **Ens**.

Morton, Sir William [Lord Chandos' regiment]
Hertford — Anderson, John **Capt**. FOOT
L. & W. — Banks, William Capt.
Gloucester — Laight, Joseph **Capt. Lieut**.
Oxon — Forty, Thomas **Ens**. to Capt. John Morton

Mostyn, Sir Roger
Flint — Price, Thomas **Capt**. FOOT
        Wynne, William Capt.

                Mostyn, Peter Capt. ⎱
                  Peirce, John Ens.   ⎰
                Jones, Ithell **Lieut.** to Capt. James Llewellin
                Williams, Edw. Lieut. †
                Powell, Thomas **Ens.** †
                Griffith, Richard Ens. †

Muddiford, Thomas
Devon   Wayes, Richard **Capt. Lieut.** HORSE

Devon   Delton, Anthony **Capt. Lieut.** ⎱   FOOT
                  Delahay Richard Ens.   ⎰
L. & W.   Moore, Richard **Ens.** to Capt. Thompson

Muller ['Miller'], Lord
Somerset   Marks, Samuel **Capt.** HORSE
L. & W.   Morris, Thaddeus Capt.   ⎫
                  Hill, Thomas Lieut.   ⎬
                  Condon, William Cor.   ⎭
Devon   Needs, Thomas **Lieut.**   ⎫
Berks   Tottle, Jeffery Lieut.   ⎬ To Lieut. Col. Marks
Somerset   Parfett, John Quart.   ⎭
Devon   Needs, Richard **Cor.** to Maj. Freehall
L. & W.   Ruddell, Christopher Cor.
                Pawlet, William **Quart.** to Capt. Clance
Cornwall   Cory, Nicholas Quart. †

Muschamp, Sir George
Northumb.   Muschamp, Robert **Capt.** FOOT

Musgrave, Sir Edward [1648]
Cumberl.   James, Hugh **Capt.** HORSE
Chester   Cudworth, Thomas **Lieut.** †
Cumberl.   Fell, John **Cor.** †

Cumberl.   Lyndsy, Francis **Capt.** FOOT
                Chambers, William **Lieut.** to Capt. Chambers
                Fisher, Thomas Lieut. †
Lincoln   Gower, Martin **Ens.** to Lieut. Col. Terwhyt
Cumberl.   Grave, William Ens. †
                Webster, Robert **Regt. Quart.**

Musgrave, Sir Phillip [1648]

Cumberl.	Musgrave, William **Capt**. HORSE
	Oglethorpe, Robert Capt.
Westmo.	Hilton, Robert Capt.
	Hilton, Lancelot Lieut.
	Garnet, Anthony Cor.
	Atkinson, Hugh Quart.
Cumberl.	Wilkinson, George **Lieut**. } To Capt. Thomas Sandford
	Jackson, George Cor.
Northumb.	Dawson, Nicholas **Cor**. } To Capt. Simon Musgrave
Warwick	Dawson, Nicholas Cor.
Durham	Ullathornes, Thomas Cor.
Cumberl.	Musgrave, Anthony Cor. †
Durham	Middleton, John **Quart**. to Capt. Phillipson
York	Reed, John Quart. to Maj. Hutchinson
Westmo.	Sleigh, John Quart. to Capt. Sandford
Cumberl.	Dowling, Matthew **Capt**. FOOT
	Barker, Richard **Lieut**. †
	Baynes, John Lieut.
Westmo.	Robinson, Matthew Lieut. †
	Smith, John **Ens**. to Capt. Sir Richard Musgrave
	Harling, Christopher Ens. to Capt. Wilson
	Fothergill, William Ens.
	Hutchinson, Thomas Ens. †

Musgrave, William

L. & W.	Musgrave, Henry **Lieut. Col**. HORSE
Cumberl.	Robinson, Michael **Capt**. FOOT
	Musgrave, Richard **Capt. Lieut**.

Mylott, Ralph*

Durham	Fenwick, Robert **Cor**. HORSE

Mynne, Nicholas

Hereford	Pye, Walter **Capt**. HORSE
Cornwall	Pendarvis, Thomas **Capt**. FOOT
Carmarth.	Price, David **Ens**. †

Mynne, Robert

York	Hough, Gilbert **Capt**. FOOT

Mynne, Colonel ___
Monmouth Harris, Henry Lieut. FOOT to Capt. Grey

Nevill, Richard*
Durham Hodgson, William Capt. HORSE
L. & W. Paslew, Richard Capt. ⎱
             Bonust, Robert Cor. ⎰
Middlesex Jewkes, Henry Lieut. to Maj. Thomas Panton
Durham Salvin, John Quart. to Capt. Richard Conquest

Nevill, William
Northam. Mason, John Capt. ⎱ HORSE
L. & W.   Colston, Daniel Lieut. ⎰
Leicester Ellis, William Capt. Lieut. ⎱
L. & W. Davis, Robert Capt. Lieut. ⎬
          Wellstead, George Cor. ⎰
Lincoln Hawes, Henry Lieut. †

L. & W. Bywaters, Thomas Maj. FOOT
Lincoln Bagshaw, Charles Capt.
Northam. Claughton, James Capt.
          Claughton, William Lieut. †

Nevill[12]
L. & W. Pen, Roger Lieut. HORSE to Maj. Trevor
Middlesex Harrison, Eusebius Lieut. to Capt. Woodward
Devon Baron, Hercules Lieut. to Capt. John Ball

Bedford Robinson, Henry Lieut. FOOT to Capt. Ed. Goodwin

Newcastle, Marquess of
L. & W. Egerton, Richard Col. HORSE & FOOT
          Holtby, Marmaduke Col. HORSE & FOOT
          Trafford, Francis Col. HORSE
          Claxton, John Capt. †
Northumb. Newton, Christopher Lieut. to Capt. Brandling
York West, John Lieut. to Capt. Turner
      Cooke, William Lieut. †
Stafford Adderly, William Lieut. †
Hereford Heaven, Rowland Lieut. to Capt. Towne †
York Atkins, Robert Cor. to Capt. Mozin †
      Hudson, Edw. Quart. to Capt. Benson
Durham Chilton, John Quart. to Capt. William Unthanke

---

[12] It is unclear whether these men claimed under Richard Neville, or William Neville, or both; Richard Neville did not command foot, but one of his officers was, like claimant Robinson above, from Bedford.

L. & W.	Le Hunt, Sir John **Col**. FOOT	
Durham	Marshall, Ingram **Capt**.	
	Hedworth, William Capt.	
Northumb.	Fenwick, Ralph Capt.	
	Selby, Ralph Capt.	
	Elrington, Nicholas **Capt. Lieut**.	
York	Nalson, Robert Lieut. to Sir Arthur Basset	
Durham	Snary, William Lieut. to Capt. John Rutter	
Hertford	Bull, Henry **Ens**. to Capt. Thomas Sharper	
Stafford	Sewell, Richard Ens.	
Northumb.	Thomson, Robert Ens. to Capt. James Swinhoe	
York	Tayler, Richard Ens. to Capt. Tirwhytt	
L. & W.	Wiseman, Samuel Ens. to Capt. Nicholas Lanyon	
Northumb.	Ripley, John Ens. to Capt. William Gower	
L. & W.	Stuart, William **Col**. DRAGOONS	

Norris, Edward

Lancaster	Lancaster, John **Capt**. FOOT

Northampton, Earl of

L. & W.	Knight, Valentine **Capt**.	HORSE
	Crane, Richard Cor.	
	Simmons, John Quart.	
Salop	Ferrers, John Quart.	
L. & W.	Tudor, Thomas **Lieut**. to Capt. George Rowly	
Essex	Whitney, William Lieut.	To Maj. Colborne
L. & W.	Woodward, John Lieut.	
Warwick	Smith, Christopher Lieut.	To Sir W. Compton
	Hopkins, George Quart.	
Leicester	Hales, Stephen Cor.	
L. & W.	Moore, Robert Lieut.	To Capt. Moore
Warwick	Burden, Moyses Lieut.	
	Powell, William Cor.	
L. & W.	Woodhall, Thomas **Cor**. †	
Warwick	Wootton, William **Quart**.	
	Blackford, Daniel Quart. to Capt. Clarke	
Northam.	Page, William Quart. to Capt. William Hickman	
	Wisdom, William Quart. to Capt. Slaney	
Surrey	Lowe, Edw. Quart. to Sir Charles Compton	
L. & W.	Massey, William Regt. Quart.	
Oxon	Smith, Francis Quart. †	
L. & W.	Gwynn, Thomas Quart. to Capt. Paslew	
Northam.	James, William **Capt**. FOOT	

L. & W.	Walrond, George **Lieut**. to Sir W. Compton
	Paris, John Lieut. †
	Underhill, John **Ens**. to Capt. Tirwhyt
Warwick	Phipps, William **Quart**. DRAGOONS

Northampton, Lord Spencer[13]

Bucks	Betts, William **Capt**. FOOT

Norwich, Earl of [1648]

L. & W.	Grove, Francis **Cor**. HORSE to Capt. Richard Weeks
L. & W.	Davison, George **Lieut**. FOOT to Capt. Pitts
Cambridge	Parlet, William Lieut. to Capt. Francis Birch

Oately, Sir Francis

Salop	Ambler, Richard **Lieut**. FOOT to Capt. Allen
	Scott, Richard **Ens**. to Capt. Pontsbury Owen
	Ursgat, John **Quart**.
L. & W.	Betton, Richard **Cor**. DRAGOONS

Ogle, Lord William

L. & W.	Hicks, Henry **Lieut**. HORSE
Montgom.	Rock, James **Cor**.
L. & W.	Green, Jerom. **Regt**. **Quart**.
Kent	Harvill, William **Quart**. to Lieut. Col. Gardiner
L. & W.	Goddard, John **Capt**. FOOT
	Thorpe, Lancelot Capt. ⎱
	Roe, John Lieut. ⎰
Southam.	Hambury, John Capt. ⎱
L. & W.	Davis, Hugh Lieut. ⎰
Southam.	Tyre, William Capt.
	Stainsby, Thomas Capt.
L. & W.	Heather, Richard **Lieut**. to Capt. Titchburne
Southam.	Colebrooke, John Lieut. to Capt. James
	Colston, John Lieut. †
	Bye, Ferdinando Lieut. †
	Silver, John Lieut. †
	Colles, Richard **Ens**.

Osborne, Sir Edward

York	Gibson, Sir John **Capt**. HORSE

---

[13] Probably Spencer Compton, Earl of Northampton; but conceivably Henry Lord Spencer, of Brington in Northants.

Owen, Sir John*
Salop	Floyd, Edward **Capt.** FOOT
	Floyd, Thomas Capt.
Anglesey	Jones, Daniel Capt.
L. & W.	Nanny, John **Capt. Lieut.**
Montgom.	Matthews, Richard Lieut.
Merion.	Floyd, David Lieut. ⎫ To Capt. Humphryes
	Humphryes. Gabriel Ens. ⎭
Denbigh	Gething, Humphry Lieut. †
Merion.	Pugh, William Lieut. to Lieut. Col. Burges
Carnarvon	Wynne, Thomas Lieut. to Capt. Robert Wynne
Anglesey	Wynne, Humphry Lieut. to Capt. Jenkins
Denbigh	Powell, Thomas Lieut. to Capt. Jones
	Matthews, Thomas Lieut. to Capt. Brunker
Carnarvon	Lewis, Richard Lieut. †
Merion.	Floyd, John **Ens.** to Capt. John Pugh
Anglesey	Roberts, John Ens. to Capt. Merrick

Owen, William
Salop	Roberts, John **Lieut.** FOOT †

Packington, Sir John [1651]
Worcester	Randal, Thomas **Capt. Lieut.** [ ]

Page, Sir Richard*
York	Lemgo, Andrew **Ens.** [ ] to Capt. Anthony Norton

Palmer, Richard
Glamorg.	Pitts, James **Capt.** HORSE
L. & W.	Leigh, Phillip **Lieut.** ⎫ To Maj. Phillip Bacon
	Allbrittayn Thomas Cor. ⎭
	Swarland, Thomas **Quart.** to Maj. Brinfield

Parry
York	Read, Leonard **Ens.** [ ] to Capt. Rooksby

Pate, Sir John
Leicester	Digby, Nathaniel **Capt.** ⎫ HORSE
Lincoln	Barnwell, Francis Cor. ⎭
Leicester	Bent, Christopher **Lieut.** ⎫ To Capt. Bent
Northam.	Randall, Andrew Cor. ⎭
Leicester	Woolland, Robert **Cor.** to Capt. Bowman
?	Bodington, George **Quart.**

Paulet, Lord [John, 1ˢᵗ Baron Paulet]*

Wilts	Kitson, John **Lieut**. HORSE to Maj. Fuller
Somerset	Plumly, Henry **Cor**.
Somerset	Beecher, John **Capt**. FOOT
	Hawkins, Thomas **Capt**. **Lieut**.

Paulet, Sir John

L. & W.	Wind, Robert **Capt**. FOOT
	Wind, Robert Capt.
Southam.	Richards, Sir Edw. Capt.
	Mill, Edw. Capt.
L. & W.	Barling, John **Lieut**. to Capt. Neve
Southam.	Newbury, John Lieut. †

Pelham, Sir William

L. & W.	Floyd, Francis **Capt**. HORSE
Lincoln	Verny, Francis **Lieut**. to Capt. Floud
	Laythorpe, William Lieut. to Capt. Saltmarsh
	Appleyard, Thomas Lieut. ⎫
	Rask, John Cor. ⎬ To Maj. Scroop
	Dawson, Christopher Quart. ⎭
	Skipwith, John Lieut. to Capt. Thomas Wright
	Sergeant John Lieut. †
L. & W.	Lovell, Thomas **Cor**.
Lincoln	Waters, Thomas Cor. to Capt. Husthwaite Wright
	Wesled, Thomas Cor. to Capt. Wesled
	Wright, Anthony Cor. ⎫ To Lieut. Col. William Booth
	Davy, John Quart. ⎭
	Bowden, Edward Cor. †
	Bestoe, Othwell Cor. †
	Gilby, Richard **Quart**. to Capt. Darrell
	Bennet, Henry Quart.
Lincoln	Hardy, James **Lieut**. FOOT to Capt. Pelham
	Sharpe, Thomas **Ens**. to Capt. Toogood

Pennyman, Sir James*

York	Norton, Anthony **Capt**. FOOT
	Jackson, John Capt.
	Sympson, John Capt.
	Bateson, Francis Capt.
Durham	Eggleston, John **Lieut**. to Capt. Mallory
York	Anderson, Thomas **Ens**.

Corpes, James Ens. to Lieut. Col. George ___[14]
Bates, William **Quart.**

Pennyman, Sir William*
Kent	Dixon, James **Lieut.** HORSE to Lieut. Col. Hutchinson
Northam.	Huthwayte, John Lieut. to Maj. Edw. Hutchinson
Lincoln	Hullock, William **Quart.** to Capt. Edw. Warder
York	Skurray, John Quart. to Lieut. Col. Franckland
York	Storre, James **Lieut.** FOOT to Capt. Blakeston
L. & W.	Tatham, Anthony Lieut. to Capt. Humphrey Elmes
	Sartan, Allen Lieut. †
Salop	Read, James **Ens.** to Capt. Lawson

Perkins, Isham
Nottingh.   Trees, George **Cor.** HORSE

Pert, Thomas
Middlesex	Segor, Thomas **Capt.** FOOT †
Glamorg.	Thomas, John Capt.
	Floyd, Walter Capt.
Carmarth.	Bowen, William **Lieut.** to Capt. Rudds
Worcester	Meysy, Francis Lieut. to Capt. Nicholas Blunt
Somerset	Lambe, Henry **Ens.** to Capt. Wingfield
Glamorg.	Roberts, Hugh Ens.

Pettus, Sir John
Suffolk	Sherman, John Capt. HORSE
L. & W.	Thornborow, Benjamin Cor. to Capt. Colt

Phelips, Edward
Somerset   Highdown, Richard **Capt.** HORSE
           Clark, Richard **Quart.** †

Phelips, Robert
Somerset	Burgh, Edw. **Capt.** HORSE
	Rush, James **Lieut.** to Capt. Rowes
	Willoughby, Richard **Cor.**
	Haine, Thomas **Quart.** to Capt. Rosse
	Cecil, Jonathan Regt. Quart.
L. & W.	Forrester, Andrew **Capt.** FOOT
Somerset	Phelipps, Arthur Capt.

---

[14] Possibly Lieutenant Colonel George Gwinn, who requested inclusion in I.O. but is not listed under any regiment.

L. & W.	Coles, John **Capt. Lieut.**
Wilts	Steadman, William Lieut. to Maj. John Morgan
L. & W.	Rose, John Lieut. to Lieut. Col. Overton
Somerset	Hyde, Thomas **Quart.** †

Phelips, Colonel ___
Wilts   Spyer, Henry **Quart.** HORSE to Capt. Lambert

Pierce, Sir Edmond
Middlesex	Raven, Roger **Capt.** HORSE
	Clarke, Thomas Capt.
Southam.	Pyne, Henry **Lieut.** ⎫
L. & W.	Cooper, Roger Cor. ⎬ To Capt. Dunce
Middlesex	Ducket, John **Cor.**
	Cotton, John Cor. †
L. & W.	Charnock, Thomas **Quart.**

Piercy, Lord Henry*
Glamorg.	Williams, Roger **Lieut.** HORSE to Sir H. Heron
Berks	Stafford, Humphry **Cor.** to Lieut. Col. Slingsby
L. & W.	Whitford, David **Capt.** FOOT
Suffolk	Theobald, Thomas **Lieut.** to Maj. Henry Crompton
L. & W.	Steley, John Lieut. to ffor

Pigott, Thomas
Somerset	Roche, Adam **Maj.** ⎫ FOOT
L. & W.	Trant, Edw. Ens. ⎭
Somerset	Leicester, Henry **Capt.**
L. & W.	Fitzgerald, Edmund **Lieut.** to Capt. King
Somerset	Crook, Thomas Lieut. to Lieut. Col. Barret

Pinchback
Suffolk   Goodrich, Thomas **Capt. Lieut.** FOOT

Playters, Thomas
L. & W.	Burton, Richard **Lieut.** HORSE to Capt. Warner
	Le Hunt, Robert **Cor.** to Capt. John Le Hunt
	Tyrrell, Anthony **Quart.**

Pollard, Ames
York	Reesby, Francis **Capt.** ⎫ HORSE
L. & W.	Jones, Morgan Quart. ⎭

Wilts	Abithell, Thomas **Lieut.** †
Somerset	Allen, Henry Lieut. †
	Buckingham, William Lieut. †
Essex	Wood, Bowyer Lieut. †
Dorset	Collinder, Edw. **Cor.** †
Devon	Bowerman, Andrew **Quart.** †
Cornwall	Carver, Thomas **Capt. Lieut.** FOOT
Devon	Summers, John Lieut. to Maj. Thomas Coe
Somerset	Knight, Francis **Ens.** †

Pollard, Sir Hugh
L. & W.	Jemmett, Warham **Capt.** FOOT
	Coffin, Thomas Capt.
Devon	Bottomly, William Capt.
	Hunt, Roger **Lieut.** †
Cornwall	Stanbury, John Lieut. †
	Richards, John **Ens.** †
	Upton, John Ens. †
Devon	Read, John Ens. †

Porter, George
Lincoln	Ogar, Edmund **Capt.** ⎫ HORSE
Cambridge	Walls, Edw. Quart. ⎭
Nottingh.	Johnson, Marmaduke **Lieut.** to Capt. Oker

Poyer, John [1648]
L. & W.	Carre, John **Cor.** HORSE †

Preston, Sir John
York	Pudsey, Peter **Maj.** ⎫ HORSE
Northumb.	How, Christopher Cor. ⎬
York	Paul, Richard Quart. ⎭
Lancaster	Knight, John **Capt.**
Durham	Salvin, John Capt.
York	Merryman, Gerrard **Lieut.** to Lieut. Col. Preston
Northumb.	How, John **Cor.** to Lieut. Col. Eure
L. & W.	Bodington, George **Quart.**
York	Copeland, Laurence Quart. †
Lancaster	Singleton, Thomas Quart. †

Prestwich, Sir Thomas
Middlesex	Prestwich, Thomas **Maj.** ⎫ HORSE
L. & W.	Percivall, Edw. Quart. ⎭
Chester	Massy, William **Capt. Lieut.**

L. & W.	Ryvely, Edw. **Quart.**	} To Lieut. Col. Richard Wiltshire
	Day, John Quart.	
Sussex	Edmonds, Thomas Quart. to Capt. Masterson	
Lancaster	Bennet, William Quart. †	

Pretty, William
L. & W.	Smith, Miles **Capt.** FOOT
Kent	King, Matthew Capt.
Gloucester	Hayward, John Capt.
Flint	Vaughan, Bithell Capt.
L. & W.	Morris, Henry **Lieut.** to Lieut. Col. Morgan
Glamorg.	Lewis, Rice Lieut. †
	Williams, Stradling **Ens.** to Maj. St. Leger
	Lewis, George Ens. †
	Lewis, Miles Ens. †
Worcester	Hayward, John Ens. †

Price, Sir Herbert
L. & W.	Price, John **Capt.** HORSE	
Hereford	Cornwall, Gilbert Capt.	
Monmouth	Croft, Richard **Lieut.**	} To Col. Morgan
	Pye, James Cor.	
	Hughes, Giles Quart.	
Brecon	Vaughan, Henry Lieut. to Capt. Bartholomew Price	
Hereford	Hoply, Richard Lieut. to Capt. Walter	
Monmouth	Crofts, Richard Lieut. †	
	James, Phillip **Cor.** †	

L. & W.	Price, Richard **Maj.** FOOT
Radnor	Price, James **Capt.**
Brecon	Davis, Edw. Capt.
	Powell, Peter Capt.
Monmouth	Roberts, John **Lieut.** to Maj. Turbervile Morgan
Brecon	Prees, William Lieut. to Capt. Thomas Vaughan
Hereford	Barrer, Thomas Lieut. to Maj. Slaughter
Monmouth	Roberts, John Lieut. †
Brecon	William, Meredith Lieut. †
	Powell, Thomas Lieut. †
	Powell, Walter Lieut. †
	Edwards, John Lieut. †
	John, Howell **Ens.** †
	William David Ens. †

Price, William
Denbigh	Fulkes Llowarch **Lieut.** FOOT to Capt. Price

Prideaux, William
Nottingh.   Walker, Richard **Cor**. DRAGOONS to Lieut. Col. Craythorne

Progers, James
Monmouth   Jones, Henry **Ens**. to Lieut. Col. Charles Progers
James, John **Regt. Quart**.

Pye, Sir Walter
Warwick   Dorcas, Edw. **Lieut**. HORSE
Hereford   Horne, Thomas **Quart**.
Barrow, John Quart.

Radford, Arthur
Dorset   Cave, Morgan **Lieut**. FOOT to Lieut. Col. Dirdo
Husy, Clifford Lieut. †
Somerset   Willys, Henry Lieut. †

Radly, Sir Henry
Lincoln   Radly, Charles **Cor**. HORSE

Ramsden, Sir John
York   Snowsdale, Henry **Lieut**. FOOT to Capt. Pilkington
Meux, Thomas Lieut. †
Ramsden, Hugh **Ens**. to Capt. Henry Grice
Wright, Robert **Quart**.

Ratcliffe, Sir William
L. & W.   Egerton, Thomas **Lieut. Col**. HORSE
Aston, Arthur **Capt. Lieut**.
Lancaster   Booker, William **Quart**.

Rawston, Edward
Lancaster   Kay, William **Capt**. HORSE

Lancaster   Greenhall, James **Ens**. † FOOT

Redhead, Arthur
York   Empson, George **Lieut**. HORSE } To Capt. Henry Redhead
Marshall, Anthony Cor.

Redman, Sir John*
York   Ogden, Thomas **Lieut**. FOOT to Capt. Cartwright

L. & W.   Maxfield, William **Lieut**. DRAGOONS to Capt. Col. Monro

Reymes, Bullen*
L. & W.	Hill, John **Capt**. FOOT
Middlesex	Cory, William **Lieut**. †
Dorset	Braddor, John **Regt. Quart**.

Riddell, Sir Thomas
Durham	Paul, Thomas **Capt**. HORSE
	Eden, Ralph **Lieut**. to Capt. Gascoyn Eden
Suffolk	Partridge, George **Capt**. FOOT
Newcastle	Errington, Christopher **Lieut**. ⎫
Durham	Marshall, Robert Ens. ⎬ To Capt. Thomas Paul
	Hanworth, Robert **Ens**. to Capt. Proctor
	Pinckard, Robert Ens. to Maj. Clark
	Allen, Robert **Cor**. DRAGOONS to Capt. Gascoyn Eden
	Urwin, Edw. **Regt. Quart**.

Rivers, Lord
Chester	Jennings, Ralph **Lieut**. HORSE †
	Parsons, George **Capt**. to Capt. Henry Savage

Robinson, John
Anglesey	Wynne, Hugh **Lieut**. FOOT to Capt. William Wynne

Robinson, Sir William
York	Scudamore, Thomas **Capt**. FOOT
	Taylor, John **Capt. Lieut**.
	Mascal, Jonas Lieut. to Capt. Thomas Mascall
	Scudamore, Henry **Ens**. †

Rodney, Sir Edward
Somerset	Rodney, William **Capt**. FOOT
	Plush, Thomas **Lieut**. ⎫ To Maj. William Morgan
	Slade, Henry Ens. ⎭

Rogers, Francis
Warwick	Crisp, Thomas **Lieut**. HORSE to Capt. Awbry
Salop	Hammond, Henry Lieut. †
Glamorg.	Butler, Lamerock **Cor**. †
Kent	Emerson, John **Quart**. †

Rolleston [William] [Ralph Eure's regiment]
Surrey	Wyndly, Robert **Quart**. HORSE

Roper, Christopher
Salop   Smith, Charles **Capt. Lieut.** FOOT

Rosecarrock, Edward
Surrey   Thomas, Humphry **Capt.** HORSE

Rosthorne
L. & W.   Ballard, Thomas **Ens.** [   ] to Capt. Penkeath
             Askew, Thomas Ens. †

Rothes, Earl of [1651]
Huntingd.   Moore, Alexander **Cor.** HORSE to Lieut. Col. Sir W. Scot

Roydon, Sir Marmaduke
L. & W.   Atterbury, William **Capt. Lieut.** HORSE
             Goddard, John Lieut. to Maj. Addison
Somerset   Bold, Thomas **Cor.**   } To Maj. Henry Hene
Southam.   Sayer, Robert Quart.
L. & W.   Amery, Robert **Capt.**   } FOOT
Cambridge   Pildrim, William Lieut.
Somerset   Brown, John **Lieut.** to Capt. Fletcher
L. & W.   Teadman, Giles **Ens.** to Capt. Isaac Rowlett
             Murrey, William Ens. to Capt. Rudyer
             Fauntleroy, John Ens. †

Rupert, Prince*
L. & W.   Walsh, Sir Robert **Col.** HORSE
             Cary, Sir Horatio Col.
             Martin, Clement **Capt.** & Quart. Gen.
Wilts   Thacham, Robert Quart. to Capt. Clement Martin
York   Davis, Hugh Capt. †
Surrey   Gardiner, Richard Capt. †
York   Blakeston, George **Lieut.**
             Walter, Thomas Cor.   } To Sir Francis Cobbe
Suffolk   Thwaytes, Thomas Quart.
Durham   Richardson, Bryan Lieut. } To Capt. John Richardson
Wilts   Jackson, Robert Quart.
Dorset   Cox, Humphry Lieut. to Capt. Smith
Kent   Crickett, Daniell Lieut. †
Salop   Wood, Henry **Cor.** to Capt. Grace
Southam.   Hooke, Edmund Cor.   } To Sir Thomas Dallison
York   Bower, Jeremy Cor.
L. & W.   Hubert, John Cor.   } To the Lord Grandison
Salop   Armstrong, Roger Quart.

Carmarth.	King, William Cor. to Capt. Warner
L. & W.	Watson, George Cor. to Sir Lewis Dives
	Montgomery, William **Quart**. to the Lifeguard
	Field, John Quart. to Col. William Legge
Durham	Young, William Quart. to Capt. William Bowes
Derby	Clay, William Quart. †
L. & W.	Lyne, Aeneas **Maj**. ⎫ FOOT
	Hinane, James Ens. ⎪
	Carty, Owen Lieut. ⎬
	O'Donoghue, Mortaugh Ens. ⎭
	White, Gerard **Capt**.
	Nicholls, Thomas Capt.
Wilts	Basket, Richard Capt.
Monmouth	Tilden, John Capt. †
L. & W.	Barker, Nicholas **Capt. Lieut**.
Kent	Joyner, Richard Capt. Lieut.
Dorset	Hillary, Roger Lieut. ⎫
Salop	Osborne, Thomas Ens. ⎭
L. & W.	Grey, George Lieut. to Lieut. Col. John Russell
Worcester	Sparrey, John Lieut.
L. & W.	Howell, Matthew Lieut. to Capt. Nelson
Worcester	Woogan, Thomas **Ens**. to Capt. Baxter
Hereford	Walwyn, Richard Ens. to Capt. Walwyn
Somerset	Pyne, William Ens. to Capt. Pyne
L. & W.	Coningsby, William Ens. †
Surrey	Broadnax, Henry **Capt**. DRAGOONS

Russell, Sir William [of Strensham]*

Worcester	Blunt, Peter **Capt**. HORSE
	Brent, Edw. Capt. ⎫
	Brent, George Lieut. ⎬
Gloucester	Prickett, Anker Quart. ⎭
Worcester	Manly, John **Lieut**. to Maj. Blunt
	Hall, Matthew Lieut. †
Kent	Bridges, William **Cor**.
Norfolk	Ellis, Francis Cor. to Capt. Watkins
Worcester	Bernard, John **Quart**. to Capt. Henry Colt
	Walker, John Quart. to Capt. Walsh
L. & W.	Osborne, Edw. **Capt**. FOOT
Worcester	Moore, Richard Capt.
	Sheldon, Thomas Capt.

Denbigh	Hughes, Robert Capt. ⎫
Salop	Normcott, Richard Lieut. † ⎭
Gloucester	Whittorne, Conway Capt. ⎫
L. & W.	Mellicheap, Thomas Ens. ⎭
Hertford	Fitch, Henry Lieut. to Maj. Harvey
Worcester	Williams, Richard Lieut. to Capt. Middlemore
	Collins, Walter Lieut. to Capt. Ingram
	Moses, John Lieut. †
	Moore, John Ens. †
	Twittey, Thomas Ens. †
L. & W.	Blumson, Thomas Quart.

Ruthen, Lord General

Durham	Barnes, Henry Capt. ⎫ HORSE
York	Key, George Quart. ⎭
Salop	Worsley, Jeroboam Lieut. to Maj. Elvis
Northam.	Harman, Samuel Lieut. ⎫
Durham	Close, William Quart. ⎭ To Maj. Goade
Hertford	Ellis, William Cor. to Capt. Fleetwood
York	Anderson, John Quart. to Lieut. Col. Hutchinson
Durham	Sedgewick, Lancelot Quart. to Capt. Shaw
Essex	Johnson, George Quart. †
L. & W.	St. Clare, William Lieut. Col. FOOT & Adj. Gen.
Berks	Batt, Thomas Capt.
Bucks	Sergeant, William Capt.
Norfolk	Draper, Thomas Capt.
L. & W.	Baxter, Walter Lieut. to Capt. Berckly
Lincoln	Bowden, Thomas Lieut.

St. Albans, Lord [Henry Jermyn; Queen's regiment]

Middlesex	Brockholles, Thomas Capt. ⎫ HORSE
Lancaster	Wilkinson, William Quart. ⎭
Durham	Dixon, George Cor. to Capt. Markham
L. & W.	Deale, John Quart. to Sir Edw. Brett
Lancaster	Butchard, Lionell Quart. to Capt. Clifton
Northam.	Grafton, John Quart. to Capt. Charles Charbo
Warwick	Reeve, Francis Quart. to Sir Thomas Smith
York	Crofts, Roger Quart. ⎫
Lancaster	Sergeant, William Quart. ⎭ To Maj. Sir John Cansfield
York	Hutchinson, Arthur Quart. to Capt. Norton
Kent	Jorey, Sidrach Capt. FOOT
Durham	Buttery, John Capt. ⎫
	Moore, Robert Ens. ⎭

L. & W.	De St. Mark, Anthony Capt.
	Crompton, James Capt.
	Poore, Francis Capt. ⎫
	Garnet, Edmund Lieut. ⎭
	Livermore, John **Lieut**. to Capt. St. Michael
	Brown, Ralph Lieut. †
	Hopkins, William Lieut. †
	Robinson, Richard Lieut. †
Cumberl.	Porter, Nicholas Lieut. †
L. & W.	Knight, John **Ens**. to Capt. Thomas Cooke
York	Buttery, Christopher Ens. to Capt. Butler
Oxon	Earle, Henry Ens. to Maj. William Blunt

St. Aubyn, Thomas

Salop	Floyd, Matthias **Maj**. FOOT
Cornwall	Arnold, Thomas **Capt**.
Somerset	Arundell, John Capt.
L. & W.	King, John Capt.
Cornwall	Cock, Maugan **Lieut**. to Capt. Munday
	Munday, John Lieut. †
	Hodden, Michael Lieut. †
	Colliver, Stephen Lieut. †
	Trenhale, George **Ens**. †
	Hutchins, William Ens. †
	Lobbe, John Ens. †
	Prideaux, Francis Ens. †
	Dingle, George Ens. †

St. George, William

Northumb.	Lorrayne, Thomas **Capt**. FOOT
	Lorrayne, Nicholas Capt.
Hereford	Jones, David **Lieut**. to Capt. Owen
York	Cartwright, Matthew **Quart**.

St. Leger, Anthony

Kent	Lee, John **Lieut**. HORSE

St. Leger, Sir William*

L. & W.	Mountayn, Richard **Lieut**. FOOT to Capt. Hill

St. Paul, Lord

York	Littlewood, Josuah **Cor**. HORSE
L. & W.	Baker, John **Quart**.

Salisbury, Sir Thomas*
Denbigh	Floyd, Nanny **Capt**. FOOT
	Broughton, William Capt.
Oxon	Jones, Matthew **Lieut**. †
Denbigh	Daulben, Hugh **Ens**. to Capt. Daulben

Salisbury, William
Denbigh	Rutter, Reynold **Capt**. FOOT
Carnarvon	Pugh, Robert Capt.
Denbigh	Price, Thomas Capt. †
	Evans, William **Lieut**. †
	Wynne, Robert Lieut. †
	Jones, Robert **Ens**. †
	Floyd, John Ens. †

Sandford, Sir Thomas
Westmo.	Ward, Henry **Capt**. FOOT
	Ecton, John **Capt. Lieut**.
	Dobson, Christopher **Ens**. †

Sandys, Henry
L. & W.	Herbert, Charles **Quart**. HORSE †

Sandys, Sir Martin
Worcester	Tyrer, Humphry **Capt**. ⎫ FOOT
	Ford, Thomas Ens. ⎭
	Batch, Thomas Capt.
	Symonds, Nicholas **Lieut**. †
	Sherman, Francis Lieut. †
	Mascall, Thomas Lieut. †
	Ockley, William **Ens**. to Capt. Knight
	Hughes, Francis Ens. to Lieut. Col. Solley
	King, Humphry Ens. to Capt. Richard Mascall

Sandys, Robert
L. & W.	Bingley, Oliver **Capt**. HORSE

Sandys, Samuel*
Carmarth.	Sandys, Martin **Capt**. ⎫ HORSE
L. & W.	Scargill, Robert Lieut. ⎬
Kent	Thurston, Ralph Cor. ⎭
L. & W.	Fisher, Thomas Capt.
	Manley, Robert Capt. ⎫
Worcester	Cartwright, John Cor. ⎭
	Stratford, Anthony Capt.

	Hanbury, John Capt.	}
	Hulford, Francis Quart.
L. & W.	Fielding, Christopher Capt. †
Stafford	Doughty, Edw. Lieut. †
Worcester	Rowles, Giles Lieut. †
	Barret, Edw. Cor.
	Durston, John Quart. } To Capt. Savage
	Martin John Quart.
	Hunt, Thomas Cor.
	Gunter, Walter Quart. } To Maj. Wild
	Price, Robert Quart.
	Batch, William Cor. †
	Mopson, William Quart. to Capt. Langston
	Lunne, John Quart.
L. & W.	Wainwright, Francis Quart. †
Gloucester	Canner, John Quart. †
Surrey	Goffe, John Quart. †
Worcester	Clare, Francis Capt. } FOOT
	Colles, Walter Lieut.
Salop	Field, Richard Capt.
Gloucester	Hunt, Richard Lieut. to Maj. More
Worcester	Freeman, Edw. Lieut. to Capt. Millington
	Salmon, John Lieut. to Capt. Sandys
Norfolk	Butts, Lewis Lieut. to Capt. Littleton
Middlesex	Copley, George Lieut. †
Montgom.	Evans, Austin Lieut.

Sandys, Sir Thomas
L. & W.   Walker, Steward Capt. HORSE
          Heskith, Bartholomew Lieut. to Lieut. Col. Palmer
          Houghton, William Cor.
          Chaloner, Francis Quart. †

Sandys, Colonel ___
Oxon   Trowe, Gilbert Quart. HORSE

Hereford Davis, Thomas Ens. FOOT†

Savile, Sir William
L. & W.   Beversham, John Maj. HORSE
York   Portington Henry Capt.
            Bishop, Richard Lieut. }
            Tayler, John Cor.

	Grymston, Christopher **Capt.** ⎫
	Chapman, William Lieut. ⎭
	Nevill, Roger Capt.
Lincoln	Markham, Phillip Capt. ⎫
Nottingh.	Sherburn, Richard Lieut. ⎭
Warwick	Sclater, William Capt.
York	Harland, Richard **Lieut**. ⎫ To Sir John Goodrick
	Justice, Emanuel Quart. ⎭
	Wentworth, Michael Lieut. ⎫
	Nunnes, Robert Lieut. ⎬ To Maj. Wentworth
	Loft, Thomas Quart. ⎭
	Keighly, Michael Lieut. to Capt. Vernatt
	Spurgen, Thomas Lieut. to Lieut. Col. Portington
	Brearcliffe, Stephen Lieut. †
Lincoln	Chambers, James **Cor**. ⎫ To Capt. Oliver Fleetwood
Nottingh.	Manwaring, John Cor. ⎭
Essex	Bright, William Cor. to Abraham Vernatt
Derby	Goodyear, Thomas Cor. †
York	Hallely, Cutbert **Quart**. to Capt. Ord
	Milner, John Quart. to Capt. John Benson
	Reddish, William Quart. to Capt. John Copley
	Settle, William Quart.
	Stoner, William Quart. to Capt. Roger Portington
	Rawson, Thomas Quart. †
	Carrington, John Quart. †
	Clough, Robert Quart. †
York	Audesly, John **Capt.** FOOT
	Jackson, Charles Capt.
	Oxley, John **Lieut**. to Sir Thomas Beaumont
	Woodrow, Joseph **Ens**. to Capt. Woodrow
	Dawson, William Ens. to Capt. Batts
	Waterhouse, Matthew Ens. †
York	Fayrbank, John **Lieut**. DRAGOONS to Capt. Dixon
	Child, James Lieut. to Capt. Bromhead

Saul, John
L. & W.	Rastall, Henry **Capt.** HORSE
L. & W.	Bell, Augustine **Capt.** FOOT

Sayers, Christopher
Hertford	Thody, Henry **Capt. Lieut.** HORSE

Salop	Phillips, Richard **Capt.**	} FOOT
	Screven, William Ens.	
	Russell, William **Ens**. to Sir Thomas Eyton	

Scroop, Sir Adrian [Lord General's regiment]
L. & W.	Shipman, John **Capt**. HORSE
Warwick	Metcalfe, Edw. **Lieut**. †
Northam.	Gibson, William Lieut. †
Middlesex	Scroop, Adrian **Cor**.
Dorset	Cousins, John **Quart**. to Capt. Fleetwood

Scroope, John
York	Walker, John **Lieut**. FOOT to Lieut. Col. James
York	Smith, John **Cor**. HORSE

Scudamore, Sir Barnaby
Kent	Walter, Thomas **Capt**. HORSE	
Hereford	Cornwall, Edw. Capt.	
	Blashfield, Richard Capt.	
L. & W.	Cox, Henry **Lieut**.	} To Maj. Charles Cox
Hereford	Tainton, Edmund Cor.	
	Williscot, Edw. Lieut.	} To Maj. John Pye
	Widrington, Oswald Lieut.	
	Smith, George **Cor**. to Sir Nicholas Throckmorton	
	Price, Edw. Cor.	
	Pittman, William Cor. †	
	Lord, Hugh **Quart**. to Capt. Walter	
	Drew, Thomas Quart.	
Hereford	Rogers, John **Capt**.	} FOOT
	Rodd, Humphry Lieut.	
	Jones, John Ens.	
	Cawarden, Thomas Capt.	}
	Shepheard, Walter Ens.	
Surrey	Goodwin, Robert Capt. †	
L. & W.	Brown, Richard Capt. †	
Hereford	Russell, Robert **Lieut**. to Capt. Price	
	Vincent, Richard Lieut.	} To Capt. Thomas Lewis
	Traherne, James Ens.	
L. & W.	Lightfoot, Toby Lieut. to Capt. Ballard	
Glamorg.	Matthew, Howell Lieut.	
Hereford	Bayly, Edward **Ens**. to Capt. Edw. Clark	
	Love, James Ens. to Maj. Norman	
	Jones, Henry Ens. to Capt. Chaplin	

Sellwyn, Sir Nicholas [City of Oxford regiment]*
Oxon	White, Robert **Lieut.** [ ] ⎫ To Capt. Peter Langsten
	Stevenson, William Ens. ⎭
	Wells, Thomas Lieut. to Maj. James Bowman
	Lello, Matthew **Ens.** to Lieut. Col. Hall
	Andrews, William Ens. to Capt. Stephens
	Wild, John Ens. to Lieut. Col. Smith

Seymore, Sir Edward
L. & W.	Phillips, Owen **Capt.** FOOT
Devon	Griffith, Thomas Capt.
	Edgecumbe, Richard **Lieut.** ⎫
	Bayly, Degory Ens. ⎭
Somerset	Barnes, William Lieut. to Maj. Wanklen
Devon	Irish, Richard Lieut. to Maj. Turner
Devon	Bond, John **Ens.** to Capt. Arthur Horton
L. & W.	Burleigh, George Ens. †
Wilts	Homerson, Ralph Ens. †
Devon	Furlong, Francis Ens. †
Cornwall	Binneck, Abraham Ens. †

Shallcrosse, John
York	Clement, William **Capt.** HORSE
Stafford	Rudyer, John **Capt. Lieut.**
Lancaster	Penketh, William Capt. Lieut.
Derby	Herod, Thomas **Cor.**
	Bradshaw, Francis **Quart.**

Shelley, Henry
Sussex	Shelley, John **Capt.** ⎫ FOOT
Somerset	Goring, Thomas Lieut. ⎬
Sussex	Rishton, Richard Ens. ⎬
	Amias, John Lieut. ⎭
L. & W.	Bold, William **Lieut.** to Maj. Davison
Lincoln	Bird, Christopher Lieut. †
Sussex	Shelly, Thomas **Ens.** †
	Haselin, John Ens. †
	Garrett, William Ens. †
Wilts	Wheatly, Drew **Quart.**

Shrewsbury, Earl of [1651]
Worcester	Penn, William **Capt.** HORSE

	Carew, George Capt. ⎫
	Horwood, Kemp Cor. ⎭
	Symonds, Thomas Capt.
Hereford	Kemble, Richard **Capt. Lieut.**
Worcester	Roan, Humphry, **Cor.**
Middlesex	Standish, Ralph Cor. †
Worcester	Theckston, Thomas **Quart.** †
Salop	Barrett, Ralph Quart. †

Sibbett
L. & W.	Makeing, Alexander **Capt. Lieut.** HORSE

Skipwith
Lincoln	Wilson, William **Cor.** HORSE †

Slanning, Sir Nicholas*
Devon	Franklin, Richard Lieut. FOOT to Capt. Bidlake
Cornwall	Carnsew, James Lieut. †
	Wall, John Ens.
	Mohun, Teage Ens.

Slaughter
Carmarth.	Morgan, John **Lieut.** FOOT to Capt. Halsy

Slingsby, Sir Arthur*
L. & W.	Lowe, Hercules **Lieut. Col.** HORSE
	Burck, Richard **Capt.** ⎫
	Murray, William Cor. ⎭
Wilts	Norborne, Edw. **Capt. Lieut.**
Bucks	Denton, Robert Capt. Lieut.
Durham	Thursby, John Lieut. to Maj. Leonard Scott
L. & W.	Clarke, James Lieut. to Capt. Thursby
	Delamot, Peter Lieut. to Maj. Barre
York	Lazenby, Seth Lieut. to Maj. Scruggs
L. & W.	Tuer, John **Cor.** †
Carmarth.	Floyd, David Cor. †
Flint	Hughes, John Cor. †
Southam.	Wheatly, Daniel **Quart.** †
L. & W.	Floyd, John Quart.
L. & W.	Edmonds, Andrew **Capt.** DRAGOONS

Slingsby, Sir Charles
Northumb.	Pryor, Robert **Ens.** [ ] to Capt. Marlay

Slingsby, Sir Henry
York	Mason, Richard **Capt. Lieut.** FOOT
	Lutton, Thomas Lieut. to Lieut. Col. Metcalfe
	Fothergill, Thomas Lieut. to Maj. Grey
L. & W.	Bales, Samuel **Ens.**
York	Holmes, Walter Ens. to Capt. Harrison
	Atkinson, Richard Ens. to Capt. Waterton
	Hesletine, George Ens. †
	Wright, Henry **Quart.**

Slingsby, Thomas*
L. & W.	Grey, Andrew **Maj.** HORSE
York	Blanchard, William **Lieut.** to Capt. Wharton
	Vavasor, Thomas **Cor.** } To Lieut. Col. Thomas Metcalfe
	Burdet, Amery Cor.

Slingsby, Colonel ___
Northumb.	Ogle, John **Capt.** FOOT

Smith, Sir James
L. & W.	Salter, John **Capt.** } HORSE
	Morley, Miles Cor.
Somerset	Nicholls, Thomas Quart.
	Warham, William Capt.
Nottingh.	Kirle, William Capt.
Wilts	Kirle, John Capt. }
L. & W.	Kirle, Thomas Lieut.
Oxon	Hawker, Hugh **Lieut.** to Maj. Crymes
Cornwall	Black John Cor. } To Maj. Humphry Arscott
	Barry, William Quart.
Somerset	Mudford, Stephen **Quart.** †
Devon	Leechland, Thomas Quart. †
Cornwall	Tregellas, Abell Quart. †

Smith, John
Durham	Booth, Ralph **Capt. Lieut.** HORSE
York	Singleton, Thomas **Cor.**
	Bullmer, William Cor.
Durham	Greenwell, William **Quart.**

Smith, Sir William
Bucks	Lambert, William **Capt.** HORSE
L. & W.	Griffith, William **Lieut.** to Capt. Smith
	Merchant, Hugh **Cor.** to Lieut. Col. Hurter

Darrell, Paul Cor. †
Bumpstead, John Regt. Quart.
Barrett, Peter Quart. to Capt. Spicer

Snead, Ralph
L. & W.	Rode, Thomas Capt. HORSE
	Doughty, William Capt. Lieut.
Stafford	Clayton, William Lieut. to Capt. Buckly
Carmarth.	Andrews, William Cor. to Capt. Rooksby
Chester	Hulme, Robert Quart. to Maj. John Connock

Somerset, Lord Charles
Hereford	Stavely, Edw. Capt. FOOT
	Pugh, William Capt.
Monmouth	Morris, Walter Capt.
Carmarthen	Weston, Ralph Ens. to Capt. Protherech
Monmouth	Elliot, George Ens. to Capt. Morgan

Somerset, Charles
Kent	Pownall, John Capt. HORSE

Somerset, Duke of
Gloucester	Best, Robert Lieut. HORSE †

Somerset, Lord John [Edmund Fortescue's regiment]
Hereford	Meeke, William Quart. HORSE to Capt. Elton

Southcott, Sir Popham
Devon	Westcott, John Ens. [ ] to Lieut. Col. Fullford

Spencer, John
Southam.	Lampray, William Quart. HORSE

Stamford, Edward [Lord Digby's / Earl of Bristol's regiment]
Stafford	Dovey, Gervase Cor. HORSE
L. & W.	Wilkins, John Quart.

Stanhop, Phillip [Duke of Gloucester's regiment]
Lincoln	Denton, Willoughby Capt. Lieut. HORSE
Nottingh.	Firman, Seymor Lieut. FOOT
Lincoln	Reniger, Richard Ens. †

Stanton, William
Essex	Colebrand, William Capt. FOOT

Surrey	Sherly, Scanderdine **Lieut.**	} To Capt. Thomas Taylor
York	Fardington, Robert **Ens.**	
Nottingh.	Hall, John **Quart.**	
Nottingh.	Kerkevall, Roger **Quart.** HORSE	

Stawell, Sir Edward

Somerset	Dyer, Stephen **Capt.** HORSE
	Langford, James **Lieut.** †
	Williams, Richard **Cor.** †
Surrey	Luccombe, Christopher Cor. } To Maj. Robert Bates
Somerset	Rogers, Elkanah Cor.
	Parfet, Richard Cor. } To Capt. Edmund Bower
	Hardwick, Robert Quart.
	Norman, Thomas **Quart.**
	Winter, John Quart.
	Foot, Robert **Regt. Quart.**

Stawell, George

Dorset	Lush, Richard **Cor.** HORSE

Stawell, Sir John

Somerset	Browne, Stephen **Lieut.** HORSE to Capt. Bowes
	Cox, Lyndley Lieut.
Somerset	Knoylle, Thomas **Capt.** FOOT
	Newcourt, Richard Capt.
	Dennis, William Capt.
	Simcocks, Thomas Capt.
	Winter, Henry Capt.
	Knoylle, William Lieut.
	Willys, John Ens.
	Warham, Thomas Ens.
Dorset	Fellow, Alexander Quart.
Somerset	Denham, Henry Capt. †
	Atherton, Phillip Capt. †
Wilts	Cousins, Andrew **Lieut.** to Capt. Stawell
Somerset	Haggard, John Lieut. to Capt. Gerard
	Bull, John Lieut. to Capt. Pittman
	Heath, Thomas Lieut. to Capt. George Bisse
	Walsh, Henry Lieut. to Capt. Overton
	Parfet, Henry **Ens.** to Maj. Clapp
	Fuzare, Thomas Ens. to Lieut. Col. Powell
Devon	Clapp, John Ens. to Capt. Francis Clark
Somerset	Allcote, Thomas **Capt.** DRAGOONS

Stepney, Sir John
Pembroke	Stepney, Thomas **Capt**. FOOT

Stocker, John
L. & W.	Salkield, Edw. **Capt**. FOOT
Carmarth.	Newsham, Thomas Capt.
Somerset	Pikes, Walter Capt.
Wilts	Knowles, John Capt.
Somerset	Day, Robert **Capt. Lieut.**
Dorset	Seymore, Richard Lieut. ⎫ To Capt. Edward Goodwyn
Somerset	Cotton, Francis Ens. ⎭
	Feltham, Francis Lieut. ⎫ To Capt. William Greenway
Wilts	Matthews, John Ens. ⎭
Somerset	Burge, John **Quart**. HORSE

Stradling, Sir Edward*
L. & W.	Hardwick, Ollivere **Capt**. ⎫ FOOT
Monmouth	Morgan, Thomas Ens. ⎭
Glamorg.	Price, William Capt.
Somerset	Roberts, Hugh **Lieut**. ⎫ To Capt. Edward Morgan
	Morgan, Alexander Ens. ⎭
Glamorg.	Thomas, Thomas Lieut. to Maj. Carne
Carmarth.	Read, John Lieut. to Capt. Hopkin Dawkins
Glamorg.	Miles, Thomas Lieut. †
	Howard, John Lieut. †
Berks	Byrd, Francis Lieut. †
Glamorg.	Nicholson, Richard **Ens**. †
Carmarth.	Davids, Lluelin Ens. to Capt. Vaughan

Stradling, Sir Henry
L. & W.	Cowles, William **Lieut**. FOOT †
Glamorg.	Glawdy, Charles **Ens**. †

Stradling, John*
Glamorg.	Wade, James **Capt**. FOOT
Carmarth.	Mansell, Robert **Lieut**. to Lieut. Col. Thomas Stradling sen.
	Mansell, Edw. Lieut. to Maj. Thomas Bushy
L. & W.	Druell, Pierce Lieut. to Capt. Arnold Morgan
Carmarth.	Rice, Morgan **Ens**. to Capt. Evans
Carmarth.	Mansell, Walter Cor. HORSE

Stradling, Thomas [Sir Edward Stradling's / John Stradling's regt.]
Monmouth	Morgan, Edw. **Capt**. FOOT

Strangewayes, Giles

Dorset	Strode, George **Capt.**	⎫ HORSE
Devon	Way, Richard Quart.	⎬
Somerset	Munday, John Quart.	⎭
Gloucester	Whitny, Courteen **Capt.** HORSE	
	Tidmarsh, John **Lieut.** to Maj. Colles	
L. & W.	Joyliffe, John Lieut. to Maj. Strangewayes	
Dorset	Samwayes, Andrew Lieut. †	
	Dawbeney, John Lieut. †	
	Dawbeney, James **Cor.** to Capt. Dawbeney	
	Turbervile, Thomas Cor.	⎫
	Hill, Henry, Quart.	⎬ To Maj. Dolling
Middlesex	Loop, Thomas Quart.	⎭
L. & W.	Cole, Charles Cor. to Lieut. Col. Chamberlain	
Dorset	Hooper, Gregory **Quart.**	
	Guy, John Quart. †	
	Crouch, Robert Quart. †	
	Barnes, Micheas Quart. †	
	Williams, William Quart. †	

Strangewayes, James

Oxon	Jones, Walter **Capt.** FOOT
Dorset	Brown, Henry Capt.
Somerset	Keymor, Harrison Capt.
Gloucester	Colles, William Lieut. †
Somerset	Keymor, Ellis Lieut. †
	Holman, Morgan Lieut. †
Dorset	Brown, Jonathan **Ens.**
Kent	Wyborn, John Ens. †
Dorset	Larder, Lewis Ens. †
Somerset	Daw, Richard Ens. †

Strickland, Sir Robert

L. & W.	Nevill, Matthias **Capt. Lieut.** FOOT	
York	Pitchard, William Lieut. to Maj. Frankland	
	Dagget, Richard Lieut.	⎫ To Capt. George Clough
	Hopps, Thomas Ens.	⎭
	Carter, Francis Lieut. to Capt. Jones	
	Harper, Arthur Lieut. to Capt. Strickland	
	Skipwith, John Lieut. to Maj. Sadlington	
	Slater, Stephen **Quart.**	

Strickland, Sir Thomas [1648]

Westmo.	Threlkeild, John **Lieut.** HORSE †

                    Graham, Richard **Cor.** to Maj. Phillipson
                    Beck, John Cor.

Strother, William
Northumb.   Strother, Edw. **Capt.** ⎫ FOOT
                    Hoodspeth, Henry Lieut. ⎭
                    Errington, David **Lieut.** to Capt. Crow
Durham   Fenwick, John **Ens.** to Lieut. Col. Forster
Northumb.   Richardson, Thomas Ens. to Maj. Armorer
                    Givings, John Ens.

Stuart, Lord Bernard
Wilts   Rutter, Thomas **Quart.** HORSE †

Stuart, Colonel [John] [Earl of Cleveland's regiment]*
L. & W.   Roche, Adam **Capt.** ⎫   HORSE
                    Morphy, John Lieut.   ⎪
                    Morley, Bartholomew Cor. ⎬
                    Barry, Phillip Quart. ⎭
                    Simons, Thomas Capt.
                    Morphy, Cornelius **Cor.** to Lieut. Col. Callaham
                    Wickham, John Cor.
Southamp.   Jeanes, Thomas **Quart.** to Lieut. Col. Lowe

Stuart, Francis
L. & W.   Scott, Walter **Capt.** HORSE
                    Duncan, Thomas Capt. ⎫
Durham   Hutton, Toby Cor.   ⎭
Northumb.   Appleby, Laurence Capt.

Stuart, [Lord] John [Earl of Cleveland's regiment]*
L. & W.   Graham, John **Lieut.** HORSE †
                    Thurston, John Lieut. ⎫
Surrey   Woodman, Thomas Cor.   ⎬ To Maj. Bill
                    Wood, John Quart.   ⎭
L. & W.   Williams, Thomas **Cor.** to Capt. Standelo
Oxon   Wood, John Cor.
Southam.   Crosse, Leonard **Quart.**

Stuart, William
L. & W.   Gordon, James **Lieut. Col.** DRAGOONS

Stukely, Sir Thomas
Somerset	Putham, Walter **Capt.** HORSE
Devon	Falby, Luke **Capt. Lieut.**
Somerset	Putham, William Lieut. to Capt. Putham
L. & W.	Sampson, Jeffery Lieut. to Lieut. Col. Prust
Devon	Snell, George **Cor.** to Capt. Goodwin
Cornwall	Holman, Degory Quart.

Styles, William
Lincoln	Wyche, Richard **Cor.** HORSE
Northam.	Traughton, Robert Cor. †
L. & W.	Lambkin, Robert **Quart.** to Capt. Styles
Lincoln	Langley, Henry **Capt.** FOOT
	Wyche, Robert **Ens.**
	Brigges, William **Quart.** to Capt. Garner

Swinhoe, Gilbert
Northumb.	Pemberton, Robert **Capt.** FOOT
	Mustchamp, Michael **Lieut.** to Capt. Mustchamp
	Hoodspeth, George **Ens.**

Swinhoe, James*
Newcastle	Potts, Eleazar **Lieut.** F. to Lieut. Col. Ord

Talbot, John [of Thornton-le-Street]
York	Winterscale, Michael **Lieut.** FOOT to Capt. Taylor
	Crosby, Robert Lieut. to Capt. Blakeston

Taylor
Somerset	Griffith, Richard **Lieut.** F. to Maj. Robert Deane
	Collins, John Lieut. to Capt. Play

Tempest, John
Durham	Conyers, Henry **Capt.** ⎫ FOOT
	Gargrave, Matthew Lieut. ⎬
	Smith, George Ens. ⎭
	Poore, Thomas Capt.
	Blakeston, Robert Capt. ⎫
	Robinson, John Ens. ⎭
Northumb.	Halsall, John **Capt. Lieut.**
Durham	Sheeres, George **Ens.** to Capt. Ralph Allenson

Tempest, Sir Richard
Durham	Duncomb, Edw. **Capt.** HORSE

	Morpeth, Richard Capt.
L. & W.	Iley, Thomas Lieut. to Capt. Clavering
Warwick	Hodgson, Richard Lieut.
Durham	Wilkinson, William Lieut. to Sir Francis Liddell
	Sober, Edmund Lieut. to Capt. Smith
Northumb.	Ord, William Lieut.
Durham	Hume, George Cor.
Northumb.	Fenwick, Ambrose Cor. to Sir William Blakeston
Lancaster	Parker, Thomas Cor.
Durham	Hedworth, Ralph Quart. to Capt. Blakeston
	Hodgson, Edw. Quart. to Capt. Tempest
Durham	Briggnell, John Capt. FOOT
	Wren, Henry Capt.
	Potter, William Lieut. to Lieut. Col. Lambton
	Phillips, Arthur Lieut. to Maj. Salvin
	Holden, Humphry Ens. to Maj. Kennet
	Stock, John Cor. DRAGOONS to Capt. Tempest

Tempest, Richard

York	Banks, Samuel Capt. HORSE
	Roe, John Capt.
L. & W.	Monck, Richard Capt.
Nottingh.	Brighouse, Tempest Capt.
Lancaster	Manknowles, John Lieut. to Capt. Roe
Durham	Sadler, William Quart. to Maj. Salvin
York	Holt, Thomas Quart.
Durham	Liddell, William Quart. FOOT

Temple, Thomas
L. & W.	Woolgrove, John Quart. HORSE to Capt. Merrick

Thelwell, Anthony*
Chester	Leigh, Peter Capt. FOOT
	Leigh, Charles Capt.
	Davenport, Edw. Ens. to Capt. Davenport

Thomas, Rice [Queen's Lifeguard of Foot]
Glamorg.	Barry, Edw. Capt. FOOT
	Edwards, James Capt.

Thomas, Colonel ___
Dorset	Dewy, William Capt. HORSE
L. & W.	Dewy, William Capt.

Thornhill, Richard
L. & W.	Moore, Giles **Cor.** } To Lieut. Col. John Marsh
	Fortune, John Quart.
Hertford	Mason, George Cor. to Capt. Robert Hill
L. & W.	Colley, Lancelot Cor.

Throckmorton, Sir Baynham [Lord Capel's regiment]
L. & W.   Lane, Daniel **Lieut.** HORSE †
Gloucester   Kirk, Richard **Quart.** †

Throckmorton, Sir William
Lancaster   Cooper, Bryan **Capt.** FOOT
L. & W.   Grames, James **Lieut.** to Maj. Dutchfield
Huntingd.   Keysar, John Lieut. to Maj. Glanvile
Carmarth.   Floyd, Samuel Lieut. †

Tildesly, Sir Thomas
Cumberl.   Whitfield, Robert **Capt.** } HORSE
    Bradwood, John Cor.
L. & W.   Beckingham, Rowland Capt.
    Westby, George Capt. }
Lancaster   Dickinson, Hugh Cor.
    Westby, Charles Capt.
    Heskith, Cutbert Capt.
    Clifton, Gervase Capt.
    Brookes, John Capt.
    Twaddell, Edmund Capt.
    Dale, Daniel Capt. †
Middlesex   Holden, Francis Capt. †
York   Tempest, Richard **Lieut.** to Capt. Bailden
Lancaster   Butler, Richard Lieut. to Capt. Butler
    Sharpe, William Lieut. †
    Waring, Richard Lieut. †
    Gerard, William Lieut. †
    Gardiner, John **Cor.** to Lieut. Col. Anderton
Middlesex   Dickinson, William Cor. } To Capt. Thomas Winckly
Lancaster   Banister, Henry Quart.
    Pearson, James Cor. to Capt. Bamber
    Ingleton, Robert Cor. to Capt. Carus
    Anderton, Christopher Cor. to Capt. Anderton
Middlesex   Waring, Edw. **Quart.** to Capt. Swinglehurst
Lancaster   Rogerson, Edw. Quart. to Capt. Holden
Cumberl.   Maughan, John Quart. †
Lancaster   Oddy, Edw. Quart. †

	Adamson, Robert Quart.
L. & W.	Draycott, John **Capt**. FOOT
Lancaster	Haughton, Thomas Capt.
	Westby, Robert Capt.
	Bradly, James Capt.
	Collier, James Capt.
	Fletcher, John **Lieut**. ⎫
	Whittingham, Thomas Ens. ⎭ To Lieut. Col. Hugh Anderton
	Tootall, Oliver Lieut. to Capt. Nicholas Anderton
	Carus, Wilfrid Lieut. to Capt. Brabant
	Dawson, John Lieut. to Capt. Bradkirk
York	Cripling, Edw. Lieut. to Maj. Ord
Lancaster	Werden, William Lieut. to Capt. Swinglehurst
	Whiteside, John Lieut.
L. & W.	Harling, Henry **Ens**. to Maj. Harling
Lancaster	Corney, Edw. Ens. to Capt. Martin
	Walmsly, Thomas Ens.
	Yates, Thomas Ens. to Capt. Butler

Till, James [1648]

Kent	Earle, John Capt. ⎫ FOOT
L. & W.	Lock, John Lieut. ⎭
Kent	Wheeler, Thomas **Lieut**. †
	Cackett, William **Ens**. †
L. & W.	Monox, Morley Ens.

Tillyer, Henry

L. & W.	Boone, William **Capt**. **Lieut**. FOOT
	Pye, Richard Lieut. ⎫
	Butler, Miles Ens. ⎭ To Capt. John Cressy
	Calthorpe, Ambrose **Ens**. to Capt. Bagnall
Monmouth	David, Lewis Ens. to Capt. Hetherington

Tourney, Colonel ___

Lincoln	Butler, Thomas **Lieut**. FOOT to Capt. Cracroft

Trafford, Francis

York	Dennis, Godfrey Maj. ⎫ HORSE
L. & W.	Hall, John Cor. ⎭
York	Hunter, Richard Capt.
Cumberl.	Wyvall, Edw. Capt. ⎫
L. & W.	Errington, John Lieut. ⎬
Cumberl.	Lowther, Thomas Cor. ⎭
York	Thimbleby, George **Capt**. **Lieut**.
	Herbert, Phillip **Quart**. to Capt. Hillyard

Jackson, Charles Quart. to Lieut. Col. Morley

Tregonnell, Thomas
Wilts   Thorpe, George **Capt**. HORSE

Trelawny, Jonathan*
Cornwall   Slemming, Roger **Capt**. FOOT
               Polewheele, Stephen Capt. ⎫
                  Bridgeman, John **Lieut**. ⎭
               Glyn, Walter Capt.
               Manaton, Ambrose Capt.
               Grills, Adam Capt. **Lieut**.
               Hawke, John Lieut. to Capt. Hunkyn
               Grills, John Lieut. †
               Venman, Thomas Lieut. †
               Cowling, Thomas Lieut. †
               Cowling, Phillip Lieut. †
               Lobbe, William **Ens**. to Maj. John Prideaux
               Floud, John Ens. †
               Richards, Pierce Ens. †
               Skantlebury, Thomas Ens. †
               Honycombe, John Ens. †
               Beare, William Ens. †
               Hill, Humphry Ens. †
               Laundry, Roger Ens. †
               Stevens, William Ens. †

Tremayne, Lewis
Devon   Rous, Walter **Capt**. ⎫ FOOT
               Norman, John Ens. ⎭
Cornwall   Dynham, Oliver Capt. ⎫
               Moores, Hugh Lieut. ⎭
               Tremayne, Phillip Capt. ⎫
               Pardew, Stephen Ens. ⎭
               Prideaux, John Capt. ⎫
               Kessell, William Lieut. ⎭
L. & W.   Speccot, Thomas Capt. ⎫
Devon   Merryfield, John Ens. ⎭
Cornwall   Robins, Robert **Capt**. **Lieut**.
               Penbertha, John Lieut. †
               Remphry, Warne Lieut. †
Devon   Frayne, Leonard Lieut. †
               Rowe, Francis **Ens**. to Capt. Cottle
Cornwall   Pierce, Thomas Ens.
               Matthews, William Ens. †

Trevanion, Sir Charles
Cornwall   Edmonds, Hugh **Capt**. FOOT
Olliver, Thomas Capt.
Edwards, John Capt.
Catcher, John Capt.   }
    Osgood, Francis Ens.
Hooker, Amethyst **Lieut**. to Lieut. Col. Tremayne
Davy, Richard Lieut. †
Weeks, Richard Lieut. †
Honywell, William Lieut. †
Hicks, Henry Lieut. †
Oliver, John **Ens**. †
Thomas, John Ens. †
John, Caleb Ens. †
White, Richard Ens. †
Rowe, Nicholas Ens. †
Tregonner, Andrew Ens. †
Davy, Richard **Quart**.

Trevanion, John
Cornwall   Williams, William **Capt**. FOOT
Saul, Francis Capt.
Nicholson, Thomas **Capt**.   }
    Howes, John Ens.
Colquit, Francis **Lieut**. to Capt. Edw. Cooke
Devon   Slee, George Lieut. †
Cornwall   Vivian, John Lieut. †
Baker, Degory Lieut. †
Hicks, Rand. **Ens**. to Capt. Rashly
Leane, Richard Ens. to Lieut. Col. Kendall
Pullen, John Ens. †
Hawky, Francis Ens. †

Trevillyan, George
Somerset   Trowbridge, John **Capt**. FOOT

Trevor, Mark*
Chester   Griffith, Robert Lieut.   } HORSE
    Vaughan, Roger Quart.   } To the Lord Killmurry
Denbigh   Floyd, Peter **Cor**.

Tucker, Charles
L. & W.   Harrison, Thomas **Cor**. HORSE
Proudlove, Hugh **Capt**. **Lieut**.

Middlesex	Kirkby, William **Quart**.
Surrey	Boat, Nicholas Quart. †

Tuke, Samuel*
Essex	Lemming, Henry **Capt**. HORSE
Lincoln	Shipman, Robert **Lieut**. to Lieut. Col. Gamull
	Julian, John **Quart**. to Capt. Barker

Tynt, Hugh
Dorset	Cardrow, Walter **Lieut**. HORSE to Maj. Williams

Tynt, John
Somerset	Dyer, John **Capt**. ⎫ HORSE
	Davis, Thomas Cor. ⎭
	Pinner, John Capt. ⎫
	Allot, George Lieut. ⎬
	Sherwood, William Cor. ⎭
	Jeffery, John **Cor**. to Capt. Edw. Tynt
Bucks	South, Francis **Quart**.
Huntingd.	Cordwell, Richard Quart. to Lieut. Col. Ascough
Somerset	Cox, William Quart. †
Somerset	Dyer, Thomas **Capt**. FOOT
	Hart, Thomas Capt.

Tyrrell, Sir Timothy
Glamorg.	Hopkins, Thomas **Capt**. FOOT

Tyrringham, Sir William
Oxon	Bulloigne, Robert **Capt**. FOOT
Bucks	Castle, George Capt.

Tyrringham, Sir William [sic]
Bucks	Campian, John **Quart**. HORSE

Usher*
L. & W.	Humphreys, Theod. **Capt**. DRAGOONS

Vampere
Nottingh.	Eagle, William **Quart**. FOOT

Vaughan, Sir George
Dorset	Fitzjames, Thomas **Cor**. HORSE
Wilts	Keetson, Richard Cor. to Capt. Grove
	Flower, John Cor. to Sir Robert Walsh

Somerset	Heytor, William Cor. †
Wilts	Goodrose, William **Quart**. to Maj. Ventris
L. & W.	Harcourt, Thomas Quart.

Vaughan, Sir Henry

Carmarth.	Jones, Thomas **Capt**. FOOT
	Floyd, John Capt.
	Jones, Thomas Capt.
	Floyd, David **Lieut**. to Lieut. Col. Williams
Salop	Haberly, Francis Lieut. †
Pembroke	Davis, Maurice **Ens**. to Capt. Marychurch
Carmarth.	Williams, Thomas Ens. to Capt. Gwyn
	Gwyn, Griffith Ens. to Maj. Gwyn
Radnor	Lewis, Hugh Ens.

Vaughan, Sir William

Montgom.	Fox, Thomas **Capt**. } HORSE
Radnor	Vaughan, Morgan Lieut. }
Salop	Jones, Edw. Capt. }
Durham	Wright, Thomas Cor. }
Salop	Hosier, George Capt.
	Sugar, William **Lieut**. to Capt. Dixy
L. & W.	Moon, Thomas Lieut. to Lieut. Col. Slater
	Ling, William **Cor**.
York	Cotton, John Cor. †
Somerset	Sherwood, Thomas Cor. †
L. & W.	Crosman, Huntington **Quart**. to Capt. Bomer
	Shelton, Alexander Quart.
Chester	Newton, John Quart. †
Salop	Lingen, Thomas **Lieut**. FOOT to Capt. Armorer

Vavasor, Sir Walter

York	Wilson, Thomas **Capt**. } HORSE
	Hutchinson, Christopher Cor. }
	Mennell, James **Lieut**. }
	Seaton, Ralph Quart. } To Capt. Thwing
	Jackson, Henry Quart. }
Stafford	Gifford, Nicholas Lieut. to Capt. Thorpe
York	Flesher, William Lieut. to Capt. Vavasor
Stafford	Gifford, John Lieut. }
York	Steude, James Quart. } To Maj. William Vavasor
	Metcalfe, Bryan **Cor**. }
	Richmond, William Quart. } To Capt. Messinger
	Hamerton, Edw. Cor.

Frank, Thomas Cor.
Prince, John **Quart**. to Maj. Bland
Tempest, Richard Quart. to Lieut. Col. Hungate
Crawford, George Quart. to Capt. Wilson
Ketling, Francis Quart. to Capt. Dolman
Thomson, Peter Quart.
Atkinson, William Quart. to Sir William Blakston

Vavasor, Sir William*

Gloucester	Carter, John **Capt**. HORSE
Hereford	Barlow, Richard **Lieut**. to Lieut. Col. John Price
	Browne, Thomas **Quart**.
L. & W.	Blackwell, John Quart. to Capt. Walsh
L. & W.	Croft, Robert **Col**. FOOT
	Robinson, Francis **Capt**.
Radnor	Monington, Thomas Capt.
Hereford	Boulcot, Joseph **Lieut**. to Capt. Barrell
Monmouth	Morris, Lewis Lieut. to Maj. Villiers †
Hereford	Traherne, Phil. **Ens**. to Lieut. Col. Traherne
Carmarth.	Morgan, Edw. Ens. to Capt. Matthewes

Veale, Thomas

Wilts	Bennet, Francis **Capt**. FOOT
Dorset	Clifford, John **Lieut**. to Maj. Veale
Gloucester	Cowling, George Lieut. to Capt. Smith
	Wrench, William Lieut. to Capt. Hicks
Monmouth	Pritchard, Thomas **Ens**. to Capt. Bridgeman
L. & W.	Creeche, Edw. **Cor**. HORSE

Vere, Edward

L. & W.	Bermingham, John **Maj**. ⎫ HORSE
Lancaster	Masham, Francis Lieut. ⎭
L. & W.	Ward, John **Capt**.
	Hamilton, John Capt.
	Bryers, John Capt. ⎫
Lancaster	Barton, John Lieut. ⎭
	Eltenhead, Richard Capt.
	Shaw, John Capt.
	Brooks, John **Capt**. **Lieut**.
	Middleton, Thomas Lieut. †
	Heald, William Lieut. †
York	Williams, James Lieut. †
Lancaster	Crosston, Jeremy **Cor**. †

Villiers, Edward
L. & W.   Johnson, John **Lieut**. HORSE

Villiers, Robert
Salop   Lacon, Francis **Capt**. FOOT
                Bishop, William **Ens**. †
                Danby, Francis **Quart**. †

Vivian, Sir Richard
Cornwall   Allen, John **Capt**.   ⎫
                Cock, Phill. Ens.   ⎬ FOOT
                Moyser, George **Ens**.
                Jewell, Nicholas Ens.

Waggstaffe, Sir Joseph
L. & W.   Downing, Thomas **Maj**. ⎫
                Webb, George Lieut.   ⎬ FOOT
                Butler, John **Capt**.

Waite, Henry
L. & W.   Storkey, Henry **Capt**. FOOT
York   Merrick, Thomas Capt.
                Craythorne, Edmund Capt.
                Bilborough, Thomas **Capt. Lieut**.
                Pasket, John Lieut.   ⎫
                Barton, Robert Ens.   ⎬ To Capt. Mennell
                Teasdale, Anthony **Ens**.

Wake, Sir Baldwyn
L. & W.   Penny, William Lieut. FOOT

Wake, Sir John
Bedford   Berry, Jac. **Capt**.   ⎫
                Foster, Thomas Cor.   ⎬ HORSE
Bucks   Moore, Francis **Capt. Lieut**.
Bedford   Lawson, William Lieut. to Maj. Crompton

Walgrave, Sir Edward
Dorset   Fowke, Henry **Lieut**. HORSE to Capt. Fowkes
Norfolk   Crane, Valentine Lieut. †
L. & W.   Oakes, Edmund **Quart**. to Capt. Lynne
Norfolk   Townsend, Robert Quart. †

Walker, Phillip
L. & W.	Larkin, Edw. **Lieut**. FOOT to Maj. Durant
Norfolk	Fowler, Richard Lieut. to Capt. Treswell

Walker, Thomas*
L. & W.	King, Thomas **Capt**. ⎫ FOOT
Devon	Barne, James Lieut. ⎭
Surrey	Todd, James **Lieut**. to Capt. Wakefield
Devon	Ballhatchett, William Lieut. to Capt. Trevillyan
	Porter, Ralph **Ens**. to Maj. William Knolles
	Sanders, Bernard Ens. to Capt. Wakefield
Somerset	Meade, John Ens. †

Walsh, Sir Robert
Somerset	French, Henry **Capt**. HORSE
L. & W.	Walsh, Walter **Lieut**.
	Walsh, Edw. **Cor**.

Walter, David
Gloucester	Master, Edw. **Capt**. HORSE
Surrey	Weston, Humphry **Quart**. †

Walton, William*
Lancaster	Barker, William **Lieut**. HORSE †
Durham	Heighington John Cor.
Lancaster	Sherborne, Thomas **Capt**. FOOT

Warren, Henry
L. & W.	Moore, Daniel **Maj**. FOOT
Gloucester	Berkly, Robert **Capt**.

Warren, Thomas
Norfolk	Le Neve, Thomas **Maj**. FOOT
L. & W.	Wright, William **Lieut**. to Capt. Finch

Washburne
Worcester	Colles, Edmund **Lieut**. FOOT to Capt. Blunt

Washington, Henry*
Essex	Tuke, William **Capt**. DRAGOONS
Bucks	Bellamy, Michael Capt. ⎫
Worcester	Hudson, Gilbert Lieut. ⎭
L. & W.	Rose, Richard **Lieut**. to Capt. Norwood
	Watson, Nicholas Lieut. to Maj. Morrison

	Lamply, Ralph **Cor**.
	Peters, William Cor. to Capt. Colthorpe
Warwick	Washington, John **Regt. Quart.**
Bucks	Smith, William Quart. to Capt. Frankish
Northumb.	Chesman, John **Lieut.** HORSE to Capt. Frank
Worcester	Hudson, Gilbert **Lieut.** FOOT to Capt. Bellamy
L. & W.	Pilkington, William **Ens.** to Capt. Robinson

Watts, Sir John
Denbigh	Dutton, Richard **Capt**. FOOT

Webbe, Maj. Gen. [Lord Treasurer's regiment]
Oxon	Chamberlain, Thomas **Capt.** HORSE †
L. & W.	Quarles, John Capt. †
Carmarthen	Beale, John Cor. †

Welby, Phillip
Lincoln	Ashton, Edmund **Capt. Lieut.** DRAGOONS
Cambridge	Trym, John **Cor**.
Lincoln	Cope, Thomas Cor. †

Wentworth, Sir George
Lincoln	Empson, William **Capt.** FOOT
Middlesex	Bretton, John Capt.
York	Wheatly, Thomas Capt. ⎫
	Jackson, Thomas Ens. ⎭
	Woolrich, Henry Capt. ⎫
	Bradsbury, Thomas Lieut. ⎭
	Morris, Nicholas **Capt. Lieut.**
	Day, Francis Lieut. to Sir Thomas Bland
	Killingbeck, Thomas **Ens.** †
	Liddell, George Ens. †
	Bullock, Richard **Quart.**

Wentworth, Lord Thomas [Prince Charles's regiment]
L. & W.	Prestwich, Sir Thomas **Col.** HORSE
	Rivers, Marcellus **Capt.** ⎫
	Piggen, Edw. Lieut. ⎭
Kent	Watson, John **Lieut.** to Capt. Mildmay
L. & W.	Hay, James **Col.** DRAGOONS
Northumb.	Widdrington, Michael **Capt.**

Werden, Robert*
L. & W.	Dewit, Cornelius Maj. HORSE
Chester	Manwaring, John Capt.
	Burchill, Richard Lieut.
Stafford	Lea, Stephen Cor.
Chester	Tayler, Robert Quart.
	Phillips, John Capt.
Salop	Arthur, Roger Lieut. to Capt. Jones
L. & W.	Meakins, Richard Quart.

Wheatly, Thomas*
L. & W.	Monro, Coll. Lieut. Col. FOOT
York	Wheatly, Francis Capt.
	Wheatly, Edw. Capt.
L. & W.	Portworthy, James Lieut. to Lieut. Col. Ashton
York	Barton, William Lieut. to Capt. Hemsworth
Lancaster	Carnes, Bryan Lieut. to Capt. Kitchin
York	Favill, John Lieut. †
	Bradbury, Nicholas Quart.

Wheeler
Nottingh.	Newton, Edw. Lieut. FOOT to Capt. Atkinson

Whittly, Roger
Flint	Mathews, John Lieut. HORSE to Capt. Ravenscroft
L. & W	Lewis, Edw. Lieut. to Capt. Walter Bushell
Lancaster	Kay, Dennis Cor.
Merion.	Vaughan, Alban Quart. to Maj. Roberts
Montgom.	Langford, John Quart. †
Flint	Davenport, Thomas Capt. FOOT
Kent	Taylor, Anthony Capt.
Flint	Evans, Roger Ens. †

Whittly, Thomas
Nottingh.	Gawthrop, John Ens. [ ] to Capt. Cartwright

Widrington, Edward
Northumb.	French, Edw. Capt. HORSE
	Hobson, James Quart.
Newcastle	Pearson, Thomas Capt.
Durham	Conyers, William Lieut. to Lieut. Col. Langley
Northumb.	Widdrington Henry Capt. Lieut.
	Fenwick, Ralph Cor.

York	Kirk, Stephen Lieut.	⎫
	Brigham, Henry Lieut.	⎬ To Capt. Ascough
	Newton, Miles Quart.	⎭
	Daniel, John Cor. to Lieut. Col. Constable	
L. & W.	Emerson, Ralph Cor.	⎫ To Sir Edward Charleton
Northumb.	Fenwick, Henry Quart.	⎭

Widrington, Lord

York	Mallory, John Capt. HORSE
Northumb.	Errington, John Capt. ⎫
	Errington, Mark Lieut. ⎬
Durham	Tempest, Charles Cor. ⎭
Cumberl.	Senhouse, Anthony Capt.
Durham	Lambton, William Capt.
	Lambton, William Cor.
Northumb.	Snawden, Gowen Lieut. ⎫ To Maj. Gilbert Errington
Durham	Read, Roger Cor. ⎭
Northumb.	Fenwick, John Lieut. ⎫
York	Smithson, Robert Cor. ⎬ To Lieut. Col. John Thornton
Northumb.	Mackow, Ralph Cor. ⎭
	Hildreth, John Quart.
	Errington, Edw. Lieut. †
York	Gayle, Matthew Lieut. to Sir William Mason
Durham	Blakeston, Marmaduke Lieut. †
	Herbert, George Lieut. ⎫ To Capt. Peter Forcer
	Winter, George Cor. ⎭
Northumb.	Nicholson, William Lieut. to Capt. Swinburne
York	Beckwith, John Cor. to Capt. Fenwick
Northumb.	Errington, John Cor. †
Durham	Mason, John Cor. ⎫
Newcastle	Shafto, Thomas Cor. ⎬ To Maj. Roger Carleton
Durham	Lodge, Nicholas Quart. ⎭
	Ogle, John Cor. to Capt. David Errington
Northumb.	Pawston, Henry Cor. ⎫ To Capt. Ralph Errington
L. & W.	Ray, George Quart. ⎭
Northumb.	Widdrington, William Cor.
Lincoln	Hutchinson, Jonathan Cor. to Capt. Thomas
Northumb.	Hodgson, Francis Quart. to Sir William Liddell
	Clennell, William Quart. to Sir Edw. Widdrington
	Weightman, Cutbert Quart.
Newcastle	Garnett, Anthony Capt. FOOT
Northumb.	Carre, John Capt. ⎫
York	Grange, Gregory Ens. ⎭
Northumb.	Cowle, Henry Capt. ⎫
	Challoner, Henry Ens. ⎭

York	Metcalfe, Thomas **Capt. Lieut.**
Northumb.	Tayler, Ralph Lieut. to Capt. Carnaby
	Errington, Frederick Lieut. †
Essex	Errington, Richard Lieut. to Capt. Errington
Durham	Allgood, Richard **Ens**.
Newcastle	Errington, Anthony Ens. ⎫
Durham	Mittford, Robert **Quart**. ⎬ To Capt. Lancelot Errington
Northumb.	Hudson, John Quart. ⎭
Durham	Millborne, Henry **Capt**. DRAGOONS
Northumb.	Reeveley, Rowland **Cor**. to Capt. Chester
York	Hildreth, William **Quart**. to Capt. Bullmer

Williams, Sir Trevor

Monmouth	Kynvin, John **Lieut**. HORSE to Capt. Lewis
Gloucester	Harris, Rowland Lieut. to Capt. Kemis
Monmouth	Tyler, John **Cor**. to Capt. Catchmay
	Jones, John Cor.
L. & W.	Gwillym, George **Lieut. Col**. FOOT
	Corney, Richard **Capt**.
Hereford	Baskevile, Edw. Capt.
Monmouth	Stevens, Matthew **Ens**. to Capt. Rumsey
	Williams, Henry **Quart**.

Willoughby, Lord

Chester	Mackworth, Edw. **Lieut**. FOOT to Capt. Walthal

Willys, Sir Richard*

Leicester	Goodman, John Capt. HORSE
Nottingh.	Wharton, Christopher Capt.
L. & W.	Doughty, Thomas Capt.
Stafford	Cotton, William Capt. †
L. & W.	Willford, Thomas **Lieut**. †
Middlesex	Trussell, John Lieut. to Maj. Hatton
L. & W.	Le Geyt, John **Cor**. to Capt. Hatton
Salop	Outon, John Cor. to Capt. Bateman
Northam.	Makepeace, Abell Cor. †
York	Davis, Robert Cor. to Maj. Broughton
	Morley, John **Quart**. to Capt. Parson

Willys, William*

L. & W.	Colles, John **Capt**. HORSE
Stafford	Awdley, Thomas Capt.

Surrey	Dawborn, Robert **Cor.** to Capt. Hill
L. & W.	Wedgegood, Giles **Quart.** to Capt. Hatton

Willys, Colonel ___
Wilts	Head, William **Lieut.**	} HORSE
L. & W.	Roberts, Thomas Quart.	} To Lieut. Col. Offly

Wills, Colonel ___
Durham	Emerson, Matthew **Quart.** HORSE to Capt. Doughty

Wilsford, Edward
L. & W.	Mann, Thomas **Capt. Lieut.** HORSE

Wilmot, Lord
L. & W.	Smith, Paul **Lieut. Col.** HORSE
	Panton, Edw. **Capt.**
Gloucester	Izod, Henry Capt.
Hereford	Lochard, Anthony **Lieut.** †
Surrey	Twining, William Lieut. †
L. & W.	Massey, George **Cor.**
Gloucester	Stringer, Anthony Cor. to Capt. Fisher
Hereford	Williams, Walter Cor. to Capt. Baskevile
L. & W.	Button, John **Quart.** †
Worcester	Dowler, William Quart. Gen. †

Winchester, Marquess of
L. & W.	Cuffand, Francis **Capt. Lieut.** HORSE
Southam.	Clancy, Hugh Lieut.
L. & W.	Tasborough, Peregrine **Capt.** FOOT
	Payne, William Capt.
	Payne, William Capt.[15]
Hertford	Snow, John Capt. }
L. & W.	Massey, Francis Lieut. }
	Quoyle, Patrick **Lieut.** } To Sir Robert Peake
	Faithorne, William Ens. }
Southam.	Cleere, John Lieut. †
L. & W.	Hankinson, Rand. **Ens.**
Lincoln	Tonstall, Thomas Ens. to Capt. Tattershall
Middlesex	Higges, Joseph Ens. †
Southam.	Wakefield, Bold Ens. †

---

[15] This second Captain Payne is probably a printing error.

Windebank, Francis [Charles Gerard's regiment]
L. & W.	Phillips, William **Capt.** ⎱ FOOT
	Michell, James Ens. ⎰
Suffolk	Smith, John Capt.
Glamorg.	Hawkins, Hugh **Lieut.**

Windham Francis
Somerset	Wyatt, Benjamin **Capt.** HORSE
	Coningsby, Humphry Capt.
	Slocombe, Richard Quart.
Somerset	Leigh, Robert **Capt.** ⎱ FOOT
	Wake, Thomas Ens. ⎰
	Byam, William Capt.
	Vicary, John **Lieut.** †

Windham
Dorset	Ansell, Christopher **Cor.** ⎱ HORSE
	Hayly, Richard Quart. ⎰ To Capt. Phillips
L. & W.	Stone, John **Capt.** FOOT

Windham Sir Hugh
Devon	Pitt, John **Lieut.** ⎱ HORSE
	Freak, Henry Cor. ⎰ To Maj. John Harvey
Somerset	Combes, William Quart.
	Bond, Abraham Lieut. ⎱ To Capt. Benjamin Wyatt
	Estmond, John Cor. ⎰
	Plinton, Anthony Lieut. ⎱ To Col. William Ancthill
	Farthing, John Cor. ⎰
	Moore, William Lieut. to Capt. Thomas Littleton
	Dynham, John Lieut. to Capt. James Fitzjames
	Walsh, Edmund **Cor.** †
	Every, Francis **Quart.**
	Backwell, Bartholomew Quart. to Capt. Francis Keene
Dorset	Clark, Hancock Quart. †
Somerset	Winter, Francis Quart. †

Windsor, Lord
Gloucester	Broadway, Humphry **Quart.** HORSE
Bucks	Williams, Roger Quart.

Wintour, Sir John
L. & W.	Abercrombe, David Capt. FOOT
Hereford	Mason, Thomas Capt. ⎱
Monmouth	Redman, Phillip Lieut. ⎰

Gloucester	Sherle, Richard Capt. †
L. & W.	Denzell, John Capt. †
Surrey	Maynard, Henry Lieut. to Capt. Colche

Wintour, William
L. & W.	Adams, Anthony **Lieut**. FOOT

Wise, Matthew
L. & W.	Rustat, Robert **Maj**. FOOT
Glamorg.	Rimbron, Herbert **Capt**.
Brecon	Morgan, John Capt.
	Morgan, William **Ens**. †
Glamorg.	Harry, Lyson Ens. †

Wolsley, Devereux
Stafford	Aston, Edw. **Cor**. HORSE
Glamorg.	Matthew, Hopkin **Lieut**. FOOT to Capt. Napper

Woodhall, Thomas
Northumb.	Ogle, Charles **Capt. Lieut**. HORSE
Durham	Tayler, John **Quart**.

Woodhouse, Sir Michael [Prince Charles's regiment]
Flint	Broughton, Oliver **Capt**. FOOT
Salop	Phillips, Richard Capt.
	Ellis, Phillip Capt.
	Dannet, Gerard Capt. ⎫
	Bishop, Dannet Ens. ⎭
	Reynolds, Samuel Capt.
Northumb.	Wadhall, Peter **Capt. Lieut**.
L. & W.	Acton, Adam Lieut. to Capt. Jones
Denbigh	Vaughan, Robert Lieut. †
L. & W.	Breakes, Thomas Lieut. †
Salop	Beddoe, William **Ens**. to Capt. Fisher
L. & W.	Williams, Andrew Ens. to Maj. Williams
Salop	Pritchard, Samuel **Quart**.

Woogan, Edward [1654]
L. & W.	Mosely, Charles **Capt**. HORSE
	King, Daniel Capt.
Northumb.	Smith, Edw. **Lieut**. to Maj. Smith
	Ellison, Edw. **Cor**.
Durham	Kemp, Ralph **Quart**. to Capt. Dingen

Woolrick, Sir Thomas
Salop   Cresset, Edw. **Capt.** FOOT

Worcester, Marquess of
L. & W.	Walmsly, William **Capt.** HORSE
	Sherwood, Laurence Capt.
Montgom.	Pugh, Robert Capt.
Salop	Astly, John Capt.
Monmouth	Faunt, John Capt. ⎫
Berks	Dudman, John Quart. ⎭
Hereford	Lingen, Thomas Capt. † & Commiss. Gen. Must.
Monmouth	Gwyllim, William Capt. †
	Herbert, Henry Capt. †
	Fountaine, Francis Capt. †
Hereford	Wiggemore, John **Lieut.** to Capt. Edw. Bacon
Monmouth	Shaw, Edmund Lieut. †
	Thomson, William Lieut. to Capt. Henry Mallory
Lancaster	Manwaring, William Lieut. to Capt. James Anderton
Warwick	Griffin, Edw. **Cor.** to the Lord Somerset
Monmouth	Maddock, Charles Cor. to Capt. Wakeman
	Ayleworth, John Cor. †
Hereford	Coleman, Thomas **Quart.** to Maj. Sillyard
Monmouth	Saxby, John Quart. ⎫ To Lieut. Col. Sillyard
Salop	Baldwin, William Quart. ⎭
L. & W.	Cardiffe, Thomas **Col.** FOOT
Monmouth	Price, Morgan **Maj.** ⎫
L. & W.	Rudston, John Lieut. ⎬
	Price, James Ens. ⎭
	Molineux, Charles **Capt.**
Middlesex	Vaughan, Roger Capt.
Monmouth	Morgan, John Capt. ⎫
	Jones, John Ens. ⎭
	Scudamore, James Capt.
	Cowles, Richard Capt. †
Surrey	Harris, John Capt.
Glamorg.	Matthews, William **Capt. Lieut.**
Monmouth	Powel, Reynold Lieut. to Capt. Michael Morgan
	Jones, John Lieut. to Capt. Gainsford
	Hughes, Thomas Lieut. to James Progers
	Dunford, Stephen Lieut. to Maj. Fortescue
	Hazzard, Henry Lieut. to Lieut. Col. Henry Somerset
Hereford	Pierepoint, William Lieut. to Capt. Young
	Abrahall, Richard Lieut. to Capt. John Abrahall
Glamorg.	Morgan, Lewis Lieut. to Humphry Matthews

Pembroke	Revel, Robert Lieut. †	
Brecon	De La Grange, Matthew Lieut. †	
L. & W.	Seaborn, Richard Lieut. † to Capt. John Gifford	
Monmouth	Kemis, John Ens. to Capt. Middlemore	
Glamorg.	David, Morgan Ens. to Capt. Prythero	
Hereford	Craddock, John Ens. Kemble, John Ens. Young, Robert Ens.	} To Capt. Mallory
Monmouth	Owens, Edmund Quart.	
L. & W.	Lynaker, Thomas Quart.	

Wortly, Sir Francis*

L. & W.	Naylor, Walter **Capt. Lieut.** HORSE
	Oglethorpe, Robert Lieut. to Capt. Bilby
Gloucester	Ruckly, Richard Cor.
York	Garnett, Thomas Quart. to Capt. Marmaduke Holtby
L. & W.	Newton, Bryan **Capt. Lieut.** FOOT
York	Rimmington, James Quart.
Stafford	Barnes, Thomas Quart. †
Worcester	Heaton, Robert Cor. } DRAGOONS
Stafford	Dudly, Jeffery Cor. } To Maj. Dud Dudly

Wraughton, James

Hereford	Weaver, Thomas Capt. [ ]
Hereford	Weaver, James Cor. DRAGOONS

Wray, Sir Chichester

L. & W.	Hammond, Charles Capt. FOOT
	Thurloe, Simon Capt.
Cornwall	Jolly, Nicholas Capt.
	Wray, William Capt.
	Stephens, John Lieut. to Capt. Goysgarne
	Dymond, Ezekiel Lieut. †
	Perkins, John Ens. †
York	Owston, Christopher Quart. †
Cornwall	Tozer, William Quart.

Wray, George*

York	Edsforth, William **Capt.** HORSE
Durham	Danby, George Capt.
Northumb.	Sympson, Henry **Capt. Lieut.**

York	Danby, Edmund Lieut.	} To Maj. John Danby
	Lazenby, Christopher Quart.	

Wharton, Richard **Cor.** to Capt. Marmaduke Frank
Durham Chicken, George **Quart.** to Lieut. Col. Robert Millet
Northumb. Katherick, Lancelot Quart.

Wyndham, Edmond

Somerset Day, John **Capt.** } HORSE
           Lemming, Robert Lieut.
           Lemming, Francis Cor.
           Lemming, John Quart.
           Hayne, John Capt.
           Curle, William Capt.
           Dowthwaite, John **Lieut.** †
           Shippy, George Lieut. †
           Kymer, Francis Lieut. to Major Humphry Sydenham
           Walter, Peter Lieut.
           Hilbron, Thomas Cor. } To Lieut. Col. William Ancthill
           Jones, Stephen Quart.
           Buncombe, John Lieut. } To Capt. William Sandford
           Paris, Lewis Quart.
Dorset Wake, William **Cor.**
Somerset Ellis, James Cor. } To Maj. Leversedge
           Thick, John Quart.
           Pittard, Amos **Quart.** †

L. & W. Buffkin, Lewin **Maj.** FOOT
Somerset Arundell, John **Capt.**
           Barret, James Capt.
           Roberts, John Capt.
Sussex Arundell, Christopher Capt. †
Somerset Keene, John Lieut. } To Lieut. Col. Ancthill
           Ancthill, Francis Ens.
           Simons, William Lieut. to Capt. Andrew Gamlyn
           Griffith, John Lieut. †
           Raymond, Edw. Lieut. †
Dorset King, Thomas **Ens.** to Capt. John Nash
Somerset Howell, Richard **Cor.** DRAGOONS to Capt. Jones

Wynne, Hugh

Denbigh Williams, John **Capt.** FOOT
           Wynne, Matthew Capt.
             Floyd, William Ens.
           Vaughan, Evan **Lieut.** } To Lieut. Col. Robert Wynne
           Lewis, David Ens.

Merion.	Floyd, Maurice Lieut. †

Wynne, William
Denbigh	Edwards, William **Capt.** FOOT
Essex	Chambers, William **Lieut.** to Maj. Francis Manly
Denbigh	Roberts, Peter Lieut. †
	Wynne, John Lieut. †
	Wynne, Owen **Ens.**
Carnarvon	Wynne, Robert Ens. †
Denbigh	Wynne, Ellis **Quart.** HORSE

York, Duke of*
Northam.	Batson, Edw. **Lieut.** HORSE to Col. Samuel Tuke
L. & W	Woodward, Richard **Maj.** FOOT
	Roche, James **Capt.**
Oxon	Gayton, Edmund **Capt. Lieut.**
L. & W.	Crook, Henry **Ens.** to Maj. Kirton
	Sewell, George Ens. to Capt. Peaker

Zouch, James
L. & W.	Sanders, Christopher **Quart.** HORSE to Capt. Zouch

Stray Officers (Horse)

Captains

L. & W.	Hudson, Richard
	Paulett, John
	Warton, Michael
	Terrick, Samuel
	Conquest, Charles
	Audly, John Capt. & Quart. Gen.
Kent	Walter, Thomas
York	Bacon, Christopher
	Savill, John
Worcester	Canning, Edmund
Cambridge	Appleyard, John
Hertford	Tayler, John
Berks	Turner, William
Surrey	Danvers, Thomas
Sussex	Mascall, Henry
Hereford	Hawly, Edmund
Oxon	Thorp, Henry
Southam.	Hall, William HORSE & FOOT
Wilts	Webb, John
Somerset	Harvy, John
	Brice, John
	Littleton, Thomas
	Byam, Francis
Devon	Brice, Worthington
Nottingh.	Holder, Toby
Leicester	Shuttlewood, George in Ashby
Derby	Walthall, Alexander
Stafford	Hulst, Thomas
Northam.	Styles, Thomas
Rutland	Hudson, Jeffery
Lancaster	Foxcraft, William
	Gorst, Ralph
	Lyme, Nicholas
	Brockholls, John
Flint	Eddow, Thomas
	Whitley, John
Cardigan	Herbert, Edw.

Lieutenants

L. & W.	Noyse, Richard Capt. Lieut.
Kent	Barrows, Henry
	Johnson, James
York	Robinson, Richard
Warwick	Goodall, Thomas
Cambridge	Morley, Richard
Essex	Stubbing, William to Capt. John Lynsell
Berks	Leigh, John
	Lybbe, Richard to Capt. John Davies
Bucks	Hartly, William
	Penn, Edward
Surrey	Tayler, Edward to Capt. John Casy
Salop	Howard, Thomas to Capt. William Barnard
Hereford	Addys, Edw.
Oxon	Playdell, Oliver
	Woodfield, David to Lieut. Col. Thomas Smith
	Tillyard, William under Maj. Francis Lovelace
Southam.	Wels, Swithen
	Batt, George
Wilts	Magothes, William
	Sadler, Henry
	Oldfield, William
	Langly, Richard
Devon	Lyndsey, Owen
Nottingh.	Grace, Godfrey to Maj. Anthony Nevill
Leicester	Everard, John to Capt. Walter Hastings
	Wiggly, Edw. to Capt. John Smith
	Wright, George
Derby	Lowe, Charles
Stafford	Ironmonger, Humphry
Lancaster	Heskith, Richard to Maj. Richard Latham
	Fletcher, Ralph to Capt. William Kay
	Turver, Thomas to Capt. Foxcraft
	Clarkson, Thomas
	Jepthson, Edmund
Flint	Matthews, John
	Edwards, Roger
	Eyton, Randolph
	Eddow, Richard
Carnarvon	Griffith, William
Denbigh	Ball, Richard to Capt. Hugh Morris

Cornets

L. & W.	Thornborow, John
	Lynde, Venables
	Holland, Thomas under Sir Jeffery Shakerly
	Watkins, Thomas to Lieut. Col. John Morgan
	White, George to Capt. Nicholas Armorer
Kent	Lanier, Endymion
York	Loftus, Francis to Capt. Laurence Apleby
	Apleby, William to Capt. Henry Messenger
	Tomms, John to Capt. Prideaux
Westmo.	Blenkinsop, Francis to Capt. Thomas Braithwait
Lincoln	Batson, Austin to Capt. William Barker
	Cooper, Hugh to Lieut. Col. Pollard
	Stow, Joseph to Capt. Thomas Cressy
	Claypoole, William to Capt. William Bale
	Sparrow, George to Capt. Edmund Raines
Worcester	Evatt, Walter to Capt. Henry Ingram
Essex	Partridge, John to Capt. John Lynsell
Berks	Soper, Francis to Capt. Stoke
	Fettiplace, Thomas
Bucks	Symonds, Edw. to Capt. John Denton
Gloucester	Griffith, William
Hereford	Seaborn, Benedict
	Bodenham Thomas
Oxon	Bond, Robert to Lieut. Col. Thomas Colepepper
	Sherwood, Henry to Capt. James Smith
Southam.	Tarrant, Hercules
Wilts	Grant, William to Capt. Staples
Somerset	Powell, Anthony to Capt. Weeks
	Farthing, John
Devon	Cottle, Bernard to Capt. Simon Cottle
	Darracot, Humphry to Capt. Prust
Nottingh.	Hollingworth, Edward to Capt. Fitzrandolph
	Nevill, Gervase to Capt. Gervase Nevill
	Chadwick, Anthony to Capt. John Bingly
	Holyman, Edw.
Stafford	Everdon, John to Capt. William Carlos
Northam.	Lynne, George
Chester	Gill, Christopher to Lieut. Col. Richard Greene
Lancaster	Watmough, Laurence
	Hewitson, William
Flint	Andrewes, John

Quartermasters

L. & W.	White Edward Quart. Gen.
Kent	Garrett, Robert
	Munnes, John
York	Sympson, Stephen to Capt. Laurence Sayer
	Kenner, Peter to Capt. William Paulden
	Bradly, William to Capt. Francis Rearsby
Northumb.	Whitfield, Richard to Sir Edw. Charlton
Lincoln	Codling, John to Capt. Hassellwood
	Sherman, John to Capt. Thomas Savile
	Dunkin, John to Capt. Christopher Grimston
	Haddon, Robert ⎫ To Capt. John Hussey
	Knight, Robert ⎭
	Crosfield, Edw. ⎫ To Capt. Charles Boads
	Rowly, Thomas ⎭
	Vokes, John to Maj. Bodenham
	Clarke, John to Lieut. Col. Whitchcote
Warwick	Jepthcott, Henry
Worcester	Powell, Richard to Capt. John Blunt
	Soule, John to Capt. William Fitter
Essex	Montfort, Thomas to Capt. John Lynsell
	Westwood, Edw. to Capt. John Aylett
Bucks	Wheatly, John to Capt. John Denton
Sussex	Faulconer, John under Maj. Crompton
Salop	Jones, Thomas under Sir Thomas Whittmore
Gloucester	Page, Richard under Thomas Acton
Oxon	Day, Philip to Capt. William Langston
Dorset	Alford, Thomas to Capt. Edw. Berkly
	Abbot, Francis under Maj. Henry Hastings
Southam.	Smith, John
Wilts	Clark, John to Maj. Henry Clark
	Clark, Thomas to Capt. Gouldsborow
	Michell, Andrew to Scoutmaster General Tristram Sturges
Somerset	Hodges, Laurence to Capt. Henry Keymer
	Broome, Philip to Capt. Ames Paulett
	Webb, Benedict to Capt. Henry Berkly
	Marler, John to Lieut. Col. Crymes
Devon	Brockden, George to Gregory Hockmore
Nottingh.	Higgins, Thomas to Capt. Tomkins
	Neale, Richard to Capt. Ralph Pudsey
Leicester	Jesson, John to Maj. William Hungate
Derby	Brince, Thomas to Capt. William Fitzherbert
	Sowter, Humphry
	Bradshaw, Edw.

	Ward, Robert
Stafford	Cartwright, Andrew to Capt. William Ogle
	Dutton, Richard to Capt. John Hasselwood
	Buckly, Ralph to Capt. John Potts
Lancaster	Aston, Thomas to Capt. Ratcliffe Duckenfield
	Heapes, Thomas to Capt. William Kay
	Hoole, John to Capt. George Westby
	Cutler, John to Lieut. Col. William Walton
	Forbes, Thomas
Flint	Milton, Randolph
	Edwards, John to Capt. Edw. Morgan
Somerset	Crosse, Stephen **Corporal** to Maj. Samuel Fitzherbert, under Sir Lewis Dives

Stray Officers (Foot & Dragoons) [16]

Captains
L. & W.	Harley, Thomas
	Holmes, William
	Gregory, Edmund
	Done, Edward
	Paulden, Thomas in Pontefract
Essex	Southcote, Henry Capt. FOOT and Frega[t]
Kent	Verrall, Christopher
Surrey	Dyer, James
Warwick	Butler, John
Norfolk	French, Robert
	Stump, Thomas
	Browne, Richard Jun.
Cornwall	Coghland, John at Sea and Land
Somerset	Harvy, Francis
Devon	Pomeroy, Hugh at Sea and Land
	Broughton, George
	Bourne, Henry in Mount Edgecumbe
Chester	Pershall, Thomas
Derby	Grant, Arthur to Sir John Harpur
Lancaster	Fox, Richard
	Orbell, Nicholas
	Kitchin, John
	Danson, Thomas
	Holt, Richard of the Free-holders
Flint	Griffith, John
	Williams, Peter
	Middleton, Hugh
	Floyd, Humphry
	Love, Thomas
Carnarvon	Morris, William
	Wynne, William
Cardigan	Floyd, Francis
Montgom.	Evans, Lewis

Lieutenants
L. & W.	Browne, George to Capt. Thomas Pound
	Bennet, Reginald to Capt. Molineux Ratcliffe
	Bates, Leonard

---

[16] The dragoons are listed together at the end of this section.

	Abernethy, George
	Wharton, Richard in Jersey
Kent	Mantell, John to Capt. Andrew James
	Rixon, John
	Gibbs, William
York	Foster, Edward to Capt. Robert Benson
Northumb.	Hodgson, Edward to Lieut. Col. Widdrington
Cumberl.	Howthwaite, Robert to Maj. Flemming
Cambridge	Reynolds, Thomas to Lieut. Col. William Blakeston
Norfolk	Barber, Edw. Capt. Lieut.
	Gambe, Harrold
	Hanham, William
	Cufand, Francis to Maj. Cufand
Berks	Latham, Luke Capt. Lieut.
	Young, Richard Capt. Lieut.
	Webber, Matthew
Salop	Bishopp, William to Lieut. Col. Thomas Wynne
	Sheldon, Richard to Capt. Bostock
Hereford	Gwilliam William, to Capt. Herbert Awbry
Dorset	Roberts, Leonard
Southam.	Linch, Anthony
Somerset	Babb, Tristram
	Porter, Atwell in Dunstar
	Crook, Henry
Devon	Goddard, John to Capt. Aaron Burdall
	Gold, Thomas
	Searell, Thomas
Cornwall	Avery, Robert to Lieut. Col. William Scawen
Nottingh.	Francis, Edward to Capt. Morris
Stafford	Wilks, William to Capt. William Hopkins
	Gifford, John to Maj. Simon Heveningham
Lancaster	Fielding, Charles under Lieut. Col. Slater
	Olivers, Robert
	Dickenson, Edward to Capt. Charles Ratcliffe
	Babot, Thomas to Capt. Hugh Matthews
	Halsal, Edward to Capt. John Walter
	Heape, Richard to Capt. Molineux Ratcliffe
Flint	Conway, William
	Powell, John
Carnarvon	Robbins, Herbert
	Morris, Griffith
Pembroke	Floyd, Joseph to Capt. William Williams

Ensigns

L. & W.	Johnson, Martin under ___ Beckman
	Whaley, William to Capt. John Aston
	Godbar, Henry to Capt. Bingham
	Agehead, George to Capt. Thomas Paulden
	Webber, John
Kent	Frost, James to Capt. Thomas Delaval
	Sawyer, Stephen
York	Denton, Lancelot to Capt. Toby Thurscrosse
	Willys, George to Maj. Godfry Ashby
Northumb.	Boult, John under Lieut. Col. Thomas Davison
	Bednall, Robert to Lieut. Col. Thomas Haggerston
Cumberl.	Nesse, Richard under Sir Edw. Cary
	Rudd, Thomas to Capt. John Caipe
Lincoln	Carlisle, John to Capt. Charles Pelham
	Anthony, Robert to Capt. Saul
Warwick	Harvy, William to Maj. Thomas Eyre
Worcester	Hall, Thomas to Maj. Thomas Wild
Berks	Browning, John to Capt. Edw. Howard
	Booth, Richard
Suffolk	Heigham, George to Maj. Henry Crompton
Surrey	Gates, Thomas
Salop	Grosvenor, Leicester to Capt. Thomas Holland
	Thornes, Francis to Capt. Armorer
Dorset	Laurence, William under Maj. Robert Mohan
	Meyo, John to Capt. John Bishopp
Somerset	Parfet, Michael
Devon	Moore, William to Capt. Nicholas Arundell
	Raddall, Thomas to Maj. John Jacob
	Pierce, Thomas
Cornwall	Wise, William to Maj. George Collins
Nottingh.	Powell, Daniel
Derby	Aston, Clifton to Lieut. Col. Clifton
Northam.	Clement, John to Capt. William Marsh
Stafford	Blunt, Walter under Sir Richard Astly
	Kirk, Zachary to Capt. Dibdale
Chester	Orrat, Thomas to Lieut. Col. Disney
	Harvey, William under Sir William Manwaring
Lancaster	Brock, Richard to Capt. Brock
Westmo.	Pattison, Robert to Lieut. Col. Dalton
Carnarvon	Williams, Edmund
Pembroke	Prethero, Philip to Capt. William Williams
Montgom.	Floyd, Morgan to Capt. Andrew Blayney
Carmarth.	Prichard, Rice to Capt. Thomas Phillips

Morris, Anthony to Capt. Robert Lewis

Quartermasters

York	Hawly, William Quart. Gen. in York
Nottingh.	Shirly, James Quart. Gen. in Newark
Stafford	Tomkins, Thomas Quart. &c.

Dragoons

Somerset	Jones, Hugh **Capt.** in Bristoll
Chester	Ranakers, Roger Capt. to Lieut. Col. Slater
L. & W.	Taylor, Francis **Lieut.** under Maj. Malbrank
Lincoln	Northam, Francis Lieut. ⎫
Somerset	Rowlinson, Richard Cor. ⎬ To Capt. William Pistor
	Jones, Edw. Lieut. ⎭
Nottingh.	Clay, Samuel **Quart.** to Capt. William Swinburn

Sea Captains

L. & W.	Turner, Christopher Capt. *Mary* Fregat, Prince Rupert
	Gills, John Capt. *John Adventure*, Sir Nicholas Crisp
	Johnson, John Capt. *Newcastle*, Marquess Newcastle
	Isbrant, Ger. Capt. *St. Patrick*, Sir Nicholas Crisp
Somerset	Roberts, John Capt. *Phoenix*, Lord Hopton
	Carteret, Phi. Capt. *Cavalier* Frc Sir John Pennington
York	Ingram, William Capt. *Friendship*, Prince Rupert
	Bilbrough, Richard Capt., Sir Matthew Boynton
L. & W.	Dowdall, George ⎫
	Jordan, Robert ⎬ Capt. *Duke of York*
	Neale, James ⎭
	Ensom, Robert Capt. of the *York* Fregat
	Pine, Robert Capt. of the *Charles* Fregat
	Young, Richard Capt. of the *Greyhound*
	Armestead, Robert Capt. of the *Charles, James*, &c.
	Cannon, Peter Capt. of the *Great Seahorse*, and *Antilope*
	Nicholls, Edw. Capt. of the *Charles* of Jersey
	Garnett, Thomas Capt. of the *True Blew*, &c.
Kent	Stanton, Robert Capt. of the *Swallow*
L. & W.	Foran, Robert Capt. †
	Covell, Allen Capt. †
	Dillon, James Capt. †
	Handricson, Harman Capt. †
	Morris, James Capt. †
	Brett, Ignatius Capt. †
	Wright, John Capt. †
	Bowden, Robert Capt. †
Kent	Anderson, Robert Capt. †
L. & W.	Dillon, Henry Lieut. of a Fregat †
Merion.	Owen, Edward Capt. of the *Lyon*. **Note:** an addition from the errata.
Salop	Mason, Francis Lieut. of a Fregat. **Note:** an addition from the errata.
Sussex	Parker, Robert Capt. **Note:** an addition from the errata.

Indigent Officers

Auxiliary Staff

Commissary Generals
L. & W.	Jay, Thomas
	Throwly, John
	Barber, George
	Langdon, Henry
Stafford	Gifford, Richard
Derby	Ward, Francis
Middlesex	Knightly, Edw.
Southam.	Whitehead, William
Somerset	Mabye, William

Commissaries
L. & W.	Batchelor, Richard
	Ellis, Robert
Flint	Yate, Robert
Somerset	Gilbert, William
	Bayly, John
	Wells, John
	Mabye, Richard
	Spicer, Thomas
	Drake, Richard
	Hungerford, John
Worcester	Mascall, Theophilus
Surrey	Couper, Thomas
Southam.	Fry, Thomas
Kent	Philcott, Peter
L. & W.	Rutherford, John
	Knapton, Reynold; Commissary & Provost Marshall General
	Loup, Thomas; Commissary & Engineer
Chester	Jackson, William; Commissary Assistant
L. & W.	White, William ⎫
	Walsh, Robert ⎬ Commissary Train
	Barnes, Thomas ⎪
Durham	Lovett, John ⎭
Cornwall	Drake, John; Deputy Commissary
Stafford	Martin, Simon; Muster Master & Commissary of Musters
Northam.	Williams, William; Muster Master
Durham	Vine, Thomas ⎫ Providor General
Stafford	Riddling, John ⎭
Northam.	Emerson, Francis; Purveyor to the Train

Adjutants

L. & W.	Newbury, James Allen John	} Adjutant General
Gloucester Bucks	Underhill, Samuel Kingston, Thomas Hollis, Nicholas	} Adjutant

Conductors of the Train

L. & W. Griffin Morgan
Hill, Alexander
Fenwick, George
Cotham, Henry
Warnock, Patrick
Brook, William
Pope, Mark
Harrison, Robert
Oxon Green, Charles

Middlesex Payne, John; Waggon Master General
Devon Blackmore, John; Waggon Master
Surrey Wells, Thomas; Bridge Master
Berks Evans, Laurence; Quart. to the Train
L. & W. Bayly, Thomas; Quart. to the Train in Oxon
Nottingh. Kempton, Christopher Quart. to the Train
Glamorg. Thomas, George; Quart. to the Train
L. & W. Skelden, Thomas; Master Cooper to the Train

Engineers

L. & W. Gastines, James
Hensman, William
Scarlet, Edw.
Derby Huxley, Anthony; Engineer & Chapl. **Note:** addition from the errata.

Comptrollers of the Ordnance

L. & W. Currey, James; Comptroller of the Ordnance
Chambers, John; Capt. Comptroller
Cornwall Tresahar, James; Comptroller
Gloucester Wadley, John; Comptroller and Master Gunner
Devon Roche, Pollidore; Master of the Ordnance
L. & W. Du Bois, Prudentius; Lieutenant of the Ordnance
Hodgkinson, Richard
Handson, Howell } Gentleman of the Ordnance
Sheeres, William

Auxiliary Staff

Provost Marshalls
L. & W.	Bate, Richard
Nottingh.	Flintham, Francis
Surrey	Thomas, Gabriel
York	Ruddock, Christopher
	Walbanck, Thomas
Southam.	Alley, Samuel
Cornwall	Christopher, William
	Bennet, James
Somerset	Lock, John
	Cayford, John

L. & W.	Smith, William	} Prov. Marsh. Gen.
Devon	Hawkins, Jonathan	

Marshalls
L. & W.	Griffith, Richard
Stafford	Wilks, Roger
Northumb.	Lishman, William
Oxon	Hollis, George
Southam.	Duncastle, James
Wilts	Bennet, John
Somerset	Smart, William
Devon	Midwinter, Robert
Glamorg.	Lewis, Saphin
Dorset	Poole, William

L. & W.	Tresahar, Thomas	
Devon	Turner, Robert	} Marsh. Gen.
Leicester	Duncombe, Nathaniel	

Captains Magazine
L. & W.	Jones, Walker
Cornwall	Thomas, Edmund

Pyoneers
L. & W.	Legge, William Capt.
	Fowler, John Capt.
Cornwall	Piper, John Capt.
Monmouth	Cowles, Richard Capt.
Devon	Somerton, Thomas Capt.
Somerset	Slape, Tristram Capt.
	Hooper, Zorobabell Capt. to Lt Coll Cupper. **Note:** an addition from the errata.
Oxon	Holland, William Capt. in Oxford

L. & W.	Pierce, John **Lieut.**
Lancaster	Clayton, John Lieut.
Nottingh.	Miller, Thomas Lieut.
Carnarvon	Polkinhorne, Edw. Capt. **Note:** an addition from the errata.
	Smith, John Capt. **Note:** an addition from the errata.
Dorset	Meadway, Richard Capt. **Note:** an addition from the errata.
Sussex	Harrold, Thomas Capt. **Note:** an addition from the errata.
?	Ellis, Robert Capt. **Note:** an addition from the errata.

Scout Masters

Stafford	Hancks, Thomas
	Smart, William
	Bradbury, George
	Cartwright, Thomas
Leicester	Holland, John
Nottingh.	Bray, Lodowick
Berks	Bennet, John
Hereford	Pierpoint, Ralph
Carmarth.	Edwards, John
Radnor	Roberts, James
Devon	Cokayne, William; Scout Master Gen. & Quart. Gen.
Devon	Halfstaffe, Peter; Armourer
Somerset	Trimme, George; Secretary at Warr
Cornwall	Visack, William; Deputy Quart.
Lancaster	Arderen, Thomas; Drum Major Gen.
Surrey	Barnes, Francis; Drum Major

Advocates

L. & W.	Lewin, William ⎫ Dr. Judge Advocat
	Floyd, Oliver ⎭

Chirurgions

L. & W.	Clark, Alexander
	Morall, John
	Porter, Benedict
	Du Gard, Anthony
	Risbrooke, Rivers
	De Choqueux, Anthony
	Pruden, John
	Lumley, Richard
	Downes, William
	Smith, James
	Nicholls, John
	De Lason, Pardous

	Seile, Thomas
	Wright, John
Chester	Warren, Thomas
Leicester	Gregory, Abraham
Newcastle	Shevyll, David
Westmo.	Gant, Bartholomew
Norfolk	Morall, John
Essex	Thompson, John
Surrey	Hord, Edmund
Sussex	Rose, William
Gloucester	Freame, William
Hereford	Hunt, Richard
	Curron, John
Southam.	Howell, Francis
Wilts	Thorpe, Roger
	Keepe, John
	Raven, Miles
Dorset	Holman, William
Kent	Dean, William
Cornwall	Clark, John
	Penwarne, Anthony
	Harris, John
	Hawke, Peter
	Pride, Thomas
Somerset	Down, John
	Shuter, Thomas
Devon	Weeks, John
	Prince, George
Glamorg.	Gamage, Morgan
Southam.	Barrows, Lancelot Barber Chirurgion

Physitians
L. & W.	Davis, Nicholas; Dr. Physick in the West
Leicester	Kinder, Philip; Physitian Licentiate
Westmo.	Steele, Michael; Physitian and Chirurgion
Norfolk	Le Febure, James Physitian

Chaplains
L. & W.	Cade, Thomas
	Alford, Theophilus
	Ogstone, William D. D.
	Buchannon, George
	Rowland, John
	Blaxton, Benjamin
	Atkins, Francis

Salop	Churchman, William
	Awnsham, Richard
Lincoln	Huntington, John
	FugilWing l, Christopher
	Gibson, Edw.
Norfolk	Feltwell, Robert
	Shepheard, Nicholas
	Anguish, Richard
Bucks	Deane, William
	Burden, Reginald
York	Forster, Christopher
Wilts	Otway, Thomas
	Bigg, Richard
Kent	Knell, Paul
	Trott, Robert
Cornwall	Thomas, John
Devon	Moore, Francis
	Nation, Francis
Somerset	Clench, George

Appendix I
Changes of Regimental Command

Anderson, Sir Francis – took over George Heron's Foot after Heron's death at Adwalton Moor in 1643.
Appleyard, Sir Matthew – took over Sir Charles Vavasour's ex-Irish foot after the regiment mutinied at Bristol in 1644. No officers claimed under Vavasour.
Apsley, Sir Allen – foot regiment taken over by Sir Edward Hopton in 1645.
Astley, Sir Bernard – took over Marquess of Hertford's Foot.
Astley, Lord [Sir Jacob Astley] – took over Richard Feilding's Foot after Fielding's disgrace at Reading in April 1643.
Aston, Sir Arthur – horse regiment commanded by George, then Sebastian Bunkly.
Bagot, Harvey – took over the remnants of his brother Richard's regiment.
Baggott, Richard – mortally wounded at Naseby in 1645; his foot regiment passed to his brother Harvey.
Basset, Sir Thomas – took over Sir Nicholas Slanning's Foot after the latter's death at Bristol in July 1643.
Bath, Earl of [Sir John Grenvile] – took over the regiment of his father, Sir Bevill Grenvile, who was mortally wounded at Lansdown in July 1643.
Beard, Richard – Beard's foot regiment was possibly commanded at some point by Colonel Edward Broughton, but if so the circumstances are unclear.
Beaumont, Sir John – k. at the siege of Gloucester in August 1643. His foot regiment passed to Col. John Godfrey.
Belassis, Sir John (later Lord) – raised two foot regiments: the first taken over by Theophilus Gilby late in 1643 when Belasyse returned to Yorkshire.
Bolle, Richard – k. Alton in December 1643. Regiment taken over By Col. George Lisle (drafted in from Oxford).
Brett, Sir Jerome – absent from I.O.; *see* Lord Herbert of Cherbury.
Broughton, Sir Edward – Broughton's foot regiment was possibly commanded at some point by Richard Beard, but if so the circumstances are unclear.
Broughton, Robert – regiment originally raised by Col. William Cromwell for Irish service. Returned to England in 1644. No officers claimed under Cromwell.
Bunkly, Sir George – commanded Sir Arthur Aston's Horse. After Boncle's capture at Naseby (and subsequent death), command seems to have passed to his brother Sebastian:
Bunkly, Sebastian – *see* George Bunkly, above.
Burgesse, Roger – commanded Sir John Owen's foot regiment at Faringdon garrison, while Owen returned to Wales to raise more cavalry.
Byron, Sir Robert – horse regiment commanded by Lieut. Col. William Walton (k. Naseby).
Capel, Lord – raised three horse regiments. The first passed to Col. Marcus Trevor late in 1643; the second was a revived Prince Charles's regiment, which Trevor's

men merged with in 1645; the third was raised in 1648.

Carnarvon, Earl of – k. at Newbury I. His regiment passed to Sir Charles Lucas, and then to Richard Neville.

Cary, Horatio – briefly commanded the Earl of Cleveland's Horse.

Cavendish, Charles – regiment also known as the Duke of York's. Cavendish was k. at Gainsborough in 1643, and it passed to Samuel Tuke.

Champernon, Philip – took over Prince Maurice's Foot towards the end of the first civil war.

Prince Charles (foot) – the title of two consecutive foot regiments: the first that of Michael Woodhouse in the Welsh Marches, the second that of Sir John Ackland in the West Country.

Cholmley, Sir Hugh (foot) – taken over by Toby Jenkins in 1645 after the fall of Scarborough, and transferred to Newark.

Cholmly, Sir Richard – son-in-law of Lord Paulet, commanded his foot until k. at Axminster in November 1644.

Lord Cholmondly [Robert, 1st Viscount] – late in 1643 his regiment taken over by Col. John Marrow, who was k. at Northwich late in 1644. Marrow's deputy Robert Werden commanded it at Naseby.

Chudleigh, James – k. Dartmouth, October 1643; regiment passed to Bullen Reymes.

Clavering, Sir Robert (horse) – regiment passed to John Forcer in July 1644, when Clavering died of fever.

Clavering, Sir Robert (foot) – regiment passed to James Swinhoe after Clavering's death.

Cleveland, Earl of – led by Horatio Cary, then Lord John Stuart who was k. at Cheriton; then passed to John Fleetwood, then to Colonel John Stuart.

Colepepper, Thomas – took over Henry, Lord Spencer's regiment after Spencer k. at Newbury I.

Crane, Sir Richard – took over Prince Rupert's Horse after Sir Thomas Dallison k. at Naseby in June 1645. Crane k. at Bristol in August.

Crofts (or Croft), Robert – claims as a colonel of foot under Sir William Vavasour: presumably commanded that regiment.

Cromwell, James – took over Sir Richard Willys's Horse in November 1645.

Cromwell, William – absent from I.O.; *see* Robert Broughton.

Dallison, Sir Thomas – commanded Prince Rupert's regiment of horse after the departure of Daniel O'Neil for Ireland late in 1643. K. Naseby.

Dalston, Sir William (foot) – Dalston ceased fighting after the Preston campaign in 1648, for reasons unknown; his foot regiment passed to George Denton.

Dalton, Thomas – colonel of his own horse regiment, but later became deputy to Sir Thomas Tyldesley.

Denton, George – took over Sir William Dalston's regiment after the Preston campaign in 1648.

Digby, John (horse) – son of the Earl of Bristol. Commanded horse, foot and dragoons; horse regiment taken over by Jonathan Trelawney in 1644.

Digby, Sir John (of Mansfield Woodhouse) – foot regiment passed to Anthony Gilby.

Drury, Edward – took over Sir Thomas Gower's dragoons, after the latter's arrest by

Appendix I - Changes of Regimental Command

the Earl (later Marquess) of Newcastle early in 1643.

Dutton, Sir Ralph – regiment passed to Sir Stephen Hawkins.

Eyre, Anthony – took over Sir Gervase Eyre's Horse, after the latter's death in 1644.

Eyre, Sir Gervase – died of wounds 1644, regiment passed to half-brother Anthony.

Fane, Sir Francis – foot regiment commanded by Lieut. Col. Edward Forbes in early 1644, while Fane was governor of Lincoln.

Fielding, Richard – disgraced after surrendering Reading in April 1643. His foot regiment taken over by Sir Jacob Astley.

Fitton, Sir Edward – died August 1643; regiment passed to Anthony Thelwell.

Fleetwood, Dutton – regiment commanded by (or passed to) Sir William Campion. A monument to Dutton's son in Putney Church states that Dutton was governor of Boston garrison.

Fleetwood, John – absent from I.O.; *see* Earl of Cleveland.

Forbes, Edward – commanded Sir Francis Fane's Foot in early 1644, while Fane was governor of Lincoln. Forbes and the regiment captured at Selby in April; Fane captured at Lincoln in May. Forbes mentioned in I.O. but does not claim.

Forcer, John – took over Sir Robert Clavering's regiment, after the latter's death from fever in July 1644.

Gerard, Sir Gilbert – k. 1645, regiment passed to younger brother Ratcliffe.

Gerard, Ratcliffe – took over brother Gilbert's regiment in 1645.

Gilby, Anthony – took over foot regiment of Sir John Digby of Mansfield Woodhouse.

Gilby, (Sir) Theophilus – took over Sir John Belassis's first foot regiment late in 1643.

Godfrey, John – took over Sir John Beaumont's foot regiment after the latter's death at Gloucester in 1643.

Gower, Sir Thomas – arrested by the Earl (later Marquess) of Newcastle early in 1643; dragoon regiment taken over by Edward Drury.

Greenvile, Sir Bevile – mortally wounded at Lansdown, July 1643. Foot regiment passed to his son John, later 1st Earl of Bath.

Hamilton, Sir James – passed to Sir William Russell of Strensham.

Hawkins, Sir Stephen – took over Sir Ralph Dutton's Foot.

Herbert, Edward Lord Herbert of Cherbury – regiment commanded successively by Sir Richard Lawdy and Sir Jerome Brett.

Heron, George – k. Adwalton Moor, June 1643. Foot regiment passed to Sir Francis Anderson.

Hertford, Marquess of – foot regiment taken over by Sir Bernard Astley.

Hooper, Sir Thomas – took over Prince Rupert's dragoons, which until at least early 1644 were commanded by John Innes.

Hopton, Sir Edward – took over Sir Allen Apsley's foot regiment in 1645.

Howard, Sir Francis – took over the dragoon regiment of his brother Thomas, who died December 1642; also the horse regiment of his (Sir Francis's) son, Thomas Howard of Corby, k. at Adwalton Moor in 1643.

Howard, Sir Robert – took over Sir Francis Wortley's Foot, date unknown.

Hungate, Francis – took over Sir Walter Vavasour's Horse in 1644, after Vavasour was wounded and went abroad. K. at Sherburn-in-Elmet in 1645.

Innes, John – absent in I.O.; *see* Sir Thomas Hooper.

Jenkins, Toby (or Tobias) – took over Sir Hugh Cholmley's Foot in 1645.

Knottsford, Sir John – took over Samuel Sandys' Foot in 1644.

Lawdy, Sir Richard – commanded Lord Herbert's Foot; k. at Coleford in February 1643 and succeeded by Sir Jerome Brett.

Legge, William – took over Sir Nicholas Sellwyn's Foot (the 'City of Oxford Regiment') when Legge became governor of Oxford in January 1645.

Lisle, George – took over Richard Bolle's foot regiment after the latter's death at Alton in December 1643.

Lloyd, Sir Charles – took over Sir Thomas Salisbury's Foot in 1643.

Lunsford, Sir Thomas – captured at Edgehill; regiment passed to his brother Henry, who led it until k. at Bristol; then became Rupert's Foot.

Lord General (horse) – originally a troop under the 1st Earl of Lindsey; after his death at Edgehill it passed into the command Lord General, Patrick Ruthven, and various deputies.

Lord General (foot) – raised by the 1st Earl of Lindsey; after his death at Edgehill it passed to the Lord General, Patrick Ruthven, and various deputies.

Lucas, Sir Charles – took over the Earl of Carnarvon's regiment after the latter's death at Newbury I in 1643. Left in 1644 to join the Northern Horse; Carnarvon's former regiment passed to Richard Neville.

Marlborough, Earl of (foot) – commanded by John Hungerford.

Marrow, John – formerly Lord Cholmondly's regiment. Marrow k. at Northwich late in 1644, the regiment passed to his deputy, Robert Werden.

Prince Maurice (foot) – taken over by Lieut. Col. Philip Champernon towards the end of the first civil war.

O'Neale, Daniel – absent from I.O.; *see* Prince Rupert (horse)

Lord Mohun – wounded(?) at Bristol 1643, regiment passed to Walter Slingsby.

Mylott, Ralph – had taken over George Wray's Horse by 1644.

Neville, Richard – regiment previously that of Sir Charles Lucas, and previous to that the Earl of Carnarvon (k. Newbury I, 1643).

Owen, Sir John – command of his foot regiment passed to Roger Burgess during its stay at Faringdon garrison in 1645-1646.

Page, Sir Richard – took over Sir James Pennyman's regiment in winter of 1644, when Pennyman resigned.

Lord Paulet – his foot regiment taken over successively by Sir Richard Cholmly (k. at Axminster in 1644) and Thomas Walker.

Pennyman, Sir James – took over Sir William Pennyman's Foot after Sir William's death from fever in August 1643. Resigned Winter 1644, regiment passed to Sir Richard Page.

Pennyman, Sir William – died August 1643, regiment taken over by his half brother Sir James Pennyman.

Percy, Lord Henry – regiment passed to Sir Arthur Slingsby, after Percy fell into disfavour with the King in August 1644.

Redman, Sir John – died 1645. Regiment taken over by Thomas Wheatly.

Reymes, Bullen – took over James Chudleigh's regiment after the latter's death at

Dartmouth in October 1643.

Prince Rupert (horse) – regiment led successively by Daniel O'Neale, Sir Thomas Dallison (k. Naseby 1645) and Sir Richard Crane (k. Bristol 1645).

Prince Rupert (foot) – was Sir Thomas Lunsford's Foot; commanded by his brother Henry until Henry's death at Bristol in 1643.

Queen's Lifeguard of Foot – absent in I.O.; see Richard Gerard

Russell, Sir William (of Strensham) – took over Sir James Hamilton's Horse.

St. Leger, Sir William – regiment returned from Ireland late in 1643, then by early 1644 was serving as the Duke of York's Foot.

Salisbury, Sir Thomas – died 1643, regiment passed to Sir Charles Lloyd.

Sandys, Samuel – regiment passed to Sir John Knottsford in 1644.

Sellwyn, Sir Nicholas – commanded the 'City of Oxford Regiment', in the Oxford garrison; command passed to William Legge when he became city governor.

Slanning, Sir Nicholas – k. Bristol 1643, foot regiment passed to Sir Thomas Basset.

Slingsby, Sir Arthur – took over Lord Percy's Horse after Percy fell into disfavour with the King in August 1644.

Slingsby, Guilford – absent from I.O.; *see* Thomas Slingsby.

Slingby, Thomas – took over Guilford Slingsby's Horse in January 1643, after the latter was mortally wounded at Guisborough.

Slingsby, Walter – absent from I.O.; *see* Lord Mohun.

Stradling, Sir Edward – captured at Edgehill, regiment passed to his younger brother John. Exchanged May 1644 but died of fever in June.

Stradling, John – *see* Sir Edward Stradling, above

Stuart, Lord John – commanded the Earl of Cleveland's Horse. K. Cheriton 1644.

Stuart, Colonel John – Scottish; *see* Earl of Cleveland.

Sunderland, Henry Spencer 1st Earl of – absent from I.O.; *see* Thomas Colepepper.

Swinhoe, James – took over Robert Clavering's Foot after Clavering's death from fever in July 1644.

Thelwell, Anthony – took over Sir Edward Fitton's regiment, August 1643. Killed at Newbury II, 1644.

Trelawney, Jonathan – took over John Digby's Horse in 1644.

Trevor, Mark (or Marcus) – took over Lord Capel's horse regiment in 1643.

Tuke, Samuel – took over the Duke of York's horse regiment after the death of Col. Charles Cavendish at Gainsborough in 1643. Eventually merged it into Prince Charles's regiment, where it had originally been raised.

Usher, James – k. Lichfield 1643, dragoon regiment passed to Henry Washington

Vavasour, Sir Charles – absent from I.O.; *see* Matthew Appleyard.

Vavasour, Sir Walter – went abroad after being wounded at Selby in April 1644; regiment passed to Francis Hungate.

Vavasour, Sir William – foot regiment appears to have been commanded by Robert Crofts (or Croft), who claims as a foot colonel under Vavasour.

Walker, Thomas – took over Lord Paulet's foot from Sir Richard Cholmly, after the latter's death at Axminster in November 1644.

Walton, William – lieut. col. of Sir Robert Byron's regiment of horse. K. Naseby.

Washington, Henry – took over James Usher's dragoons after the latter's death at

Lichfield in 1643.

Werden, Robert – lieut. col. of John Marrow's regiment. Took command after Marrow's death at Northwich late in 1644.

Wheatley, Thomas – took over Sir John Redman's Foot after Redman's death in 1645.

Willys, Sir Richard – regiment briefly commanded by his brother William in 1644. Taken over by James Cromwell in November 1645.

William Willys – lieut. col. to his brother Sir Richard. Took full command after the latter's capture at Ellesmere in 1644.

Wortley, Sir Francis – regiment passed to Sir Robert Howard, date unknown.

Wray, George – regiment taken over by Ralph Mylott by 1644.

Duke of York (horse) – raised by Charles Cavendish; taken over by Samuel Tuke after Cavendish's death at Gainsborough in 1643.

Duke of York (foot) – formerly William St. Leger's regiment; became the Duke's regiment after its return from Ireland late in 1643.

Appendix II
Brief Statistics

The list contains the names of 7,442 Royalist officers and auxiliary staff, although at least 65 names are possible duplications created by compilation or printing errors in 1663. Ignoring possible duplicates, of the 7,442 names 5,351 were living claimants and the rest were absentees, named but not claiming for themselves. Of these 2,091 absentees 68 were peers of some description (of whom at least 31 were dead), and 279 were knights (at least 115 of whom were dead). The fate of the remaining 1,945 is largely unknown; whilst some higher-ranking military officers are known to have died in or before 1662, in the majority of cases the reasons for not claiming are presently unclear.

Subsequent public scrutiny of the list after its publication, and the elimination of duplicate claims, probably changed the claimant total slightly. However, if the allocated £60,000 is divided equally amongst the initial 5,351 claimants, each would have received £11 4s 2d in old money; which today is worth £1,366.

The 1662 Act specified that qualifying claimants,

'have had reall Command of Souldiers according to their severall Commissions, and who had never deserted his Majestyes nor his blessed Fathers Service, dureing the late times of Rebellion and Usurpation, and who have not a sufficient Livelyhood of their owne, nor have since his Majestyes Returne obtained any Reward Office or Imployment sufficient for a Livelyhood by such wayes, meanes and proportions...'

The intention of publishing the list in 1663 was to allow other old soldiers and former Royalists to compare claimants' names against the qualifying criteria, and object to anyone who did not in fact qualify for the reward, or whose claim was entirely bogus. As Stuart Reid points out, sadly there is no record of any such objections, which would have been a great help in resolving many of the question marks and absences in the information that has come down to us.

The 'sufficient Livelyhood' qualification immediately disqualified anyone with an existing income from landed estates, thus no peers are to be found amongst the claimants, although 13 knights claimed: bestowal of knighthood, particularly in a military scenario, did not necessarily presume or require established family wealth, so presumably these men were in straightened circumstances and had not benefited from any other largesse from the restored monarch. One or two absentees were known turncoats (in either direction), and a few more were foreigners and may have left the country.

Further research and comparison of I.O. with contemporary sources such as the records of the Committee for Compounding will fill in many gaps, and provide more information about the circumstances and fate of many of these officers. To that end, the present editor welcomes contributions, corrections and comments from other researchers working in the same field.

Bibliography

Modern sources / reprints of contemporary sources

Howard, J. and Crisp, F. (eds.). *Visitation of England and Wales*. Volume 9. Privately printed, 1911.

Manwaring, G. E. (ed.). *The Life and Works of Sir Henry Manwaring*. Two volumes. Navy Records Society, 1920.

Money, W. *The First and Second Battles of Newbury and the Siege of Donnington Castle During the Civil War, A.D. 1643-6*. Second edition. London: Simpkin, Marshall, and Co., 1884.

Newman, P. R. *The Old Service. Royalist regimental colonels and the Civil War, 1642-46*. Manchester: Manchester University Press, 1993.

Newman, Peter. *The Battle of Marston Moor 1644*. Chichester: Antony Bird Publications, 1981.

Roy, Ian (ed.) *The Royalist Ordnance Papers 1642-1646*. Two volumes. Banbury: Oxfordshire Record Society, 1964, 1975.

Salzman, L. F. (ed.). *A History of the County of Northampton: Volume 4*. London: Victoria County History, 1937.

Shaw, W. A. *The Knights of England*. Two volumes. London: Sherratt and Hughes, 1906.

Symonds, Richard (Charles Edward Long, ed.). *Diary of the Marches of the Royal Army During the Great Civil War*. Camden Society: 1859.

Toynbee, M. & Young, P. *Strangers in Oxford. A Side Light on the First Civil War 1642-1646*. Chichester: Phillimore & Co. Ltd., 1973.

Tucker, Norman. *Royalist Officers of North Wales 1642-1660*. Denbigh: published by the author, 1961.

Young, Peter. *Marston Moor 1644. The Campaign and the Battle*. Moreton-in-Marsh: Windrush Press, 1998.

Calendar of State Papers, Domestic Series, of the Reign of Charles I. 1644-1645. Preserved in Her Majesty's Public Record Office. Hamilton, William Douglas (Ed.). London: Eyre and Spottiswoode, 1890.

Internet sources

Journal of the House of Commons (at http://www.british-history.ac.uk/)
Journal of the House of Lords (http://www.british-history.ac.uk/)
The History of Parliament (http://www.historyofparliamentonline.org)
Oxford Dictionary of National Biography (http://www.oxforddnb.com/) – requires subscription.

Contemporary sources

TT E.42[21] / Wing (2nd edn.) T2682
A True Discovery Of The Great And Glorious Victory of that Victorious and ever renowned patriott Sir William Waller Knight, at Christ Church in Hampshire. With a List of the Names of the Commanders taken there. London. Printed for Matthew Walbancke, 1644.

TT E.84[22] / Wing (2nd edn.) T2956
A True Relation Of The Fortunate S. William Waller Collonel Under His Excellency the Earle of Essex, Concerning, The manner of the beseeging and taking of Chichester, Together with the Names of all such Commanders and others taken Prisoners there and brought up to London. London. Printed for Henry Twyford, 1643.

Mercurius Aulicus, Week 14, 31st March-6th April 1644. TT E.43[18]

Mercurius Civicus
    No. 34, 4th-11th January 1644. TT E.82[22]
    No. 47, 11th-18th April 1644. TT E.43[10]

Perfect Occurrences, 11th Week, 7th-14th March 1645. TT E.258[35]

The Kingdomes Weekly Intelligencer, No. 27, 18th-25th July 1643. TT E.61[22]

Index

* Individuals in *italics* were mentioned by former colleagues but did not claim.
* Claimants who did not name their regiment are marked as 'stray'.
* To aid identification, the names of commanding officers are added to entries where adjacent claimants have similar names, ranks and locations.
* Names are indexed 'as is': if looking for a particular officer, readers should consider alternative spellings.

BL: British Library
ODNB: Oxford Dictionary of National Biography
JHC: Journal of the House of Commons
JHL: Journal of the House of Lords
THoP: The History of Parliament (online resource)
TT: Pamphlet from the 'Thomason Tracts' at the British Library

Abarrow, W___ Maj. F., 103
Abbot, Francis Quart. H., Dorset, stray, 160
Abercrombe/Abercromb, David Capt. F., L. & W., 151
Abernethy, George Lieut. F., L. & W., stray, 164
Abithell, Thomas Lieut. H., Wilts, 115
Abrahall, John Capt. F., 153
Abrahall, Richard Lieut. F., Hereford, 153
Abraham, Richard Lieut. F., Cornwall, 50
Ackland, Arthur Lieut. H., Devon, 77
Ackland, Hugh Capt. F., Cornwall, 36
Ackland, Sir John Col. H. & F. (d. 1647), 13. Foot regiment known as Prince Charles's Foot; the second consecutive regiment to bear that title.
Acton, Adam Lieut. F., L. & W., 152
Acton, Samuel Lieut. H., L. & W., 94
Acton, Thomas ___ H., stray, 160
Adams, Anthony Lieut. F., L. & W., 152
Adams, Edward Quart. H., Salop, 59
Adams, John Lieut. F., Cornwall, 43
Adams, John Lieut. H., Pembroke, 91
Adams, Richard Ens. F., Northampton, 42
Adams, Thomas Lieut. H., L. & W., 72
Adams, Thomas Regt. Quart. F., L. & W., 104
Adams, William Quart. H., Wilts, 95
Adamson, Robert Quart. H., Lancaster, 138
Adamson, William Lieut. H., Derby, 68
Adderly, William Lieut. H., Stafford, 108
Addinson, Thomas Lieut. F., Cumberland, 49
Addison, ___ Maj. H., Sir William Courtenay, 44
Addison, ___ Maj. H., Sir Marmaduke Royden, 119
Addison, Richard Quart. H., Northumberland, 34

Addys, ___ Capt. H., 19
Addys, Edw. Lieut. H., Hereford, stray, 158
Adway, ___ Capt. H., 41
Ady, Thomas Lieut. F., Wilts, 53
Agehead/Adgehead, George Ens. F., L. & W., stray, 165
Albion, Philologus Lieut. F., L. & W., 98
Alcock, William Quart. H., Nottingham, 97
Alden, Richard Quart. H., L. & W., 84
Aldersey, John Ens. F., Chester, 92
Aldridge, Rowland Capt. H., Kent, 94
Alexander, Paul Lieut. F., L. & W., 27
Alford, Gregory Capt. H., 23
Alford, Robert Capt. F., Somerset, 51
Alford, Theophilus, Chaplain, L. & W., 173
Alford, Thomas Quart. H., Dorset, stray, 160. Claims under a Captain Edward Berkly, possibly the Somerset captain mentioned under Lord John Berkly.
Alford, William Cor. H., Somerset, 23
Allbrittayn Thomas Cor. H., L. & W., 111
Allcote/Alcott, Thomas Capt. Dr., Somerset, 131
Allen, ___ Capt. H., Sir Humphrey Bennet, 23
Allen, ___ Capt. H., Rowland Eyre, 57
Allen, ___ Capt. F., 110
Allen, Edw. Quart. H., Derby, 60
Allen, Henry Lieut. H., Somerset, 115
Allen, John Capt. F., Cornwall, 144
Allen John Adjutant General, L. & W., 170
Allen, Leonard Lieut. H., Cornwall, 14
Allen, Robert Cor. Dr., Durham, 118
Allen, Thomas Quart. H., York, 90
Allen, William Capt. F., 16
Allenson, John Capt. F., Durham, 53
Allenson, Ralph Capt. F., 135
Allestry, Richard Cor. H., Derby, 89
Alley, Samuel Provost Marshall, Southampton, 171
Allgood, Richard Ens. F., Durham, 149
Allman, Richard Quart. F., L. & W., 88
Allot, George Lieut. H., Somerset, 141
Allwin, John Capt. H., Southampton, 23
Alsop, Durand Capt. H., Lincoln, 75
Alsop, Durand Capt. H. & F., L. & W., 75. The same regiment, and so probably the same man as above.
Alsop, Richard Capt. H., L. & W., 63
Alsop, Thomas Cor. H., L. & W., 75
Alsop, Thomas Quart. H., Derby, 17
Ambler, John Quart. H., York, 61

Index

Ambler, Richard Lieut. F., Salop, 110
Amery, Robert Capt. F., Sir William Courtenay, 44
Amery, Robert Capt. F., L. & W., Sir Marmaduke Royden, 119
Amhurst, Giles Ens. F., Kent, 77. I.O. does not give an arm of service, but the rank of ensign indicates foot.
Amias, John Lieut. F., Sussex, 127
Ancthill, ___ Capt. H., 13
Ancthill, Francis Ens. F., Somerset, 155
Ancthill, Nicholas Cor. H., Dorset, 91
Ancthill, William Col. H., 13, 151, 155. Mentioned by officers under Sir Hugh Windham and Sir Edmond Wyndham; one officer claims under him directly.
Anderkin, Philip Lieut. H., L. & W., 25
Anderson, ___ Capt. H., 90
Anderson, Bartram Sen. Lieut. F., Newcastle, 100
Anderson, Edward Lieut. F., Durham, 58
Anderson, Sir Francis Col. H. (d. 1679), 13
Anderson, Francis Lieut. F., Newcastle, 88
Anderson, John Capt. F., Hertford, 105
Anderson, John Ens. F., York, 73
Anderson, John Quart. H., York, 121
Anderson, Peregrine Lieut. F., L. & W., 22
Anderson Robert Sea Capt., Kent, 167
Anderson, Thomas Ens. F., York, 112
Anderton, ___ Lieut. Col. H., 137. Same regiment as lieutenant colonel of foot Hugh Anderton, below; probably the same man.
Anderton, ___ Capt. H., 137
Anderton, Christopher Cor. H., Lancaster, 137
Anderton, Hugh Lieut. Col. F., 138
Anderton, James Capt. H., 153
Anderton, Nicholas Capt. H., 138
Andrewes/Andrews, John Lieut. F., Suffolk, 42
Andrewes/Andrews, John Cor. H., Flint, stray, 159
Andrews, ___ Capt. Dr., 70
Andrews, Richard Capt. F., Lincoln, 32
Andrews, Thomas Capt. Lieut. F., Glamorgan, 96
Andrews, Thomas Ens. F., Wilts, 24
Andrews, William Cor. H., Carmarthen, 130
Andrews, William Ens. F., Oxon, 127
Angel, Richard Cor. H., Berks, 74
Anguish, John Capt. F., 79
Anguish, Richard, Chaplain, Norfolk, 174
Anne, John Lieut. H., York, 56
Anne, Thomas Lieut. H., Wilts, 17
Ansell/Anselme, Christopher Cor. H., Dorset, 151
Anthony, John Quart. H. Lincoln, 78. I.O. does not give an arm of service, but

he claims under Lieutenant Colonel Richard Neville in Sir John Henderson's regiment; which was a cavalry unit.

Anthony, Robert Ens. F., Lincoln, stray, 165

Anton, James Cor. H., L. & W., 84

Appleby, Cutbert Capt. F., Durham, 53

Appleby, Laurence Capt. H., Northumberland, 134, 159. Claims under Sir Francis Stuart; also mentioned by a stray cornet.

Appleby, William Cor. H., York, stray, 159. Claims under Captain Henry Messenger, who in turn claims under Sir Robert Clavering.

Appleton, Robert Cor. H., York, 68

Appleyard, John Capt. H., Cambridge, stray, 157

Appleyard, Sir Matthew Col. F. (d. 1670), 13. Knighted 2nd June 1645, after the storming of Leicester.

Appleyard, Thomas Lieut. H., Lincoln, 112

Apsley, Sir Allen Col. H. & F. (d. 1683), 13

Apsley, James Col. ___, 14. I.O. gives no arm of service for Apsley's men, but of the three who claim under him, two are indexed as foot officers and one as horse.

Apsley, John Col. H., 14

Archer, ___ *Capt. H.*, 96

Archibald, Henry Lieut. F., Northumberland, 100

Archibald, Robert Ens. F., Newcastle, 100

Arderen, Thomas Drum Major Gen., Lancaster, 172

Aris, Nicholas Cor. H., Bucks, 23

Armestead, Robert Sea Capt. 'of the *Charles, James,* &c.', L. & W., 167

Armorer, ___ *Maj. F.*, William Strother, 134

Armorer, ___ *Maj. Dr.*, Sir Robert Clavering, 40

Armorer, ___ *Capt. F.*, Sir William Vaughan, 142

Armorer, ___ *Capt. F.*, stray, 165. Possibly the man above, as both are mentioned by Shropshire officers.

Armorer, Nicholas Capt. H. (d. 1686), stray, 159. Commanded garrison at High Ercall in Shropshire. Knighted in 1662.

Armstrong, Roger Quart. H., Salop, 119

Armstrong, William Lieut. F., Durham, 54

Arnold, Stephen, Quart. H., York, 37

Arnold, Thomas Capt. F., Cornwall, 122

Arscott, Humphry Maj. H., 128

Arscott, Richard Lieut. H., Devon, 82

Arscott/Arscot, William Lieut. H., L. & W., 101

Arthur, Roger Lieut. H., Salop, 147

Arundell, ___ *Lieut. Col. H.*, 19. Reid states that this is Ezekiel Arundell from Camborne in Cornwall.

Arundell, Christopher Capt. F., Sussex, 155

Arundell, John ('Jack') Col. F. (d. 1654-1656), 14. Governor of Pendennis Castle.

Arundell, John Col. H. (k. 1644; Plymouth), 14. Son of Colonel John Arundell above.

Arundell, John Capt. H., Cornwall, 77

Index

Arundell, John Capt. F., Somerset, 122
Arundell, John Capt. F., L. & W., 155
Arundell, John Lieut. F., Cornwall, 54
Arundell, Nicholas Capt. F., stray, 165
Arundell, Richard Col. F. (d. 1687), 15. Son of Colonel John ('Jack') Arundell, above. In 1645 appointed colonel of the trained bands and garrison at Pendennis Castle, where his father was governor.
Arundell, William Col. F., 15
Ascough, ___ Lieut. Col. H., 141
Ascough, ___ Capt. H., 148
Ascough, Hugh Lieut. F., Cumberland, 85
Ascough, Thomas Lieut. F., York, 56
Ash, William Capt. H., 23
Ashburnham, William Col. H. & F. (d. 1679), 15
Ashby, Godfrey Col. H. (& F.?), 9, 165. Requests own inclusion. Mentioned by a stray ensign of foot, so presumably also an infantry colonel.
Ashly, Craithorne/Ashley, Crathorne Capt. Lieut. Dr., York, 55
Ashly, Francis Capt. H., 55
Ashly Cooper, [Anthony] Col. F. (d. 1683), 16. Ashly Cooper switched to the Parliament's side soon after raising his regiment in 1643.
Ashton, ___ Lieut. Col. F., 147
Ashton, Edmund Capt. Lieut. Dr., Lincoln, 146
Ashton, Henry Capt. F., Lancaster, 38
Ashton, John Lieut. F., Lancaster, 38
Askew, Charles Lieut. F., York, 67
Askew, George Ens. F., Surrey, 96
Askew, Thomas Ens. F., L. & W., 119
Aslaby, Bartholomew Lieut. H., York, 61
Asmall, Thomas Capt. H., York, 103
Aspenwell, Matthew Quart. H., York, 102
Astley, [Jacob] 1ˢᵗ Baron Astley of Reading, Col. H. & F. (d. 1652), 16. Created Baron in November 1644.
Astley, Sir Bernard Col. F. (k. 1645; Bristol), 16
Astly, John Capt. H., Salop, 153
Astly, Sir Richard Capt. H. & F. (d. 1688), 96, 165. Mentioned by a quartermaster of horse, and a stray ensign of foot.
Astly, Thomas Quart. H., Hereford, 33
Astly, Wootton/Wootten Cor. H., L. & W., 33
Aston, Sir Arthur Col. H. & F. (k. 1649; Drogheda, Ireland), 16. Governor of Oxford 1643-1644. Broke his leg in a riding accident in December 1644; it was amputated, and legend has it that he was beaten to death with the wooden substitute when the Royalist garrison at Drogheda was massacred in 1649.
Aston, Arthur Capt. Lieut. H., L. & W., 117
Aston, Clifton Ens. F., Derby, stray, 165
Aston, Edw. Cor. H., Stafford, 152

Aston, James Capt. F., Oxon, 14
Aston, John Capt. F., stray, 165
Aston, Ralph Col. H., 17
Aston, Sir Thomas Col. H. (woun. Nov 1645, Bridgnorth; d. in prison Mar 1646), 17
Aston, Thomas Quart. H., Lancaster, stray, 161
Aston, [Walter] 2nd Lord Aston, Col. H. (d. 1678), 17
Atherton, Phillip Capt. F., Somerset, 131
Athrelpho/Atrelpho, John Quart. H., L. & W., 44
Atkins, Francis, Chaplain, L. & W., 173
Atkins, Jonathan Col. F., 17
Atkins, Richard Capt. H., 40
Atkins, Robert Cor. H., York, 108
Atkins, Thomas Capt. Lieut. F., L. & W., 76
Atkinson, ___ Capt. H., 40
Atkinson, ___ Capt. F., 147
Atkinson, Francis Ens. F., York, 105
Atkinson, Hugh Quart. H., Westmorland, 107
Atkinson, Miles Quart. H., Lancaster, 68
Atkinson, Ralph Capt. F., York, 49
Atkinson, Richard Ens. F., York, 129
Atkinson, Robert Lieut. F., Somerset, 76
Atkinson, William Lieut. F., Salop, 84
Atkinson, William Quart. H. (Brigade), York, 26, 143. Atkinson claims both as brigade quartermaster to Sir William Blakeston of Archdeacon Newton, and as quartertmaster in Sir Walter Vavasour's regiment. Presumably that regiment was in Blakeston's brigade.
Atterbury, William Capt. Lieut. H., L. & W., 119
Atthow, William Ens. F., Southampton, 23
Aubin, Germain Ens. F., L. & W., 65
Audesly/Awdesly, John Capt. F., York, 125
Audly/Awdly, John Capt. H. & Quart. Gen., L. & W., stray, 157
Austin, Peter Lieut. H., Devon, 72
Avery, Robert Lieut. F., Cornwall, stray, 164
Awbry, ___ Capt. H., 118
Awbry, Anthony Maj. F., 94
Awbry, Edw. Capt. H., Worcester, 54
Awbry, Herbert Capt. F., stray, 164
Awbry, John Quart. Gen. F., Carmarthen, 33
Awbry, Richard Cor. H., Carmarthen, 33
Awbry/Awbrey, Thomas Capt. H., Devon, 23
Awde, John Lieut. Dr., Durham, 81
Awdley/Awdly, Thomas Capt. H., Stafford, 149
Awnsham/Awmsham, Richard, Chaplain, Salop, 174
Aylet/Aylett, John Capt. H., L. & W., Sir Charles Lucas, 97
Aylet, John Capt. H., Lord John Lucas, 98. Possibly the captain who claimed under

the command of Lucas's brother Charles, above.
Aylett, John Capt. H., stray, 160. Possibly the man above, as both officers are cited by claimants from Essex.
Ayleworth, John Cor. H., Monmouth, 153
Ayliffe, William Col. F., 17
Babb, Tristram Lieut. F., Somerset, stray, 164
Babbidge, Greg. Cor. H., Dorset, 91
Babington, Ferdinando Ens. F., Nottingham, 25
Babot/Babbot, Thomas Lieut. F., Lancaster, stray, 164
Backwell, Bartholomew Quart. H., Somerset, 151
Bacon, Christopher Capt. H., York, stray, 157
Bacon, Edw. Capt. H., 153
Bacon, George Lieut. H., Westmorland, 30
Bacon, Phillip Maj. H., 111
Bacon, Robert Capt. H., L. & W., 97
Badcock, Henry Ens. F., Cornwall, 24
Badger, Thomas Ens. F., L. & W., 21
Badghot/Badgehot, Thomas Capt. H., Bucks, 34
Bagaley, ___ Lieut. Col. F., 21
Bagaley/Bagaly, Humphrey Capt. F., L. & W., 22
Bagaley/Bagaly, Simon Lieut. F., L. & W., 22
Bagge, George Capt. F., Devon, 35
Bagnall, ___ Maj. F., 16
Bagnall, ___ Capt. F., 138
Bagott, Harvey Col. F., 17
Bagott, Richard Col. H. & F. (k. 1645; Naseby), 18. Originally a captain of foot under Colonel Richard Bolle. Appointed governor of Lichfield, by Prince Rupert, in March 1643. Mortally wounded at Naseby in June 1645 and died three weeks later on 7th July. Interred in Lichfield Cathedral. I.O. wrongly calls him 'Sir Richard'.
Bagshaw, Charles Capt. F., Lincoln, 108
Bailden, ___ Capt. H., 137
Bailey – *see* Bayly
Baines, ___ Lieut. Col. H., 105
Baker, Degory Lieut. F., Cornwall, 140
Baker, Francis Col. F. & Dr., 18
Baker, John Cor. H., L. & W., 76
Baker, John Quart. H., L. & W., 122
Baker, Robert Lieut. F., L. & W., 19
Baker, Thomas Capt. F., Denbigh, 31
Baker, William Lieut. F., L. & W., 42
Bakewell, Zach. Ens. F., Stafford, 18
Baldwin, Edw. Capt. Dr., 43
Baldwin, William Quart. H., Salop, 153
Baldwyn/Baldwin, Thomas Lieut. F., Middlesex, 16

Bale, ___ Maj. H., Lord Langdale, 90
Bale, ___ Maj. H., Lord Loughborough, 96
Bale, John Lieut. F., Somerset, 39
Bale, William Col. H., 18. As his officers claimed from Leicester, this is probably the Lieutenant Colonel William Bale listed below under Lord Loughborough.
Bale, William Lieut. Col. H., Lord Loughborough, 96
Bale, William Capt. H., stray, 159
Bale, William Lieut. H., Southampton, 44
Bales (Bale), Samuel Ens. F., L. & W., 129
Balgy, ___ Capt. F., 57
Ball, John Capt. H., 108
Ball, John Ens. F., Somerset, 98
Ball, Richard Lieut. H., Denbigh, stray, 158
Ball, Thomas Lieut. F., Stafford, 60
Ball, William Lieut. F., Oxon, 52
Ballard, ___ Capt. F., 126
Ballard, Thomas Ens. F., L. & W., 119. I.O. does not give an arm of service, but the rank of ensign indicates foot.
Ballhatchett, William Lieut. F., Devon, 145
Bamber, ___ Capt. H., 137
Bambridge, Francis Lieut. H., L. & W., 38
Bambrigge/Bambridge, Arthur Cor. Dr., Durham, 80
Bamfield/Bampfield, James Cor. H., Dorset, 74
Bampfield, Joseph Col. F. (d. 1685), 18
Bancks/Banks, Robert Cor. H., Chester, 101
Banister, ___ Capt. F., 97
Banister, Henry Quart. H., Lancaster, 137
Banister, John Lieut. H., Hereford, 38
Banister, John Cor. H., Lancaster, 99
Banister, Ralph Capt. F., York, 86
Banks, Francis Lieut. F., York, 58
Banks, James Lieut. F., York, 91
Banks, John Capt. H., York, 36
Banks, John Lieut. F., York, 38
Banks, Samuel Capt. H., York, 136
Banks, William Capt. F., L. & W., 105
Barber, ___ Capt. H., 40
Barber, Edmund Capt. H., Suffolk, 25
Barber, Edw. Capt. Lieut. F., Norfolk, stray, 164
Barber, George Commissary General, L. & W., 169
Barber, John Capt. F., Suffolk, 25
Bard, [Henry] Lord, Col. F. (d. 1656), 18
Bardsey (Bardsy), James Lieut. Col. F., L. & W., 9, 19
Barker, ___ Capt. H., 141
Barker, ___ Capt. F., 97

Index

Barker, George Cor. Dr., York, 91
Barker, John Capt. F., 67
Barker, Leonard Cor. H., Somerset, 82
Barker, Matthew Cor. H., Derby, 57
Barker, Nicholas Capt. Lieut. F., L. & W., 120
Barker, Richard Lieut. F., Cumberland, 107
Barker, Thomas Cor. H., Lancaster, 31
Barker, William Capt. H., stray, 159
Barker, William Lieut. H., Lancaster, 145
Barletson, Thomas Quart. Dr., Northumberland, 40
Barling, John Lieut. F., L. & W., 112
Barlow George Ens. F., L. & W., 69
Barlow, John Col. H., 19
Barlow, John Capt. H., 54
Barlow, Richard Lieut. H., Hereford, 143
Barlow, Thomas Quart. H., Stafford, 18
Barnard, ___ Capt. H., 53
Barnard, John Col. H., 19
Barnard, John Lieut. F., Somerset, 83
Barnard, Laurence Capt. F., Middlesex, 77
Barnard, William Capt. H., stray, 158
Barne, James Lieut. F., Devon, 145
Barner, Thomas Capt. F., 56
Barnes, Bartholomew Capt. H., 95
Barnes, Francis Drum Major, Surrey, 172
Barnes, George Col. F., 19
Barnes, Henry Capt. H., Durham, 121
Barnes, Micheas Quart. H., Dorset, 133
Barnes, Nicholas Lieut. F., Cornwall, 19
Barnes, Robert Quart. F., Wilts, 46
Barnes, Thomas Quart. F., Stafford, 154
Barnes, Thomas 'Commissary Train', L. & W., 169
Barnes, Walter Lieut. H., Dorset, 82
Barnes, William Lieut. F., Somerset, 127
Barnsly, Charles Capt. H., Derby, 59
Barnsly, Henry Ens. F., Worcester, 92
Barnston, Richard Capt. Lieut. F., Chester, 64
Barnwell, Francis Cor. H., Lincoln, 111
Barnwell, John Lieut. H., L. & W., 96
Baron/Barons, Hercules Lieut. H., Devon, 108
Barraclough, Richard Ens. F., Lincoln, 57
Barre, ___ Maj. H., 128
Barree, ___ Lieut. Col. H., 91
Barrell, ___ Capt. F., Fitzwilliam Coningsby, 42
Barrell, ___ Capt. F., Sir William Vavasor, 143

Barrer, Thomas Lieut. F., Hereford, 116
Barret, ___ Lieut. Col. F., 114
Barret, Edw. Cor. H., Worcester, 124
Barret, James Capt. F., Somerset, 155
Barrett/Barret, Bonaventure Lieut. F., Carmarthen, 52
Barrett/Barret, Lewis Lieut. H., Cornwall, 19
Barrett/Barret, Peter Quart. H., L. & W., 130
Barrett/Barret, Ralph Quart. H., Salop, 128. Served in 1651.
Barrow, John Quart. H., Hereford, 117
Barrow, William Ens. Dr., Chester, 61
Barrows, Henry Lieut. H., Kent, stray, 158
Barrows, Lancelot Barber Chirurgion, Southampton, 173
Barry, Edw. Capt. F., Glamorgan, 136
Barry, Miles Capt. F., L. & W., 76
Barry, Phillip Quart. H., L. & W., 134
Barry, William Quart. H., Cornwall, 129
Barton, ___ Capt. H., 98
Barton, Edw. Cor. H., Northampton, 98
Barton, John Lieut. H., Lancaster, 143
Barton, Robert Ens. F., York, 144
Barton, Roger Quart. H., Wilts, 34
Barton, William Lieut. F., York, 147
Bartram, Francis Capt. H., York, 61
Bartram, John Quart. Dr., Northumberland, 55
Bartram, William Quart. H., Cumberland, 101
Basket, Richard Capt. F., Wilts, 120
Baskeville, ___ Capt. H., 150
Baskeville, ___ Capt. F., 42
Baskevile/Baskerville, Edw. Capt. F., Hereford, 149
Basset, Sir Arthur Col. F., 19. Regiment based in Cornwall.
Basset, Sir Arthur, ___ F., Marquess of Newcastle, 109. There is much debate as to whether this officer and the man above are the same person.
Basset/Bassett, Charles Lieut. H., Glamorgan, 64
Basset/Bassett, Charles Cor. H., L. & W., 64
Basset, James Lieut. F., Glamorgan, 65
Basset, Sir Thomas Col. H. F. & Dr., 19
Basset, William Capt. F., Glamorgan, 65
Bassett, Arthur Capt. F., 104
Baston, John Ens. F., L. & W., 16
Batch, Thomas Capt. F., Worcester, 123
Batch/Bach, William Cor. H., Worcester, 124
Batchelor/Bachelor, Richard Commissary, L. & W., 169
Bate, Richard Provost Marshall, L. & W., 171
Bateman, ___ Capt. H., 149
Bateman, James Lieut. H., Kent, 39

Bates, Leonard Lieut. F., L. & W., stray, 164
Bates, Robert Maj. H., 131
Bates, Robert Ens. F., Wilts, 84
Bates, Thomas Capt. H., L. & W., 44
Bates, William Capt. F., Nottingham, 63
Bates, William Quart. F., York, 113
Bateson, Francis Capt. F., York, 112
Bateson, Henry Cor. H., Middlesex, 103
Bath, [Sir John Grenville] 1st Earl of, Col. F. (d. 1701), 20. Took over regiment of father, Beville, k. Lansdown July 1643. Created Earl of Bath in 1661.
Batmanson/Batemanson, John Lieut. F., Durham, 53
Batson/Bateson, Austin Cor. H., Lincoln, stray, 159
Batson/Bateson, Edw. Lieut. H., Northampton, 156
Batt, George Lieut. H., Southampton, stray, 158
Batt, Henry Capt. H., Bedford, 60
Batt, Thomas Capt. F., Berks, 121
Battersby, John Capt. F., Cornwall, 50
Batts, ___ Capt. F., 125
Batts, James Quart. H., L. & W., 96
Batts, John Capt. H., 37
Battyn, Christopher Lieut. H., Devon, 23
Bavand, ___ Capt. H., Lord John Byron, 30
Bavand, Daniel Capt. H., Chester, 64, 104. Claimed at Chester under Lord Molineux; cited by two Chester officers under Sir Francis Gamul.
Bawden, Tobias Ens. F., Cornwall, 20
Bawden, William Ens. F., Cornwall, 15
Bawds, Maurice Col. H. (k. 1645; Naseby), 20
Baxter, ___ Capt. F., 120
Baxter, Richard Quart. F., L. & W., 96
Baxter, Walter Lieut. F., L. & W., 121
Bayly, Edward Ens. F., Hereford, 126
Bayly, Degory Ens. F., Devon, 127
Bayly, Giles Lieut. F., Westmorland, 22
Bayly, John Commissary, Somerset, 169
Bayly, Thomas Capt. F., Thomas Blague, 25
Bayly, Thomas Capt. F., Leicester, Lord Loughborough, 96
Bayly, Thomas Lieut. F., Devon, 14
Bayly, Thomas 'Quart. to the Train in Oxon', L. & W., 170
Bayly, William Capt. F., Wilts, 18
Baynes, Francis Lieut. Col. H., 21. Deputy of his brother's 1651 regiment, above. Mentioned in I.O. by his cornet; the man does not give Baynes's first name, but we know it from Robert Lilburne's account of the Wigan Lane skirmish, where he gives a list of the captured and the dead. Baynes was a prisoner.
Baynes, John Col. H. & F., 21. Baynes's regiment was a 1651 unit defeated at Wigan Lane.

Baynes, John Capt. H., L. & W., 21. Served in 1651.
Baynes, John Lieut. F., Cumberland, 107
Bayton, Edw. Cor. H., Salop, 49
Beal/Beale, Roger Capt. F., Hereford, 94
Bealby, ___ Capt. H., Lord Mansfield, 100. Probably the Captain Bilby mentioned under Henry Cavendish; Mansfield and Cavendish were brothers.
Beale, John Cor. H., Carmarthen, 146
Beales, Francis Capt. F., Kent, 24
Beard, Richard Col. F., 21. An officer mentioned in his regiment, Major Timothy Blencow, is also mentioned under Colonel Edward Broughton: Reid has taken this to mean that Beard took over Broughton's regiment at some point, although he offers no source.
Beardmore, Walter Lieut. H., Stafford, 18
Beare, John Cor. H., Cornwall, 54
Beare, Simon Ens. F., Devon, 72
Beare, William Ens. F., Cornwall, 139
Bearperk, William Ens. F., York, 49
Beaumont, J___ Lieut. Col. F., 93. Reid believes this was John Beaumont, who served as a captain in 1640.
Beaumont, Sir John Col. F. (k. 1643; siege of Gloucester), 21
Beaumont, John Cor. H., Somerset, 82
Beaumont, Sir Thomas ___ F., 125
Beaumont, William Cor. H., York, 86
Beck, Anthony Quart. Dr., York, 99
Beck, John Cor. H., Westmorland, 134. Served in 1648.
Beck, John Ens. F., Westmorland, 22
Beck, Thomas Capt. F. & Dr., L. & W., 18
Beckalack/Beckalacke, William Lieut. H., Devon, 70
Beckingham, Rowland Capt. H., L. & W., 137
Beckman, ___ ___ F., stray, 165
Beckwith, John Cor. H., York, 148
Beckwith, Thomas Lieut. H., York, 39
Beckwith, W___ Maj. H., 102
Bedborough, Thomas Capt. F., 40
Bedborrow/Bedborough, Thomas Capt. H., L. & W., 85
Beddingfield, Edmund Capt. F., Norfolk, 80
Beddingfield, Henry Cor. H., Norfolk, 31
Beddingfield, Thomas Col. H. & F., 21
Beddoe, William Ens. F., Salop, 152
Bednall, Robert Ens. F., Northumberland, stray, 165. Listed as a stray, but claims under Lieutenant Colonel Thomas Haggerston, deputy to his father Sir Thomas Haggerston.
Beecher, John Capt. F., Somerset, 112
Beeton, John Capt. F., Berks, 98
Beeton, Sigismund Col. F. (k. 1643; Gainsborough), 21

Belassis, [John] Lord, Col. H. & F. (d. 1689), 21
Belfore, ___ Maj. H., Sir Henry Cary, 35
Belfore, ___ Maj. H., Robert Harris, 75
Bell, Albany Capt. Lieut. Dr., Northumberland, 34
Bell, Augustine Capt. F., L. & W., 125
Bell, Christopher Quart. H., Westmorland, 47
Bell, Edw. Cor. H., Northumberland, 34
Bell, John Lieut. H., Newcastle, 62
Bell, Phillip Capt. Lieut. H., L. & W., 40
Bell, Robert Cor. H., Cumberland, 101
Bell, Thomas Quart. H., Northumberland, 34
Bellamy, Michael Capt. Dr., Bucks, 146
Bellasis, ___ Lieut. Col. H., 58. Usually 'Belasyse'.
Bellingham, Sir Henry Col. F. (d. 1650), 22
Belson, John Cor. H., Derby, 104
Benchkin, Samuel Capt. F., L. & W., 96
Bend, Henry Lieut. H., Nottingham, 96
Bendish, Roger Capt. F., 98
Bennet, Anthony Capt. H., Derby, 59
Bennet, Francis Capt. F., Wilts, 143
Bennet, Henry Maj. F., 27
Bennet, Henry Quart. H., Lincoln, 112
Bennet, Sir Humphrey Col. H. & F. (d. 1667), 23. Knighted 1645/5 after Newbury II.
Bennet, James Provost Marshall, Cornwall, 171
Bennet, John, Marshall, Wilts, 171
Bennet, John Scoutmaster, Berks, 172
Bennet, Nicholas Capt. F., Devon, 35
Bennet, Reginald Lieut. F., L. & W., stray, 163
Bennet, Thomas Ens. F., Lincoln, 103. I.O. does not give an arm of service, but the rank of ensign indicates foot.
Bennet, William Quart. H., Lancaster, 116
Bennett/Bennet, Richard Lieut. F., Devon, 50
Benson, ___ Capt. H., 108
Benson, ___ Capt. F., 89
Benson, John Capt. H., 125
Benson, Robert Lieut. F., stray, 164
Benson, Robert Ens. F., York, 56
Bent, ___ Capt. H., 111
Bent, Christopher Lieut. H., Leicester, 111
Bentall/Benthall, Sampson Capt. F., Worcester, 63
Benthall, Laurence Capt. H., 32
Bently, William Lieut. ___, Somerset, 66. Bently claims under a Captain Croker in the regiment of an unidentified 'Gerard': this was probably Lord Gerard's horse, where a Captain Croker is mentioned.
Berckly, ___ Capt. F., 121

Berisford/Berrisford, William Cor. H., Lincoln, 79
Berkenhead, Roger Capt. H., L. & W., 30
Berkenhead, William Ens. F., L. & W., 98
Berkly, Sir Edward Col. F. (d. 1654), 23
Berkly, Edw. Capt. H., stray, 160. Possibly the Captain Edward Berkly mentioned by a stray Dorset quartermaster.
Berkly, Henry Capt. H., stray, 160
Berkly, Lord John Col. H. & F. (d. 1678), 23
Berkly, Robert Capt. F., Gloucester, 145
Bermingham, John Maj. H., L. & W., 10, 143
Berminsham, ___ Maj. F., 92
Bernard, John Quart. H., Worcester, 120
Berridge, George Maj. F., 19
Berry, Jacob Capt. H., Bedford, 144
Berry, Nicholas Lieut. F., Cornwall, 71
Berty, Edw. Capt. F., 25
Berty, Nicholas Capt. F., L. & W., 98
Berty, Sir Peregrine Col. H. & F., 24
Best, Cuthbert Capt. F., 58
Best, Matthew Cor. H., Wilts, 59
Best, Robert Lieut. H., Gloucester, 130
Best, Samuel Lieut. F., Worcester, 76
Best, Thomas Capt. F., York, 60
Bestoe, Othwell/Othowell Cor. H., Lincoln, 112
Betton, Richard Cor. Dr., L. & W., 110
Betts, William Capt. F., Bucks, 110
Betty, William Lieut. F., Radnor, 91
Bevan, Thomas David Capt. F., Carmarthen, 105
Bevan, Thomas Capt. F., Monmouth, 105. Reid believes this is the officer above.
Beverly, ___ Capt. F., Conyers Darcy, 49
Beverly, John Maj. F., Theophilus Gilby, 67
Beverly, John Cor. H., L. & W., 55
Beverly, Lenox Ens. F., L. & W., 28. I.O. does not give an arm of service, but the rank of ensign indicates foot.
Beverly, Thomas Capt. H., 55
Beverly, Thomas Capt. F., Chester, 92
Beversham, John Maj. H., L. & W., 10, 63, 124. The I.O. main text lists him under John Frechevile and Sir William Savile, but the index only lists him under Frechevile.
Beynon, Henry Capt. F., L. & W., 65
Beynon, John Lieut. F., Salop, 46
Bidlake, ___ Capt. F., Sir Nicholas Slanning, 128
Bidlake, Henry Capt. F., Sir Thomas Basset, 20. Possibly the Captain Bidlake above, as Basset took over Slanning's regiment after the latter's death
Bigg/Bigge, Richard, Chaplain, Wilts, 174

Bilbrough/Bilborough, Richard Sea Capt., Sir Matthew Boynton, York, 167
Bilborough/Bilborough, Thomas Capt. Lieut. F., York, 144
Bilby, ___ Capt. H., Lord Henry Cavendish, 36. Probably the Captain Bealby mentioned under Lord Mansfield: Mansfield and Cavendish were brothers.
Bilby, ___ Capt. H., Sir Francis Wortley, 154
Bill, ___ Maj. H., 134
Billet, William Capt. F., 24
Billing, Richard Quart. H., Lancaster, 55
Billing, Robert Quart. H., Cornwall, 54
Billingsly, Francis Col. F. (k. 1646; Bridgnorth), 25
Billingsly, Francis Maj. F., 25, 88. Not to be confused with Colonel Francis Billingsly. Major Billingsly was cited by an officer in Sir Lewis Kirke's foot, and also by an officer in Colonel Billingsly's foot.
Billingsly, George Capt. F., Warwick, 25
Bilton, Ralph Cor. H., York, 68
Bincks/Binks, Ambrose Ens. F., Durham, 85
Bingham, ___ Capt. F., stray, 165
Bingham, George Lieut. F., Somerset, 25
Bingley/Bingly, Oliver Capt. H., L. & W., 123
Bingly, John Capt. H., stray, 159
Binneck, Abraham Ens. F., Cornwall, 127
Binns/Binnes, John Cor. H., York, 29
Birch, Francis Capt. F., 110
Birch, John Capt. Lieut. H., Stafford, 93
Bird – *see also* Byrd
Bird/Byrd, Christopher Lieut. F., Lincoln, 127
Bird/Byrd, John Cor. H., Dorset, 77
Birssing, John Capt. F., 42
Birt – *see* Burt
Bis___, John Capt. H., 30
Bishop, Dannet Ens. F., Salop, 152
Bishop, Sir Edward Col. Dr. (d. 1649), 25
Bishop, Edward Capt. H., Salop, 49
Bishop, John Capt. F., Devon, John Digby, 50
Bishop, John Capt. F., L. & W., Lord Hawly, 76
Bishop, Richard Lieut. H., York, 124
Bishop, Thomas Lieut. H., York, 39
Bishop, William Ens. F., Salop, 144
Bishopp/Bishop, William Lieut. F., Salop, stray, 164
Bishoppe, John Capt. F., 37
Bishopp, John Capt. F., stray, 165
Bisse, Edward Col. H. & F. (will proved February 1647), 25
Bisse, George Capt. F., 131
Bissett/Bisset, Tristram Lieut. F., Devon, 20
Bissett/Bisset, Tristram Lieut. F., Cornwall, 20. Same regiment, and probably

the same man as above. Most likely a mistake in the original list.
Black – *see also* Blake
Black, John Cor. H., Cornwall, 129
Blackford, Daniel Quart. H., Warwick, 109
Blackmore, John Waggon Master, Devon, 170
Blackwell, John Quart. H., L. & W., 143
Blackwell, Marmaduke Quart. F., Durham, 30
Blackwell, Sir Thomas Col. F. (d. 1653), 25
Bladwell, ___ Capt. F., 65
Blague, Thomas Col. F., 25
Blake – *see also* Black
Blake/Black, George Capt. F., Somerset, 82
Blake, John Capt. F., Cornwall, 86
Blake, John Capt. F., L. & W., 86. The same regiment, and possibly the same man as above.
Blake, William Lieut. H., L. & W., 35
Blake, William Lieut. F., Cornwall, 13
Blakeston – *see also* Blaxton
Blakeston, ___ Capt. H., 136
Blakeston, ___ Capt. F., Sir William Pennyman, 113
Blakeston, ___ Capt. F., John Talbot, 135
Blakeston, Francis Lieut. H., York, 61
Blakeston, George Lieut. H., York, 119
Blakeston, Marmaduke Lieut. H., Durham, 148
Blakeston, Robert Capt. F., Durham, 135
Blakeston, Sir William Col. H., 26, 143. Of Archdeacon Newton, Durham; knighted in 1643. A quartermaster in Sir Walter Vavasor's regiment claims Blakeston as his senior officer; presumably Vavasor's unit served in Blakeston's brigade.
Blakeston, Sir William ___ H., 136. Of Gibside. Served under Sir Richard Tempest.
Blakeston, William Lieut. Col. H. (d. 1685), 26, 38, 164. Of Newton Hall, Durham. A distant cousin of Sir William of Archdeacon Newton (above), and served as his deputy. Later an MP for Durham. Also mentioned by a stray Cambridge lieutenant, and a lieutenant in Sir Hugh Cholmley's foot; the military connection between Blakeston and Cholmley is not clear.
Blanchard, William Lieut. H., York, 129
Bland, ___ Maj. H., 143
Bland, Christopher Ens. F., Durham, 85
Bland, Sir Thomas Lieut. Col. F., (d. 1657) 146
Blaney/Blayny, Edward Cor. H., L. & W., 64
Blashfield, Richard Capt. H., Hereford, 126
Blashford, Richard Cor. Dr., Southampton, 83
Blaxly, Lancelot/Blaxley, Laurence Ens. F., Northampton, 32
Blaxton/Blakeston, Benjamin, Chaplain, L. & W., 173
Blaume, Robert Quart. H., Essex, 105
Blaymyre/Blaymire, Robert Quart. H., Cumberland, 48

Index 201

Blayne, William Maj. H., 64
Blayny/Blayney, Andrew Capt. F., Montgomery, 78, 165. Claims under Edward Herbert, Lord Cherbury; also mentioned by a stray Montgomery ensign.
Blayney, John Col. Dr., 26. Lieutenant colonel to Sir Francis Mackworth.
Blechenden/Blechinden, Robert Lieut. F., Devon, 24
Blencow, Timothy Maj. F., 21, 28
Blenkensoppe/Blenkinsop, Jacob Capt. F., Newcastle, 68
Blenkhorn/Blenkhorne, John Lieut. H., Lincoln, 46
Blenkhorne, Robert Lieut. F., Stafford, 18
Blenkinsop, Francis Cor. H., Westmorland, stray, 159
Blewet, John Capt. F., 62
Blewet/Blewitt, William Capt. F., Devon, 13
Blewit/Blewitt, Valentine Capt. H., Cornwall, 81
Blewitt, Richard Capt. F., Cornwall, 14
Blewitt, Samuel Lieut. H., Cornwall, 82
Blight, John Capt. F., Cornwall, 15
Blight, John Cor. H., Cornwall, 78
Blight, Nevill Capt. F., 43
Blodwell, John Capt. F., 78
Blodwell, Nathaniel Ens. F., Montgomery, 78
Blodwell, Richard Ens. F., Denbigh, 55
Bluckmore, John Capt. F., 24
Bludd, ___ Capt. H., 51
Blumson, Thomas Quart. F., L. & W., 121
Blundell, Edmund Quart. H., L. & W., 21
Blunt, ___ Lieut. Col. H., 76
Blunt, ___ Maj. H., 120
Blunt, ___ Capt. F., 145
Blunt, Francis Capt. F., Hereford, 45
Blunt, John ___ H., 26. Blunt's single claiming officer mentions Major John Haslewood, who was in Sir Francis Mackworth's horse; possibly Blunt was also an officer in that regiment.
Blunt, John Capt. H., Sir James Hamilton, 74
Blunt, John Capt. H., stray, 160
Blunt, Nicholas Capt. F., 113
Blunt, Peter Capt. H., Worcester, 120
Blunt, Walter Ens. F., Stafford, stray, 165. Listed as a stray, but claims under Sir Richard Astly, a captain under Lord Loughborough.
Blunt, William Maj. F., 122
Blunt, William Capt. H., Oxon, 37
Boad, Nathaniel Cor. H., L. & W., 36
Boads, Charles Capt. H., stray, 160
Boat, Nicholas Quart. H., Surrey, 141
Bodington, George Quart. H., L. & W., Sir John Preston, 115
Boddington, George Quart. H., ___, Sir John Pate, 111. An addition from the errata;

I.O. gives no place of claim. Probably the man above.
Bodeley/Bodely, William Capt. F., L. & W., 18
Bodenham, ___ Maj. H., stray, 160
Bodenham Thomas Cor. H., Hereford, stray, 159
Bodenham, Sir Wingfield Col. H., 26
Body, George Ens. F., Somerset, 18
Bold, John Lieut. F., Nottingham, 57
Bold, Thomas Cor. H., Somerset, 119
Bold, William Lieut. F., L. & W., 127
Bolles – *see also* Bowles
Bolles, ___ Lieut. Col. H., 95
Bolles, Sir Charles ___ H. (d. 1661), 25, 26
Bolles, Richard Col. F. (k. 1643; Alton), 26
Bolt, James Maj. F., 54
Bomer, ___ Capt. H., 142
Boncle – *see* Bunkly
Bond, Abraham Lieut. H., Somerset, 151
Bond, Christopher Capt. H., Cornwall, 54
Bond, Ezekiel Ens. F., Cornwall, 24
Bond, John Ens. F., Devon, 127
Bond, John Ens. F., Essex, 97
Bond, Robert Cor. H., Oxon, Thomas Colepepper, 41, 159. Claims under Sir Thomas Colepepper, but also listed as a stray.
Bond, William Capt. F., Cornwall, 20
Bonny, George Quart. H., L. & W., 74
Bonust, Robert Cor. H., L. & W., 108
Bonvill/Bonvile, John Capt. F., Somerset, 18
Booker, Richard Capt. Lieut. H., Sussex, 14
Booker, William Quart. H., Lancaster, 117
Boone, Peter Capt. H., 35
Boone/Boon, William Capt. Lieut. F., L. & W., 138. Listed as a captain lieutenant in the main I.O. text, but only as a lieutenant in the index.
Booth, Beeston Capt. H., York, under 'Danby', 49
Booth, Beeston Cor. H., Lancaster, Sir Thomas Danby, 49
Booth, Charles Capt. F., Hereford, 42
Booth, Coningsby Capt. F., Salop, 42
Booth, John Capt. F., Hereford, 42
Booth, Ralph Capt. Lieut. H., Durham, 129
Booth, Richard Ens. F., Berks, stray, 165
Booth, Thomas Capt. F., Lincoln, 22
Booth, William Lieut. Col. H., 112
Booth, William Maj. F., 22
Bordman, John Ens. F., Lancaster, 40. Although I.O. does not give Bordman's arm of service, officers subsequent to him are listed as cavalry, making him foot by elimination. His rank as ensign confirms this.

Borlace, James Lieut. H., Cornwall, 26
Borlace, Nicholas Col. H., 26
Bosa, Samuel Col. Dr., 26
Bostock, ___ Capt. F., stray, 164
Bostock, Henry Capt. H., 92
Boswell, ___ Maj. H., 41
Boteler – *see* Butler
Bottomly, William Capt. F., Devon, 111
Bouck, Hercules Capt. Lieut. F., Durham, 30
Boughey, John Lieut. F., Stafford, 65
Boulcot, Joseph Lieut. F., Hereford, 143
Boult, John Ens. F., Northumberland, stray, 165
Bourne, Anthony Capt. F., Cambridge, 65
Bourne, Henry Capt. F. 'in Mount Edgecumbe', Devon, stray, 163
Bow/Bowes, John Lieut. F., Cumberland, 85
Bowbank, George Lieut. F., Durham, 53
Bowden, Edward Cor. H., Lincoln, 112
Bowden, Robert Sea Capt., L. & W., 167
Bowden, Thomas Lieut. F., Lincoln, 121
Bowen, Griffith Lieut. F., Carmarthen, 55
Bowen, John Cor. H., Montgomery, 32
Bowen, Owen Capt. F., Pembroke, 65
Bowen, Phillip Capt. F., Pembroke, 91
Bowen, Thomas Capt. H., 70
Bowen, William Lieut. F., Carmarthen, 113
Bower, Edmund Capt. H., 131
Bower, Jeremy Cor. H., York, 119
Bower, William Capt. F., Lancaster, 50
Bowerman, Andrew Quart. H., Devon, 115
Bowes, ___ Capt. H., 131
Bowes, Sir George ___ H. (k. 1643; Winceby), 27, 79. Mentioned by officers under Robert Brandling and George Heron
Bowes, Henry Cor. H., Newcastle, 100
Bowes, Ralph Capt. H. & F., Newcastle, 100
Bowes, William Capt. H., 120
Bowles – *see also* Bolles
Bowles, Francis Lieut. F., L. & W., 16
Bowman, ___ Capt. H., 111
Bowman, James Maj. F., 127
Bowyer, Thomas Quart. H., Derby, 57
Box, Thomas Capt. F., Devon, 24
Boynton, Sir Matthew Col. H. & F. (k. 1651; Wigan Lane), 27, 167. Boynton was killed in 1651, but it is unclear whether the men claiming under him did so from that period. Also mentioned by a naval officer.
Boys, Sir John Col. H. & F. (d. 1664), 26

Boys, John Capt. H., Somerset, 25
Boys, John Capt. H., 77
Bozoun, ___ Capt. H., 79
Brabant, ___ Capt. F., 138
Brabant, Ralph Lieut. H., Durham, 38
Brace, Francis Ens. F., Hereford, 45
Brace, James Lieut. F., Hereford, 42
Bradbury, H. Capt. F., 21
Bradbury, George Scoutmaster, Stafford, 172
Bradbury, Henry Maj. F., 10. Requests inclusion, but no officers claim so his regiment is unknown.
Bradbury, John Lieut. F., Derby, 57
Bradbury, Nicholas Quart. F., York, 147
Bradbury, Thomas Quart. H., Salop, 92
Braddor, John Regt. Quart. F., Dorset, 118
Bradford, Barnaby Capt. F., Hereford, 94
Bradgstow, Francis Capt. H., 99
Bradkirk, ___ Capt. F., 138
Bradley, Thomas Lieut. H., Lincoln, 26
Bradly, Edward Capt. F., York, 58
Bradly, Hillary Ens. F., Westmorland, 85
Bradly, James Capt. F., Lancaster, 138
Bradly, William Lieut. H., Westmorland, 90
Bradly, William Quart. H., York, stray, 160. Claims under Captain Francis Rearsby, possibly 'Captain Francis Reesby' of Ames Pollard's regiment who also claimed from York.
Bradsbury, Thomas Lieut. F., York, 146
Bradshaw, Edmund Lieut. F., L. & W., 33
Bradshaw, Edward Quart. H., Derby, stray, 160
Bradshaw, Francis Quart. H., Derby, 127
Bradshaw, James Capt. F., L. & W., 52
Bradshaw, John Capt. F., Carmarthen, 33
Bradshaw, Richard Capt. H., Lincoln, 46
Bradshaw, Robert Capt. H., Middlesex, 45
Bradshaw, Sir William Col. H., 27
Bradwood, John Cor. H., Cumberland, 137
Bragge/Bragg, John Capt. F., Somerset, 102
Braithwait, Thomas Capt. H., stray, 159
Bramble, Samuel Capt. F., Dorset, 102
Brampston, John Capt. H., Essex, 41
Brandling, ___ Maj. H., 90
Brandling, ___ Capt. H., Marquess of Newcastle, 108
Brandling, Charles Col. H., 27
Brandling, Francis Capt. H., Edward Grey, Northumberland, 72
Brandling, Ralph Maj. H., 28

Brandling, Robert Col. H., 27
Brandling, Robert Lieut. Col. F., 27
Brandling, Robert Capt. F., 27
Bransden/Brantsden, John Cor. H., Sussex, 70
Brathwayt/Brathwaite, Geo. Quart. H., Cumberland, 58
Bray, Anthony Ens. F., Cornwall, 70
Bray, Edward Capt. F., Surrey, 16
Bray, John Quart. H., Somerset, 53
Bray, Joseph Lieut. F., Cornwall, 19
Bray, Lodowick Scoutmaster, Nottingham, 172
Breakes/Breaks, Thomas Lieut. F., L. & W., 152
Brearcliffe/Brerecliffe, Stephen Lieut. H., York, 125
Brellisford, George Capt. F., L. & W., 98
Brent, ___ Capt. H., Earl of Carnarvon, 34
Brent, Edward Capt. H., Worcester, Sir William Russell, 120
Brent, George Lieut. H., Worcester, 120
Brereton, Henry Capt. F., 64
Brereton, Richard Capt. F., Chester, 31
Brett, Sir Edward [Capt.] H. (d. 1684), 121. I.O. gives no rank, but Brett was known to have been a captain in the Queen's Regiment. Knighted August 1644.
Brett, Henry Lieut. H., Somerset, 91
Brett, Ignatius Sea Capt., L. & W., 167
Bretton, John Capt. F., Middlesex, 146
Bretton, Robert Lieut. F., Middlesex, 31
Brewine/Bruine, Thomas Quart. H., Derby, 60
Brice, John Capt. H., Somerset, stray, 157
Brice, Worthington Capt. H., Devon, stray, 157
Bridgeman, ___ Lieut. Col. H., 17
Bridgeman, ___ Capt. F., 143
Bridgeman, John Lieut. F., Cornwall, 139
Bridges, George Capt. F., Somerset, 28
Bridges, Edward Capt. F., Somerset, 16
Bridges, Edward Quart. H., Wilts, 95
Bridges, Henry Cor. H., Bucks, 34
Bridges, Richard Capt. H., Bucks, 34
Bridges, Sir Thomas Col. H., 28
Bridges, Sir William Maj. F., 28
Bridges, William Cor. H., Kent, 120
Bridle, Francis Quart. H., Somerset, 76
Brigges/Briggs, Edward Ens. F., Glamorgan, 87
Brigges/Briggs, William Quart. F., Lincoln, 135
Briggnell/Brignell, John Capt. F., Durham, 136
Briggs, Edward Ens. F., Westmorland, 22
Briggs, Richard Capt. F., Gloucester, 57. *Mercurius Civicus* names him as 'Captain Richard Riggs' (TT E.43[10]).

Briggstock, Edward Quart. H., Surrey, 44
Brigham, Henry Lieut. H., York, 148
Brighouse, Tempest Capt. H., Nottingham, 136
Bright, ___ Capt. F., 51
Bright, William Capt. H., L. & W., 102
Bright, William Cor. H., Essex, 125
Brightman, Richard Capt. F., Nottingham, 31
Brince, Thomas Quart. H., Derby, stray, 160
Brinch Thomas Quart. H., York, 73
Brinfield, ___ Maj. H., 111
Brisby, Edw. Lieut. F., Cumberland, 88
Brisby, Edw. Lieut. F., Leicester, 88. The same regiment, and therefore possibly the same man as above.
Brisby, Richard Lieut. F., Cumberland, 60
Brisco/Briscoe, John Capt. F., L. & W., 19
Briscoe, George Capt. H., Cumberland, John Lamplaw, 89. Possibly the man below.
Briscoe, George Capt. H., Cumberland, Sir Christopher Lowther, 96
Bristol, [George Digby] 2nd Earl of, Col. H. (d. 1677), 28. Lord George Digby, who succeeded as Earl of Bristol in 1653.
Broad, Edmund Maj. H., 55
Broadhead, William Lieut. F., Nottingham, 67
Broadnax, Henry Capt. Dr., Surrey, 120
Broadway, Humphry Quart. H., Gloucester, 151
Brock, ___ Capt. F., stray, 165
Brock, Howard Capt. H., Derby, 57
Brock, Richard Ens. F., Lancaster, stray, 165
Brockden, George Quart. H., Devon, stray, 160
Brockden, Henry Capt. F., L. & W., 50
Brockhills/Brockholles, Thomas Capt. H., Lancaster, 27
Brockholls, John Capt. H., Lancaster, stray, 157
Brockholles, Thomas Capt. H., Middlesex, 121
Brocklesby, Thomas Ens. F., Lincoln, 25. I.O. gives no arm of service, but the rank of ensign indicates foot.
Bromfield, Edward Capt. H., Surrey, 41
Bromhall, John Cor. H., Salop, 28
Bromhead, ___ Capt. Dr., 125
Brook, Henry Lieut. H., L. & W., 36
Brook, John Lieut. H., Suffolk, 82
Brook/Brookes, William 'Conductor of the Train', L. & W., 170
Brookes, John Capt. H., Lancaster, 137
Brooking, John Capt. H., Devon, 77
Brooks/Brookes, John Capt. Lieut. H., Lancaster, 143
Broome, Andrew Capt. F., Lincoln, 98
Broome, Hugh Cor. H., York, 99
Broome, John Cor. H., Stafford, 30

Broome, Philip Quart. H., Somerset, stray, 160
Broster, Charles Ens. F., Chester, 64
Brotherton, John Quart. H., Lancaster, 31
Brough, Thomas Capt. H., Stafford, 89
Broughton, ___ Maj. H., 149
Broughton, Sir Edward Col. F. (k. 1665), 28. I.O. gives no arm of service for Broughton or the ensign who claimed under him, but the rank of ensign indicates foot, and Broughton is known as a foot officer. The ensign mentions another regimental officer, Timothy Blencow, who is also mentioned as a major under Richard Beard; Reid has taken this to mean that Beard took over Broughton's regiment at some point. This may indeed be the case, but unfortunately Reid offers no other source to support it. Tucker gives a full account of Broughton's service before, during and after the Civil War (pp.18-19). He served under his uncle, Colonel Robert Broughton, in Ireland in 1641; was knighted in 1663, 'died of wounds sustained in sea fight against the Dutch, 1665', and was buried at Westminster Abbey.
Broughton, George Capt. F., Devon, stray, 163
Broughton, Oliver Capt. F., Flint, 152
Broughton, Robert Col. F., 28. Uncle of Colonel Sir Edward Broughton.
Broughton, William Capt. F., Denbigh, 123
Broughton, William Capt. Dr., 61
Brown, ___ Capt. H., 86
Brown, Henry Capt. F., Dorset, 133
Brown, Henry Cor. Dr., Northumberland, 85
Brown, John Capt. H., L. & W., 48
Brown, John Lieut. F., Somerset, 119
Brown, Jonathan Ens. F., Dorset, 133
Brown, Ralph Lieut. F., L. & W., 122
Brown, Richard Capt. F., L. & W., 126
Brown, Robert Capt. F., Somerset, 79
Brown, Thomas Ens. F., Gloucester, 53
Brown, William Capt. F., L. & W., 88
Brown, William Cor. H., Surrey, 96
Brown, William Quart. H., York, 56
Brown, Valentine Lieut. Col. H., 48
Brown, Valentine Capt. H., L. & W., 48. Unlikely to be the lieutenant colonel above, as it seems implausible that he would claim as captain if he was later a more senior officer.
Browne, ___ Capt. H., 59
Browne, Sir Adam Col. H. (d. 1690), 29
Browne/Brown, Christopher Capt. H., York, 70
Browne/Brown, Edward Capt. F., Derby, 38
Browne/Brown, Francis Quart. H., L. & W., 35
Browne/Brown, George Lieut. H., L. & W., 77
Browne/Brown, George Lieut. F., L. & W., stray, 163

Browne/Brown, John Quart. H., L. & W., 64
Browne/Brown, Richard Jun. Capt. F., Norfolk, stray, 163
Browne/Brown, Sir Robert Capt. H., Northampton, 36
Browne/Brown, Stephen Lieut. H., Somerset, 131
Browne/Brown, Thomas Quart. H., Hereford, 143
Browne, William Ens. F., Surrey, 76
Browning, John Ens. F., Berks, stray, 165
Browning, Mark Capt. F., Devon, 24
Bruce, Francis Capt. F., Bedford, 103
Brudenell, John Capt. H., 32
Brunker, ___ Capt. F., 111
Brunly/Brundly, Francis Capt. H., Stafford, 33
Brydon, Jasper Lieut. F., Suffolk, 25
Brydon, John Ens. F., Suffolk, 75. Served in 1648.
Bryers, John Capt. H., L. & W., 143
Buchannon, George, Chaplain, L. & W., 173
Buchannon, Walter Cor. H., L. & W., 73
Buck, Brutus Col. F. (k. 1643; storming of Bristol), 29
Buckeridge, Ralph Ens. F., Salop, 17
Buckingham, [George Villiers] Duke of, Col. H. (d. 1687), 29. Buckingham's troop or regiment of horse, raised in 1648, participated in the Earl of Holland's ill-fated rebellion, in which Buckingham's younger brother Francis was killed.
Buckingham, William Lieut. H., Somerset, 115
Buckland, William Ens. F., Devon, 36
Buckly, ___ Capt. H., 130
Buckly, ___ Capt. F., 96
Buckly/Buckley, Benjamin Lieut. F., Salop, 45
Buckly, Ralph Quart. H., Stafford, stray, 161
Buckly, Richard Col. H. (k. 1650; Anglesey), 29. Properly, 'Bulkeley'. Killed by a rapier during an argument.
Buffing, John Quart. H., Somerset, 50
Bufkin/Buffkin, Lewin Maj. F., L. & W., 10, 155
Bull, Henry Capt. F., Somerset, 28
Bull, Henry Ens. F., Hertford, 109
Bull, John Lieut. F., Somerset, 131
Bull, Richard Capt. F., 28
Bull, Robert Ens. F., Somerset, 16
Buller, John Col. F., 29
Bullmer, ___ Capt. Dr., 149
Bullmer, William Capt. Dr., Bucks, 97
Bullmer, William Cor. H., York, 129
Bullock, Richard Quart. F., York, 146
Bullock, Robert Capt. Dr., York, 74
Bullock, Robert Quart. H., Nottingham, 63
Bullock, William Capt. H., Derby, 75

Bulloigne, Robert Capt. F., Oxon, 141
Bumpstead, John Regt. Quart. H., L. & W., 130
Buncombe, John Lieut. H., Somerset, 155
Bunkly, ___ Maj. H., 16. Sir Arthur Aston's horse. Probably Sebastian Bunkly.
Bunkly, Sir George Lieut. Col. H. (prisoner 1645, Naseby; d. in prison), 29. Properly, 'Boncle'. Lieutenant Colonel to Sir Arthur Aston's regiment of horse.
Bunkly, Sebastian Capt. H. (d. after 1651), 29. Properly, 'Boncle'. Commanded Sir Arthur Aston's horse regiment, after George Bunkly captured at Naseby.
Bunter, Thomas Lieut. H., Somerset, 53
Burchall, John Lieut. F., Berks, 31
Burchill, Richard Lieut. H., Chester, 147
Burck, Richard Capt. H., L. & W., 128
Burdall, Aaron Capt. F., stray, 164
Burden, Moyses Lieut. H., Warwick, 109
Burden, Reginald, Chaplain, Bucks, 174
Burdet/Burdett, Amery Cor. H., York, 129
Burge, John Quart. H., Somerset, 132
Burges, John Capt. F., 77
Burgess/Burgesse, Francis Col. F., L. & W., 9, 29, 82. Requests inclusion, and also claims under Sir Ralph Hopton. Two officers claim under him directly.
Burgesse, John Capt. F., L. & W., 41
Burgesse/Burges, Roger Lieut. Col. F., 29, 111. Sir John Owen's regiment. Two officers claim directly under Burgess; another as his lieutenant under Owen.
Burgh, Edward Capt. H., Somerset, 113
Burghill, Arthur Capt. F., 42
Burgoyn, Peter Capt. F., York, 103
Burleigh, Bernard/Barnard Capt. H., Southampton, 70
Burleigh/Burly, George Ens. F., L. & W., 127
Burre, Thomas Lieut. F., Kent, 75. Served in 1648.
Burrel/Burrell, Benjamin Capt. H., Cornwall, 23
Burrell, James Lieut. F., Cornwall, 54
Burrell, Redmain Maj. F., 57
Burrow/Burrough, Reynold Quart. H., Cornwall, 78
Burt, Edward Capt. F., Devon, 24
Burt/Birt, James Lieut. H., Dorset, 49
Burt/Birt, John Lieut. F., Somerset, 83
Burt/Birt, Thomas Quart. H., Dorset, 81
Burton, Bryan Ens. F., Lancaster, 68
Burton, Ralph Cor. H., York, 68
Burton, Richard Lieut. H., L. & W., 114
Burton, Richard Quart. H., L. & W., 74
Burton, Roger Quart. H., Salop, 44
Bury, Richard Cor. H., Bucks, 34
Busbridge, ___ Lieut. Col. H., 56
Busbridge, Joseph Capt. Dr., L. & W., 25

Busbridge, Robert Maj. H., 56
Busby, Thomas Capt. F., 75. Served in 1648.
Busfield, Thomas Capt. F., York, 89
Bush, Nicholas Ens. F., L. & W., 19
Bushel, William Capt. H., 45
Bushell, Walter Capt. H., 147
Bushy, Thomas Maj. F., 132
Buston, William Lieut. F., Durham 58
Butchard, Lionell/Lyonell Quart. H., Lancaster, 121
Butcher, John Lieut. H., Middlesex, 45
Butler, ___ Capt. H., 137
Butler, ___ Capt. F., Lord St. Albans, 122
Butler, ___ Capt. F., Sir Thomas Tyldesly, 138
Butler, Arnold Capt. F., 30. I.O. gives no arm of service for Butler or the ensign who cited him, but the rank of ensign indicates foot.
Butler, Hugh Capt. H., L. & W., 64
Butler, John Capt. F., L. & W., 144
Butler, John Col. F., 29
Butler, John Capt. F., Earl of Carbery, 33
Butler, John Capt. F., Rowland Laughorne, 91
Butler, John Capt. F., Warwick, stray, 163
Butler, Lamerock Cor. H., Glamorgan, 118
Butler, Miles Ens. F., L. & W., 138
Butler, Richard Lieut. H., Lancaster, 137
Butler, Thomas Col. F., 30. I.O. gives no arm of service for Butler or the ensigns who cited him, but the rank of ensign indicates foot.
Butler, Thomas Lieut. F., Lincoln, 138. Prisoner at Gainsborough, 28th July 1643 (TT E.61[22]); listed as 'Lieut. Thomas Boteler'.
Butler, Sir William Col. H. (k. 1644; Cropredy Bridge), 30
Butt, William Lieut. F., Cornwall, 71
Buttery, Christopher Ens. F., York, 122
Buttery, John Capt. F., Durham, 121
Buttman/Butman, Thomas Lieut. F., L. & W., 25
Button, Abell Quart. H., L. & W., 40
Button, John Quart. H., L. & W., 150
Button, Martin/Martyn Capt. H., L. & W., 84
Button, Miles Lieut. Col. F., 87
Button, William Capt. F., 83
Butts, Joseph Cor. H., Somerset, 81
Butts, Lewis Lieut. F., Norfolk, 124
Butts, William Capt. H., Somerset, 81
Buxton, William Capt. H. & Dr., L. & W., 81, 83. Served under Lord Hopton. Claimed as a captain of horse; mentioned as a captain of dragoons.
Byam, Francis Capt. H., Somerset, stray, 157
Byam, John Lieut. H., Somerset, 28

Byam, Laurence Lieut. H., Somerset, 19
Byam, William Capt. F., Somerset, 151
Bye, Ferdinando Lieut. F., Southampton, 110
Byerly, Anthony Col. F., 30
Byram, John Capt. F., 66
Byrd – *see also* Bird
Byrd, Francis Lieut. F., Berks, 132
Byrd, James Ens. F., York, 17
Byrd, John Cor. H., L. & W., 78
Byrd, Theophilus Lieut. H., L. & W., 16
Byron, Gilbert Lieut. Col. H., 30
Byron, Henry Capt. F., 104
Byron, [Sir John] Lord, Col. H. & F. (d. 1652), 30
Byron, Sir Nicholas Col. F. (d. 1648), 31. Uncle of Lord John Byron. Although I.O. does not give an arm of service, an officer of Byron's included in the errata is listed as a lieutenant of foot; and he is known to have led foot at Newbury I.
Byron, Sir Philip Col. F. (k. 1644; York), 31
Byron, [Richard] Lord, Col. H. & F. (d. 1679), 31
Byron, Robert Col. H. (d. 1664), 31. Governor of Liverpool.
Byron, William Maj. H., 30
Bywaters, Thomas Maj. F., L. & W., 10, 108
Cackett, William Ens. F., Kent, 138. Served in 1648.
Cade, John Capt. F., 16
Cade, John Quart. H., Nottingham, 21
Cade, Thomas, Chaplain, L. & W., 173
Caesar, John Capt. Lieut. H., L. & W., 95
Caethmayde, Thomas Lieut. F., Carmarthen, 42
Caipe, John Capt. F., stray, 165
Cake, Roger Lieut. H., Devon, 23
Calcot – *see* Colcott
Calendar, [James Livingston] 1st Earl of, Col. H. (d. 1674), 32
Callaham, ___ Lieut. Col. H., 134
Callcroft/Calcroft, Robert Capt. F., Lincoln, 80
Calthorpe, Ambrose Ens. F., L. & W., 138
Calverly, Robert Quart. H., York, 68
Calvert, John Lieut. F., York, 60
Calvert, Richard Cor. H., Lancaster, 85
Came, Thomas Lieut. H., Devon, 26
Campanet, Gilbert Quart. H., Kent, 100
Campden, Lord, Col. H. & F., 32. The cavalry officers claiming under 'Lord Cambden' could have served under Edward Noel, 2nd Viscount Campden (d. 1643) or his son Baptist Noel (d. 1682); both of whom were militarily active and both of whom were cavalry colonels. The foot officers probably served under the 2nd Viscount, who raised three foot regiments.
Campian, Arthur Cor. H., Devon, 78

Campian, John Quart. H., Bucks, 141
Campian, Josias Ens. F., Devon, 37
Campian, Sir William Col. H., 32
Caney, Richard Lieut. H., Stafford, 93
Canham, Simon Capt. F., L. & W., 35
Canne, William Ens. F., Cornwall, 71
Canner, John Quart. H., Gloucester, 124
Canning/Cannyng, Edmund Capt. H., Worcester, stray, 157
Cannon, James Capt. Lieut. F., Somerset, 44
Cannon, Peter Sea Capt. 'of the *Great Seahorse*, and *Antilope*', L. & W., 167
Cannyng, Endymion Capt. F., Rutland, 42
Cansfield, Sir John Col. H., 32, 121. Queen's Regiment of Horse. Three officers claim under him directly, and another claim him as their major under 'Lord St. Albans' (Henry Jermyn, the regiment's colonel). Reid lists Cansfield as a lieutenant colonel.
Cantloe, John Capt. F., Dorset, 79
Capel, [Arthur] Lord, Col. H. & F. (executed 1649), 32
Capell, John Capt. H., Middlesex, 45
Capplewood, William Ens. F., Stafford, 93
Carbery, [Richard Vaughan] 2nd Earl of, Col. H. & F. (d. 1686), 33
Cardiffe, Edmund Lieut. F., Lincoln, 78
Cardiffe, Lancelot Capt. F., L. & W., 33
Cardiffe, Thomas Col. F., L. & W., 9, 33, 153. Claims under the Marquess of Worcester; mentioned by three officers directly.
Cardiffe, Thomas Capt. F., 42
Cardinall, Thomas Capt. F., Lincoln, 53
Cardrow, Walter Lieut. H., Dorset, 141
Carew, George Capt. H., Worcester, 128. Served in 1651.
Carew, John Lieut. H., L. & W., Thomas Colepepper, 41
Carew, John Lieut. H., L. & W., ___ Layland, 91
Carleton, ___ Lieut. Col. F., 60
Carleton, John Cor. H., Cumberland, 30
Carleton, Nicholas Quart. F., Northumberland, 33
Carleton, Roger Maj. H., 148
Carleton, Thomas Capt. H., Cumberland, Lord John Byron, 30
Carleton, Thomas Capt. H., Col. Francis Carnaby, 34
Carleton, Sir William Col. F., 33. A 1648 regiment.
Carlisle, [James Hay] 2nd Earl of, Col. H. (d. 1660), 34
Carlisle, Francis Capt. H., L. & W., 56
Carlisle, John Ens. F., Lincoln, stray, 165
Carlos, William Col. H. & F. (d. 1689), 33. Carlos served under Thomas Leveson at Dudley Castle, then as governor of Lapley House in Staffordshire and of Tong Castle; captured December 1644, eventually released and went abroad. Joined the fugitive Charles II in 1651 and famously helped hide him in the oak tree at Boscobel.

Index

Carlos, William Capt. H., stray, 159
Carmigall/Carmighall, Thomas Cor. H., Durham, 41
Carnaby, ___ Capt. F., 149
Carnaby, Francis Col. H. (k. 1645; Sherburn-in-Elmet), 34
Carnaby, Ralph Col. H., 34
Carnaby, Ralph Capt. H., Northumberland, 34
Carnaby, Reignald Lieut. Col. H., 34
Carnaby, Richard Capt. H., Northumberland, 34
Carnaby, Thomas Maj. H., 34
Carnarvon, [Robert Dormer] 1ˢᵗ Earl of, Col. H. (k. 1643; Newbury I), 34
Carne, ___ Maj. F., 132
Carne, Edward Col. F., 34
Carne, Thomas Ens. F., Cornwall, 15
Carnes, ___ Capt. H., 103
Carnes, Bryan Lieut. F., Lancaster, 147
Carnock, John Maj. H., 72
Carnsew, James Lieut. F., Cornwall, 128
Carpenter, Edward Ens. F., Devon, 36
Carpenter, Walter Lieut. Dr., Cambridge, 83
Carr, Richard Capt. F., 18
Carre, ___ Lieut. Col. H., 74
Carre/Carr, Andrew Cor. H., Northumberland, 35
Carre/Carr, Ephraim Lieut. H., Northumberland, 58
Carre, Francis Lieut. Col. H., Sir Richard Dacres, 47
Carre, Francis Lieut. Col. H., Edward Grey, 72. Probably the Francis Carre listed above. Reid thinks so, although he offers no specific evidence. In 1663 Carre's name was 'delivered to be inserted' after the list was ready to go to print, and is only included in the errata (he was probably related to Maj. George Carre, below, whose name arrived at the same time). He is noted as serving under Grey, but no location is given for his claim.
Carre, George Maj. F., ___, 99. An addition from the errata; I.O. gives no place of claim. Probably related to Lieut. Col. Francis Carre, above.
Carre/Carr, John Capt. F., Durham, Sir William Carleton, 33
Carre, John Capt. F., Sir Robert Clavering, 39. Almost certainly the man above. Carre and his subordinate, Lieutenant Thomas Rountree, appear together in both Clavering's regiment and that of Sir William Carleton.
Carre/Carr, John Capt. F., Northumberland, Lord Widrington, 148
Carre/Carr, John Cor. H., L. & W., 115. Served in 1648 under Colonel John Poyer, so may be a former Parliamentarian.
Carre, Ralph Capt. F., 73
Carre/Carr, Ralph Lieut. F., Northumberland, 27
Carre/Carr, Ralph Quart. H., L. & W., 73
Carre, Sir Robert ___ H., 87
Carre, Robert Col. H., 35
Carre, Robert Capt. F., 80

Carre/Carr, William Capt. H., Northumberland, 72
Carrington, John Quart. H., York, 125
Carter, Francis Lieut. F., York, 133
Carter, John Capt. H., Gloucester, 143
Carter, Joseph Cor. H., Cumberland, 85
Carter, Robert Lieut. F., Devon, 24
Carter, Thomas Quart. F., L. & W., 53
Carter, William Quart. H., Hertford, 79
Carteret, Abraham Capt. F., 101
Carteret, Sir George Col. F. (d. 1680), 35. Lieutenant-Governor of Jersey. Knighted January 1645; commissioned as Vice-Admiral December 1644.
Carteret, Phil. Sea Capt., *Cavalier*, Frc. Sir John Pennington, Somerset (k. 1672; Solebay, naval battle), 167. What 'Frc' means is not known; as Carteret was a naval officer, it may be a printing error for 'Frg' ('Fregat'). Son of Sir George Carteret.
Carthy, Richard Ens. F., Monmouth, 94
Carts, Thomas Capt. H., 103
Cartwright, ___ Capt. F., Sir John Redman, 117
Cartwright, ___ Capt. F., Thomas Whittly, 147
Cartwright, Andrew Quart. H., Stafford, stray, 161
Cartwright, Francis Capt. Lieut. H., Nottingham, 31
Cartwright, John Cor. H., Worcester, 123
Cartwright, Matthew Quart. F., York, 122
Cartwright, Thomas Scoutmaster, Stafford, 172
Carty, Owen Lieut. F., L. & W., 120
Carus, ___ Capt. H., 137
Carus, Wilfrid Lieut. F., L. & W., 138
Carver, Thomas Capt. Lieut. F., Cornwall, 115
Carver, Walter Lieut. F., Somerset, 83
Carvis, ___ Lieut. Col. H., 103
Cary, ___ Capt. F., 53
Cary, Edmond ___ F., 35. I.O. gives no arm of service for Cary or the ensign who cited him, but the rank of ensign indicates foot.
Cary, Sir Edw. ___ F., stray, 165
Cary, Edw. Capt. F., 35
Cary, Edward Lieut. F., Devon, 35
Cary, George Ens. F., L. & W., 36
Cary, Sir Henry Col. H. & F., 9, 35, 71. Cary claimed under Sir Richard Greenvile, despite having his own regiment; it probably fell under Greenvile's purview.
Cary, Sir Horatio Col. H., L. & W., 9, 36, 119. Fought for Parliament until June 1643. Numerous officers claim directly under Cary; he claims under Prince Rupert.
Cary, John Lieut. H., L. & W., 86
Cary, Peter Cor. H., L. & W., 91
Cary, Theodore Col. F., L. & W., 9, 36, 72

Cary, Thomas Maj. H., 13
Cassada, Patrick Lieut. H., Durham, 68
Casson, Edward Capt. H., Norfolk, 97
Castle, George Capt. F., Bucks, 141
Casy, John Capt. H. 'in Oxon', L. & W., Sir Thomas Glenham, 68
Casy, John Capt. H., stray, 158
Catcher, John Capt. F., Cornwall, 140
Catchmay, ___ Capt. H., 149
Catesby, John Quart. H., Northampton, 25
Catesby, Richard Capt. Dr., Warwick, 84
Catherick/Cathericke, Robert Quart. H., Cumberland, 46
Catterell, Arthur Lieut. H., York, 99
Catterell, Edward Capt. H., York, 99
Cave, Henry Cor. H., L. & W., 40
Cave, Morgan Lieut. F., Dorset, 117
Cave, Robert Lieut. H., Berks, 37
Cave, William Lieut. F., Southampton, 24
Cavely, John Capt. Dr., Salop, 61
Cavendish, Charles Col. H. (k. 1643; Gainsborough), 36. His regiment was raised around his troop from the Prince of Wales's horse, and was known as The Duke of York's regiment. He was *not* Charles Cavendish, Lord Mansfield (*see*), the eldest son of the Marquess of Newcastle; or Newcastle's younger brother Charles, who shared exile with the Marquess in 1644.
Cavendish, Lord Henry Col. H. (d. 1691), 36. Younger son of the Marquess of Newcastle. His older brother Charles, Lord Mansfield (*see*), also commanded a cavalry regiment. Henry succeeded as Viscount Mansfield when Charles died in 1659, therefore men claiming under 'Mansfield' may have been referring to either brother.
Cavendish, William – *see* Marquess of Newcastle
Cawarden/Carwarden, Thomas Capt. F., Hereford, 126
Cawdron, Anthony Cor. H., Lincoln, 36
Cawsey, John Capt. F., Lancaster, 60
Cayford, John Provost Marshall, Somerset, 171
Cayley, Sir Arthur ___ H., 88
Caywood, John Capt. H., 32
Cecil/Cecill, Jonathan Regt. Quart. H., Somerset, 113
Chaderton/Chadderton, Francis Lieut. F., York, 69
Chadwick, Anthony Cor. H., Nottingham, stray, 159
Chaloner/Challoner, Francis Quart. H., L. & W., 124
Challoner, Anthony Ens. F., L. & W., 61
Challoner, Frederick Capt. Dr., York, 99
Challoner, Henry Ens. F., Northumberland, 148
Challoner, Robert Capt. F., 61
Chamberlain, ___ Lieut. Col. H., 133
Chamberlain, Robert Ens. F., L. & W., 98

Chamberlain, Thomas Capt. H., Oxon, 146
Chamberlain, William Col. H., L. & W., 71
Chamberlain, William Cor. H., Dorset, 95
Chamberlaine/Chamberlain, John Cor. H., L. & W., 84
Chamberlane, William ___ F., 33
Chamberlayn, Joshua/Chamberlain, Josua Capt. H., Devon, 23
Chamberlayn/Chamberlain, William Col. H., L. & W., 9, 72
Chambers, ___ Capt. F., 106
Chambers, James Cor. H., Lincoln, 125
Chambers, John Ens. F., York, 22
Chambers, John Capt. Comptroller, L. & W., 170
Chambers, Matthew Cor. H., Durham, 56
Chambers, Robert Cor. H., Westmorland, 36
Chambers, William Lieut. F., Cumberland, 106
Chambers, William Lieut. F., Essex, 156
Champernon, Philip Col. H., 37. Lieut. Col. to Prince Maurice's Foot.
Champion, John Quart. H., L. & W., 30
Champnes, John Cor. H., Somerset, 36
Chandois, [George Brydges] Lord, Col. H. & F. (d. 1655), 37
Channyn, Mich. Quart. H., L. & W., 91
Chaplin, ___ Capt. F., 126
Chappel, ___ Maj. H., 47
Chappel, John Capt. H., 47
Chapman, Edmund Col. H., L. & W., 9, 32
Chapman, Henry Capt. F., Somerset, 28
Chapman, John Ens. F., Lincoln, 97
Chapman, Richard Capt. F., L. & W., 16
Chapman, Simon Capt. H., Somerset, 95
Chapman, William Lieut. H., York, 125
Chanon, William Capt. F., Devon, 13
Chantrell, Robert Lieut. F., Chester, 65
Charbo, Charles Capt. H., 121
Charlesworth, Thomas Quart. H., L. & W., 56
Charleton, Sir Edward ___ H. (d. 1675), 148, 160. Mentioned by two officers under Sir Edward Widrington, and a stray quartermaster.
Charlton, Richard Quart. H., Northumberland, 28
Charley, Walter Quart. H., Lancaster, 103
Charnock, ___ Capt. F., 21
Charnock, Thomas Quart. H., L. & W., 114
Charter, Alexander Capt. Dr., 45
Chattris, William Cor. H., Northampton, 32
Chauke, Jacob Capt. H., L. & W., 36
Cheator, Henry Col. F. (k. 1644; Marston Moor), 38
Cheator, Nicholas Col. F., 53
Chegwin, Thomas Ens. F., Cornwall, 15

Chesman, John Lieut. H., Northumberland, 146. Claimed as a horse officer, but served in Henry Washington's dragoons.
Chester, ___ Capt. Dr., 149
Chester, Henry Col. H. & F., 9. Requests inclusion, but no officers claim.
Chesterfield, [Phillip Stanhope] Earl of, Col. F. (d. 1656), 38
Chetmell, Arthur Lieut. F., Dorset, 14
Chichester, Henry Capt. F., 14. I.O. does not give Chichester's arm of service in the main list, but the officer who claims under him is indexed as a foot officer.
Chicken, George Quart. H., Durham, 155
Chilcot, John Capt. Dr., 49
Child, James Lieut. Dr., York, 125
Chiles, Edw. Cor. H., Warwick, 18
Chilton, John Quart. H., Durham, 108
Ching, George Quart. H., Devon, 78
Chipchase, Thomas Ens. F., Durham, 80
Chippingdale, Francis Capt. H., Lincoln, 56
Chippingdale, John Capt. H., L. & W., Sir Robert Dallison, 48
Chippingdale, John Capt. H., Ralph Eure, 56
Chisnall, Edward Col. H. & F., 38. A 1648 regiment.
Chock, Sir Francis Capt. H., 79
Cholmeley/Cholmely, Richard Capt. H., Durham, 21
Cholmly, Sir Hugh Col. H. & F. (d. 1657), 38
Cholmly, James Capt. F., Durham, 38
Cholmly, Sir Richard Col. F. (k. 1644; Axminster), 39. Son-in-law of Lord Paulet, whose regiment he was killed leading in 1644.
Cholmondly, [Robert, 1ˢᵗ Viscount], Col. H. (d. 1681), 39. Known as 'Lord Cholmondly'.
Chowles, John Lieut. F., Middlesex, 44
Christopher, Thomas Lieut. F., Dorset, 15
Christopher, William Provost Marshall, Cornwall, 171
Chudleigh, ___ ___ ___. The ensign who claims under 'Chudleigh' intended either Sir George Chudleigh or his son James, both of whom initially fought for Parliament. It is most likely that he intended James, who fought under the King as a foot colonel until his death at Dartmouth in October 1643.
Church, ___ Capt. H., 35
Church, Thomas Ens. F., Chester, 101. I.O. does not give an arm of service, but the rank of ensign indicates foot.
Churchhill/Churchill, Matthew Cor. H., Dorset, 50
Churchman, William, Chaplain, Salop, 174
Churnel/Churnell, Francis Lieut. F., Cumberland, 22
Chute, George Col. H., 39
City of Oxford Regiment – *see* Sir Nicholas Sellwyn and William Legge
Clance, ___ Capt. H., 106
Clancy, Hugh Lieut. H., Southampton, 150
Clapp, ___ Maj. F., 131
Clapp/Clap, John Ens. F., Devon, 131

Clare, Francis Capt. F., Worcester, 124
Clark, ___ Lieut. Col. H., 59
Clark, ___ Maj. H., Earl of Cleveland, 40
Clark, ___ Maj. H., Richard Manning, 100
Clark, ___ Maj. F., 118
Clark, ___ Capt. H., Sir John Digby (of Gayhurst), 51
Clark, Abraham Capt. F., 43
Clark/Clarke, Alexander Chirurgion, L. & W., 172
Clark, Edw. Capt. F., 126
Clark, Francis Capt. F., 131
Clark/Clarke, Hancock Quart. H., Dorset, 151
Clark, Henry Maj. H., stray, 160
Clark, Henry Lieut. H., L. & W., 36
Clark, John Capt. H., Cornwall, 84
Clark, John Capt. Lieut. H., Worcester, 37
Clark, John Ens. F., Cornwall, 20
Clark, John Quart. H., Wilts, stray, 160
Clark, John Chirurgion, Cornwall, 173
Clark, Ralph Capt. F., 16
Clark, Richard Quart. H., Somerset, 113
Clark, Roger Quart. H., Lincoln, 32
Clark, Thomas Capt. F., 25
Clark, Thomas Quart. H., Dorset, 40
Clark, Thomas Quart. H., Wilts, stray, 160
Clarke, ___ Capt. H., 109
Clarke/Clark, James Lieut. H., L. & W., 128
Clarke/Clark, John Quart. H., Lincoln, stray, 160
Clarke, Thomas Capt. H., Middlesex, 114
Clarke/Clark, William Capt. H., Dorset, 77
Clarkson, Thomas Lieut. H., Lancaster, stray, 158
Claughton, James Capt. F., Northampton, 108
Claughton, William Lieut. F., Northampton, 108
Clavering, ___ Capt. H., 136
Clavering, Sir Robert Col. H. & F. (d. 1644), 39
Clavering, Thomas Capt. H., Durham, 39, 61. Mentioned by a quartermaster under Sir Robert Clavering, then claimed in his own right under Colonel John Forcer (who took over the regiment after Sir Robert's death).
Claxton, John Capt. H., L. & W., 108
Clay, Samuel Quart. Dr., Nottingham, stray, 166
Clay, William Quart. H., Derby, 120
Claypoole, William Cor. H., Lincoln, stray, 159
Clayton, Henry Col. F., 40
Clayton, John Lieut. Pioneers, Lancaster, 172
Clayton, John Cor. H., York, 101
Clayton, Richard Quart. H., L. & W., 28

Clayton, William Lieut. H., Stafford, 130
Cleaver, John Lieut. F., L. & W., 88
Cleere, John Lieut. F., Southampton, 150
Clement, John Ens. F., Northampton, stray, 165
Clement, William Capt. H., York, 127
Clench, George, Chaplain, Somerset, 174
Clennell, William Quart. H., Northumberland, 148
Clerk, Sir Francis Col. F. (d. 1686), 40. A 1648 regiment.
Cleveland, [Thomas Wentworth] 1ˢᵗ Earl of, Col. H. (d. 1667), 40
Cleves/Clecves, Henry Quart. H., Dorset, 77
Cliffe, Daniel Ens. F., York, 38
Clifford, John Lieut. F., Dorset, 143
Clifton, ___ Lieut. Col. F., stray, 165
Clifton, ___ Capt. H., 121
Clifton, Cuthbert Col. H. & F. (d. 1645), 40. Governor of Liverpool. Captured when it fell in 1645, and died in prison.
Clifton, Francis Capt. H., 104
Clifton, Gervase Capt. H., Lancaster, 137
Clifton, Gervase Cor. H., Lancaster, 104
Clifton, Thomas Quart. H., Lancaster, 104
Close, William Quart. H., Durham, 121
Clough, Francis Ens. F., York, 60
Clough, George Maj. F., 133
Clough, Robert Quart. H., York, 125
Clyes, Ralph Ens. F., Cornwall, 70
Coates/Cotes, John Lieut. F., L. & W., 35
Cobb, Sir Francis Capt. H./Col. F., 40, 119. Sir Francis Cobb of Burnham (later Ottringham; d. 1648) had a son, also Sir Francis Cobb (d. 1666); it is unclear whether the two instances of the name in I.O. refer to father or son, or both. One of them commanded the garrison of Clifton Tower at York.
Cobb, James Cor. H., L. & W., 45
Cobbe, Sir Francis ___ H., 119
Cock, John Ens. F., Cornwall, 72
Cock, Maugan Lieut. F., Cornwall, 122
Cock, Philip Ens. F., Cornwall, 144
Cocker, Edward Ens. F., L. & W., 21
Cockram, Roger Ens. F., Devon, 36
Codling, John Quart. H., Lincoln, stray, 160
Coe, Thomas Maj. F., 115
Coffin, Thomas Capt. F., L. & W., 115
Coghland, John Capt. F. 'at Sea and Land', Cornwall, stray, 163
Cokayn, William Capt. H., 24
Cokayne, William 'Scout Master Gen. & Quart. Gen.', Devon, 172
Coke, Edward Lieut. H., L. & W., 97
Coker, Sir Henry Col. H., 40, 79 (d. 1681). Three men cite Coker as their officer under

the Marquess of Hertford, and six claim under him directly.
Colborne, ___ Maj. H., 109
Colby, William Capt. H., Rutland, 98
Colche, ___ Capt. F., 152
Colcott/Calcot, Arthur Ens. F., L. & W., 52
Cole, Charles Cor. H., L. & W., 133
Cole, John Capt. F., 69
Cole, Sir Nicholas Col. H., 41
Cole, Richard Capt. H., Sir Francis Anderson, 13
Cole, Richard Capt. H., Sir Nicholas Cole, 41
Cole, Richard Capt. H., James King (Lord Eythin), 87
Cole, Thomas Ens. F., Salop, 53
Cole, William Maj. F., 31
Colebrand, Sir James ___ H., 82
Colebrand, William Capt. F., Essex, 130
Colebrooke, John Lieut. F., Southampton, 110
Coleman/Colman, Henry Quart. H., L. & W., 50
Coleman/Colman, Thomas Quart. H., Hereford, 153
Colepepper, Sir Thomas Col. H. & F., 41, 159
Coles, John Capt. Lieut. F., L. & W., 114
Coles, Laurence Lieut. F., L. & W., 105
Colles, ___ Maj. H., 133
Colles/Coles, Charles Capt. Lieut. F., L. & W., 93
Colles, Edmund Lieut. F., Worcester, 145
Colles, Francis Capt. F., Stafford, 93
Colles, John Capt. H., L. & W., 149
Colles, Richard Ens. F., Southampton, 110
Colles, Thomas Quart. H., L. & W., 62
Colles, Walter Lieut. F., Worcester, 124
Colles, William Lieut. F., Gloucester, 133
Colley/Colly, Lancelot Cor. H., L. & W., 137
Collier – *see also* Collyer
Collier, Christopher Ens. F., Cornwall, 104
Collier, Francis Capt. Lieut. H., Stafford, Lord Aston, 17
Collier, Francis Capt. F., Harvey Bagott, 18. Possibly the Francis Collier above, who claimed under Lord Aston, as both Bagott's and Aston's regiments were part of the Lichfield garrison.
Collier, James Capt. F., Lancaster, 138
Collier, Richard Lieut. H., Stafford, 93
Collinder, Edward Cor. H., Dorset, 115
Colling/Collings, Samuel Lieut. H., Bedford, 60
Collingridge, Richard Quart. Gen. H. (Brigade), Bucks, 51
Collings, George Capt. F., Cornwall, 14
Collingson, John Lieut. F., York, 38
Collingwood, John Capt. F., Northumberland, 27

Index

Collingwood, John Cor. H., Northumberland, 61
Collins, ___ Maj. Gen. F., 35
Collins, Barnaby Ens. F., Dorset, 51
Collins, Degory Maj./Col. F., 9, 41, 82. Mentioned as a major in Sir Ralph Dutton's foot; claimed as a colonel under Lord Hopton. Also mentioned directly by several other officers, although his rank is not given. I.O. indexes as colonel.
Collins, Edward Cor. H., Somerset, 50
Collins, Edward Ens. F., Cornwall, 33
Collins, George Maj. F., Sir Richard Grenvile, 72
Collins, George Maj. F., stray, 165. Mentioned by a stray Cornish ensign, therefore possibly the officer above, as Grenvile served in Devon and Cornwall.
Collins, John Lieut. F., Somerset, 135
Collins, John Ens. F., Cornwall, 35
Collins, Thomas Lieut. Col. F., L. & W., 9, 41
Collins, Walter Lieut. F., Worcester, 121
Colliver, Stephen Lieut. F., Cornwall, 122
Collyer/Collier, John Capt. Dr., Worcester, 74
Colmer, Edward Lieut. F., Cornwall, 44
Colquit, Francis Lieut. F., Cornwall, 140
Colster, ___ Capt. H., 97
Colston, Daniel Lieut. H., L. & W., 107
Colston, John Lieut. F., Southampton, 110
Colston, Thomas Cor. H., York, 62
Colt, ___ Capt. H., Sir John Pettus, 113
Colt, Henry ___ H., 41. Rank not given. Mentioned by one officer claiming from Gloucester under a captain of Colt's.
Colt, Henry Capt. H., Sir William Russell (of Strensham), 120
Colthorpe, ___ Capt. Dr., 146
Colvell, Adam Capt. Lieut. Dr., Durham, 26
Colverly, Peter Lieut. H., Devon, 82
Combe, Henry Lieut. F., Somerset, 28
Combe, John Ens. F., Somerset, 28
Combe, Matthew Ens. F., L. & W., 103
Comberford, Thomas Col. H., 41
Combes, ___ Capt. H., 59
Combes, William Quart. H., Somerset, 151
Comer, John Cor. H., Devon, 26
Comings, Peter Ens. F., Devon, 24
Compton, ___ Capt. H., 24
Compton, John Quart. F., Salop, 18
Compton, Sir Charles Capt. H. (d. 1661), 109. Brother of James, 3rd Earl of Northampton.
Compton, Sir William Capt. H./Col. F. (d. 1663), 42, 110. Mentioned by three first civil war cavalry officers, under his brother James, 3rd Earl of Northampton;

raised his own foot regiment in 1648.
Condon, William Cor. H., L. & W., 106
Conell/Conel, Jeffery Capt. H., Monmouth, 71
Coningsby, ___ Capt. ___, 35
Coningsby, ___ Capt. H., 71
Coningsby, Fitzwilliam Col. H. (d. 1666), 42. Hereford garrison.
Coningsby, Fitzwilliam Lieut. F., Hereford, 16, 94. Claimed at Hereford as a lieutenant of foot under Lord Astley, and also as a captain of foot under Sir Henry Lingen. Available genealogical records indicate only one Fitzwilliam Coningsby, suggesting he may also be the cavalry colonel above.
Coningsby, [Humphrey] Lieut. Col. H. (d. 1671), 42. Son of Fitzwilliam Coningsby, MP. his first name is not given in I.O., however this man was deputy to Fitzwilliam, who is known to have employed his son Humphrey as his lieutenant colonel (Newman, *Old Service*, p.111).
Coningsby, Humphry Capt. H., Somerset, 151
Coningsby, Robert Lieut. H., L. & W., 44
Coningsby/Conyngsby, Thomas Lieut. Col. F., Hereford, 9, 16. Possibly Thomas, second son of Fitzwilliam Coningsby, whose three sons Humphrey, Thomas and Henry all fought for the King (Newman, *The Old Service*, p. 111).
Coningsby, William Ens. F., L. & W., 120
Conner, Charles Lieut. Dr., L. & W., 81
Connock, John Col. F., 42
Connock, John Maj. H., 130. Reid believes this is the man listed above.
Conquest, Charles Capt. H., L. & W., stray, 157
Conquest, Richard Capt. H., 42, 108. Mentioned without regiment by an officer from Bedford, then by another man from Durham serving under Richard Neville.
Consett, John Capt. H., York, 92
Constable, ___ Lieut. Col. H., 148
Constable, Edward Capt. H. & Advocate General, L. & W., 90
Constable, George Cor. H., York, 68
Constable, Peter Lieut. H. York, 90
Constable, Ralph Maj. H., York, 10, 90
Conway, William Lieut. F., Flint, stray, 164
Cony, Richard Maj. ___, 88
Conyers, ___ Capt. H., 52
Conyers, Cuthbert Col. F. (k. 1644; Malpas), 42
Conyers, Henry Capt. F., Durham, 135
Conyers, Henry Cor. H., L. & W., 30
Conyers, John Cor. H., Durham, 79
Conyers, Thomas Maj. Dr., 10. Requests inclusion, but no officers claim, so his regiment is unknown.
Conyers, Thomas Lieut. F., York, 49
Conyers, William Lieut. H., Durham, 147
Cooban, William Quart. H., Lancaster, 40
Cook/Cooke, Andrew Lieut. Dr., Salop, 75

Cook/Cooke, Anthony Quart. H., Somerset, 79
Cook, Francis Col. H. & F., 43
Cook/Cooke, John Quart. H., Wilts, 79
Cook/Cooke, Richard Cor. H., Hereford, 94
Cook/Cooke, Robert Lieut. H., Southampton, 59
Cooke, ___ Capt. H., 90
Cooke, Edw. Capt. F., 140
Cooke, Edward Lieut. F., L. & W., 84
Cooke, George Capt. H., 88
Cooke/Crooke, Henry Capt. Lieut. H., Wilts, 40
Cooke, Humphry Capt. H., 41
Cooke, John Capt. H., 100
Cooke, Jonathan Capt. H., Warwick, 95
Cooke, Nathaniel Lieut. F., Cornwall, 15
Cooke, Thomas Capt. F., 122
Cooke, William Lieut. H., York, 108
Cooling, Bartholomew Capt. H., York, 102
Cooling, George Quart. H., Nottingham, 102
Cooling, Godfrey Lieut. H., L. & W., 102
Cooly, Anthony Lieut. F., L. & W., 44
Cooper – *see also* Couper
Cooper, Bryan Capt. F., Lancaster, 137
Cooper, George Ens. F., Kent, 102. I.O. does not give an arm of service, but the rank of ensign indicates foot.
Cooper, Hugh Cor. H., Lincoln, stray, 159
Cooper, John Capt. F., 51
Cooper, John Lieut. H., York, 92
Cooper, Michael Ens. F., Nottingham, 51
Cooper, Roger Cor. H., L. & W., 114
Cooper, William Quart. H., Montgomery, 71
Coot, John Capt. H., 22
Cope, Thomas Cor. Dr., Lincoln, 146
Copeland, Laurence Quart. H., York, 115
Copley, George Lieut. F., Middlesex, 124
Copley, John Capt. H., 125
Coppleston, ___ Maj. F., 36
Corbet, William Lieut. Dr., Salop, 84
Corbett, John ___ F., 43
Corbett, Richard Capt. Dr., Salop, 75
Corbett, Thomas Capt. F., 94
Corbett, Sir Vincent Col. H. & Dr. (d. 1656), 43
Corbyne, Robert Cor. Dr., Dorset, 45
Cordwayne/Cordwayn, Thomas Lieut. F., L. & W., 98
Cordwell, Richard Quart. H., Huntingdon, 141
Corney, Edward Ens. F., Lancaster, 138

Corney, Richard Capt. H., L. & W., 149
Cornwall, Edward Capt. H., Hereford, 126
Cornwall, Gilbert Capt. H., Hereford, 116
Cornwall, Humphry Capt. F., 45
Cornwall Humprey Capt. F., Hereford, 45, 94. Mentioned by an ensign under Sir William Crofts; claimed in his own right under Sir Henry Lingen.
Cornwallis, Francis Maj. H., 10. Requests inclusion, but no officers claim, so his regiment is unknown.
Cornwallis, ___ Maj. Dr., 81
Cornwallis, Francis Capt. H., 42
Cornwallis, John Cor. H., Middlesex, 42
Cornwallis, Thomas Lieut. H., L. & W., 42
Corpes, Edward Lieut. F., York, 19
Corpes, James Ens. F., York, 113
Cory, Andrew Capt. F., Cornwall, 71
Cory, Degory Lieut. H., L. & W., 30
Cory, Nicholas Quart. H., Cornwall, 106
Cory, Thomas Capt. F., Norfolk, 99
Cory, William Lieut. F., Middlesex, 118
Coryton, John ___ F. (d. 1680), 24. Son of William Coryton. Served under Sir John Berkeley, but later commanded his own regiment (THoP). Reid states that he was a lieut. col. under Berkeley, but does not give his source.
Coryton, William Col. F. (d. 1651), 43
Coster, John Quart. H., Gloucester, 17
Coswarth, John Maj. F., 50
Cotes, William Capt. Lieut. H., York, 98
Cotham, Henry 'Conductor of the Train', L. & W., 170
Cotterell, ___ Capt. F., 65. Possibly Sir Charles Cotterell.
Cotterell, Sir Charles, ___ F. (d. 1701), 65
Cotterell, Francis Ens. F., Derby, 103
Cotterell John Capt. F., L .& W., 33
Cottle, ___ Capt. F., 139
Cottle, Bernard Cor. H., Devon, stray, 159
Cottle, Simon Capt. H., stray, 159
Cotton, Charles Lieut. H., Middlesex, 79
Cotton, Francis Ens. F., Somerset, 132
Cotton, John Cor. H., Middlesex, 114
Cotton, John Cor. H., York, 142
Cotton, Thomas Quart. H., Stafford, 60
Cotton, William Capt. H., Stafford, 149
Cottrell, Simon Capt. H., 50
Couch, Richard Ens. F., Cornwall, 50
County, Peter Capt. H., 91
County/Countye, Peter Capt. H., Devon, 23
Couper/Cooper, Thomas Commissary, Surrey, 169

Court, Edward Capt. H., Somerset, 23
Court, Henry Lieut. H., Somerset, 23
Courtenay, James Quart. H., Wilts, 44
Courtenay, Sir Peter Col. F., 43, 71. Knighted June 1642, York.
Courtenay, Peter Capt. F., Cornwall, John ('Jack') Arundell, 14
Courtenay, Peter Capt. F., Cornwall, Richard Arundell, 15
Courtenay, Reskemmer Capt. F., Cornwall, 14
Courtenay, Sir William Col. H. & F. (d. 1702), 43. Of Powderham. Reid notes that a number of the men listed under his name were in fact probably ex-Irish veterans claiming under Sir William Courtney of Boggatt, in Hampshire.
Courtenay, William Lieut. H., Cornwall, 14
Cousins/Cousines, Andrew Lieut. F., Wilts, 131
Cousins/Cousines, John Quart. H., Dorset, 126
Covell/Coven, Allen Sea Capt., L. & W., 167
Covely, Sir Hugh ___ F., 44
Coventry, John Col. F. (d. 1652), 44
Covert, John Col. H., 44
Cowle, Henry Capt. H., Northumberland, 148
Cowles, Richard Capt. F., Monmouth, 153
Cowles, Richard Capt. Pioneers, Monmouth, 171
Cowles, William Lieut. F., L. & W., 132
Cowling, George Lieut. F., Gloucester, 143
Cowling, Phillip Lieut. F., Cornwall, 139
Cowling, Robert Ens. F., York, 86
Cowling, Thomas Lieut. F., 139
Cownly, William Capt. H., L. & W., 40
Cowsly, ___ Capt. H., 80
Cox, Alexander Lieut. F., L. & W., 101
Cox, Charles Maj. H., 126
Cox, Francis Lieut. F., Somerset, 28
Cox, Griffith Capt. H., L. & W., 40
Cox, Henry Lieut. H., L. & W., 126
Cox, Humphry Lieut. H., Dorset, 119
Cox, John Quart. F., Dorset, 28
Cox, Lyndley Lieut. H., Somerset, 131
Cox, Nicholas Lieut. F., Somerset, 83
Cox, Patrick Capt. F., 67
Cox, Philip Cor. H., Somerset, 45
Cox, Richard Ens. F., L. & W., 21
Cox, Roger Ens. F., Hereford, 94
Cox, Thomas Lieut. H., Wilts, 49
Cox, Thomas Lieut. F., L. & W., 83
Cox, William Quart. H., Somerset, 141
Coxhead, ___ Capt. H., 29
Coxhead, Thomas Lieut. H., L. & W., 99

Coxhead, William Capt. H., Lincoln, 99
Coxwell, John Capt. H., Gloucester, 53
Coyesgarne, William Capt. F., Cornwall, 72
Coyney, Thomas Lieut. H., Stafford, 44
Crabbe/Crabb, John Lieut. F., Cornwall, 71
Cracroft, ___ Capt. F., 138
Cracroft/Craycroft, John Capt. Lieut. H., 48
Craddock/Cradock, John Ens. F., Glamorgan, 154
Cradock, Richard Capt. F., Glamorgan, 34
Cradock, William Cor. H., Durham, 54
Crafford, John Lieut. F., L. & W., 92
Craister, George Capt. F., Northumberland, 73
Craithorne, ___ Maj. H., 61
Cranbury, William Ens. F., Kent, 51
Crane, Henry Lieut. H., Northampton, 63
Crane, Sir Richard Lieut. Col. H. (k. 1645; Bristol), 44
Crane, Richard Cor. H., L. & W., 109
Crane, Valentine Lieut. H., Norfolk, 144
Crane, William Lieut. H., Middlesex, 50
Crasfield – *see* Crossfield
Craw, Thomas Capt. F., 100
Crawford, George Quart. H., York, 143
Crawford, [Ludovic Lindsay] 16th Earl of, Col. H. (d. 1652), 44
Crawhall, John Lieut. H., Durham, 26
Craythorn, Thomas Capt. H., 39
Craythorne, ___ Lieut. Col. Dr., 117
Craythorne, Edmund Capt. F., York, 144
Creech, Henry Ens. F., Somerset, 28
Creeche, Edward Cor. H., L. & W., 143
Cresheld, Arthur Lieut. F., L. & W., 31
Cresset/Cressett, Edward Capt. F., Salop, 153
Cresswell, ___ Capt. F., 51
Cresswell, Richard Quart. F., Salop, 94
Cressy, ___ Capt. H., 48
Cressy, Thomas Capt. H., stray, 159. Mentioned by a stray cornet from Lincoln, therefore probably the man above, who was mentioned by three Lincoln officers under Sir Robert Dallison.
Cressy, John Capt. F., 138
Crickett, Daniell Lieut. H., Kent, 119
Cripling, Edward Lieut. F., York, 138
Crisp, Sir Nicholas Col. H. (d. 1666), 45. Also mentioned by two naval officers.
Crisp/Crisps, Thomas Lieut. H., Warwick, 118
Crisp, Thomas Cor. H., L. & W., 37
Crispe/Crisp, Arthur Quart. F., Durham, 80
Croft/Crofts, Richard Lieut. H., Monmouth, 116. Same regiment as the officer

Index

below; probably the same man.

Crofts, Christopher Capt. F., York, 49

Crofts, Richard Lieut. H., Monmouth, 116

Crofts, Robert Col. F., L. & W., 9, 45, 143. Claims as as a (lieutenant?) colonel under Sir William Vavasour, but a number of men claim directly under Crofts. Sometimes 'Croft'.

Crofts, Roger Quart. H., York, 121

Crofts, Sir William Col. F. (k. 1645; Stokesay), 45

Croker, Gerard Col. H., 46, 64, 66. Formerly a captain in Lord Gerard's horse. Promoted to colonel early in 1643 (Newman, *The Old Service*, p.297).

Crome, Henry Lieut. F., York, 31

Crompton, ___ Maj. H., Sir John Wake, 144

Crompton, ___ Maj. H., stray, 160. Mentioned by an officer claiming from Bucks, therefore possibly the man above as Wake's regiment was based around Bedford/Bucks.

Crompton, ___ Capt. H., 68

Crompton, Henry Maj. F., 114, 165. Mentioned by two Suffolk officers, one a stray and the other claiming under Lord Henry Piercy (Percy).

Crompton, James Capt. F., L. & W., 122

Cromwell, Gregory Maj. H. & Adjut. Gen., Norfolk, 10, 46

Cromwell, Henry Col. H., 46

Crook, Henry Lieut. F., Somerset, stray, 164

Crook/Crooke, Henry Ens. F., L. & W., 156

Crook/Crooke, Thomas Lieut. F., Somerset, 114

Crooke, John Col. F., 46

Crosby, Robert Lieut. F., York, 135

Crosfield, Edward Quart. H., Lincoln, stray, 160

Crosland, Sir Jordan Col. H. (d. 1670), 46. Knighted July 1642.

Crosland, Nathaniel Capt. H., 58

Crosman, Huntington Quart. H., L. & W., 142

Crosse, Henry Lieut. H., Surrey, 62

Crosse, Leonard Quart. H., Southampton, 134

Crosse, Stephen Corporal H., Somerset, 161. Listed as a stray, but claims under Sir Lewis Dives.

Crossfield/Crasfield, Thomas Quart. H., Sussex, 74

Crossland, John Capt. H., 22

Crosston/Croston, Jeremy Cor. H., Lancaster, 143

Crouch, Robert Quart. H., Dorset, 133

Crow, ___ Capt. F., Godfry Floyd, 60

Crow, ___ Capt. F., William Strother, 134

Crow, Henry Col. F. & Dr., L. & W., 9, 33, 46. Crow claims as a dragoon colonel under Lord Capel (Reid lists him as a lieutenant colonel), and three officers cite him directly as their colonel of foot.

Crowder, William Lieut. F., L. & W., 97

Crump, Edward Capt. Lieut.F., Monmouth, 87

Crymes, ___ Lieut. Col. H., stray, 160
Crymes, ___ Maj. H., 129
Cudlip, Richard Lieut. F., Cornwall, 54
Cudworth, Thomas Lieut. H., Chester, 106
Cufand, ___ Maj. F., stray, 164
Cufand, Francis Lieut. F., Norfolk, stray, 164
Cuffand, Francis Capt. Lieut. H., L. & W., 150
Culme, Phil. Capt. F., 83
Cumberland, [Henry Clifford] 5th Earl of, ___ F. (d. 1643), 46
Cummin, Edward Quart. H., Durham, 29
Cupper, ___ Lieut. Col. Pioneers, 171
Cupper, Henry Capt. H., L. & W., 66
Curbyn/Curbin, John Ens. F., Cornwall, 54
Curle, William Capt. H., Somerset, 155
Currey/Curry, James Comptroller of the Ordnance, L. & W., 170
Curron, John Chirurgion, Hereford, 173
Curwen, Sir Patricius Col. H. & F., 46
Curtys, John Cor. H., Berks, 37
Curtys, Richard Capt. F., Durham, 39
Curtys, Thomas Maj. H., 26
Cusse, William Capt. H., Wilts, 95
Cutbert, Edward Lieut. H., Somerset, 79
Cutbert, John Lieut. F., Durham, 80
Cutbert, Robert Quart. Dr., Durham, 99
Cutler, Benjamin Cor. H., Wilts, 73
Cutler, John Quart. H., Lancaster, stray, 161. Claims under William Walton, Lieutenant Colonel of Robert Byron's horse.
Dabbs, Daniel Capt. F., York, 39
Dacres, John Quart. H., L. & W., 32
Dacres, Sir Richard Col. H. (k. 1644; Marston Moor), 47. Usually 'Dacre'.
Dacres, Sir Thomas Col. H., 47. Usually 'Dacre'.
Dagget, Richard Lieut. F., York, 133
Dalben, ___ Capt. F., 55
Dale, Daniel Capt. H., Lancaster, 137
Dale, Thomas Capt. H., York, 90
Dallison, Sir Charles Col. H., 47
Dallison, Sir Robert Col. H., 48
Dallison, Sir Thomas Col. H. (k. 1645; Naseby), 48, 119. Mentioned by two officers under Prince Rupert and by four more directly. Sources disagree as to whether he was a lieutenant- or a full colonel at the time of his death, commanding Prince Rupert's regiment and lifeguard at Naseby.
Dalston, Sir William Col. H. & F. (d. 1683), 48. A 1648 regiment, taken over by George Denton for reasons unknown. Perhaps Dalston had withdrawn to settle his his personal battles with the Committee for Compounding, which had rumbled on since he first submitted in November 1645.

Dalton, ___ Lieut. Col. F., 49. Reid gives his first name as Sutton.
Dalton, ___ Lieut. Col. F., stray, 165. An addition from the errata.
Dalton, Thomas Col. H. (k. 1643; Newbury I), 48. Commanded his own cavalry regiment early in the war, then became deputy to Sir Thomas Tyldesley at some point before September 1643. Mortally wounded at Newbury; Money (p. 61, fn.), records that he died at Andover on 2nd November and was buried at St. Mary's church in the town.
Dalton, Thomas Cor. H., Surrey, 85
Danby, ___ ___ H., York, 49. Probably Sir Thomas Danby.
Danby, ___ Capt. Dr., 85
Danby, Christopher Cor. H., Lancaster, 103
Danby, Edmund Lieut. H., York, 155
Danby, Francis Quart. F., Salop, 144
Danby, George Capt. H., Durham, 154
Danby, John Maj. H., 155
Danby, John Capt. H., 39
Danby, Sir Thomas ___ H., 49. Reid places him as a lieutenant colonel under John Belasyse.
Dancy, William Capt. F., 42
Dangell, ___ ___ F., 49
Dangerfield, Fulk Lieut. F., L. & W., 16
Dangerfield, George Lieut. H., Worcester, 40
Daniel – see also Danyell
Daniel, ___ Lieut. Col. H., 23
Daniel, James Cor. H., York, 34
Daniel, John Cor. H., York, 148
Daniel, Robert Capt. Dr., Leicester, 96
Daniel, Sir Thomas ___ H., 49. I.O. offers no rank, but Reid states that he was major of horse to Prince Charles's regiment in 1643.
Daniell, ___ Capt. H., 91
Dannet/Dannett, Gerard Capt. F., Salop, 152
Danson, Thomas Capt. F., Lancaster, stray, 163
Dansy, De Labere/Dansey, Delabere Lieut. F., L. & W., 42. Included in the body of the list as 'Dausy'; however 'n' and 'u' seem to have been frequently muddled by the printers, therefore the name is probably 'Dansy', as per its inclusion as 'Dansey' in the original index.
Danvers, Thomas Capt. H., Surrey, stray, 157
Danyell/Daniell, John Ens. F., Somerset, 18
Darcy, ___ ___ F., 49. The regiment intended is undoubtedly that of Lord Conyers Darcy, although it is not clear under which of his commanders these men claimed.
Darcy, Lord Conyers, F. (d. 1654), 49. The regiment was run by Lord Conyers' sons, initially by his heir and namesake Colonel Conyers Darcy. P. R. Newman (*Old Service*, pp. 94-95) states that the younger Conyers was crippled at Burton in July 1643, and that command passed to his younger brother Marmaduke.

this suggests that Marmaduke was the 'Colonel Darcy' wounded at Newbury in September, and not Conyers, as secondary commentators usually state. As a 'Colonel Darcy' commanded a brigade just prior to this at Gloucester, in August, Newman's suggestion implies that that commander must also have been Marmaduke and not Conyers.
Darcy, Henry Lieut. Col. F., 22
Darcy, Lewis Capt. F., York, 68
Darcy, Marmaduke Maj. F., 49. First name not given in I.O., but regiment's major known to be Lord Darcy senior's son.
Darcy, Thomas Capt. F., 49
Darracot/Darracott, Humphry Cor. H., Devon, stray, 159
Darracot/Darracott, William Quart. H., Devon, 77
Darrell, ___ Capt. H., 112
Darrell, Paul Cor. H., L. & W., 130
Dart, Charles Capt. F., Devon, 44
Dart, Phil. Maj. F., 15
Darell/Darrell, Peter Capt. H., Bucks, 32
Daulben, ___ Capt. F., 123
Daulben, Hugh Ens. F., Denbigh, 123
Dausy – *see* Dansy
Davaleere, John Col. H., 49
Davenport, ___ Capt. F., 136
Davenport, Edward Ens. F., Chester, 136
Davenport, Thomas Capt. F., Flint, 147
Davenport, William Capt. F., 59
David, Evan Ens. F., Carmarthen, 105
David, Lewis Ens. F., Monmouth, 138
David, Morgan Ens. F., Glamorgan, 154
Davids, Lluelin/Luellin Ens. F., Carmarthen, 132
Davies, [Edward] Capt. F., 25
Davies, John Capt. H., stray, 158
Davill, Thomas Capt. H., York, 102
Davis, Chauncy Lieut. H., Pembroke, 54
Davis, Edward Capt. F., Brecon, 116
Davis, Hugh Capt. H., York, 119
Davis, Hugh Lieut. F., L. & W., 110
Davis, John Cor. H., Pembroke, 54
Davis, John Quart. H., Dorset, 76
Davis, Maurice Ens. F., Pembroke, 142
Davis, Nicholas 'Dr. [of] Physick in the West', L. & W., 173
Davis, Owen Lieut. H., Anglesey, 50
Davis, Robert Capt. Lieut. H., L. & W., 108
Davis, Robert/Richard Cor. H., York, 149
Davis, Thomas Col. F., 49
Davis, Thomas Capt. H., Pembroke, 54

Davis, Thomas Cor. H., Somerset, 141
Davis, Thomas Ens. F., Hereford, 124. I.O. does not give an arm of service, but the rank of ensign indicates foot.
Davis, William Capt. H., Suffolk, 26
Davison, ___ Maj. F., 127
Davison, Benjamin Quart. H., Lincoln, 25
Davison, George Lieut. F., Durham, 27
Davison, George Lieut. F., L. & W., 110
Davison, Joseph Capt. F., 100
Davison, Robert Capt. F., Northumberland, 39
Davison, Robert Ens. F., L. & W., 102. I.O. does not give an arm of service, but the rank of ensign indicates foot.
Davison, Samuel Maj. H., 13
Davison, Thomas Lieut. Col. F., stray, 165
Davison, William Ens. F., Durham, 88
Davy, John Quart. H., Lincoln, 112
Davy, Ralph Ens. F., Cornwall, 50
Davy, Richard Capt. H., 79
Davy, Richard Lieut. F., Cornwall, 140
Davy, Richard Quart. F., Cornwall, 140
Daw, Richard Ens. F., Somerset, 133
Dawbeney, ___ Capt. H., 133
Dawbeney/Dawbeny, James Cor. H., Dorset, 133
Dawbeney/Dawbeny, John Lieut. H., Dorset, 133
Dawborn, Robert Cor. H., Surrey, 150
Dawkins, Hopkin Capt. F., Carmarthen, 132
Dawson, Anthony Cor. H., York, 22
Dawson, Christopher Quart. H., Lincoln, 112
Dawson, George Capt. H., Lord Bellasis, 22
Dawson, George Capt. Dr., Sir John Mallory, 99
Dawson, John Capt. H., 56
Dawson, John Lieut. F., L. & W., 138
Dawson, John Quart. H., Northumberland, 34
Dawson, John Quart. H., Chester, 61
Dawson, Lancelot Ens. F., Durham, 58
Dawson, Nicholas Cor. H., Northumberland & Warwick, 107. Listed twice, in the same regiment and under the same captain, but in different locations.
Dawson, Stephen Capt. F., 61
Dawson, Thomas Quart. H., Northumberland, 73
Dawson, William Ens. F., York, 125
Day, Francis Lieut. F., York, 146
Day, John Capt. H., Somerset, 155
Day, John Quart. H., L. & W., 116
Day, Philip Lieut. Col. Dr., 9, 83
Day, Philip Quart. H., Oxon, stray, 160

Day, Robert Capt. Lieut. F., Somerset, 132
De Choqueux, Anthony Chirurgion, L. & W., 172
De Gomme, Bernard Capt. F. (d. 1685), 25. Best known as an engineer serving under Prince Rupert.
De La Grange, Matthew Lieut. F., Brecon, 154
De Lason, Pardous Chirurgion, L. & W., 172
De St. Mark, Anthony Capt. F., L. & W., 122
Deale, John Quart. H., L. & W., 121
Dean/Deane, Edward Capt. H., L. & W., 30
Dean/Deane, William Chirurgion, Kent, 173
Deane, ___ Capt. F., 65
Deane, Edward Lieut. H., Cambridge, 55
Deane, Robert Maj. F., 135
Deane, William ___ H. & Dr., 49
Deane, William Lieut. Col. H., 9, 81. Claimed under Lord Hopton. Possibly the William Deane listed above.
Deane, William, Chaplain, Bucks, 174
Dearelove, Thomas Capt. F., York, 86
Debee, ___ Maj. H., 36
Debee, John Capt. H., 36
Deeyell, ___ ___ F., 49
Deighton – *see also* Dighton
Deighton/Dighton, Francis Quart. H., York, 26
Delahay/De la Hay, Richard Ens. F., Devon, 106
Delahay/De la Hayer, Thomas Quart. H., Carmarthen, 33
Delamot/De la Mot, Peter Lieut. H., L. & W., 128
Delaval/De Lavall, John Capt. F., Salop, 31
Delaval, Thomas Capt. F., stray, 165
Delavall/De la Val, Henry Lieut. H., Northumberland, 79
Delton, Anthony Capt. Lieut. F., Devon, 106
Demaret, John Lieut. H., L. & W., 25
Dutton, Richard Capt. F., Denbigh, 145
Denham, George Capt. H., Lincoln, 74
Denham, Henry Capt. F., Somerset, 131
Dennis, ___ Capt. Dr., 74
Dennis, Godfrey Maj. H., York, 10, 138
Dennis, William Capt. F., Somerset, 131
Denton, George Lieut. Col. H., 48. Sir William Dalston's regiment, 1648. Took over the regiment for reasons unknown.
Denton, James Capt. F., Northumberland, 38
Denton, John Capt. H., stray, 159, 160. Mentioned by a stray cornet and stray quartermaster, both from Bucks.
Denton, Lancelot Ens. F., York, stray, 165
Denton, Robert Capt. Lieut. H., Bucks, 128
Denton, Willoughby Capt. Lieut. H., Lincoln, 130

Denzell/Denzhell, John Capt. F., L. & W., 152
Derby, [James Stanley] 7th Earl of, Col. H. & F. (executed 1651), 50
Derby, Michael Capt. F., L. & W., 97
Deschato/De Schato, John Cor. H., L. & W., 16
Deverell, Francis Lieut. Dr., Wilts, 83
Dewen, Thomas Ens. F., Cornwall, 72
Dewes, Roger Lieut. F., Suffolk, 97. Almost certainly a member of the D'Ewes family of Suffolk, which included parliamentary diarist Sir Symonds.
Dewit/Dewitt, Cornelius Maj. H., L. & W., 10, 147
Dewxtell, John Capt. F., 87
Dewy, William Capt. H., Dorset, 136
Dewy, William Capt. H., L. & W., 136. This claim and the identical one above are the only ones made under an unidentified Colonel Thomas, a cavalry officer. The entries are probably duplicates.
Dibble, Henry Quart. H., Somerset, 53
Dibble, Richard Lieut. H., Somerset, 53
Dibdale, ___ Capt. F., stray, 165
Dickenson, Edward Lieut. F., Lancaster, stray, 164
Dickenson, Hugh Quart. H., Lancaster, 48
Dickenson, Robert Ens. F., York, 22
Dickenson, Thomas Ens. F., York, 86
Dickenson, William Capt. Lieut. F., Cumberland, 89
Dickinson/Dickenson, Hugh Cor. H., Lancaster, 137
Dickinson, William Cor. H., Middlesex, 137
Digby, George – *see* Earl of Bristol
Digby, Sir John Col. H. (k. 1645; Taunton), 51. Of Gayhurst, Bucks. Younger brother of Sir Kenelm Digby.
Digby, Sir John Col. F. (d. 1684), 51. Of Mansfield Woodhouse.
Digby, John Col. H., F. & Dr. (d. 1664), 51. Son of the 1st Earl of Bristol; younger brother of George Digby.
Digby, Sir Kenelme, ___ H. (d. 1665), 28
Digby, Kenelm Gen. Ordnance, Bucks, 70. Possibly the eldest son of Sir Kenelm, above; Kenelm senior had returned from Paris with his sons in 1645.
Digby, Nathaniel Capt. H., Leicester, 111
Digger, R___ Quart. H., Oxon, 46. The claimant only gives his initial.
Dighton – *see also* Deighton
Dighton, Gervase Ens. F., Lincoln, 88. I.O. does not give an arm of service, but the rank of ensign indicates foot.
Dillingham, Roger Quart. F., York, 31
Dillon, Christopher Capt. F., L. & W., 76
Dillon, Henry Lieut. 'of a Fregat', L. & W., 167
Dillon, James Sea Capt., L. & W., 167
Dingen, ___ Capt. H., 152. Served in Scotland, 1654.
Dingle, George Ens. F., Cornwall, 122
Dinham – *see also* Dynham

Dinham, John Quart. H., Cornwall, 14
Dinsdale/Densdale, Ralph Lieut. F., York, 25
Dirdo, ___ Lieut. Col. F., 117
Disney, ___ Lieut. Col. F., stray, 165
Dives, Sir Lewis Col. H. & F. (d. 1669), 51, 120. Usually 'Dyve'. A cornet in Prince Rupert's regiment claims Dives as his captain, and a large number of officers claim under him directly. Also mentioned by a stray quartermaster.
Dixon, ___ Capt. H., 38. Served in 1648.
Dixon, ___ Capt. Dr., 125
Dixon, Andrew Lieut. F., Northumberland, 93
Dixon, George Cor. H., Durham, 121
Dixon, George Cor. H., York, 92
Dixon, James Lieut. H., Kent, 113
Dixon, John Lieut. H., L. & W., 95
Dixon, Joseph Quart. H., York, 92
Dixon, Nicholas Cor. H., York, 47
Dixon, Richard Lieut. H., York, 99. An addition from the errata.
Dixon, Robert Capt. H., 92
Dixwell, Thomas Cor. H., Derby, 60
Dixy, ___ Capt. H., 142
Dobson, Christopher Ens. F., Westmorland, 123
Dobson, Robert Quart. H., Durham, 13
Dod, ___ Capt. H., 101
Dod, Thomas Lieut. H., Stafford, 54
Dod, Thomas Lieut. F., L. & W., 84
Dod, Thomas Quart. H., L. & W., 64
Doddington, Sir Francis Col. H., 52
Doddington, John Capt. H., 49
Doddington, William Cor. H., L. & W., 89
Dodson, Miles Quart. Gen. in Oxon, L. & W., 32
Dolby, James Lieut. H., Lincoln, 56
Dolby, Thomas Quart. H., Lincoln, 56
Dolling, ___ Maj. H., 133
Dolling, John Capt. H., 77
Dolman, ___ Capt. H., 143
Dolman, John Cor. H., York, 85
Dolman, Philip ___ H., 56
Dolman, Thomas Quart. H., York, 102
Dolman, William Capt. H., William Eure, 56. Young says k. Marston Moor (p.246).
Dolman, William Capt. H., Francis Hungate, 85
Donne, Daniel Ens. F., Carmarthen, 30. I.O. does not give an arm of service, but the rank of ensign indicates foot.
Done, Edmund Capt. H., 27
Done, Edward Capt. F., L. & W., stray, 163
Done, Henry Quart. H., Wilts, 95

Done, Valentine Lieut. F., L. & W., 27
Donnell, Richard Col. F., 52
Dorcas, Edward Lieut. H., Warwick, 117
Dormer, ___ Capt. F., 98
Dormer, Anthony Capt. F., Stafford, 21
Dormer, Francis Ens. F., Warwick, 66
Dormer, William Capt. Lieut. F., Berks, 76
Doubleday, Francis Capt. H., L. & W., 64
Doughty, ___ Capt. H., 150
Doughty, Edward Lieut. H., Stafford, 124
Doughty, Thomas Capt. H., L. & W., 149
Doughty, William Capt. Lieut. H., L. & W., 130
Douglass, ___ Capt. H., Sir William Blakeston, 26
Douglas, ___ Capt. H., Sir Jordan Crosland, 46
Douglasse/Douglas, Thomas Cor. H., Northumberland, 93
Dover, [Henry Carey] 1st Earl of, Col. F. (d. 1666), 52
Dovey, Gervase Cor. H., Stafford, 130
Dovy/Dovey, Richard Cor. H., Salop, 76
Dowdall, George Sea Capt. *Duke of York*, L. & W., 167
Dowglasse/Douglas, Ferdinando Ens. F., L. & W., 93
Dowle, Theophilus Cor. H., L. & W., 86
Dowler, William Quart. Gen. H., Worcester, 150
Dowling, Matthew Capt. F., Cumberland, 107
Down, John Chirurgion, Somerset, 173
Downe, R. Capt. H., 50
Downes, William Chirurgion, L. & W., 172
Downing, Thomas Maj. F., L. & W., 10, 144
Dowset, John Ens. F., Bucks, 16
Dowthwaite, John Lieut. H., Somerset, 155
Dowthwaite/Douthwaite, Nicholas Cor. H., Somerset, 45
Drake, John Capt. F., Devon, 35
Drake, John Deputy Commissary, Cornwall, 169
Drake, Richard Commissary, Somerset, 169
Drake, Thomas Capt. H., 77
Draper, Thomas Capt. F., Norfolk, 98, 121. Lord General's foot. Mentioned by a lieutenant under the Earl of Lindsey; claims in his own right under Patrick Ruthven.
Draycott/Draycot, John Capt. F., L. & W., 138
Draycott/Draycot, Phillip Ens. F., L. & W., 93
Drew, Thomas Quart. H., Hereford 126
Drewit/Drewitt, John Quart. H., Southampton, 23
Driffield, Symon Quart. H., York, 68
Dring, Lewis Capt. F., Surrey, 86
Drue/Drew, George Lieut. F., Somerset, 62
Druel/Druell, George Lieut. F., L. & W., 80

Druell, Pierce Lieut. F., L. & W., 132
Drury, Edward Col. Dr., 52
Dryden, George Lieut. F., Northumberland, 77
Du Bois, Prudentius Lieutenant of the Ordnance, L. & W., 170
Du Gard, Anthony Chirurgion, L. & W., 172
Duckenfield, Ratcliffe Capt. H., stray, 161
Ducket, John Cor. H., Middlesex, 114
Duckett, Charles L. H., Westmorland, 103
Dudly, Dud Maj. Dr. (d. 1684), 154
Dudley, Sir Gamaliel Col. H., 52
Dudly, Henry Capt. Lieut. H., L. & W., 89
Dudly, Henry Lieut. H., Leicester, 95
Dudly, Jeffery Cor. Dr., Stafford, 154
Dudly, Richard Capt. H., Leicester, 95
Dudly, William Quart. H., Leicester, 96
Dudman, John Quart. H., Berks, 153
Duffield, Thomas Lieut. Dr., York, 99
Duhurst, ___ Lieut. Col. F., 60
Duhurst, John Lieut. H., Lancaster, 27
Duke, George Capt. Dr., Wilts, 83
Duke, Robert Capt. Dr., 83
Duncalf/Duncalfe, William Lieut. H., Cornwall, 50
Duncan, Thomas Capt. H., L. & W., 134
Duncastle/Dancastle, James, Marshall, Southampton, 171
Dunce, ___ Capt. H., 114
Duncomb, Sir Edward Col. H. & Dr., 52
Duncomb/Duncombe, Edward Capt. H., Durham, 135
Duncombe, ___ Capt. H., 52. Of Sir Edward Duncomb's horse; mentioned by a subordinate. Possibly Captain William Duncombe in Sir Edward's dragoons.
Duncombe, Nathaniel Lieut. H., Middlesex, 96
Duncombe, Nathaniel Marshall General, Leicester, 171
Duncombe, William Capt. Dr., York, 52
Dun, ___ Capt. F., 25
Dunford, Stephen Lieut. F., Monmouth, 153
Dunhill, ___ Capt. H., 27
Dunkin, John Quart. H., Lincoln, stray, 160. Claims under a Captain Christopher Grimston, perhaps he of Sir William Savile's Horse.
Dunkin, William Ens. F., Cornwall, 15
Dunnell, Nicholas Quart. H., York, 92
Dunnell, William Capt. H., 90
Duport, James Capt. H., Leicester, 95
Durant, ___ Maj. F., 145
Durant, John Lieut. F., Huntingdon, 82
Durant, John Quart. H., Leicester, 96
Durham, Anthony Cor. H., York, 90

Durston/Dureston, John Quart. H., Worcester, 124
Dussing, John Capt. F., L. & W., 42
Dutchfield, ___ Maj. F., 137
Duteil, John Baptista Cor. H., L. & W., 70
Dutton, Sir Ralph Col. H. & F. (d. 1646), 52
Dutton, Richard Capt. F., Denbigh, 146
Dutton, Richard Quart. H., Stafford, stray, 161
Dutton, Thomas Lieut. F., York, 27
Dyer, Edward Col. H., 53
Dyer, James Capt. F., Surrey, stray, 163
Dyer, John Capt. H., Somerset, 141
Dyer, Sir Lodowick ___ H. (d. 1669), 53
Dyer, Stephen Capt. H., Edward Dyer, 53
Dyer, Stephen Capt. H., Somerset, Sir Edward Stawell, 131. Possibly the man above, as Edward Dyer's regiment was also based in Somerset.
Dyer, Thomas Capt. F., Somerset, 141
Dymock, ___ ___ H., 53. Mentioned by a single officer; possibly the Cressy Dymock below
Dymock, Cressy Col. H., L. & W., 9, 52
Dymock, William Capt. H., Flint, 30
Dymond, Ezekiel Lieut. F., Cornwall, 154
Dynham – *see also* Dinham
Dynham, John Capt. ___, 39
Dynham, John Lieut. H., Somerset, 151
Dynham/Dinham, Oliver Capt. F., Cornwall, 139
Dyott, Anthony Capt. F., 18
Dyve – *see* Dives
Eagle, William Quart. F., Nottingham, 141
Ealand, Robert Quart. H., Lincoln, 47
Eaman, Timothy, Cor. Dr., Berks, 18
Earl/Earle, Henry Lieut. H., Devon, 23
Earle, ___ Capt. H., 59
Earle, Henry Ens. F., Oxon, 122
Earle, John Capt. F., Kent, 138. Served in 1648.
Earnly, Sir Michael Col. F. (k. 1645; Shrewsbury, circumstances unclear), 53
Earnly, Robert Capt. F., 65
East, Michael Lieut. F., Stafford, 18
Easton, William Capt. H., John Digby, 50
Easton, William Capt. Dr., Devon, Sir Richard Greenvile, 72. Possibly the William William Easton above, who was mentioned by an officer also claiming in Devon.
Eaton, John Quart. H., Leicester, 96
Ecton, John Capt. Lieut. F., Westmorland, 123
Eddow, Richard Lieut. H., Flint, stray, 157
Eddow, Thomas Capt. H., Flint, stray, 157
Eden, Gascoygne Capt. H., 26, 118. Mentioned by two officers under Sir William

Blakeston, and by two (one an officer of dragoons) under Sir Thomas Riddell.
Eden, Henry Capt. H., L. & W., 48
Eden, John Col. H. & F., 53
Eden, John Cor. H., Durham, 26
Eden, Ralph Lieut. H., Durham, 118
Eden, Robert Maj. F., 80
Edgecumbe, ___ Maj. F., 54
Edgecumbe, Pierce Col. H. & F., 54
Edgecumbe, Richard Lieut. F., 127
Edlington, Edmund Quart. H., Nottingham 90
Edmonds, Andrew Capt. Dr., L. & W., 128
Edmonds, Henry Lieut. F., Bucks, 62
Edmonds, Hugh Capt. F., Cornwall, 140
Edmonds, Thomas Quart. H., Sussex, 116
Edsforth, William Capt. H., York, 154
Edwards, David Ens. F., Denbigh, 55
Edwards, Edward Ens. F., Cornwall, 15
Edwards, Humphry Lieut. H., Huntingdon, 41
Edwards, James Capt. F., Glamorgan, 136
Edwards, James Ens. F., L. & W., 97
Edwards, John Capt. F., Denbigh, 55
Edwards, John Capt. F., Cornwall, 140
Edwards, John Lieut. F., Brecon, 116
Edwards, John Quart. H., Flint, stray, 161
Edwards, John Quart. F., Warwick, 89
Edwards, John Scoutmaster, Carmarthen, 172
Edwards, Rice Lieut. F., Merioneth, 55
Edwards, Robert Cor. H., Cornwall, 54
Edwards, Roger Lieut. H., Flint, stray, 158
Edwards, Thomas Ens. F., Wilts, 88
Edwards, William Capt. F., Hereford, 46
Edwards, William Capt. F., Denbigh, 156
Eedy, John Ens. F., Cornwall, 20
Egerton, ___ Lieut. Col. H., 17
Egerton, Randolph Col. H., 54
Egerton, Richard Col. H. & F., L. & W., 9, 55, 108. Egerton claimed as a colonel of horse and foot under the Marquess of Newcastle; one officer of horse claimed under him directly.
Egerton, Richard Capt. H., 16
Egerton, Thomas Lieut. Col. H., L. & W., 9, 117
Egerton, William Capt. F., L. & W., 37
Eggleston, John Lieut. F., Durham, 112
Eglesfield, John Ens. F., Cumberland, 49
Eldridge, John Lieut. Dr., L. & W., 17
Elgar, Henry Ens. F., Kent, 75. Served in 1648.

Eliot/Elliot, John Lieut. F., L. & W., 57
Ellery, Anthony Capt. H., Cornwall, 72
Ellesden, William Capt. H., 23
Elliot, George Ens. F., Monmouth, 130
Elliot, James Capt. H., 102
Elliot, John Lieut. F., Devon, 36
Elliot, John Ens. F., Cornwall, 20
Elliot, Richard Lieut. H., L. & W., 102
Elliot, Thomas Ens. F., L. & W., 97
Elliot, William Quart. H., Bucks, 93
Elliott/Elliot, John Lieut. F., Pembroke, 33
Ellis, David Capt. F., Derby, 103
Ellis, Francis Cor. H., Norfolk, 120
Ellis, Henry Capt. F., 72
Ellis, James Cor. H., Somerset, 155
Ellis, John Ens. F., Montgomery, 65
Ellis, Phil. Capt. F., 31
Ellis, Phillip Capt. F., Salop, 152
Ellis, Philip/Phillip Capt. Lieut. H., Cumberland, 48
Ellis, Robert Commissary, L. & W., 169
Ellis, Robert Col. F., 55
Ellis, Robert Capt. F., 73
Ellis, Robert Capt. Pioneers, 172. An addition from the errata; I.O. gives no place of claim.
Ellis, William Capt. Lieut. H., Leicester, 108
Ellis, William Cor. H., Hertford, 121
Ellison, Edward Cor. H., Northumberland, 152. Served in Scotland, 1654.
Elmes, Humphrey Capt. F., 113
Elrington, Francis Capt. H., Northumberland, 35
Elrington, George Capt. H., 38
Elrington, Nicholas Capt. Lieut. F., Northumberland, 109
Eltenhead, Richard Capt. H., Lancaster, 143
Elton, ___ Capt. H., 130
Elvis, ___ Maj. H., 121
Ely, William Cor. H., Lincoln, 24
Emerson, Francis 'Purveyor to the Train', Northampton, 169
Emerson, John Quart. H., Kent, 118
Emerson, Matthew Quart. H., Durham, 150
Emerson, Ralph Cor. H., L. & W., 148
Emerson, Robert Quart. H., Durham, 55
Emmett/Emmet, John Cor. H., Cornwall, 54
Emotson, Thomas Cor. H., L .& W., 48
Empson, George Lieut. H., York, 117
Empson, William Capt. F., Lincoln, 146
England, George Capt. H., Devon, 59

Enett/Ennet, Richard Capt. H., Hereford, 94
Englefield, Thomas Capt. F., Oxon, 92
Ennis, Thomas Ens. F., L. & W., 69
Ennys, ___ ___ H., 55
Ensom/Ensam, Robert Sea Capt. 'of the *York* Fregat', L. & W., 167
Eratt, William Quart. H., York, 85
Errington, ___ Maj. H., 35
Errington, ___ Capt. F., 149. Possibly Captain Lancelot Errington, of the same regiment.
Errington, Anthony Ens. F., Newcastle, 149
Errington, Christopher Lieut. F., Newcastle, 118
Errington, David Capt. H., 148
Errington, David Lieut. F., Northumberland, 134
Errington, Edward Lieut. H., Northumberland, 148
Errington, Frederick Lieut. F., Northumberland, 149
Errington, George Capt. F., Newcastle, 100
Errington, Gilbert Maj. H., 148
Errington, John Col. H., 55
Errington, John Maj. F., 17
Errington, John Capt. H., Durham, 55
Errington, John Capt. H., Northumberland, 148
Errington, John Capt. F., 18
Errington, John Lieut. H., L. & W., 138
Errington, John Cor. H., Northumberland, 148
Errington, Lancelot Capt. F., 149
Errington, Mark Lieut. H., Northumberland, 148
Errington, Martin Capt. F., 77
Errington, Ralph Capt. Lieut. H., Northumberland, 47
Errington, Ralph Capt. H., 148
Errington, Ralph Cor. H., L. & W., 35
Errington, Ralph Ens. F., Northumberland, 27
Errington, Richard Lieut. F., Essex, 149
Escrick/Eskrick, John Quart. H., York, 90
Esmond, Thomas Lieut. H., Somerset, 44
Estmond, John Cor. H., Somerset, 151
Eubanke, Henry Capt. H., 34
Eubanke/Eubank, Tobias Cor. H., Durham, 34
Eure, ___ Lieut. Col. H., 115
Eure, Matthew ___ H., 55
Eure, Ralph Col. H., 56
Eure, Thomas Maj. H., 56
Eure, William Col. H. & F. (k. 1644; Marston Moor), 56. Buried York Minster on 7th July 1644 (Young, p.245).
Evans, ___ Capt. F., 132
Evans, Austin Lieut. F., Montgomery, 124

Evans, Edward Lieut. Dr., Salop, 61
Evans, Laurence 'Quart. to the Train', Berks, 170
Evans, Lewis Capt. F., Montgomery, stray, 163
Evans, Leyson Capt. F., Glamorgan, 52
Evans, Randolph Capt. H., Surrey, 67
Evans, Richard Lieut. H., L. & W., 104
Evans, Roger Ens. F., Flint, 147
Evans, Thomas Lieut. F., L. & W., 72
Evans, Thomas Quart. F., Salop, 78
Evans, William Lieut. F., Denbigh, 123
Evatt/Evat, Walter Cor. H., Worcester, stray, 159
Eveleigh, George Capt. F., Devon, 24
Eveleigh, John Capt. F., Devon, 24
Eveleigh, Miles Quart. H., Devon, 23
Everard, John Lieut. H., Leicester, 96, 158. Claims under Lord Loughborough, but is also listed as a stray.
Everdon, John Cor. H., Stafford, stray, 159
Every, Francis Quart. H., Somerset, 151
Ewer, Thomas Maj. Dr., 84
Ewins, Edward Cor. H., Devon, 75
Exton, Anthony Quart. H., Hereford, 44
Eyre, ___ Lieut. Col. H., 57
Eyre, Anthony Col. H., 56. Half-brother of Sir Gervase Eyre.
Eyre, Edw. Capt. H., 81
Eyre, George Cor. H., Derby, 59
Eyre, Sir Gervase Col. H. (d. 1644), 57. Died of wounds at Newark. Half-brother of Anthony Eyre.
Eyre, John Capt. H., Derby, Sir John Fitzherbert, 59
Eyre, John Capt. H., John Frechevile, 63. Mentioned by subordinate claiming from Derby; this suggests he was possibly the same Captain Eyre as above.
Eyre, John Cor. H., Derby, 59
Eyre, Reynold Lieut. H., York, 59
Eyre, Rowland Col. H., F. & Dr., 57
Eyre, Thomas Maj. F., stray, 165
Eyre, Thomas Capt. F., 21
Eyre, Thomas Lieut. H., Derby, 63
Eyre, Thomas Quart. H., Derby, 63
Eyres, Edw. Capt. H., 82
Eyton, Edward Lieut. Col. H., Bucks, 9, 93
Eyton, Randolph Lieut. H., Flint, stray, 158
Eyton, Sir Thomas ___ F., 126. Also, 'Eaton'. Knighted October 1642, at Shrewsbury.
Eyves, Thomas Quart. H., Lancaster, 85
Fairbrother, Anthony Quart. H., Kent, 20
Fairely/Fairly, Richard Lieut. H., L. & W., 89
Fairely/Fairly, William Cor. H., L. & W., 87

Faithorne, William Ens. F., L. & W., 150
Falby, Luke Capt. Lieut. H., Devon, 135
Fame, ___ Maj. H., 37
Fane, Sir Francis Col. H. & F., 57. Most historical sources suggest he may have died in 1681, although none offer their evidence.
Fanning, James Lieut. H., Somerset, 44
Fanshaw, Sir Simon ___ H. (d. 1679), 97
Fardington, Robert Ens. F., York, 131
Farly/Fairley, John Capt. F., Worcester, 76
Farmer, [William] Maj. F., 38. I.O. gives no first name, but Young names him as William Farmer, and states that he was k. at Marston Moor (p.245); Reid states that he was a Scottish professional soldier.
Farmer, John Lieut. H., Carmarthen, 54
Farmer, Sir William ___ H. (d. 1661), 57. Knighted 1661. Sometimes 'Fermor'. Captain of horse at Edgehill, but later ranks, if any, are unknown.
Farmer, William Lieut. F., Carmarthen, 14
Farr, Henry Col. F., 57. Former Parliamentarian, defected to the Royalists in 1648 and narrowly escaped execution by fleeing after the surrender of Colchester.
Farrant, Nathaniel Quart. H., Devon, 24
Farrock – *see* Parrock
Farrow, Gerard Quart. H., Durham, 28
Farside, William Lieut. F., York, 38
Farthing, John Cor. H., Somerset, 151, 159. Claims under Sir Hugh Windham, but also listed as a Somerset stray.
Faulconer/Falconer, John Quart. H., Sussex, stray, 160
Faunt, John Capt. H., Monmouth, 153
Fauntleroy/ Faunt le Roy, John Ens. F., L. & W., 119
Fauston, Robert Cor. H., Wilts, 79
Favill/Favil, John Lieut. F., York, 147
Fawcet, James Capt. H., Durham, 72
Fawcett, Samuel ___ ___, 58
Fawkett/Fawket, George Lieut. F., L. & W., 16
Fayrbank/Fayrebanck, John Lieut. Dr., York, 125
Fazacarle, William Capt. H., 104
Fell, John Cor. H., Cumberland, 106
Fellow, Alexander Quart. F., Dorset, 131
Feltham, Francis Lieut. F., Somerset, 132
Feltwell, Robert, Chaplain, Norfolk, 174
Fenton, Charles Cor. H., Nottingham, 47
Fenwick, ___ Capt. H., Sir Nicholas Cole, 41
Fenwick, ___ Capt. H., Lord Widrington, 148
Fenwick, ___ Capt. Dr., 58
Fenwick, Ambrose Cor. H., Northumberland, 136
Fenwick, George Capt. H., Northumberland, 58
Fenwick, George 'Conductor of the Train', L. & W., 170

Fenwick, Henry Capt. F., L. & W., 74
Fenwick, Henry Quart. H., Northumberland, 148
Fenwick, John Col. H. (k. 1644; Marston Moor), 58. MP for Morpeth. Son of Sir John Fenwick, MP for Northumberland.
Fenwick, John Capt. Dr., Northumberland, 73
Fenwick, John Lieut. H., Northumberland, 148
Fenwick, John Ens. F., Durham, 134
Fenwick, Ralph Capt. Lieut. H., Northumberland, 58
Fenwick, Ralph Capt. F., Northumberland, 109
Fenwick, Ralph Cor. H., Northumberland, 147
Fenwick, Robert Capt. H., Northumberland, 34
Fenwick, Robert Cor. H., Durham, 107
Fenwick, Thomas Capt. H., Northumberland, 34
Fenwick, Thomas Cor. Dr., Northumberland, 34
Fenwick, Tristram Maj. H., 34
Fenwick, William Capt. H., 39
Fenwick, William Lieut. F., Northumberland, Charles Brandling, 27
Fenwick, William Lieut. F., Northumberland, Sir Thomas Glenham, 68. An addition from the errata.
Fenwick, William Ens. F., L. & W., 73
Fermor – *see also* Farmer
Fermor, Edmund Cor. H., L. & W., 105
Ferrers, John Quart. H., Salop, 109
Ferris, John Lieut. F., Cornwall, 71
Fetherston, Sir Henry ___ H., 47
Fetherston, Sir Henry Col. F. (k. 1651; Worcester), 58. Usually 'Fetherstonhaugh'; Sir Henry came from a prominent Cumbrian family.
Fetherston, John Col. F., 58. Reid believes this to be John Fetherstonhaugh of Stanhope in Weardale; the assumption seems reasonable, as Fetherstonhaugh is mentioned several times in the records of the Committee for Compounding, and paid a large fine. Also, most of 'Fetherstone's' officers claimed from Durham.
Fetherston, John Quart. H. (Brigade), Surrey, 59
Fetherston/Fetherstonhalgh, Ralph Capt. H., L. & W., 85
Fetherston, Sir Timothy Col. F. (executed 1651), 58. Usually 'Fetherstonhaugh'.
Fettiplace, Thomas Cor. H., Berks, stray, 159
Field, Abell Cor. H., Bedford, 104
Field, John Quart. H., L. & W., 120
Field, Richard Capt. F., Salop, 124
Fielding, Charles Lieut. F., Lancaster, stray, 164
Fielding, Christopher Capt. H., L. & W., 124
Fielding, Richard Col. F. (d. 1650; Lisbon), 59. Usually 'Feilding'.
Filks, Edward Capt. F., L. & W., 73
Filldowne/Fildown, Henry Quart. H., Wilts, 82
Finch, ___ Capt. F., 145
Finch, Charles Col. H., 59

Finelay, James Capt. H., L. & W., 62
Fines, Norris Maj. H., Lincoln/L. & W., 10, 104. Listed twice in the same regiment, at both Lincoln and London.
Fines, ___ Capt. H., 86
Finister, Christopher Quart. H., York, 45
Firman, Seymor Lieut. F., Nottingham, 130
Fish, John Quart. H., York, 99
Fishborn/Fishborne, George Cor. H., L. & W., 100
Fisher, ___ Capt. H., 150
Fisher, ___ Capt. F., 152
Fisher, John Capt. Dr., L. & W., 46
Fisher, John Lieut. F., Northampton, 83
Fisher, Lawrence/Laurence Ens. F., L. & W., 96
Fisher, Robert Lieut. F., Carmarthen, 29
Fisher, Thomas Capt. H., L. & W., 123
Fisher, Thomas Lieut. F., Cumberland, 106
Fisher, Thomas Quart. H., York, 64
Fisher, William Lieut. H., Kent, 44
Fitch, Henry Lieut. F., Hertford, 121
Fitch, Thomas Capt. F., Essex, 65
Fitchett, Edward Quart. H., Southampton, 103
Fitter, William Capt. H., stray, 160
Fitton, Sir Edward Col. F. (d. 1643; circumstances unclear), 59
Fitzgerald/Fitz Gerard, Edmund Lieut. F., L. & W., 114
Fitzgerald/Fitz-Gerard, Edward Capt. H., L. & W., 37
Fitzgerald/Fitz Gerald, John Capt. Lieut. F., Dorset, 62
Fitzherbert, ___ Maj. H., 51
Fitzherbert, Sir John Col. H. & F. (d. 1649), 59
Fitzherbert, Samuel Maj. H., stray, 161
Fitzherbert, William Capt. H., Sir John Fitzherbert, 60
Fitzherbert, William Capt. H., stray, 160
Fitzjames, James Capt. H., 151
Fitzjames/Fitz-James, John Lieut. H., L. & W., 102
Fitzjames/Fits James, John Ens. F., Dorset, 66
Fitzjames/Fitz James, Thomas Cor. H., Dorset, 141
Fitzrandolph, ___ Capt. H., stray, 159
Fitzrandolph, Edward Capt. H., 60
Fitzrandolph/Fitz-Randolph, George Capt. H., Derby, 59
Fl___, Walter Capt. F., 29
Fleetwood, ___ Capt. H., Lord General Ruthen, 121
Fleetwood, ___ Capt. H., Sir Adrian Scrope, 126
Fleetwood, Dutton Col. H., 60
Fleetwood, Henry Capt. H., Stafford, 95
Fleetwood, Oliver Capt. H., 125
Fleetwood, Sir Richard Col. F. (d. 1649), 60

Fleetwood, Robert Capt. F., Stafford, 21
Fleetwood, William Capt. H., Stafford, 95
Flemin, Thomas Quart. F., Cornwall, 70
Flemin, William Maj. F., 60
Fleming/Flemen, Nicholas Capt. H., York, 56
Flemming, ___ Maj. F., stray, 164
Flemming, ___ Capt. H., 17
Flesher, George Cor. H., York, 90
Flesher, William Lieut. H., York, 142
Fleshier/Flesher, William Capt. F., Somerset, 82
Fletcher, ___ Capt. F., 119
Fletcher, Sir Henry Col. F. (d. 1645), 60
Fletcher, John Maj. F., 24
Fletcher, John Lieut. F., Lancaster, 138
Fletcher, John Quart. H., Lincoln, 56
Fletcher, Ralph Lieut. H., Lancaster, stray, 158. A stray, but claims Captain William Kay as his officer, and Kay claims under Colonel Edward Rawston.
Fletcher, Roger Cor. H., Derby, 89
Fletcher, Simon Quart. H., Salop, 96
Fletcher, William Lieut. H., Derby, 63
Flintham, Francis Provost Marshall, Nottingham, 171
Floud, ___ Capt. H., 112
Floud/Floyd, John Ens. F., Cornwall, 139
Flower, John Cor. H., Wilts, 141
Flower, Peter Capt. H., 46
Flower, Thomas Capt. Lieut. F., Monmouth, 60
Flower, Thomas Lieut. H., Surrey, 45
Flower, William ___ F., 61
Floyd. **Note:** the name 'Lloyd' was usually rendered as 'Floyd'. Most of the men listed below were probably Lloyds.
Floyd, ___ ___ F., 60. Listed immediately below Colonel Godfry Floyd; probably the same man.
Floyd, ___ Maj. F., 55
Floyd, ___ Capt. F., 74
Floyd, Bevis Maj. F., 26
Floyd, Sir Charles Col. H. & F. (d. 1661), 61. Usually 'Lloyd'. Knighted December 1644.
Floyd, Charles Quart. Dr., Montgomery, 84
Floyd, David Capt. F., L. & W., 78
Floyd, David Capt. Dr., Merioneth, 61
Floyd, David Lieut. H., Carmarthen, 54
Floyd, David Lieut. F., Carmarthen, Anthony Morgan, 105
Floyd, David Lieut. F., Carmarthen, Sir Henry Vaughan, 142
Floyd, David Lieut. F., Merioneth, 111
Floyd, David Cor. H., Carmarthen, 128
Floyd, Edw. Capt. H., 32

Floyd, Edward Capt. F., Flint, Thomas Davis, 49
Floyd, Edward Capt. F., Edward Gerard, 66
Floyd, Edward Capt. F., Salop, Sir John Owen, 111
Floyd, Edw. Capt. Dr., 61
Floyd, Sir Evan Col. F., 60
Floyd, Sir Francis, ___ H., 33
Floyd, Francis Capt. H., L. & W., 112
Floyd, Francis Capt. F., Cardigan, stray, 163
Floyd, Godfry Col. F., 60
Floyd, Hugh Capt. F., Carmarthen, 66
Floyd, Hugh Capt. H., Merioneth, 68
Floyd, Hugh Cor. Dr., Merioneth, 61
Floyd, Humphry Capt. F., Flint, stray, 163
Floyd, John Capt. H., Denbigh, 81
Floyd, John Capt. F., Carmarthen, 142
Floyd, John Ens. F., Denbigh, 123
Floyd, John Ens. F., Merioneth, 111
Floyd, John Quart. H., L. & W., 128
Floyd, Jonathan Capt. H., 54
Floyd, Joseph Lieut. F., Pembroke, stray, 164
Floyd, Lewis Ens. F., Merioneth, 65
Floyd, Matthias Maj. F., Salop, 10, 122
Floyd, Maurice Lieut. F., Merioneth, 156
Floyd, Maurice Ens. F., Carmarthen, 66
Floyd, Meredith Cor. H., Montgomery, 71
Floyd, Morgan Ens. F., Montgomery, stray, 165. Listed as a stray, but claims under Captain Andrew Blayney, who claims under Edward Herbert, Lord Cherbury.
Floyd, Nanny Capt. F., Denbigh, 123
Floyd, Oliver Dr. Judge Advocate, L. & W., 172
Floyd, Peter Cor. H., Denbigh, 140
Floyd, Phee. Ens. F., Carmarthen, 66
Floyd, Robert Ens. F., Denbigh, 65
Floyd, Sir Richard Col. H., 61
Floyd, Richard Lieut. F., Denbigh, 65
Floyd, Rowland Lieut. F., Carmarthen, 66
Floyd, Samuel Lieut. F., Carmarthen, 137
Floyd, Thomas ___ F., 61. I.O. gives no arm of service for Floyd or the ensign who cited him, but the rank of ensign indicates foot.
Floyd, Thomas Capt. F., Salop, 111
Floyd, Thomas Cor. H., Bucks, 44
Floyd, Walter Capt. F., Glamorgan, 113
Floyd, Walter Lieut. H., Carmarthen, Randolph Egerton, 54
Floyd, Walter Lieut. F., Carmarthen, Edward Gerard, 66
Floyd, William Maj. F., 10. Requests inclusion, but no officers claim so his regiment is unknown.

Floyd, William Ens. F., Denbigh, 155
Follenssby/Follensby, Robert Capt. Lieut. F., Durham, 80
Foot, Robert Regt. Quart. H., Somerset, 131
Foran, Robert Sea Capt., L. & W., 167
Forbes, [Edward] Lieut. Col. F., 57. I.O. does not give his first name, but it is supplied by a prisoner list from 1644 (*Mercurius Civicus* No. 47, E.43[10]).
Forbes, Alexander Lieut. Col. F., Newcastle, 9, 100
Forbes, Thomas Quart. H., Lancaster, stray, 161
Forcer/Forser, Barnaby Quart. H., L. & W., 90
Forcer, John Col. H., 61
Forcer, Peter Capt. H., John Forcer, 62
Forcer, Peter Capt. H., Lord Widrington, 148
Forcer, Thomas Quart. H., Durham, 62
Ford, Christopher Lieut. F., Cornwall, 72
Ford, Sir Edward Col. H. (d. 1670), 62
Ford, Gilbert Ens. F., Devon, 15
Ford, Henry Ens. F., Devon, 83
Ford, John Capt. Dr., 81
Ford, Robert Capt. H., 82
Ford, Robert Quart. H., Somerset, 41
Ford, Thomas Ens. F., Worcester, 123
Ford, William Capt. H., L. & W., 101
Ford, William Capt. F., Devon, 82
Ford, William Capt. Lieut. H., Southampton, 62
Fordred, William Lieut. F., Gloucester, 98
Forrest, John Lieut. H., Middlesex, 32
Forrester, Andrew Capt. F., L. & W., 113
Forrester, Lord James ___ H. (k. 1679), 62. Scottish. Forrester's real name was James Baillie. He had inherited the title of Lord Forrester from his father-in-law Sir George Forrester in 1654. Baillie/Forrester was murdered in 1679.
Forster, ___ Lieut. Col. F., 134
Forster, Christopher, Chaplain, York, 174
Forster, Clement Lieut. H., Northumberland, 61
Forster, George Lieut. F., Northumberland, 62
Forster, John Lieut. Col. F., 62
Forster, John Capt. F., Northumberland, 62
Forster, Martin Capt. F., 80
Forster, Matthew Cor. H., Northumberland, 35
Forster, Matthew Ens. F., Northumberland, 62
Forster, John Quart. H., Northumberland, 28
Forster, Peter Quart. H., Northumberland, 58
Forster, Richard Capt. F., Newcastle, 77
Forster, Stephen Lieut. F., York, 67
Forster, Thomas Col. F., 62
Forster, Thomas Ens. F., Northumberland, 62

Forster, Thomas Ens. F., Newcastle, 62
Forster, Thomas Quart. H., York, 90
Fortescue, ___ Maj. F., 153
Fortescue, Sir Edmund Col. H. & F. (d. 1647), 62
Fortescue, Sir Faithful Col. H. (d. 1666), 63
Fortescue, Francis Lieut. H., Warwick, 93
Fortescue, Sir N[icholas] [Lieut. Col] H. (k. 1644; Marston Moor), 102. I.O. does not give the officer's first name or rank, but he is known to be Sir Nicholas Fortescue, Sir John Mayney's lieutenant colonel, who was mortally wounded at Marston Moor.
Fortescue, Nicholas Capt. F., Devon, 37
Fortescue, Peter Capt. F., 62. Brother of Sir Edmund Fortescue.
Fortune, John Quart. H., L. & W., 137
Forty, Thomas Ens. F., Oxon, 105
Fosse, James Lieut. F., York, 22
Foster, ___ Capt. H., 73
Foster, Edward Lieut. F., York, stray, 164
Foster, John Cor. H., York, 27
Foster/Forster, Matthew Cor. H., Northumberland, 73
Foster/Forster, Robert Ens. F., Newcastle, 58
Foster, Robert Quart. H., Rutland, 32
Foster, Thomas Lieut. F., L. & W., 14
Foster, Thomas Cor. H., Bedford, 144
Fothergill, Thomas Lieut. F., York, 129
Fothergill, William Ens. F., Westmorland, 107
Fountaine/Fountain, Francis Capt. H., Monmouth, 153
Fountaine/Fountain, William Lieut. H., Middlesex, 86
Fowke, Henry Lieut. H., Dorset, 144
Fowkes, ___ Capt. H., 144
Fowle/Fowler, John Capt. H., Kent, 74
Fowler, Bartholomew Lieut. F., L. & W., 31
Fowler, Henry Lieut. H., Gloucester, 81
Fowler, John Capt. Pioneers, L. & W., 171
Fowler, Richard Lieut. F., Norfolk, 145
Fowler, Thomas Capt. H., L. & W., 76
Fox, Charles Capt. F., L. & W., 98
Fox, Edward Ens. F., L. & W., 28
Fox, Henry Lieut. F., L. & W., 65
Fox, Jeffery Ens. F., Cumberland, 85
Fox, John Ens. F., L. & W., 16
Fox, Richard Capt./Maj. H., Sir Richard Crane, 44. Mentioned by two officers who give him different ranks. Conceivably there were two Richard Foxes, one a captain and one a major, but it is most likely that they were the same man.
Fox, Richard Capt. F., Lancaster, stray, 163
Fox, Somerset Col. F., 63

Fox, Thomas Capt. H., Montgomery, 142
Fox, Thomas Capt. F., 63
Foxcraft, William Capt. H., Lancaster, stray, 157
Foxcroft, William Capt. H., 103
Foxton, John Cor., L. & W., 37
Francis, Edward Lieut. F., Nottingham, stray, 164
Francis, John Lieut. F., Kent, 79
Francis, Matthew Capt. F., 67
Francis Matthew Lieut. H., L. & W., 59
Francis, Rowland Lieut. F., Derby, 57
Franckland, ___ Lieut. Col. H., 113
Francklin/Franklin, Robert Ens. F., L. & W., 98
Francklin/Franklin, Walter Cor. H., Carmarthen, 30
Frank, ___ Capt. H., 146. Mentioned by an officer in Henry Washington's dragoons. Possibly the 'Captain Frankish' mentioned elsewhere.
Frank, Marmaduke Capt. H., 155
Frank/Franck, Thomas Cor. H., York, 143
Frankish, ___ Capt. Dr., 146
Frankland, ___ Maj. F., 133
Frankland, Richard Capt. F., Salop, 105
Frankland, William Cor. H., York, 97
Franklin, Richard Lieut. F., Devon, 128
Frayne, Leonard Lieut. F., Devon, 139
Freak, Henry Cor. H., Devon, 151
Freak/Freake, William Ens. F., Dorset, 102
Freake, ___ Capt. H., 102
Freame, David/Davy Ens. F., Glamorgan, 83
Freame, William Chirurgion, Gloucester, 173
Freath, Charles Quart. H., Chester, 95
Frechevile, John Col. H. & F., 63
Freehall, ___ Maj. H., 106
Freeman, Edward Lieut. F., Worcester, 124
Freeman, Gabriel Capt. H., York, 47
Freeman, Ralph Capt. H., 37
Freeman, Richard Ens. F., Berks, 25
Freeman, Thomas Quart. H., L. & W., 93
Freestone, ___ Capt. F., 29
French, Edward Capt. H., Northumberland, 147
French, Giles Ens. F., Dorset, 15
French, Henry Capt. H., Somerset, 145
French, Hugh Quart. H., Chester, 17
French, Robert Capt. F., Norfolk, stray, 163
Frickly, Samuel Lieut. Dr., Durham, Sir Thomas Gower, 70
Frickly/Frickley, Samuel Lieut. Dr., York, John Hilton, 80
Friend, George Quart. H., Wilts, 79

Frizell, William Capt. F., Durham, 88
Frobisher, Martin Capt. F., Lincoln, 67
Frost, James Ens. F., Kent, stray, 165
Frothingham, Michael Lieut. H., L. & W., 52
Frowd, Philip Col. H. & F., 63
Fry, Hugh Capt. H., Somerset, 81
Fry, Robert Capt. H., 51
Fry, Robert Quart. H., Somerset, 51
Fry, Stephen Cor. H., Somerset, 51
Fry, Thomas Ens. F., Somerset, 16
Fry, Thomas Commissary, Southampton, 169
Fry___, Jer. Capt. H., 30. The truncated surname is probably 'Fryer', as there is another man of that name in the regiment.
Fryer, John Cor. H., Chester, 30
Fugill, Christopher, Chaplain, Lincoln, 174
Fulford/Fullford, William Capt. H., Devon, 23
Fulk, Gerard Lieut. Col. H., Sir Fulk Hunks, 85
Fulke, Gerard Cor. H., L. & W., Randolph Egerton, 55
Fulkes/Fulks, Llowarch Lieut. F., Denbigh, 116
Fulks, ___ ___ H., 63
Fuller, ___ Maj. H., 112
Fullford, ___ Lieut. Col. F., 130
Fullwood, Thomas Lieut. H., York, 86
Furber, Henry Lieut. Dr., Somerset, 49
Furlong, Francis Ens. F., Devon, 127
Furmidge, William Lieut. H., Dorset, 41
Furnis, Rowland Cor. H., Derby, 57
Furnivall, Henry Maj. F., 96
Fursdon, Philip/Phillip Capt. Lieut. H., Middlesex, 44
Fuzare, Thomas Ens. F., Somerset, 131
Gadford, Thomas Cor. H., 44
Gage, ___ Capt. H., 62
Gage, John Ens. F., Cornwall, 13
Gage, William Lieut. Col. H., 41
Gaines/Gaynes, Francis Capt. Lieut. F., L. & W., 30
Gainsford, ___ Capt. F., 153
Gainsford, John Colonel F., 64
Gale, Richard Ens. F., Bedford, 51
Gale, Robert Capt. F., 22
Galliard, Jo. Lieut. Col. H., 101
Gallop, ___ Capt. Dr., Lord Hopton, 83. Mentioned by a quartermaster of dragoons. Possibly the captain below.
Gallop, Thomas ___ F., 63. Mentioned directly by an ensign in Dorset. Possibly the captain below, given that Hopton's foot were largely from the West Country.
Gallopp, Thomas Capt. F., Lord Hopton, 83

Gamage, ___ __ F., 63. The major who claimed under Gamage did so from Glamorgan, which suggests Gamage might be related to Captain Thomas below.
Gamage, Morgan Chirurgion, Glamorgan, 173
Gambe, Harrold Lieut. F., Norfolk, stray, 164
Games, William Capt. F., Brecon, 105
Gammage/Gamage, Thomas Capt. F., Glamorgan, 34
Gamlyn, ___ Lieut. Col. H., 41
Gamlyn, Andrew Capt. F., 155
Gamul, Sir Francis Col. F., 64
Gamull, ___ Lieut. Col. H., 141
Gant, Bartholomew Chirurgion, Westmorland, 173
Gantley/Gantly, Cutbert Quart. H., Durham, 34
Garaway, William Ens. F., L. & W., 61
Garbut/Garbutt, William Cor. Dr., York, 55
Garbutt, Christopher Quart. H., York, 26
Gardiner, ___ Lieut. Col. H., 110
Gardiner, ___ Maj. H., 44
Gardiner, ___ Capt. H., Conyers(?) Griffin, 73
Gardiner, ___ Capt. H., George Heron, 79
Gardiner, John Capt. H., 44
Gardiner, John Cor. H., Lancaster, 137
Gardiner, Richard Capt. H., Surrey, 119
Gardiner, Thomas Capt. F., L. & W., 80
Gardiner, Timothy Lieut. H., Surrey, 59
Gargrave, Anthony Lieut. Dr., Durham, 40
Gargrave, John Quart. H., L. & W., 70
Gargrave, Matthew Lieut. F., Durham, 135
Garland, John Ens. F., Carmarthen, 42
Garlick, John Lieut. F., Nottingham, 51
Garner, ___ Capt. F., 135
Garnet, Anthony Cor. H., Westmorland, 107
Garnet, Edmund Lieut. F., L. & W., 122
Garnet, John Cor. H., York, 85
Garnet, Henry Cor. H., York, 102
Garnett/Garnet, Anthony Capt. F., Newcastle, 148
Garnett/Garnet, Thomas Quart. H., York, 154
Garnett/Garnet, Thomas Sea Capt. 'of the *True Blew*, &c.', L. & W., 167
Garnier, ___ Maj. F., 83
Garnons, Roger Capt. F., Hereford, 63
Garnons, Thomas Ens. F., Hereford, 42
Garret, Cutbert Ens. F., Durham, 80
Garrett, John Capt. F., 38
Garrett/Garret, Robert Quart. H., Kent, stray, 160
Garrett/Garret, William Ens. F., Sussex, 127
Gascoyne, Sir Bernard ___ H. (d. 1687), 70. Italian. Served under Colonel Richard

Neville in 1644 (Symonds, ed. Long, p.48). Narrowly escaped execution at Colchester in 1648.

Gascoyne, Francis Ens. F., Durham, 80

Gastines/Gastine, James Engineer, L. & W., 170

Gates, Christopher Ens. F., L. & W., 36

Gates, Thomas Ens. F., Surrey, stray, 165

Gaughegan, ___ Capt. H., Sir Henry Griffith, 73. Gaughegan's officer claimed from London, raising the possibility that this Gaughegan was the Captain John from London, below. As Griffin laid down his arms in 1644, those officers of his who remained loyal would have moved on to other commanders.

Gaughegan, John Capt. H., L. & W., Lord Gerard, 64

Gaultier, John Capt. H., 91. I.O. misprints as 'Gualtier'.

Gaultier, William Capt. H., Kent, 93

Gawthrop, John Ens. F., Nottingham, 147. I.O. does not give an arm of service, but the rank of ensign indicates foot.

Gay, Thomas Capt. H., 82

Gayle, Matthew Lieut. H., York, Lord Widrington, 148

Gayle, Matthew Lieut. F., York, Godfry Floyd, 60. Possibly the man above.

Gaynes, John Lieut. F., Durham, 58

Gayre, Thomas Capt. F., Northumberland, 39

Gayton, Edmund Capt. Lieut. F., Oxon, 156

Gaywood, Laurence Lieut. H., Stafford, 17

Gaywood, T. Capt. H., 17

Geare, James Capt. F., 16

Geddy/Geedy, Nicholas Ens. F., Cornwall, 43

Geich, John Quart. H., Cornwall, 72

Geldart, William Ens. F., York, 22

Gent___, Henry Capt. H., 48

George, Henry Ens. F., L. & W., 29

Gerard, ___ Capt. F., 131

Gerard, [Charles] Lord, Col. H. & F. (d. 1694), 64

Gerard, Edward Col. F., L. & W., 9, 64, 66. Younger brother of Lord Gerard. Newman notes that he began the war as a captain under Viscount Grandison (William Villiers) but became a colonel in 1644 (*The Old Service*, p.99). Listed twice in the list of officers requesting inclusion: once as a colonel, once as a lieutenant colonel.

Gerard, Sir Gilbert Col. H. (k. 1645; Ludlow), 64, 66. Uncle of Lord Gerard; *not* Sir Gilbert Gerard of Harrow-on-the-Hill, Middlesex, who was a prominent Parliamentarian.

Gerard, John Lieut. H., Monmouth, 71

Gerard, Ratcliffe Lieut. Col. F., 66. Uncle of Lord Gerard; brother of Sir Gilbert.

Gerard, Richard Col. F., 66 (d. 1686). Of Garwood, Lancs. Family branch known as 'Gerard of Bryn', related to but separate from Lord Gerard's side. Regiment also known known as the Queen's lifeguard of foot.

Gerard, Thomas Capt. H., L. & W., 104

Gerard, William Lieut. H., Lancaster, 137

Gero, Abraham Lieut. H., L. & W., 38
Gething/Gethinge, Humphry Lieut. F., Denbigh, 111
Getly, Richard Quart. Dr., Wilts, 45
Gheast, William Lieut. H., Leicester, 48
Gibbons, ___ ___ H., 66
Gibbons, Charles Capt. Lieut. F., Warwick, 89
Gibbons, Owen Quart. H., Dorset, 79
Gibbons, W. Capt. H., 18
Gibbs, Roger Cor. H., Northampton, 96
Gibbs, Thomas Lieut. H., Somerset, 82
Gibbs, Walter Cor. H., Somerset, 82
Gibbs, William Lieut. F., Kent, stray, 164
Gibson, Edw., Chaplain, Lincoln, 174
Gibson, Sir John Capt. H., York, 67, 110. Gibson claimed in his own right under Sir Edward Osborne; a quartermaster claimed directly under Gibson.
Gibson, John Quart. H., Somerset, 40
Gibson/Gipion, John Quart. H., York, 73. The I.O. index lists this officer amongst several Gibsons, despite spelling the name as 'Gipion'; it is probably a printing error for 'Gibson'.
Gibson, Richard Col. F., 67
Gibson, Thomas Lieut. Col. Dr., L. & W., 9, 45
Gibson, Thomas Cor. H., York, 90
Gibson, William Lieut. H., Northampton, 126
Giddy, William Lieut. F., Cornwall, 20
Gifford, John Col. F., 67
Gifford, John Capt. H., Earl of Bristol, 28
Gifford, John Capt. H., Sir Thomas Hele, 77
Gifford, John Capt. H., Marquess of Hertford, 79
Gifford, John Capt. H., Somerset, Lord Hopton, 81
Gifford, John Capt. F., 154
Gifford, John Lieut. H., Stafford, 142
Gifford, John Lieut. F., Stafford, stray, 164. Listed as a stray, but claims under Simon Heveningham, deputy to Sir John Fitzherbert.
Gifford, John Cor. H., Devon, 35
Gifford, Nicholas Lieut. H., Stafford, 142
Gifford, Richard Commissary General, Stafford, 169
Gifford, Thomas Capt. F., Stafford, 93
Gifford, Thomas Cor. H., Devon, 77
Gifford, Walter Lieut. Col. H., 93
Gilbert, Francis Capt. F., Cornwall, 72
Gilbert, Nicholas Lieut. F., Cornwall, 104
Gilbert, Thomas Lieut. H., Leicester, 96
Gilbert, William Quart. H., Somerset, 40
Gilbert, William Commissary, Somerset, 169
Gilberthorp/Gilberthorpe, Francis Ens. F., Derby, 35. I.O. does not give an arm of

service, but the rank of ensign indicates foot.
Gilborne, Henry ___ H., 67
Gilby, Anthony Col. H. & F., 67
Gilby, Emmanuel Maj. F., 56
Gilby, Richard Quart. H., Lincoln, 112
Gilby, Sir Theophilus Col. F., 67. Took over Sir John (later Lord) Belasyse's foot late in 1643. Knighted at Newark in December 1645. Brother of Anthony and Emmanuel Gilby, above.
Giles, ___ Capt. F., 22
Giles, Lawrence/Laurence Capt. F., York, 58
Gill, Christopher Cor. H., Chester, stray, 159
Gill, John Capt. Dr., Cornwall, 50
Gillmore, ___ Maj. F., 55
Gills, John Sea Capt., *John Adventure*, Sir Nicholas Crisp, L. & W., 167
Girdler, Christopher Ens. F., York, 68
Girling, William ___ F., 67
Girlington, Sir John Col. H. & F. (k. 1645; Melton Mowbray), 68
Givings/Gimings, John Ens. F., Northumberland, 134
Glanvile, ___ Maj. F., 137
Glasier, Thomas Maj. F., 22
Glawdy, Charles Ens. F., Glamorgan, 132
Gleane, Peter Capt. F., 28
Glendore, Lord ___ F., 68
Glenham, Sack. Capt. H., 87
Glenham, Sir Thomas Col. H. & F. (d. 1649), 68
Gloucester, [Henry] Duke of, Col. H., 69. Gloucester was a child, colonel only in name. Sir Phillip Stanhope commanded on his behalf.
Glover, Robert/Fobert Lieut. F., Cornwall, 24. The I.O. index gives the first name as 'Fobert'; possibly there is a confusion with the French name 'Faubert', but most likely it is a printing error for 'Robert'.
Glyn/Glynne, Walter Capt. F., Cornwall, 139
Glynne, Edmund Capt. Dr., Montgomery, 26
Goade, ___ Maj. H., 121
Godbar, Henry Ens. F., L. & W., stray, 165
Goddard, John Capt. F., L. & W., 110
Goddard, John Lieut. H., L. & W., 119
Goddard, John Lieut. F., Devon, stray, 164
Godfrey, John Col. F. (k. 1644; Tewkesbury), 69. Godfrey's regiment was originally that of Sir John Beaumont, k. 1643 at the siege of Gloucester. No men claim under Beaumont in I.O.
Godolphin, Sir William Col. F. (d. 1663), 69
Goffe, Clement Ens. F., L. & W., 98
Gold/Goulds, Thomas Lieut. F., Devon, stray ,164
Goldsmith, Thomas Capt. H., L. & W., 43
Goldston, Philip/Phillip Lieut. H., Wilts, 59

Gomersal/Gomersall, John Capt. H., York, 68
Good, Walter Quart. H., Cornwall, 19
Goodall, Thomas Lieut. H., Warwick, stray, 158
Goodman, John Capt. H., Leicester, 149
Goodrich/Goodrick, Thomas Capt. Lieut. F., Suffolk, 114
Goodrick, Sir John ___ H. (d. 1670), 125
Goodrick, Philip/Phillip Quart. F., Durham, 27
Goodridge, Arthur Lieut. F., Bucks, 16
Goodrose, William Quart. H., Wilts, 142
Goodwin, ___ Capt. H., 135
Goodwin, Ed. Capt. F., Richard or William Nevill, 108
Goodwyn, Edward Capt. F., John Stocker, 132
Goodwin, Robert Capt. F., Surrey, 126
Goodwin, William Lieut. F., Lancaster, 38
Goodyear, Thomas Cor. H., Derby, 125
Gordon, James Lieut. Col. Dr., L. & W., 9, 134
Gordon, James Maj. F., L. & W., 9, 88
Gore, David Capt. F., 22
Gore Edward Quart. H., Lancaster, 104
Gore, Matthew Capt. F., L. & W., 16
Gorford, Richard Ens. F., Devon, 24
Goring, Lord Charles Col. H. (d. 1671), 70. A 1648 regiment. Goring was not ennobled until his elder brother's death in 1657. Succeeded his father as 2nd Earl of Norwich in 1663.
Goring, Lord George Col. H. & F. (d. 1657), 70
Goring, Thomas Lieut. F., Somerset, 127
Gorst, Ralph Capt. H., Lancaster, stray, 157
Gosnold, Robert Capt. F., 69
Gosse, John Quart. H., Surrey, 124
Goston, John Quart. H., Durham, 29
Goswel/Goswell, George Capt. F., L. & W., 29
Gouldsborow, ___ Capt. H., stray, 160. Mentioned by a claimant from Wiltshire, so possibly one of the two officers below.
Gouldsborough, George Capt. H., Wilts, 95
Gouldsborough, Robert Capt. H., Wilts, 23
Gowen, Thomas Capt. H., 95
Gower, ___ Capt. Dr., 91
Gower, Doyly Capt. F., York, 22
Gower, Edmund Capt. Dr., 70
Gower, Edw. Maj. H., 87
Gower, Martin Ens. F., Lincoln, 106
Gower, Sir Thomas Col. H., F. & Dr. (d. 1651), 70. Arrested by the Earl of Newcastle early in 1643 on suspicion of a plot to seize the Queen, but later cleared.
Gower, Thomas Capt. F., 100
Gower, William Capt. H., Dorset, 81

Gower, William Capt. F., Northumberland, 109
Goysgarne, ___ Capt. F., 154
Grabham, Hector Cor. H., Somerset, 53
Grace, ___ Capt. H., 119
Grace, Godfrey Lieut. H., Nottingham, stray, 158
Gradell, William Lieut. H., Lancaster, 31
Grady, Henry Col. H., 71
Grady, John Capt. H., L. & W., 71
Grafton, John Quart. H., Northampton, 121
Graham, Arthur Quart. F., York, 38
Graham, George Regt. Quart., L. & W., 45
Graham, John Capt. H., L. & W., 28
Graham, John Lieut. H., L. & W., 134
Graham, Sir Richard Col. H. (d. 1654), 71
Graham, Richard Cor. H., Westmorland, 134. Served in 1648.
Graham, William Ens. F., Cumberland, 94
Grames, James Lieut. F., L. & W., 137
Grandison, Viscount 'Lord Grandison', Col. H. & F., 71, 119. William Villiers, 2nd Lord Grandison, died of wounds in September 1643; his title passed to his younger brother John, who was a captain in Rupert's horse in 1643 and may have risen higher. John died in 1661 and the title passed to his younger brother George; born in 1617, it is entirely possible that he also fought for the King in some capacity. Therefore the two men claiming directly under 'Lord Grandison' in 1663 could have meant William or John, or, as I.O. claimants frequently claimed under an officer's present title, even George. Two further officers in Prince Ruperts Horse claim Grandison as their captain; this was probably John Villiers, who was wounded at Marston Moor in 1644 while serving under Rupert (Young, p.247).
Grange, Gregory Ens. F., York, 148
Grange, Ralph Lieut. F., York, 30
Granger, Hugh Quart. H., Stafford, 28
Grant, Arthur Capt. F., Derby, stray, 163. Listed as a stray but claims Sir John Harpur as his senior officer.
Grant, William Cor. H., Wilts, stray, 159
Grave, William Ens. F., Cumberland, 106
Greaves, George Capt. F., Derby, 100
Greaves, John Lieut. H., Lincoln, 53
Green/Greene, Alexander Ens. F., Durham, 53
Green, Charles 'Conductor of the Train', Oxon, 170
Green, Edmund Maj. F., 10. Requests inclusion, but no officers claim so his regiment is unknown.
Green, Francis Quart. H., L. & W., 59
Green, Humphrey Ens. F., Devon, 18
Green, Jerom. Regt. Quart. H., L. & W., 110
Green, Richard Cor. Dr., Somerset, 83

Green, Thomas Capt. F., Chester, 59
Green, William Capt. F., L. & W., 92
Greene, Arthur Quart. F., L. & W., 81
Greene, Edmund Maj. H. & F., Cambridge, 85. Greene claims for himself as a foot officer, and is mentioned by a cornet of horse in the same regiment.
Greene, Richard Lieut. Col. H., stray, 159
Greene/Green, Thomas Capt. F., Lancaster, 68
Greenhall, James Ens. F., Lancaster, 117
Greenho___, John Capt. H., 30
Greenvile – *see also* Grenville
Greenvile, ___ Capt. F., 71
Greenvile, Sir Bevile Col. F. (k. 1643; Lansdown), 71. Usually 'Grenville'. Mortally wounded at Lansdown, and died the next day.
Greenvile, Chammon Capt. F., Cornwall, 20
Greenvile, John Lieut. F., Devon, 24
Greenvile, Sir Richard Col. H., F. & Dr. (d. 1659), 71. Usually 'Grenville'.
Greenway, William Capt. F., 132
Greenwell, Samuel Cor. H., Durham, 36
Greenwell, William Cor. H., Northumberland, 58
Greenwell, William Quart. H., Durham, 129
Greenwood, Edward Capt. F., Devon, 72
Gregge/Gregg, Robert Quart. H., Nottingham, 69
Gregory, ___ Capt. H., Sir Nicholas Crisp, 45
Gregory, ___ Capt. H., Lord Loughborough, 96
Gregory, Abraham Chirurgion, Leicester, 173
Gregory, Edmund Capt. F., L. & W., stray, 163
Gregory, John Lieut. F., Salop, 55
Gregory, Thomas Ens. F., Cornwall, 70
Gregory, William Quart. H., L. & W., 37
Grenville – *see also* Greenvile
Grenville, Sir John – *see* Earl of Bath
Grey, ___ Maj. F., 129
Grey, ___ Capt. F., 108
Grey, Ambrose Lieut. H., Stafford, 96
Grey, Andrew Maj. H., L. & W., 11, 129
Grey, Barnard Capt. H., L. & W., 97
Grey, Edward Col. H., F. & Dr. (d. 1676), 72
Grey, George Lieut. F., L. & W., 120
Grey, John Capt. H., 97
Grey, Ralph Capt. H., 73
Grey, Ralph Cor. H., Northumberland, 73
Grey, Robert Cor. H., Northumberland, 73
Greys, Henry Capt. H., 79
Grice, Henry Capt. F., 117
Griffen, ___ Col. H., 73. Possibly Colonel Conyers Griffin, below, as the cornet citing

'Griffen' was also from Wiltshire; although Griffin is not usually thought to have commanded cavalry.

Griffin, Conyers Col. F., 73
Griffin/Griffith, Edw. Cor. H., Warwick, 153
Griffin, Morgan 'Conductor of the Train', L. & W., 170
Griffin, Thomas Ens. F., L. & W., Sir William Compton, 42
Griffin, Thomas Ens. F., L. & W., Sir Lewis Dives, 51
Griffith, Edw. Cor. H., Somerset, 82
Griffith, Evan Lieut. F., Glamorgan, 87
Griffith, Sir Henry Col. H. & F. (d. 1656), 73
Griffith, John Capt. F., Flint, stray, 163
Griffith, John Lieut. F., Somerset, 155
Griffith, Richard Lieut. F., Somerset, 135
Griffith, Richard Ens. F., Flint, 106
Griffith, Richard, Marshall, L. & W., 171
Griffith, Robert Lieut. H., Chester, 140
Griffith, Thomas Capt. F., Devon, 127
Griffith, Thomas Lieut. H., Flint, 29
Griffith, William Lieut. H., L. & W., 129
Griffith, William Lieut. H., Carnarvon, stray, 158
Griffith, William Cor. H., Gloucester, stray, 159
Grigger, Nicholas Capt. H., Middlesex, 45
Grigson, John Lieut. F., Durham, 80
Grills, Adam Capt. Lieut. F., Cornwall, 139
Grills, Hanniball/Hannibal Ens. F., Cornwall, 54
Grills, John Lieut. F., Cornwall, 139
Grills, William Capt. F., Cornwall, 54
Grills, William Cor. H., Cornwall, 102
Grimes, George Capt. F., Kent, 53
Grimes, John Quart. H., Norfolk, 79
Grimshaw, Robert Lieut. H., Lancaster, 34
Grimston, Stephen Capt. H., Cumberland, 71
Gromett, Samuel Lieut. H., Lincoln, 29
Grosvenor, Leicester Ens. F., Salop, stray, 165
Grosvenor, Richard Quart. F., Salop, 63
Grosvenor, William Quart. H., Chester, 17
Grove, ___ Capt. H., 141
Grove, Francis Cor. H. L. & W., 110
Grove, William Capt. H., L. & W., 51
Grover, James Quart. H., Middlesex, 32
Grundy, William Lieut. F., Nottingham, 67
Grymston/Grimston, Christopher Capt. H., York, 125. Mentioned by a stray Lincoln quartermaster; claims for himself under Sir William Savile.
Gudgeon, Henry Quart. H., York, 99
Guise, George Lieut. H., Gloucester, 102

Index 259

Gully, Francis Capt. F., Cornwall, 15
Gully, John Cor. H., Cornwall, 82
Gully, Thomas Lieut. H., Somerset, 81
Gully, William Capt. H., Cornwall, 71
Gunne, John Capt. Lieut. F., Cornwall, 69
Gunter, George Col. H., 74
Gunter, Walter Quart. H., Worcester, 124
Guy, Charles Lieut. F., Cornwall, 19
Guy, John Quart. H., Dorset, 133
Guy, William Capt. F., Westmorland, 22
Guy, William Lieut. F., Hereford, 79
Gwatkin, Thomas Capt. Lieut. F., L. & W., 69
Gwilliam/Gwylliam, William Lieut. F., Hereford, stray, 164
Gwillim/Gwillym, George Lieut. Col. F., L. & W., 9, 149
Gwinn, George Lieut. Col. F., 10, 112(?). Although Gwinn requested inclusion, his claim is not included under any regiment in the list. Possibly he is the 'Lieut. Col. George ___' mentioned by an officer in Sir James Pennyman's regiment, whose surname is omitted in error.
Gwyllim/Gwillym, William Capt. H., Monmouth, 153
Gwyn, ___ Maj. F., 142
Gwyn, ___ Capt. F., 142
Gwyn/Gwynne, Griffith Ens. F., Carmarthen, 142
Gwynn/Gwynne, Thomas Quart. H., L. & W., 109
Gwynne, ___ ___ F., 74
Gwynne, John Capt. F., L. & W., 80
Gwynne Richard Ens. F., Glamorgan, 83
Gwynne, Rowland Capt. F., 33
Gynnet/Gynnett, Richard Lieut. H., Gloucester, 37
Haberly, Francis Lieut. F., Salop 142
Hack, Fane Capt. F., L. & W., 76
Hacker, Rowland Maj. H., Lincoln, 11, 95
Hacket, ___ Capt. H., Sir William Butler, 30
Hackett, Richard Capt. H., Sir Nicholas Crisp, 45
Hackworth, James Ens. F., Durham 80
Haddock, Walter Quart. H., Stafford, 18
Haddon, Robert Quart. H., Lincoln, stray, 160
Hadds, Christopher Ens. F., Kent, 92
Hadonett, ___ Capt. F., 51
Hagedot, Peter Maj. H., 18
Haggard, John Lieut. F., Somerset, 131
Haggerston, George Cor. H., Essex, 13
Haggerston, Ralph Capt. F., Northumberland, 74
Haggerston, Sir Thomas Col. F. (d. 1673), 74. His son, below, was his deputy.
Haggerston, Thomas Lieut. Col. F. (d. 1710), stray, 164
Haine, Thomas Quart. H., Somerset, 113

Hales, Sir Edward Col. H. (d. 1684), 74. This is Sir Edward Hales junior, who was only sixteen in 1642. His father, Sir Edward senior, was a Parliamentarian.
Hales, Stephen Cor. H., Leicester, 109
Halfstaffe, Peter, Armourer, Devon, 172
Hall, ___ Lieut. Col. F., 127
Hall Alexander Ens. F., Bucks, 75. I.O. does not give an arm of service, but the rank of ensign indicates foot.
Hall, Armelius Quart. H., L. & W., 97
Hall, Basill/Bazill Quart. H., York, 90
Hall, Edmund Quart. H., Nottingham, 57
Hall, John Capt. F., Salop, 100
Hall, John Cor. H., L. & W., 138
Hall, John Quart. H., Northumberland, 62
Hall, John Quart. H., Warwick, 95
Hall, John Quart. F., Nottingham, 131
Hall, Matthew Lieut. H., Worcester, 120
Hall, Richard Capt. F., 83
Hall, Richard Cor. H., Stafford, 57
Hall, Thomas Maj. F., York, 30
Hall, Thomas Lieut. H., Kent, 41
Hall, Thomas Ens. F., Worcester, stray, 165
Hall, William Capt. H., Somerset, 81
Hall, William H. & F., Southampton, stray, 157
Hall, William Capt. F., L. & W., 28
Hall, William Lieut. H., York, 48
Hallamore, John Lieut. F., Cornwall, 15
Hallely/Halley, Cutbert Quart. H., York, 125
Hallford/Halford, Matthew Cor. H., Lincoln, 90
Hally/Halley, George Ens. F., York, 58
Halley, John Ens. F., Bedford, 59
Halsal/Halsall, Edward Lieut. F., Lancaster, stray, 164
Halsall, ___ Maj. F., 65
Halsall, John Capt. Lieut. F., Northumberland, 135
Halsall, Thomas Lieut. H., Lancaster, 31
Halsy, ___ Capt. F., 128
Halton, ___ Capt. F., 57
Halyburton/Hallyburton, William Lieut. H., Warwick, 32
Ham, Henry Cor. H., Devon, 78
Hambden, John Capt. F., Middlesex, 14
Hambridge, Henry Quart. H., Somerset, 24
Hambury, John Capt. F., Southampton, 110
Hamerton/Hammerton, Edward Cor. H., York, 142
Hamilton, Claudius Maj. H., 87
Hamilton, Sir James Col. H., 74
Hamilton, James Col. H., 74. Scottish. *Not* the man above.

Index 261

Hamilton, John ___ F., 75. I.O. gives no arm of service for Hamilton or the ensign who cited him, but the rank of ensign indicates foot.
Hamilton, John Capt. H., L. & W., 143
Hamilton, John Cor. H., L. & W., 74
Hamilton, M. Capt. F., 75
Hamilton, Patrick Lieut. H., L. & W., 74
Hamlett/Hamlet, John Quart. H., L. & W., 30
Hamlyn, William Cor. H., Devon, 35
Hamme/Ham, Richard Cor. H., Somerset, 52
Hammond, Anthony Regt. Quart. F., Somerset, 83
Hammond, Charles Capt. F., L. & W., 154
Hammond, Edward Col. H. & F., 75
Hammond, Henry Lieut. H., Salop, 118
Hammond, Robert Capt. F., Dorset, 50
Hampson, ___ Capt. F., 79
Hanbury, John Capt. H., Worcester, 124
Hanby, Christopher Capt. F., York, 85
Hancks/Hanckes, Thomas Scoutmaster, Stafford, 172
Hancock, Jonathan Cor. H., L. & W., 97
Handricson/Handrickson, Harman Sea Capt., L. & W., 167
Handson, Howell Gentleman of the Ordnance, L. & W., 170
Hanes/Haynes, Thomas Quart. H., L. & W., 32
Hanham, William Lieut. F., Norfolk, stray, 164
Hankinson, Rand. Ens. F., L. & W., 150
Hanmer, John Capt. H., 50
Hanse, Thomas Capt. F., Devon, 44
Hanslop, Thomas. Cor. H., L. & W., 17
Hanson, Edward Capt. H., York, 86
Hanworth, Robert Ens. F., Durham, 118
Harber, William Quart. H., L. & W., 56
Harbyn, John Capt. H., 81
Harbyn, Robert Cor. H., Somerset, 81
Harbyn, William Lieut. H., Somerset, 81
Harcourt, Thomas Quart. H., L. & W., 142
Hardcastle, Christopher Cor. H., York, 56
Hardcastle, Edward Cor. H., York, 36
Hardcastle, William Capt. Dr., York, 99
Harding, ___ Capt. H., 98
Harding, Anthony Maj. F., 79
Harding, Giles Quart. H., Somerset, 45
Harding, John Quart. H., Hereford, 42
Hardwick, Ollivere/Olivere Capt. F., L. & W., 132
Hardwick, Robert Quart. H., Somerset, 131
Hardy, James Lieut. F., Lincoln, 112
Hardy, John Lieut. F., Lincoln, 21

Hardy, Nicholas Quart. H., York, 25
Hardy, Richard Lieut. H., Cambridge, 79
Hare, James Capt. F., L. & W., 96
Hare, Richard Quart. H., York, 86
Hare, William Quart. F., York, 86
Harebread, W___ Capt. H., 100
Hargett, Francis Quart. H., Wilts, 64
Harland, Christopher Cor. H., York, 37
Harland, George Quart. H., York, 87
Harland, Michael Capt. Dr., York, 74
Harland, Richard Lieut. H., York, 125
Harley, Thomas Capt. F., L. & W., stray, 163
Harling, ___ Maj. F., 138
Harling, Christopher Ens. F., Westmorland, 107
Harling, Henry Ens. F., L. & W., 138
Harlow, ___ Capt. F., 31
Harman, Francis Lieut. H., Somerset, 35
Harman, James Lieut. F., L. & W., 74
Harman, Samuel Lieut. H., Northampton, 121
Harmer, Thomas Lieut. H., Norfolk, 72
Harper, Arthur Lieut. F., York, 133
Harper, Roger Ens. F., Durham, 80
Harpur, Sir John Col. H. & Dr., 75
Harpur/Harper, John Capt. H., Hereford, 70
Harriman, Francis Capt. H., Oxon, 90
Harrington, James Cor. H., Leicester, 96
Harris, ___ Lieut. Col. H., 46
Harris, Christopher Lieut. H., Lancaster, 103
Harris, Edmund Capt. F., Cambridge, 65
Harris, Henry Lieut. F., Monmouth, 108
Harris, Humphry Cor. H., Carmarthen, 64
Harris, John Capt. H., Surrey, 153
Harris, John Quart. H., Dorset, 51
Harris, John Quart. H., Derby, 63
Harris, John Chirurgion, Cornwall, 173
Harris, Robert Col. H., 75
Harris, Robert Ens. F., Salop, 93
Harris, Rowland Lieut. H., Gloucester, 149
Harris, Thomas Capt. F., L. & W., 39
Harris, Thomas Lieut. F., Cornwall, 69
Harris, Thomas Quart. F., Worcester, 19
Harrison, ___ Capt. H., 84
Harrison, ___ Capt. F., Sir Richard Hutton, 86
Harrison, ___ Capt. F., Sir Henry Slingsby, 129
Harrison, Cutbert Ens. F., Durham, 42

Harrison, Eusebius Lieut. H., Middlesex, 108
Harrison, Lionel/Lionell Cor. H., Somerset, 13
Harrison, Michael Ens. F., York, 22
Harrison, Ralph Ens. F., L. & W., 65
Harrison, Richard Capt. H., 44
Harrison, Robert Quart. H., Westmorland, 101
Harrison, Robert 'Conductor of the Train', L. & W., 170
Harrison, Stephen Quart. H., Durham, 28
Harrison, Thomas Cor. H., L. & W., 140
Harrison, William Lieut. H., Nottingham, 31
Harrison, William Lieut. Dr., Worcester, 45
Harrison, William Quart. Dr., York, 91
Harrold, Thomas Capt. Pioneers, Sussex, 172
Harry, Lyson Ens. F., Glamorgan, 152
Hart, John Lieut. H., Surrey, 95
Hart, Thomas Capt. F., Somerset, 141
Hart, Thomas Lieut. F., Somerset, 16
Hart, Thomas Cor. H., Kent, 66
Hart, Sir William Col. F., 76. A 1651 regiment.
Hartford, Anthony Quart. H., Devon, 50
Hartford, John Quart. H., Sussex, 62
Hartgill, Arthur Ens. F., Somerset, 83
Hartly/Hartley, William Lieut. H., Bucks, stray, 158
Hartshorne, Maurice Quart. H., Salop, 32
Harvey, ___ Maj. F., 121
Harvey, John Maj. H., 151
Harvey, William Ens. F., Chester, stray, 165
Harvill, William Quart. H., Kent, 110
Harvy, Francis Capt. F., Somerset, stray, 163
Harvy, John Capt. H., Somerset, stray, 157
Harvy/Harvey, William Ens. F., Warwick, stray, 165
Harwell, George Lieut. F., Devon, 71
Harwood, James Cor. H., York, 90
Harwood, John Quart. F., Northumberland, 27
Harwood, Laurence Lieut. H., York, 68
Harwood, Richard Cor. H., Wilts, 79
Harwood, Thomas Cor. H., Gloucester, 37
Haselin, John Ens. F., Sussex, 127
Haslewood, John Maj. H., L. & W., 11, 26, 99. Claims under Sir Francis Mackworth; also mentioned by an officer claiming under a John Blunt, who may also have been in Mackworth's.
Hasselwood, ___ Maj. H., 81
Hassellwood, ___ Capt. H., George Heron, 79
Hassellwood, ___ Capt. H., stray, 160. Possibly the man above, as both are mentioned by officers claiming from Lincoln.

Hasselwood, John Capt. H., stray, 161
Hasset, John Capt. F., 76
Hastings, Henry Maj. H., stray, 60.
Hastings, Henry Capt. H., 77. Possibly the man above, as both officers are mentioned by men from Dorset.
Hastings, Sir Richard Col. H., 76
Hastings, Walter Capt. H., 96
Haswel/Haswell, James Maj. H., L. & W., 11, 98
Hatcher, Nicholas Capt. H., Surrey, 41
Hathaway, Thomas Cor. H., L. & W., 46
Hatton, ___ Maj. H., 149
Hatton, ___ Capt. H., 150
Hatton, Robert Col. H., 76
Haughton, John Lieut. F., Lancaster, 50
Haughton, John Ens. F., Cornwall, 43
Haughton, Thomas Capt. H., Lancaster, 31
Haughton, ___ Lieut. Col. H. (k. 1643; Newbury I), 48. Reid gives his first name as William.
Haughton, Thomas Capt. F., Lancaster, 138
Haughton, William Lieut. F., Devon, 43
Haulgh, Robert Lieut. H., Lancaster, 17
Havercamp, Robert Lieut. F., L. & W., 98
Hawes, Henry Lieut. H., Lincoln, 108
Hawes, John Capt. F., 102
Hawes, Nicholas Capt. H., Cornwall, 19
Hawes, Reynold Cor. H., Cornwall, 14
Hawes, Thomas Lieut. H., Cornwall, 19
Hawk/Hawke, Josias Capt. H., Cornwall, 19
Hawk/Hawke, Nicholas Lieut. H., Cornwall, 19
Hawke, Charles Capt. F., 72
Hawke, John Lieut. F., Cornwall, 139
Hawke, Nevill Ens. F., Cornwall, 72
Hawke, Peter Chirurgion, Cornwall, 173
Hawker, Hugh Lieut. F., Oxon, 129
Hawkes, John Lieut. F., L. & W., 42
Hawkins, Edward Lieut. F., Cornwall, 72
Hawkins, Hugh Lieut. F., Glamorgan, 151
Hawkins, Jonathan Provost Marshall General, Devon, 171
Hawkins, Peter Lieut. H., York, 39
Hawkins, Sir Stephen Col. F., 76
Hawkins, Thomas Capt. Lieut. F., Somerset, 112
Hawksly, Gregory Quart. H., L. & W., 56
Hawky, Francis Ens. F., Cornwall, 140
Hawley, ___ Maj. F., 83
Hawley, Christopher Capt. F., Leicester, 43

Index   265

Hawley, William Lieut. Col. F., L. & W., 21
Hawly, Edmund Capt. H., Hereford, stray, 157
Hawly, [Sir Francis] Lord, Col. H. & F. (d. 1684), 76
Hawly, William 'Quart. Gen. in York', York, stray, 166
Haxby, ___ Capt. H., 90
Hay, James Col. Dr., L. & W., 9, 146
Hay, John Ens. F., Cornwall, 71
Hayly, Richard Quart. H., Dorset, 151
Hayme, John Lieut. F., Cornwall, 69
Hayne, George Ens. F., Dorset, 63
Hayne, John Capt. H., Somerset, 155
Hayne/Haynes, Zachary Quart. H., Devon, 35
Haynes, Edward Cor. H., Northumberland, 58
Haynes, John Quart. H., Warwick, 89
Hayward, Henry Quart. H., Derby, 57
Hayward, John Capt. F., Gloucester, 116
Hayward, John Ens. F., Worcester, 116
Hayward, Robert Cor. H., Wilts, 41
Hazard/Hazzard, Thomas Ens. F., L. & W., 66
Hazzard, Henry Lieut. F., Monmouth, 153
Hea__, John Capt. H., 30
Head, William Lieut. H., Wilts, 150
Heald, William Lieut. H., Lancaster, 143
Healing, Edward Lieut. F., Salop, 25
Heap/Heape, Thomas Lieut. H., L. & W., 64
Heape, Richard Lieut. F., Lancaster, stray, 164
Heapes/Heape, Thomas Quart. H., Lancaster, stray, 161. Claims under Captain William Kay, who claims under Edward Rawston.
Hearle, Francis Lieut. H., Cornwall, 19
Heaten/Heaton, Samuel Capt. F., Cornwall, 82
Heath, Francis ___ F., 76
Heath, John ___ ___, 77
Heath, Thomas Lieut. F., Somerset, 131
Heather, Richard Lieut. F., L. & W., 110
Heaton, Robert Cor. Dr., Worcester, 154
Heaven, Rowland Lieut. H., Hereford, 108
Hebburn, Ralph Col. F., 77
Hebden, Edward Quart. H., York, 102
Heddon, Edmund Ens. F., Cornwall, 20
Hedge, Matthew Ens. F., Essex, 58
Hedly/Headly, Martin Lieut. H., York, 102
Hedworth, Ralph Quart. H., Durham, 136
Hedworth, William Capt. F., Durham, 109
Hedworth, William Ens. F., Durham, 19
Heigham, George Ens. F., Suffolk, stray, 165. Listed as a stray, but claims under

Major Henry Crompton of Lord Piercy's (Percy's) regiment.
Heighington John Cor. H., Durham, 145
Heighington, Robert Capt. F., Durham, 39
Hele, Sir John Col. H., 77
Hele, John Ens. F., Devon, 36
Hele, Lewis Capt. H., Devon, 77
Hele, Philip/Phillip Ens. F., Essex, 20
Hele, Sir Thomas Col. H. (d. 1670), 77
Helme, Richard Quart. H., Wiltshire, 82
Helyer, William Col. H., 78
Hemmings/Hemings, John Ens. F., Gloucester, 79
Hemsworth, ___ Capt. F., 147
Henderson, Sir John, 78. I.O. does not offer this officer's first name, rank or arm of service, but his single claiming officer claims under Lieutenant Colonel Richard Neville, who was known to be Sir John Henderson's deputy. Spent much time in foreign service (*see* ODNB). Still alive in January 1658, when he was court-martialled after surrendering in Danish-Norwegian service. Pardoned after British intervention. His death is obscure.
Hene, Henry Maj. H., 119
Henne, Hugh Capt. F., 18
Hensman, William Engineer, L. & W., 170
Herbert, Charles Proger ___ F., 78. Charles Proger; the family sometimes used 'ap Herbert' as a suffix (Salzman, p.217).
Herbert, Charles Quart. H., L. & W., 123
Herbert, Edward Lord Cherbury, F. (d. 1648), 78. Herbert did not command the regiment himself, but appointed Sir Richard Lawdy.
Herbert, Edward Capt. H., Cardigan, stray, 157
Herbert, Edward ___ F., 78
Herbert, George Lieut. H., Durham, 148
Herbert, Henry Capt. H., Monmouth, 153
Herbert, Sir John Capt. H., 105
Herbert, John Ens. F., Hereford, 53
Herbert, Phillip Quart. H., York, 138
Herbert, [Richard] Lord, Col. F. (d. 1655), 28, 78. Eldest son of Edward Herbert, Lord Cherbury. Commissioned in the same month to raise a regiment of foot; in October commissioned as a captain of horse (ODNB; meaning he must be the 'Colonel Richard Herbert' mentioned by an officer under Lord Digby).
Herbert, Richard Col. F., 78. Reid believes this to be Lord Richard Herbert, above.
Herbert, Walter Capt. H., Brecon, 64
Herlackenden, Thomas Col. F., 79
Hernaman, Richard Lieut. H., Devon, 14
Herod, Thomas Cor. H., Derby, 127
Heron, George Col. H. (k. 1643; Adwalton Moor), 79
Heron, Sir H__ ___ H., 114
Heron, John Col. H. (k. 1643; Gainsborough), 79

Heron, John Capt. Lieut. H., 46
Heron, Ralph Lieut. F., Newcastle, 100
Heron, Richard Lieut. H., Rutland, 48
Heron, Thomas Maj. H., 48
Heron, William Lieut. F., L. & W., 26
Herris, Christopher Lieut. H., Essex, 98
Hertford, [William Seymour] Marquess of Col. H. & F. (d. 1660), 79
Heskith, Bartholomew Lieut. H., L. & W., 124
Heskith, Cutbert Capt. H., Lancaster, 137
Heskith, Richard Lieut. H., Lancaster, stray, 158
Heskith, Richard Lieut. F., L. & W., 52
Heskith, Robert Capt. F., 38
Heskith, Thomas Capt. F., Lancaster, 58
Hesletine, George Ens. F., York, 129
Hetherington, ___ Capt. F., 138
Hetherington, George Lieut. F., L. & W., 33
Hetherington, William Quart. H., Cumberland, 30
Hett, John Ens. F., Durham, 43
Heveningham, Christopher Maj. H., 93
Heveningham, Nathaniel Col. H., 79
Heveningham, Simon Lieut. Col. F., L. & W., 10, 60, 93. Mentioned by an ensign under Thomas Leveson; mentioned as a major by a stray lieutenant from Stafford; claims as a lieutenant colonel under Sir John Fitzherbert.
Hewit/Hewitt, Thomas Capt. H., Kent, 102
Hewitson, William Cor. H., Lancaster, stray, 159
Heymor, ___ Capt. H., 79
Heymor, Richard Col. H. & F., 79
Heytor, William Cor. H., Somerset, 142
Hichmough/Hitchmough, Thomas Quart. H., Norfolk, 102
Hickin, Samuel Ens. F., Stafford, 16
Hickman, William Capt. H., 109
Hickmans/Hickman, William Ens. F., Stafford, 93
Hicks, ___ Capt. F., 143
Hicks, Henry Lieut. H., L. & W., 110
Hicks, Henry Lieut. F., Cornwall, 140
Hicks, John Capt. F., L. & W., 21
Hicks, Randall Ens. F., Cornwall, 140
Hicks, William Capt. F., L. & W., 97
Hier, William Quart. H., Somerset, 76
Higges, Joseph Ens. F., Middlesex, 150
Higgins/Higgen, Thomas Quart. H., Nottingham, stray, 160
Highdown, Richard Capt. H., Somerset, 113
Highmore, Robert Capt. F., Cumberland, 47
Hilbron, Thomas Cor. H., Somerset, 155
Hildreth, John Quart. H., Northumberland, 148

Hildreth, William Quart. Dr., York, 149
Hildsly, William Lieut. H., Oxon, 16
Hill, ___ Capt. H., 150
Hill, Alexander 'Conductor of the Train', L. & W., 170
Hill, Anthony Lieut. F., Hereford, 42
Hill, George Capt. F., L. & W., 65
Hill, Henry, Quart. H., Dorset, 133
Hill, Humphry Ens. F., Cornwall, 139
Hill, James Quart. H., L. & W., 46
Hill, John Capt. F., L. & W., 118
Hill, John Cor. H., Hereford, 94
Hill, John Ens. ___, Denbigh, 98. I.O. does not give an arm of service, but besides his rank indicating he was a foot officer he claims under Sir Thomas Lunsford, whose foot regiment was well known.
Hill, Richard Lieut. F., Worcester, 94
Hill, Robert Capt. H., Richard Thornhill, 137
Hill, Robert Capt. H., L. & W., Earl of Cleveland, 40
Hill, Robert Capt. H., Devon, Sir Thomas Hele, 77
Hill, Thomas Capt. F., Hereford, 94
Hill, Thomas Lieut. H., L. & W., 106
Hill, William Quart. H., Dorset, 15
Hillary, Roger Lieut. F., Dorset, 120
Hillyard, ___ Capt. H., 139
Hillyard, Henry Col. F., 80
Hillyard, John Maj. F., 22
Hillyard/Hylliard, Ralph Lieut. H., Southampton, 81
Hillyard, Sir Robert ___ H. (d. 1685), 90. Usually 'Hildyard'.
Hilton, John Col. F. & Dr., 80
Hilton, John Capt. F., 80
Hilton, Lancelot Lieut. H., Westmorland, 107
Hilton, Robert Capt. H., Westmorland, 107
Hinane, James Ens. F., L. & W., 120
Hinchcliffe/Hinchliffe, Thomas Quart. F., York, 88
Hinckly/Hincly, Edward Cor. H., L. & W., 41
Hindmarsh, James Ens. F., York, 80
Hindmer/Hinmer, William Ens. F., Westmorland, 49
Hinton, Daniel Capt. F., L. & W., 65
Hinton, Roger Cor. H., Stafford, 16
Hitchcock, George Capt. F., Wilts, 96
Hittson, John Lieut. F., Cornwall, 15
Hobart/Hobbart, George Cor. H., Norfolk, 79
Hobbs, Arthur Capt. H., 82
Hobbs, Peter Quart. H., Southampton, 84
Hobbs, William Capt. Lieut. F., Somerset, 14
Hobman, William Lieut. H., York, 96

Index   269

Hobson, James Quart. H., Northumberland, 147
Hockmore, Gregory ___ H., stray, 160
Hodden, Michael Lieut. F., Cornwall, 122
Hoddenot, ___ Capt. F., 24
Hodder, Fabian Lieut. F., Dorset, 16
Hodder, John Ens. F., Dorset, 16
Hoddy, Henry Quart. H., Dorset, 34
Hodenot, Peter Quart. H., L. & W., 99
Hodge, Peter Ens. F., Cornwall, 20
Hodge, Walter Quart. H., Cornwall, 72
Hodges, Henry Quart. H., Somerset, 28
Hodges, John Cor. H., Somerset, 59
Hodges, Laurence Quart. H., Somerset, stray, 160
Hodges, William Capt. H., Somerset, 59
Hodgeson/Hodgson, Francis Cor. H., Durham, 62
Hodgeson/Hodgson, Leonard Cor. H., Newcastle, 13
Hodgekin/Hodgkin, Michael Lieut. F., Chester, 64
Hodgekin/Hodgkin, Ralph Quart. H., Chester, 30
Hodginson, George Lieut. H., York, 80
Hodgkinson, Richard Gentleman of the Ordnance, L. & W., 170
Hodgson, Alexander Lieut. H., Cumberland, 48
Hodgson, Andrew Quart. H., L. & W., 48
Hodgson, Edward Lieut. F., Northumberland, stray, 164
Hodgson, Edward Quart. H., Durham, 136
Hodgson, Eleazer Capt. F., 100
Hodgson, Francis Quart. H., Northumberland, 148
Hodgson, Lawrence/Laurence Quart. H., York, 97
Hodgson, Matthew Cor. H., Durham, 34
Hodgson, Ralph Cor. H., York, 90
Hodgson, Richard Lieut. H., Warwick, 136
Hodgson, Thomas Lieut. H., York, 97
Hodgson, Thomas Cor. H., Stafford, 60
Hodgson, William Capt. F., Northumberland, 68
Hodgson, William Capt. H., Durham, 108
Hoginson, George Lieut. ___, York, 88
Holden, ___ Capt. H., 137
Holden, Francis Capt. H., Middlesex, 137
Holden, Humphry Ens. F., Durham, 136
Holden, John Capt. F., L. & W., 96
Holder, Henry Capt. F., Nottingham, 51
Holder, Toby Capt. H., Nottingham, stray, 157
Holdich, Philip/Phillip Ens. F., Devon, 72
Holdich, Nicholas Lieut. H., Devon, 84
Holland, ___ ___ H., 80. Listed after the Earl of Holland; possibly him. I.O. gives no
   name, rank or arm of service, but the lieutenant who claims under him is indexed

as a cavalry officer.
Holland, [Henry Rich] Earl of, Col. F. (executed 1649), 80
Holland, Edward Quart. H., Nottingham, 104
Holland, John Cor. H., York, 100
Holland, John Scoutmaster, Leicester, 172
Holland, Peter Quart. H., York, 87
Holland, Thomas Capt. F., stray, 165
Holland, Thomas Cor. H., L. & W., stray, 159. Claims under Sir Jeffery Shakerly, known to be deputy to Robert Werden, who latterly commanded John Marrow's Horse after Marrow's death in 1644.
Holland, William Capt. Pioneers 'in Oxford', Oxon, 171
Hollingworth, Edward Cor. H., Nottingham, stray, 159
Hollis, George, Marshall, Oxon, 171
Hollis, Gervase Col. F. (d. 1675), 80
Hollis, Nicholas Adjutant, Bucks, 170
Hollyland, Hercules Col. F., 80
Holm/Holmes, Henry Capt. H., York, 47
Holman, Andrew Regt. Quart. Dr., Devon, 83
Holman, Degory Quart. H., Cornwall, 135
Holman, Henry Lieut. F., Worcester, 94
Holman, John Lieut. F., Cornwall, 71
Holman, Morgan Lieut. F., Somerset, 133
Holman, William Chirurgion, Dorset, 173
Holme/Holmes, John Ens. F., Derby, 100
Holme/Holmes, Thomas Ens. F., Lancaster, 38
Holmes, Thomas Capt. H., Somerset, 50
Holmes, Walter Ens. F., York, 129
Holmes, William Capt. F., L. & W., stray, 163
Holt, Richard Capt. F. 'of the Free-holders', Lancaster, stray, 163
Holt, Robert Ens. F., Lancaster, 66
Holt, Thomas Cor. H., Middlesex, 51
Holt, Thomas Quart. H., York, 136
Holtby, Marmaduke Capt. Dr./Col. H. & F., 9, 73, 84, 108, 154. Mentioned as a captain of horse under Sir Francis Wortley; as a lieutenant colonel of horse under Sir Robert Howard (who took over from Wortley); as an officer of unknown rank, by two officers of horse and one of foot; and claims in his own right as a colonel of horse and foot, under the Marquess of Newcastle.
Holyman/Hollyman, Edward Cor. H., Nottingham, stray, 159
Homerson, Ralph Ens. F., Wilts, 127
Honycombe, John Ens. F., Cornwall, 139
Honywell, William Lieut. F., Cornwall, 140
Hoodspeth, George Ens. F., Northumberland, 135
Hoodspeth, Henry Lieut. F., Northumberland, 134
Hooke, Edmund Cor. H., Southampton, 119
Hooker, Amethyst Lieut. F., Cornwall, 140

Hoole, John Quart. H., Lancaster, stray, 161. Claims under Captain George Westby, who in turn claims under Sir Thomas Tildesly.
Hooper, Gregory Quart. H., Dorset, 133
Hooper, Henry Lieut. F., Devon, 35
Hooper, Sir Thomas Col. H., 16, 80. Mentioned by a cornet under Sir Arthur Aston, and directly by a number of dragoon officers.
Hooper, Zorobabell Capt. Pioneers, Somerset, 171
Hope, John Lieut. H., York, 90
Hopkins, George Quart. H., Warwick, 109
Hopkins, Thomas Capt. F., Glamorgan, 141
Hopkins, William Capt. F., stray, 164
Hopkins, William Lieut. F., L. & W., 122
Hoply/Hopley, Richard Lieut. H., Hereford, 116
Hopps/Hoppes, Thomas Ens. F., York, 133
Hopton, ___ Lieut. Col. H., Lord Hopton, 81
Hopton, Sir Edward [Lieut.] Col. F. (d. 1668), 81. Knighted at Leicester, 1645.
Hopton, Joseph Lieut. F., Somerset, 83
Hopton, Sir Ralph (later Lord Hopton) Col. H., F. & Dr. (d. 1652), 81. Besides a great many horse and foot officers, also mentioned by a naval officer.
Hopton, William ___ F., 84. Reid suggests this unranked officer could be the lieutenant colonel Hopton, above, who claims under Lord Hopton; and also that a Captain John Waldron mentioned under William Hopton is probably the same man who claims under Lord Hopton.
Hopton, William Ens. F., L. & W., 66
Hord, Edmund Chirurgion, Surrey, 173
Hore, John Capt. F., Dorset, 20
Hore, Matthew Ens. F., Cornwall, 54
Hornabrook/Hornbook, Henry Quart. H., Devon, 40
Horne, Thomas Quart. ___, York, 58
Horne, Thomas Quart. H., Hereford, 117
Horne, William Ens. F., Devon, 35
Horner, Joseph Capt. Lieut. H., Gloucester, 36
Horsey, John Quart. H., Somerset, 91
Horsman, Thomas Quart. F., Stafford, 17
Horsmanden, Warham Capt. F., Kent, 41
Horton, Arthur Capt. F., 127
Horton, Robert Capt. H., Chester, 39
Horton, William Capt. F., Worcester, 63
Horton, William Lieut. H., Gloucester, 102
Horwood/Harwood, Kemp Cor. H., Worcester, 128. Served in 1651.
Hory/Hovy, Robert Capt. Dr., York, 88
Hosier, George Capt. H., Salop, 142
Hoskins, ___ Capt. F., 53
Hoskins, Henry Capt. F., Devon, 39
Hoskins, James Lieut. F., Dorset, 15

Hoskins, Thomas Ens. F., Cornwall, 20
Hosyer, George Capt. F., 55
Hough, Gilbert Capt. F., York, 107
Houghton, Sir Gilbert Col. Dr. (d. 1648), 84
Houghton/Haughton, William Cor. H., L. & W., 124
How/Howe, Christopher Cor. H., Northumberland, 115
How, John Cor. H., Northumberland, 115
Howard, ___ Capt. F., 84
Howard, Alexander Quart. H., Bucks, 30
Howard, Edw. Capt. F., stray, 165
Howard, Sir Francis Col. H. & Dr., (d. 1659), 84. Took over the dragoon regiment of his brother, k. in 1642, and the horse regiment of his son, k. in 1643. Both brother and son were called Thomas Howard, which has caused some confusion in I.O., further complicated by men claiming under a third Thomas Howard, brother of Lord Andover.
Howard, John Lieut. F., Glamorgan, 132
Howard, Sir Robert Col. H., F. & Dr. (d. 1653), 84
Howard, Thomas Col. H. (d. 1706), 84. Younger brother of Viscount Andover; not connected to Sir Francis Howard, above (whose son and brother were also called Thomas, and also fought for the King).
Howard, Thomas Col. Dr. (k. 1642; Piercebridge), 85
Howard, Thomas Lieut. H., Surrey, 63
Howard, Thomas Lieut. H., Salop, stray, 158
Howarth, Humphry Ens. F., Hereford, 42
Howel/Howell, Benjamin Ens. F., Carmarthen, 29
Howell, David Capt. F., 65
Howell, Francis Chirurgion, Southampton, 173
Howell, John Quart. H., Pembroke, 33
Howell, Matthew Lieut. F., L. & W., 120
Howell, Nicholas Ens. F., Cornwall, 50
Howell, Richard Cor. Dr., Somerset, 155
Howes, John Ens. F., Cornwall, 140
Howson, William Ens. F., Lincoln, 67
Howthwaite/Howthwait, Robert Lieut. F., Cumberland, stray, 164
Hoyden/Hoydon, Thomas Ens. F., Essex, 58
Hubberstay, Robert Ens. F., L. & W., 98
Hubert, John Cor. H., L. & W., 119
Huckwell, Edward Lieut. F., Oxon, 79
Hudleston, James Capt. F., Sir Francis Gamul, 64
Huddleston, Edward Maj. F., L. & W., 11, 73, 85. Claims under Edward Grey; also mentioned by an ensign under Sir William Huddleston.
Huddleston, Ingoldby Capt. F., 85
Huddleston, James Capt. F., Richard Beard, 21
Huddleston, Joseph Capt. H., Cumberland, 85. Also mentioned as a captain of foot in the same regiment.

Huddleston, Sir William Col. H. & F., 85
Huddleston, William Capt. F., Cumberland, 88
Huddy, John Quart. H., Cornwall, 14
Hudson, Edw. Quart. H., York, 108
Hudson, Gilbert Lieut. Dr., Worcester, 146. Claims as foot, but served in Henry Washington's dragoons.
Hudson, Jeffery Capt. H., Rutland, stray, 157
Hudson, John Quart. F., Northumberland, 149
Hudson, Michael Col. H. & F., 85
Hudson, Richard Capt. H., L. & W., stray, 157
Hugh, Thomas Lieut. F., Cornwall, 20
Hughes, Charles Capt. F., 33
Hughes, Charles Ens. F., L. & W., 45
Hughes, David Capt. F., Cornwall, 33
Hughes, Francis Ens. F., Worcester, 123
Hughes, Giles Quart. H., Monmouth, 116
Hughes, John Maj. F., L. & W., 11, 66
Hughes, John Cor. H., Flint, 128
Hughes, Richard Quart. H., Lincoln, 22
Hughes, Robert Capt. F., Denbigh, 121
Hughes, Robert Lieut. Dr., Denbigh, 61
Hughes, Thomas Lieut. F., Monmouth, 153
Hughes, Walter Ens. F., Monmouth, 87
Hughes, William Capt. F., Gloucester, 45
Hughes, William Lieut. F., L. & W., 31
Hulford, Francis Quart. H., Worcester, 124
Hull, Samuel Lieut. F., Berks, 53
Hull, Thomas Capt. F., L. & W., 53
Hulland, Lewis Lieut. F., Devon, 35
Hullock, William Quart. H., Lincoln, 113
Hulme, Robert Quart. H., Chester, 130
Hulse, Richard Capt. H., 39
Hulst, Thomas Capt. H., Stafford, stray, 157
Hume, George Cor. H., Durham, 136
Hume, James Capt. H., L. & W., 87
Humes, ___ Lieut. Col. Dr., 45
Humphrevile, William Capt. F., Lincoln, 76
Humphreys, David Capt. F., 64
Humphreys, Richard Cor. H., Merioneth, 64
Humphryes, ___ Capt. F., 111
Humphryes/Humphreys, Gabriel Ens. F., Merioneth, 111
Humphreys, Theod. Capt. Dr., L. & W., 141
Humphryston, Edw. Ens. F., Westmorland, 88
Hungate, Francis Lieut. Col. H. (k. 1645; Sherburn-in-Elmet), 85, 143. Deputy to Sir Walter Vavasor; took over in 1644 after Vavasor was badly wounded at Selby

and subsequently went abroad. Mentioned by one officer under Vavasor and several directly.
Hungate, William Maj. H., stray, 160
Hungerford, John Lieut. Col. F., 85, 101. Mentioned by a lieutenant under the Earl of Marlborough, and directly by a captain.
Hungerford, John Commissary, Somerset, 169
Hunks, Sir Fulk Col. H. & F., 85
Hunkyn, ___ Capt. F., 139
Hunlock, Sir Henry ___ H., 63
Hunt, ___ Maj. H., 23
Hunt, Edw. Lieut. H., L. & W., 23
Hunt, John Ens. F., Lincoln, 26
Hunt, John Cor. H., Southampton, 26
Hunt, Richard Lieut. F., Gloucester, 124
Hunt, Richard Chirurgion, Hereford, 173
Hunt, Robert Capt. F., 16
Hunt, Roger Lieut. F., Devon, 115
Hunt, Thomas Cor. H., Worcester, 124
Hunt, Valentine Quart. H., Northampton, 57
Hunt, William Quart. H., Stafford, 96
Hunter, Andrew Cor. H., Northumberland, 62
Hunter, Anthony Capt. F., Cumberland, 85
Hunter, Francis Ens. F., Westmorland, 22
Hunter, George Lieut. H., Durham, 39
Hunter, Richard Capt. H., York, 138
Hunter, Thomas Ens. F., Lancaster, 38
Huntington, John, Chaplain, Lincoln, 174
Huntrayds, William Quart. H., York, 38
Hurter, ___ Lieut. Col. H., Sir William Smith, 129. Possibly the officer below.
Hurter, John Phillip Col. H., 86
Huskyn, ___ Lieut. Col. F., 42
Hussey, John Capt. H., stray, 160
Hussy, James Capt. F., 15
Hussy, John Capt. H., 79
Husy, Clifford Lieut. F., Dorset, 117
Hutchins, Abraham Quart. H., Cornwall, 50
Hutchins, Francis Capt. F., Devon, 69
Hutchins, Thomas Capt. F., Devon, 37
Hutchins, Thomas Lieut. F., Somerset, John Digby, 50
Hutchins, Thomas Lieut. F., Cornwall, Sir Bevil Greenvile, 71
Hutchins, William Lieut. F., Devon, 37
Hutchins, William Ens. F., Cornwall, 122
Hutchinson, ___ Lieut. Col. H., Sir William Pennyman, 113
Hutchinson, ___ Lieut. Col. H., Lord General Ruthen, 121
Hutchinson, ___ Maj. H., Sir Phillip Musgrave, 107

Hutchinson, Arthur Quart. H., York, 121
Hutchinson, Christopher Cor. H., York, 142
Hutchinson, Edw. Maj. H., Sir William Pennyman, 113
Hutchinson, Hugh Lieut. F., Northumberland, 69
Hutchinson, Jonathan Cor. H., Lincoln, 148
Hutchinson, Joseph Quart. H., Lincoln, 48
Hutchinson, Nicholas Ens. F., Cumberland, 58
Hutchinson, Robert Lieut. H., York, 92
Hutchinson, Thomas Ens. F., Westmorland, 107
Huthwayte, John Lieut. H., Northampton, 113
Hutton, John Quart. H., Durham, 37
Hutton, Ralph Quart. Dr., Durham, 73
Hutton, Sir Richard Col. F. (k. 1645; Sherburn-in-Elmet), 86
Hutton, Toby Cor. H., Durham, 134
Hutton, William Lieut. H., L. & W., 76
Huxley, Anthony 'Engineer and Chaplain', Derby, 170. An addition from the errata.
Hyde, Anthony Capt. H., Kent, 59
Hyde, Humphry Capt. H., 45
Hyde, Mandevile/Mandivile Lieut. H., Dorset, 75
Hyde, Martin Quart. H., Nottingham, 90
Hyde, Richard Capt. H., Lincoln, 90
Hyde, Thomas Quart. F., Somerset, 114
Ilsley, George Quart. H., Stafford, 89
Iley, Thomas Lieut. H., Durham, 136
Ily/Iley, Thomas Cor. H., Durham, 22
Ingledew, John Quart. H., Durham, 55
Ingleton, Robert Cor. H., Lancaster, 137
Ingram, ___ Capt. F., 121
Ingram, Henry Capt. H., stray, 159
Ingram, William Sea Capt. *Friendship*, Prince Rupert, York, 167
Innes, Alexander Cor. Dr., L. & W., 81
Irish, James Quart. H., L. & W., 37
Irish, Richard Lieut. F., Devon, 127
Ironmonger, Humphry Lieut. H., Stafford, stray, 158
Ironmonger, Nicholas Quart. H., Leicester, 62
Ironmonger, William Quart. H., Bedford, 42
Irton, Christopher Cor. H., Cumberland, 85
Irton, Roger Capt. F., Cumberland, 85
Isaac, Erasmus Lieut. H., Devon, 23
Isbrant, Gerard Sea Capt., *St. Patrick*, Sir Nicholas Crisp, L. & W., 167
Ivat, Thomas Capt. F., Devon, 14
Ivy, Ferdinando Cor. H., Somerset, 28
Ivy, William Capt. F., Dorset, 79
Izod, Henry Capt. H., Gloucester, 150
Jackson, ___ Lieut. Col. F., 60

Jackson, ___ Maj. H., 73
Jackson, ___ Capt. Dr., 80
Jackson, Andrew Quart. H., L. & W., 48
Jackson, Charles Capt. F., York, 125
Jackson, Charles Quart. H., York, 139
Jackson, George Cor. H., Cumberland, 107
Jackson, Henry Quart. H., York, 142
Jackson, John Maj. H., 37
Jackson, John Capt. F., York, 112
Jackson, John Lieut. H., L. & W., Prince Charles, 37
Jackson, John Lieut. H., Devon, Sir Thomas Hele, 77
Jackson, John Lieut. H., York, Lord Langdale, 90
Jackson, Robert Quart. H., Wilts, 119
Jackson, Thomas Capt. H., Durham, Sir Francis Anderson, 13
Jackson, Thomas Capt. H. & Dr., Newcastle, Sir John Marlay, 100
Jackson, Thomas Ens. F., York, 146
Jackson, Thomas Quart. H., Lincoln, Sir Peregrine Berty, 25
Jackson, William Cor. H., Lincoln, 29
Jackson, William Commissary Assistant, Chester, 169
Jacob, John Maj. F., 35, 165. Mentioned by two Devon officers, one a stray and the other claiming under Sir Henry Cary.
James, ___ Lieut. Col. F., 126
James, ___ Capt. F., 110
James, Andrew Capt. F., stray, 164
James, Hugh Capt. H., Cumberland, 106
James, John Regt. Quart. F., Monmouth, 117
James, Phillip/Philip Cor. H., Monmouth, 116
James, Richard Cor. H., Nottingham, 69
James, Richard Ens. F., L. & W., 105
James, Robert Quart. H., L. & W., 66
James, William Capt. F., L. & W., 18
James, William Capt. F., Northampton, 109
James, William Ens. F., Salop, 63
Janines, Richard Lieut. F., Chester, 64
Jansey, Lewis Ens. F., Hereford, 94
Jaques, Francis Lieut. H., York, 49
Jarvis, Henry Capt. H., 75
Jauncy, John Capt. Lieut. F., Radnor, 76
Jay, Stephen Ens. F., Cornwall, 104
Jay, Thomas Commissary General, L. & W., 169
Jeanes, George Lieut. F., Carmarthen, 65
Jeanes, Thomas Quart. H., Southampton, 134
Jefferson, William Quart. H., York, 100
Jeffery/Jefferyes, John Cor. H., Somerset, 141
Jefferyes, Thomas Cor. H., Stafford, 17

Index

Jefferies/Jefferyes, Edw. Capt. F., Denbigh, 27
Jellico, John Lieut. H., Worcester, 75
Jemmett/Jemmet, Warham Capt. F., L. & W., 115
Jenkin, John Ens. F., Cornwall, 72
Jenkin, Patrick Capt. F., Cornwall, 20
Jenkin, Petherick/Pethereck Capt. F., Cornwall, 69
Jenkins, ___ Capt. F., 111
Jenkins, Thomas Cor. H., Devon, 23
Jenkins, Toby [or Tobias] Capt. H./Maj. H./Maj. F., 38, 86. Took over Sir Hugh Cholmly's Foot in 1645 after the surrender of Scarborough, and transferred it to Newark. Mentioned as a captain and a major of horse, and as a major of foot.
Jennings, Charles Col. F., 86
Jennings, John Lieut. F., L. & W., 51
Jennings, Ralph Lieut. H., Chester, 118
Jennings, Richard Capt. F., Essex, 57
Jennings, Thomas Maj. F., 19
Jepthcott, Henry Quart. H., Warwick, stray, 160
Jepthson, Edmund Lieut. H., Lancaster, stray, 158
Jervis, John Ens. F., L. & W., 78
Jesson, John Quart. H., Leicester, stray, 160
Jewel/Jewell, John Quart. H., L. & W., 19
Jewell, Joseph Lieut. F., Cornwall, 14
Jewell, Nicholas Ens. F., Cornwall, 144
Jewkes, Henry Lieut. H., Middlesex, 108
Job, Richard Lieut. F., Cornwall, 69
John, Caleb Ens. F., Cornwall, 140
John, Howell Ens. F., Brecon, 116
Johnson, ___ ___ H., 86
Johnson, Archibald Capt. H., L. & W., 74
Johnson, George Quart. H., Carmarthen, 30
Johnson, George Quart. H., Essex, 121
Johnson, James Lieut. H., Kent, stray, 158
Johnson, John Lieut. H., L. & W., 144
Johnson, John Sea Capt., *Newcastle*, Marquess of Newcastle, L. & W., 167
Johnson, Laurence/Lawrence Quart. H., L. & W., 98
Johnson, Marmaduke Lieut. H., Nottingham, 115
Johnson, Martin Ens. F., L. & W., stray, 165
Johnson, Oswald Lieut. F., Durham, 58
Johnson, Robert Capt. F., L. & W., 35
Johnson, Robert Lieut. H., Lincoln, 56
Johnson, Thomas Cor. H., Durham, 13
Johnson, Thomas Ens. F., L. & W., 29
Jolly, Nicholas Capt. F., Cornwall, 154
Jones, ___ Capt. H., 147
Jones, ___ Capt. F., Sir John Owen, 111

Jones, ___ *Capt. F.*, Sir Robert Strickland, 133
Jones, ___ *Capt. F.*, Sir Michael Woodhouse, 152
Jones, ___ *Capt. Dr.*, 155
Jones, Daniel Capt. F., Anglesey, 111
Jones, David Lieut. F., Hereford, 122
Jones, David Ens. F., Carmarthen, 33
Jones, Edw. Capt. H., Salop, 142
Jones, Edw. Lieut. Dr., Somerset, stray, 165
Jones, Edw. Cor. H., Montgomery, 95
Jones, Edw. Ens. F., Salop, 30
Jones, Evan Lieut. H., Denbigh, 30
Jones, Henry Ens. F., Glamorgan, 87
Jones, Henry Ens. F., Hereford, 126
Jones, Henry Ens. F., Monmouth, 117
Jones, Howel/Howell Lieut. F., Gloucester, 76
Jones, Hugh Capt. F., 61
Jones, Hugh Capt. Dr. 'in Bristoll', Somerset, stray, 166
Jones, Ithell/Ithel Lieut. F., Flint, 106
Jones, John Lieut. F., Monmouth, 153
Jones, John Cor. H., Monmouth, 149
Jones, John Ens. F., L. & W., 67
Jones, John Ens. F., Hereford, 126
Jones, John Ens. F., Monmouth, 153
Jones, John Quart. H., Kent, 41
Jones, Lewis Ens. F., Somerset, 76
Jones, Matthew Lieut. F., Oxon, 123
Jones, Morgan Quart. H., L. & W., 114
Jones, Richard Maj. F., Denbigh, 11, 60
Jones, Richard Lieut. F., Montgomery, 78
Jones, Richard Lieut. F., L. & W., 83
Jones, Robert Ens. F., Denbigh, 123
Jones, Robert Ens. F., Montgomery, 61
Jones, Stephen Quart. H., Somerset, 155
Jones, Thomas Capt. F., Carmarthen, 142
Jones, Thomas Capt. F., Carmarthen, 142. Same regiment as above. Possibly the same man, but the surname is common enough that he could be a second individual.
Jones, Thomas Lieut. H., Flint, 61
Jones, Thomas Lieut. F., Carmarthen, 105
Jones, Thomas Quart. H., Salop, stray, 160
Jones, Walker/Walter 'of the Captain's Magazine', L. & W., 171
Jones, Walter Capt. F., Oxon, 133
Jones, William Capt. H., 76
Jones, William Lieut. F., Monmouth, 78
Jones, William Ens. F., Salop, 31
Jordan, Edw. Ens. F., L. & W., 76

Jordan, Richard Capt. F., Devon, 35
Jordan, Robert Sea Capt. *Duke of York*, L. & W., 167
Jordan, Samuel Lieut. F., Devon, 24
Jorey, Sidrach Capt. F., Kent, 121
Joyliffe, John Lieut. H., L. & W., 133
Joyliffe, John Cor. H., Dorset, 45
Joyner, Richard Capt. Lieut. F., Kent, 120
Julian, James Cor. H., L. & W., 36
Julian, John Quart. H., Lincoln, 141
Justice, Emanuel Quart. H., York, 125
Justice, Richard Capt. H., Kent, 100
Kanett, ___ ___ H., 86
Katherick, Lancelot Quart. H., Northumberland, 155
Kay, Dennis Cor. H., Lancaster, 147
Kay, Sir John Col. H. (d. 1662), 86
Kay, William Capt. H., Lancaster, 117, 115, 161. Claims under Edward Rawston, and mentioned by a lieutenant and a quartermaster on the strays list.
Kay, William Ens. F., York, 67
Keat, Ralph Lieut. F., Cornwall, 15
Keene, Francis Capt. H., 151
Keene, John Lieut. F., Somerset, 155
Keene, John Quart. H., Salop, 18
Keepe, John Chirurgion, Wilts, 173
Keetson, Richard Cor. H., Wilts, 141
Keighly, Michael Lieut. H., York, 125
Keightly, ___ Capt. H., 90
Keirnane, Terence/Terrence Cor. Dr., L. & W., 81
Keliow, Henry Capt. F., Cornwall, 69
Kell, Randolph Quart. H., Chester, 101
Kelly, [Alexander Erskine] 3rd Earl of (d. 1677), 86. Usually 'Kellie'. His officer claims from Worcester and Kellie was captured there, so presumably a 1651 regiment.
Kelly, Dennis Lieut. F., L. & W., 66
Kelly, John Ens. F., L. & W., 21
Kelton, William Lieut. F., L. & W., 96
Kemble, John Ens. F., Hereford, 154
Kemble, Richard Capt. Lieut. H., Hereford, 128. Served in 1651.
Kemis, ___ Capt. H., 149
Kemis/Kemys, John Ens. F., Monmouth, 154
Kemp/Kempe, Ralph Quart. H., Durham, 152. Served in Scotland, 1654.
Kempson, Edw. Cor. H., Stafford, 41
Kempson, George Capt. F., Cornwall, 14
Kempton, Christopher 'Quart. to the Train', Nottingham, 170
Kemys, Sir Charles Col. F. (d. 1658), 87
Kemys, Sir Nicholas Col. H. & F. (k. 1648; Chepstow), 87. A 1648 regiment; Parliamentarian turncoats.

Kendall, ___ Lieut. Col. F., 140
Kendall, Philip Quart. H., York, 70
Kendall, Zachary Ens. F., Devon, 71
Kenion, George Quart. F., Durham, 88
Kenner/Kennor, Peter Quart. H., York, stray, 160
Kennet, ___ Maj. F., 136
Kennet, Jordan Quart. H., Surrey, 70
Kent, William Lieut. Dr., Wilts, 83
Kerchwall, Roger Quart. H., York, 57
Kere, Nicholas Capt. H., L. & W., 39
Kerkevall/Kerckivall, Roger Quart. H., Nottingham, 131
Kessell, William Lieut. F., Cornwall, 139
Kestell, Thomas Lieut. F., Cornwall, 15
Ketling, Francis Quart. H., York, 143
Key/Kay, George Quart. H., York, 121
Keymor, Ellis Lieut. F., Somerset, 133
Keymor, Harrison Capt. F., Somerset, 133
Keymer, Henry Capt. H., stray, 160. Mentioned by a claimant from Somerset; possibly the dragoon officer below, as many dragoons claimed as horse or foot.
Keymor, Henry Capt. Dr., Somerset, 83
Keymor, John Ens. F., Somerset, 16
Keymor, Lionell Lieut. F., Somerset, 15
Keysar/Keyser, John Lieut. F., Huntingdon, 137
Kidny, William Quart. H., York, 70
Kidson, Thomas Capt. H., 103
Killingbeck, Thomas Ens. F., York, 146
Killinghall, ___ Capt. H., 90
Killinghall, John Capt. F., 43
Killyow, William Lieut. F., Cornwall, 54
Kilmurray, [Robert Needham] 2nd Viscount, ___ H. (d. 1653), 140. Properly 'Kilmorey'.
Kinder, Philip Physitian Licentiate, Leicester, 173
King, ___ Capt. F., 114
King, ___ Capt. H., 53
King, Daniel Capt. H., L. & W., 152. Served in Scotland, 1654.
King, Humphry Ens. F., Worcester, 123
King, James Lord Eythin Col. H., F. & Dr. (d. 1652), 87
King, John Capt. F., L. & W., 122
King, Matthew Capt. F., Kent, 116
King, Richard Capt. H., Sir Peregrine Berty, 25
King, Richard Capt. H., Sir Robert Dallison, 48
King, Roger Cor. H., Lincoln, 25
King, Thomas Capt. F., L. & W., 145
King, Thomas Lieut. F., Norfolk, 21
King, Thomas Ens. F., Dorset, 155
King, William Capt. H., Lincoln, 48

Index   281

King, William Cor. H., Carmarthen, 120
King's Lifeguard of Foot – *see* Earl of Lyndsy
Kingsly, ___ Capt. H., 32
Kingsmill, Sir William ___ ___ (d. 1661), 88
Kingston, *[Robert Pierrepont] Earl of* (k. 1643; accident, by his own side), 88. I.O. does not give an arm of service, but Kingston had recently been appointed lieutenant general of five eastern counties, therefore effectively commanding all forces.
Kingston, Thomas Adjutant, Gloucester, 170
Kirby, ___ Capt. Dr., 84
Kirk/Kirke, Charles Maj. F., L. & W., 11, 76
Kirk, John Capt. F., York, 57
Kirk, John Lieut. F., L. & W., 53
Kirk, Michael Lieut. H., York, 26
Kirk, Richard Quart. H., Gloucester, 137
Kirk, Stephen Lieut. H., York, 148
Kirk, William Quart. H., York, 46
Kirk, Zachary Ens. F., Stafford, stray, 165
Kirkbank, John Cor. H., Cumberland, 85
Kirkbride, ___ Capt. H., 13
Kirkby, ___ ___ F., 88. No first name or rank is given, but Reid believes this to be Richard Kirkby.
Kirkby, William Quart. H., Middlesex, 141
Kirke, Sir Lewis Col. F. (d. 1660), 88
Kirkebride, Richard Col. F., 88
Kirkham, Walter Capt. H., 32
Kirle, John Capt. H., Wilts, 129
Kirle, Thomas Lieut. H., L. & W., 129
Kirle, William Capt. H., Nottingham, 129
Kirton, ___ Maj. F., 156
Kirton, ___ Capt. H., 31
Kitchin, ___ Capt. F., 147
Kitchin, John Capt. F., Lancaster, stray, 163. Claims from Lancaster, so possibly the man above, who is mentioned by a Lancaster officer.
Kitson, John Lieut. H., Wilts, 112
Knaggs/Knagges, John Quart. H., Durham, 29
Knap/Knapp, Christopher Lieut. H., Essex, 49
Knapper, Shelton Capt. H., Dorset, 76
Knapton, Reynold 'Commissary & Provost Marshall General', L. & W., 169
Kneebone, Gilbert Lieut. F., L. & W., 81
Knell, Paul, Chaplain, Kent, 174
Knight, ___ Capt. F., 123
Knight, Francis Capt. F., Southampton, 23
Knight, Francis Ens. F., Somerset, 115
Knight, John Capt. H., Lancaster, 115

Knight, John Capt. F., 23
Knight, John Ens. F., L. & W., 122
Knight, Robert Quart. H., Lincoln, stray, 160
Knight, Valentine Capt. H., L. & W., 109
Knight, William Lieut. H., Cornwall, Sir Thomas Basset, 19
Knight, William Lieut. H., L. & W., Sir Thomas Dallison, 48
Knightly, Edw. Commissary General, Middlesex, 169
Knill, Anthony Ens. F., Devon, 39. I.O. does not give an arm of service, but the rank of ensign indicates foot. Additionally the officer he claims under, James Chudleigh, was known as a foot officer.
Knill, Thomas Lieut. F., Radnor, 94
Knipe, Francis Capt. F., Middlesex, 23
Kniveton, ___ Capt. H., 75
Knolles, William Maj. F., 145
Knottsford/Knotsford, Francis Capt. H., Warwick, 89
Knottsford, Sir John Col. H. & F., 89
Knottsford/Knotsford, Richard Cor. H., Worcester, 89
Knowles, John Capt. F., Lord Hopton, 83
Knowles, John Capt. F., Wilts, John Stocker, 132
Knowlles, Thomas Capt. H., L. & W., 32
Knoylle/Knoyll, Thomas Capt. F., Somerset, 131
Knoylle, William Lieut. F., Somerset, 131
Knyveton, Sir Andrew Col. H. (d. 1669), 89
Knyveton, Peter Lieut. Col. H., 89
Knyveton, Thomas Cor. H., L. & W., 89
Kymer/Keymor, Francis Lieut. H., Somerset, 155
Kynnaston, Richard Capt. F., L. & W., 67
Kynvin, John Lieut. H., Monmouth, 149
La Plane, ___ Col. H., 91. A French regiment.
Lacon, Francis Capt. F., Salop, 144
Lacon, William Ens. F., Lincoln, 80
Laight, John Cor. H., Gloucester, 45
Laight, Joseph Capt. Lieut. F., Gloucester, 105
Lake, John Capt. F., 100
Lakin, Nicholas Cor. H., York, 27
Lakin, Robert Capt. H., York, Lord Henry Cavendish, 36
Lakin, Robert Capt. H., York, Sir Hugh Cholmly, 38
Lambe, Henry Ens. F., Somerset, 113
Lambe, Nicholas Cor. H., L. & W., 56
Lambe, William Lieut. F., Gloucester, 27
Lambert, ___ Capt. F., 114
Lambert, William Capt. H., Bucks, 129
Lambkin, Robert Quart. H., L. & W., 135
Lambton, ___ Lieut. Col. F., 136. Reid states that this is Henry Lambton.
Lambton, Robert Ens. F., Durham, 89

Index

Lambton, Sir William Col. F. (k. 1644; Marston Moor), 89
Lambton, William Capt. H., Sir William Blakeston, 26
Lambton, William Capt. H., Durham, Lord Widrington, 148
Lambton, William Cor. H., Durham, 148
Lamerton, Richard Quart. H., Cornwall, 82
Lamplaw, Edw. Capt. H., Cumberland, 89
Lamplaw, John Col. H., 89. Usually 'Lamplugh'.
Lamply/Lampley, Ralph Cor. Dr., L. & W., 146
Lampray/Lamprey, William Quart. H., Southampton, 130
Lancake, Thomas Quart. F., Cumberland, 58
Lancaster, John Capt. F., Lancaster, 109
Lancaster, John Quart. H., Derby, 60
Lancaster, Thomas Quart. H., Derby, 32
Lane, ___ Capt. H., 64
Lane, Daniel Lieut. H., L. & W., 137
Lane, John Col. H., 28, 89
Lane, Rich Quart. H., L. & W., 41
Langdale, [Sir Marmaduke] Lord, Col. H. (d. 1661), 90. Created Baron Langdale by the exiled Charles II in 1658.
Langdon, Henry Commissary General, L. & W., 169
Langford, James Lieut. H., Somerset, 131
Langford, John Quart. H., Montgomery, 147
Langford, Thomas Quart. F., Wilts, 14
Langhorne/Laughorne, John Quart. H., Cornwall, 82
Langley, ___ Lieut. Col. H., 147
Langley, ___ Capt. H., 81
Langley, Henry Capt. F., Lincoln, 135
Langley, Richard Capt. H., York, 90
Langly, John Lieut. F., Chester, 64
Langly, Joseph Quart. H., Lincoln, 69
Langly, Richard Lieut. H., Wilts, stray, 158
Langsten, Peter Capt. F., 127
Langston, ___ Capt. H., 124
Langston, William Capt. H., stray, 160
Lanham, William Quart. H., Lincoln, 48
Lanier, Endymion Cor. H., Kent, stray, 159
Lanyon, Nicholas Capt. F., 109
Larder, Lewis Ens. F., Dorset, 133
Larguise, Walter Lieut. H., Wilts, 59
Larkin, Edw. Lieut. F., L. & W., 145
Larkworthy, Anthony Lieut. H. & Capt. F., Devon, 77
Lasenby, Edw. Quart. H., Somerset, 24
Lassells, Francis Capt. H., York, 92
Lassells, George Lieut. H., Nottingham, 56
Lassells, John Capt. H., Derby, 89

Latham, Edw. Cor. H., Lancaster, 104
Latham, John Lieut. H., Warwick, 36
Latham, Luke Capt. Lieut. F., Berks, 164
Latham, Richard Maj. H., stray, 158
Latham, Richard Capt. F., Lancaster, 104
Latus, William Lieut. F., Cumberland, 85
Latymer, ___ Lieut. Col. H., 45
Latymer, Thomas Capt. F., 44
Laughorne, Rowland Maj. Gen. H. & F. (d. 1675), 91. Usually 'Laugharne'. Formerly a Parliamentarian, changed sides in 1648. Narrowly missed being executed after the surrender of Pembroke.
Launder, John Quart. H., Hereford, 48
Laundry, Roger Ens. F., Cornwall, 139
Laurence, John Quart. H., Dorset, 82
Laurence, Robert Col. H., 91
Laurence, Thomas Lieut. H., York, 68
Laurence, William Ens. F., Dorset, stray, 165
Lavers, John Capt. F., Cornwall, 43
Lavers, Paul Ens. F., Cornwall, 54
Law, Thomas Quart. H., Westmorland, 46
Lawdy, Sir Richard Lieut. Col. H. (k. 1643; Coleford), 91. Commanded Lord Herbert's Foot; however it is a cornet of horse who mentions Lawdy in I.O.
Lawlyn, Bartholomew Quart. H., Cornwall, 19
Lawson, ___ Capt. F., 113
Lawson, John Capt. Lieut. F., Northumberland, 18
Lawson, Richard Capt. F., Northumberland, 39
Lawson, William Capt. Lieut. H., L. & W., 74
Lawson, William Lieut. H., Bedford, 144
Layburne, ___ Capt. H., 103
Layburne, Thomas Lieut. H., Westmorland, 103
Layland, ___ ___ H., 91
Laythorpe/Laythorp, William Lieut. H., Lincoln, 112
Lazenby/Lasenby, Christopher Quart. H., York, 155
Lazenby, Seth Lieut. H., York, 128
Le Febure, James Physitian, Norfolk, 173
Le Geyt, John Cor. H., L. & W., 149
Le Geyt, Noah Quart. H., L. & W., 64
Le Hunt, Sir John Col. F., L. & W., 9, 92, 109. Three officers claim under him directly; claims in his own right under the Marquess of Newcastle.
Le Hunt, John Capt. H., 114
Le Hunt, Robert Cor. H., L. & W., 114
Le Neve, Thomas Maj. F., Norfolk, 11, 145
Lea, Stephen Cor. H., Stafford, 147
Leadham, Samuel Lieut. H., Durham, 55
Leake, Charles ___ H., 91

Leane, Richard Ens. F., Cornwall, 140
Leapenny, ___ Capt. H., 37
Leatherden, Hugh Lieut. F., Cornwall, 20
Leaver, William Ens. F., Durham, 80
Leay, John Quart. H., Devon, 14
Ledsam, Edw. Lieut. Dr., Denbigh, 61
Lee, ___ ___ F., 92. Reid believes this to be a Colonel Woolley Lee.
Lee/Leigh, John Lieut. H., Kent, 122
Lee, Thomas Capt. F., 96
Leech, Jeremy Capt. Dr., L. & W., 52
Leech, Lewis Lieut. F., Monmouth, 87
Leech, William Quart. F., Cumberland, 85
Leechland, Thomas Quart. H., Devon, 129
Legerd/Le Gerd, Richard Capt. F., L. & W., 38
Legge, William Col. H. & F. (d. 1670), 92, 120. A quartermaster in Prince Rupert's regiment claims Legge as his captain; two men claim under him directly.
Legge, William Capt. of Pioneers, L. & W., 171
Leicester, Henry Capt. F., Somerset, 114
Leicester, John Capt. Dr., York, 99. Possibly the Captain John Lister mentioned by another officer in the regiment.
Leigh, ___ Maj. F., 65
Leigh, ___ Capt. F., 65
Leigh, Charles Capt. F., Chester, 136
Leigh, Sir Ferdinando Col. H. (d. 1654), 92
Leigh, Francis Capt. H., L. & W., 74
Leigh, John Capt. H., 92
Leigh, John Lieut. H., Berks, stray, 158
Leigh, Miles Cor. H., Surrey, 29
Leigh, Patrick Capt. H., L. & W., 81
Leigh, Peter Capt. F., Chester, 136
Leigh, Phillip Lieut. H., L. & W., 11
Leigh, Robert Capt. F., Somerset, 151
Leigh, Thomas Col. F. (d. 1644; Chester garrison), 92
Leigh, Urian Lieut. Col. F., L. & W., 10, 59. Nephew of Col. Thomas Leigh, above.
Leighton, Edward Capt. F., L. & W., 78
Leighton, Henry Capt. Lieut. F., Oxon, 42
Leighton, Robert Lieut. H., York, 13
Leighton, Sir William Lieut. Col. F., L. & W., 10, 92, 98. Claims under the Earl of Lyndsy (King's Lifeguard of Foot); four officers claim under him directly. Promoted to lieutenant colonel of the Lifeguard at some point before January 1645. Escaped capture at Naseby, when the regiment was destroyed. Knighted at Hereford September 1645; fought at Colchester in 1648.
Lello, Matthew Ens. F., Oxon, 127
Lem, John Sen. Ens. F., Salop, 88

Lemming, Francis Cor. H., Somerset, 155
Lemming, Henry Capt. H., Essex, 141
Lemming, John Quart. H., Somerset, 155
Lemming, Robert Lieut. H., Somerset, 155
Lemgo/Lengo, Andrew Ens. F., York, 111. I.O. does not give Lemgo's arm of service, but his rank as ensign indicates he was a foot officer, and his colonel, Sir Richard Page, commanded a foot regiment.
Leney, Nicholas Lieut. H., Carmarthen, 64
Lenthall, Peter Cor. H., Devon, 59
Leonard, John Capt. H., Wilts, 74
Leonard, William Cor. H., Wilts, 74
Leppington, Thomas Cor. Dr., York, 70
Lesley/Lesly, Talbot Capt. F., Northumberland, 89
Levens, Robert Capt. F., 98
Leversedge, ___ Maj. H., 155
Leveson, Sir Richard Col. H. (d. 1661), 92
Leveson, Thomas Col. H. & F. (d. 1651), 93
Levett/Levet, Thomas Lieut. F., Sussex, 51
Levingston, John Capt. F., Somerset, 105
Lewin, Lewins – *see also* Lewyn, Lewyns
Lewin, John Lieut. H., Southampton, 103
Lewin, William Dr. Judge Advocate, L. & W., 172
Lewins, ___ Maj. F., 69
Lewins, Thomas Capt. H., Northumberland, 27
Lewins, Thomas Capt. Lieut. H., Northumberland, 27
Lewis, ___ Capt. H., 149
Lewis, David Lieut. F., Denbigh, 55
Lewis, David Ens. F., Denbigh, 155
Lewis, Edw. Lieut. H., L. & W., 147
Lewis, George Capt. F., Cardigan, 33
Lewis, George Ens. F., Glamorgan, 116
Lewis, Hugh Ens. F., Radnor, 142
Lewis, Hugh Quart. H., Denbigh, 50
Lewis, Miles Ens. F., Glamorgan, 116
Lewis, Rees, Cor. H., Carmarthen, 54
Lewis, Rees Ens. F., Montgomery, 78
Lewis, Rice Lieut. F., Glamorgan, 116
Lewis, Richard Maj. F., 87
Lewis, Richard Lieut. F., Carnarvon, 111
Lewis, Robert Capt. F., stray, 166
Lewis, Saphin, Marshall, Glamorgan, 171
Lewis, Thomas Capt. F., 126
Lewis, Thomas Lieut. Col. H., 87
Lewis, Thomas Capt. F., Somerset, 49
Lewis, William Capt. F., 76

Lewkenor, ___ Capt. Dr., 84
Lewkenor, Anthony Col. H., 93
Lewkenor, Sir Christopher Col. H., 93. Recorder of Chichester; elected MP for the town in November 1640. Disabled from sitting 2nd September 1642 (JHC, 3, 1640-43, p.750); captured after the siege of Chichester in December (TT E.84[22]), and imprisoned at Windsor (JHL, 5, 1642-43, p.590). Released or exchanged at some point, as he sat in the Oxford parliament and was knighted 18th December 1644. Made his will when sick in mid-1653, but his date of death is unknown (THoP; Shaw, vol. II p.219).
Lewyn, Lewyns – *see also* Lewin, Lewins
Lewyn/Lewin, Edw. Capt. F., Southampton, 29
Lewyns/Lewyns, Lucian Lieut. H., Kent, 100
Leyborn/Leyborne, Ralph Quart. H., L. & W., 56
Liddell, Sir Francis Lieut. Col. H., 41, 93, 136. Deputy to Sir Richard Tempest's, and then Sir Nicholas Cole's horse. Mentioned by one officer under Tempest, one under Cole, and directly by three other officers.
Liddell, George Ens. F., York, 146
Liddell, Sir William ___ H., 148
Liddell, William Quart. F., Durham, 136
Lightfoot, Toby Lieut. F., L. & W., 126
Lightfoot, William Ens. F., York, 56
Lill, ___ Major F., 28
Lillington, Francis Quart. H., 44
Linch, Anthony Lieut. F., Southampton, stray, 164
Linch, Theophilus Quart. H., L. & W., 40
Lindly, John Quart. H., York, 80
Lindore, [James Leslie] Lord (d. before July 1667), 93. Properly, 'Lindores'.
Lindsey – *see* Lyndsy
Ling, William Cor. H., L. & W., 142
Lingen, Sir Henry Col. H. & F. (d. 1661/2; at Gloucester, of smallpox), 94. Knighted July 1645.
Lingen, Thomas Capt. H. & Commiss. Gen. Must., Hereford, 153
Lingen, Thomas Lieut. F., Salop, 142
Lingly, John Capt. H., 60
Linton, John Quart. Dr., York, 99
Lishman, William, Marshall, Northumberland, 171
Lisle, Anthony Quart. H., Cornwall, 72
Lisle, Sir George Col. F. (executed 1648; Colchester), 94. Knighted December 1645 at Oxford.
Lisle, George Capt. H., Southampton, 95. *Not* Colonel George Lisle, above, who started the war as a lieutenant colonel; and in any case was not alive to claim in 1663.
Lisle, Richard Regt. Quart. Dr., Middlesex, 81
Lisle, Talbot Capt. F., Durham, 89. 'Lisle' is properly pronounced 'Lisley', which suggests this man might be the Captain Talbot Lesley also listed in the regiment.

Lister, Edw. Cor. H., Somerset, 101
Lister, John Capt. Dr., York, 99. A Captain John Leicester is cited by another officer in the regiment; it is likely that he was same man.
Lister, John Lieut. H., York, 92
Lister, Nathaniel Quart. H., York, 92
Litchfield, [Lord Bernard Stewart] Earl of (k. 1645; Rowton Heath), 94. Was due to be created Earl of Lichfield, but was killed before the title could be formally bestowed. It was given to his six-year-old nephew the same year; obviously the boy was not militarily active so the claiming officers cannot be referring to him. Stewart must have been using it well before it was official.
Little, Henry Maj. F., 23
Littleboys/Littleboyes, George Cor. H., York, 41
Littlefare, William Lieut. H., L. & W., 30
Littlepage, John Cor. H., Northampton, 37
Littler, Richard Ens. F., Chester, 64
Littler, William Lieut. F., Chester, 59
Littleton, ___ Capt. F., 124
Littleton, Edward Lord Keeper Col. F. (d. 1645), 94. I.O. gives no arm of service for Littleton or the ensign who cited him, but the rank of ensign indicates foot.
Littleton, James Ens. F., Stafford, 26
Littleton, John Cor. H., Warwick, 86
Littleton, Rugely Capt. F., Stafford, 94
Littleton, Thomas Capt. H., Sir Hugh Windham, 151
Littleton, Thomas Capt. H., Somerset, stray, 157. Possibly the man above, as Windham's regiment was a Somerset unit.
Littlewood, Josuah [*sic*] Cor. H., York, 122
Livermore, John Lieut. F., L. & W., 122
Llewellin, James Capt. F., 106
Lloyd – *see* Floyd
Loanes, ___ Capt. H., 86
Lobb/Lobbe, Nathan Quart. H., Cornwall, 24
Lobbe, John Ens. F., Cornwall, 122
Lobbe, William Ens. F., Cornwall, 139
Lochard, Anthony Lieut. H., Hereford, 150
Lock, ___ Capt. H., 79
Lock, John Lieut. F., L. & W., 138. Served in 1648.
Lock, John Provost Marshall, Somerset, 171
Locket, Edw. Capt. H., 54
Lockey/Locky, James Quart. H., Northumberland, 84
Lodge, Nicholas Quart. H., Durham, 148
Loft, Thomas Quart. H., York, 125
Loftus, Francis Cor. II., York, stray, 159. Claims under Captain Laurence Appleby, who in turn claims under Sir Francis Stuart.
Loker, Joseph Lieut. F., Essex, 98
Lone, Highgate Lieut. F., L. & W., 76

Long, Henry Lieut. H., Gloucester, 41
Long, Sir James Col. H. (d. 1692), 95
Long, Richard Ens. F., L. & W., 21
Long, Thomas Capt. H., 95
Long, Walter Cor. H., Wilts, 95
Long, William Capt. F., L. & W., 53
Loop/Loope, Thomas Quart. H., Middlesex, 133
Loope, George Capt. F., 69, 99, York. Claims from York under Sir Francis Mackworth; mentioned by a lieutenant under Sir Thomas Glenham.
Loosmore, George Lieut. F., Cambridge, 96
Lord, Hugh Quart. H., Hereford, 126
Lorrayne/Loraine, Nicholas Capt. F., Northumberland, 122
Lorrayne/Loraine, Thomas Capt. F., Northumberland, 122
Lorymer/Lorimer, Roger Maj. F., Southampton, 11, 93
Lotherington/Lothrington, Thomas Quart. H., York, 39
Loudell/Lowdell, Thomas Lieut. F., Suffolk, 25
Loughborough, [Henry Hastings] 1ˢᵗ Baron, Col. General (d. 1667), 95
Loup/Loupe, Thomas 'Commissary & Engineer', L. & W., 169
Love, Hastings Capt. H., Nottingham, 56
Love, James Ens. F., Hereford, 126
Love, Robert Capt. H., Southampton, 23
Love, Thomas Capt. F., Flint, stray, 163
Loveday, John Lieut. F., Warwick, 16
Lovelace, Dudley Capt. H., Kent, 39
Lovelace, Francis Col. F. (d. 1675), 96. Governor of Carmarthen Castle; lost it to Parliamentarian forces in October 1645, and went abroad. Appointed governor of New York in 1667.
Lovelace, Francis Maj. H., stray, 158. Perhaps Francis Lovelace son of Richard, 1ˢᵗ Baron, and brother of Royalist John, 2ⁿᵈ Baron. If so, is often confused with Colonel Francis Lovelace, above.
Lovell, Thomas Cor. H., L. & W., 112
Lovett, John 'Commissary Train', Durham, 169
Low/Lowe, Arthur Capt. H., Derby, 59. A Parliamentarian report of April 1644 (TT E.42[21]) reports a 'Captaine Arthur Loe' drowned in the Trent during a skirmish with Prince Rupert's forces, but it is likely that the author was mistaken, and he was the officer who claimed in 1663.
Low/Lowe, Ferdinando Lieut. H., Derby, 59
Low, John Capt. H., John Frechevile, 63
Low, John Capt. H., Sir John Harpur, 75
Lowdon, ___ Capt. F., 93
Lowe, ___ Lieut. Col. H., 134
Lowe, Charles Lieut. H., Derby, stray, 158
Lowe, Edw. Quart. H., Surrey, 109
Lowe, Hercules Lieut. Col. H., L. & W., 10, 128
Lowe, Hercules Capt. F., 31

Lower, George Maj. H., 84
Lower, Thomas Lieut. F., Cornwall, 20
Lower, Sir William Lieut. Col. F. (d. 1662), 25
Lowick, Thomas Lieut. F., L. & W., 21
Lowther, Sir Christopher ___ H. (d. 1644; Whitehaven), 96. Merchant, only in nominal command of his regiment. Governor of Whitehaven and Cockermouth castle.
Lowther, George Lieut. H., Cumberland, 48
Lowther, Gerard Col. H. & F., 97
Lowther, John ___ H., 97
Lowther, Thomas Cor. H., Cumberland, 138
Lowyck, John Maj. H., 31
Lucas, Sir Charles Col. H. & F. (executed 1648; Colchester), 97. Commanded cavalry during the first civil war, also raised foot during the second in 1648.
Lucas, Sir Gervase Col. H. & F., L. & W. (d. 1667; as governor of Bombay), 9, 95, 97. Lucas claims under Lord Loughborough; then a number of officers claims directly under Lucas.
Lucas, [John] Lord Lucas, Col. H. (d. 1671), 98. Elder brother of Sir Charles. Fought with the Oxford Army.
Lucas, Thomas Lieut. F., Glamorgan, 66
Luccombe, Christopher Cor. H., 131
Luccombe, Thomas Ens. F., Devon, 35
Lugg, Jasper Quart. H., Gloucester, 42
Lugge, Peter Lieut. F., L. & W., 25
Lugger, Nicholas Lieut. H., Devon, 75
Lugger, Peter Quart. H., Cornwall, 78
Luke, John Ens. F., Cornwall, 69
Lumley, Richard Chirurgion, L. & W., 172
Lunne, John Quart. H., Worcester, 124
Lunsford, Sir Herbert Lieut. Col. F. (d. in or after 1667), 98. Knighted July 1645.
Lunsford, Sir Thomas Col. H. & F. (d. in or before 1656), 98. Only one foot officer claims under Lunsford; probably because he was captured at Edgehill and his regiment taken on first by his brother Henry, and then by Prince Rupert.
Luntly, John Lieut. Col. H., 10, 45
Lurcock, John Lieut. F., Worcester, 84
Lush, Richard Cor. H., Dorset, 131
Lusher, John Capt. H., 82
Lusher, Thomas Maj. H., 82
Lutton, Thomas Lieut. F., York, 129
Lybbe, Richard Lieut. H., Berks, stray, 158
Lyddal/Lyddall, John Ens. F., L. & W., 39
Lyde, Edw. Capt. F., Devon, 35
Lyme, Nicholas Capt. H., Lancaster, stray, 157
Lynaker, Thomas Quart. F., L. & W., 154
Lynde, Venables Cor. H., L. & W., stray, 159
Lyndsey, ___ Capt. H., James King (Lord Eythin), 87

Lyndsey/Lindsey, Owen Lieut. H., Devon, stray, 158
Lyndsey/Lindsey, Richard Capt. H., Sussex, Sir Christopher Lewknor, 93
Lyndsey, Thomas Capt. H., Cumberland, Earl of Calendar, 32
Lyndsy, [Montagu Bertie] 2nd Earl of, Col. H. F. & Dr. (d. 1666), 98. Colonel of the King's Lifeguard of Foot.
Lyndsy, Andrew Col. H., 98
Lyndsy/Lindsey, Francis Capt. F., Cumberland, 106
Lyndsy, Robert Capt. H., 74
Lyne, Aeneas Maj. F., L. & W., 11, 120
Lyne, Richard Lieut. F., Cornwall, 14
Lynne, ___ Capt. H., 144
Lynne, George Cor. H., Northampton, stray, 159
Lynne, John Capt. H., Norfolk, 32
Lynsell, John. Capt. H., stray, 158, 159, 160. Mentioned by a lieutenant, a cornet and a quartermaster of horse, all of whom claim from Essex.
Lyon, Henry Cor. H., Lancaster, 102
M. Donough, Kelley/Mac-Donough, O Kelly Ens. F., Middlesex, 65
Mab/Mabe, John Ens. F., Pembroke, 91
Mabye, Richard Commissary, Somerset, 169
Mabye, William Commissary General, Somerset, 169
Macgill, Bryan Capt. F., L. & W., 92
Machell, John Quart. F., Westmorland, 88
Machell, Marmaduke Lieut. H., Durham, 13
Mackafrey, Spencer Capt. F., Worcester, 76
Mackerly, Darly Capt. F., 69
Macklen, Adam Ens. F., Monmouth, 87
Mackmoyler/Macmoyler, Richard Lieut. Col. H., L. & W., 10, 52
Mackow, Ralph Cor. H., Northumberland, 148
Macvicar/Mackvicar, Archibald Lieut. H., L. & W., 90
Mackworth, Edw. Lieut. F., Chester, 149
Mackworth, Sir Francis Col. H. (d. c. 1672), 99. Fled abroad with the Marquess of Newcastle in 1644, after the defeat at Marston Moor.
Maddock, Charles Cor. H., Monmouth, 153
Maddock, John Lieut. F., Devon, 24
Mageon, Edmund Quart. H., L. & W., 71
Magothes, William Lieut. H., Wilts, stray, 158
Maine, Edw. Ens. F., Northumberland, 39
Maine, William Ens. F., Cornwall, 15
Makeing, Alexander Capt. Lieut. H., L. & W., 128
Makepeace, Abell Cor. H., Northampton, 149
Malbrank, ___ Maj. H., 62. Mentioned under Sir Edward Ford, so possibly the man below, who was captured with Ford at Arundel.
Malbrank, ___ Maj. Dr., stray, 166
Malbrank, Francis Lieut. H., Sussex, 62
Malham, Sir Francis Col. H., 99

Mallome, Thomas Capt. F., Norfolk, 67
Mallory, ___ Capt. F., Sir James Pennyman, 112
Mallory, ___ Capt. F., Marquess of Worcester, 154. Possibly the Captain Henry Mallory mentioned in the Marquess's horse regiment.
Mallory, Edward Capt. F., Cambridge, 28
Mallory, Henry Capt. H., 153
Mallory, Sir John Col. H., F. & Dr. (d. 1655), 99. Governor of Skipton Castle.
Mallory, John Capt. H., York, 148
Mallory, Richard Quart. H., L. & W., 30
Mallory, Robert Quart. H., Wilts, 23
Malpas, Richard Ens. F., Chester, 32
Man/Mann, Thomas Quart. H., York, 52
Manaton, Ambrose Capt. F., Cornwall, 139
Manaton, Sampson Capt. H., 23, 103. Possibly the father of Richard and Pierce Manaton of Stoke Climsland, Cornwall; the former of whom claims in 1652 for rents from land sequestered from Pierce, but which had been given to Richard by their father, whom he names as Sampson (CCC IV, p.2936). Possibly the Sampson Mannaton listed below, in the foot.
Mand, George Quart. F., L. & W., 21
Mandsly/Maudsley, John Lieut. F., Lancaster, 38
Manger/Mainger, Henry Quart. H., Durham, 41
Manknowles, John Lieut. H., Lancaster, 136
Manley, Robert Capt. H., L. & W., 123
Manly, ___ ___ F., 99. I.O. gives no arm of service for Manly or the ensign who cited him, but the rank of ensign indicates foot.
Manly, Francis Maj. F., 156
Manly, John Capt. Lieut. H., Northampton, 89
Manly, John Lieut. H., Worcester, 120
Manly/Manley, Roger Capt. F., Denbigh, 31
Mann, Thomas Capt. Lieut. H., L. & W., 150
Mannaton/Manaton, Sampson Capt. F., Cornwall, 103. Possibly the Sampson Manaton listed above, although it is not clear if that officer was still alive in 1663.
Manning, Ambrose Capt. F., 43
Manning, Henry Capt. H., 59
Manning, [Richard] Col. H. (k. 1644; Cheriton), 100. I.O. does not give Manning's first name or rank, but he is identifiable by the Lieutenant Colonel Scott mentioned in his regiment: the Royalist newsbook *Mercurius Aulicus* reports the death of both Manning and Scott at Cheriton in 1644 (TT E.43[18]).
Mansell, Edw. Lieut. F., Carmarthen, 132
Mansell, Robert Lieut. F., Carmarthen, 132
Mansell, Walter Cor. H., Carmarthen, 132
Mansfield, [___ Cavendish] Viscount, Col. H., 36, 100. Most I.O. claimants cited their former commander's titles as they existed in 1661, rather than those they used in the 1640s, therefore the men claiming under Mansfield could have been referring to Charles Cavendish (d. 1659), or his brother Henry (d. 1691), both of

whom fought as cavalry colonels during the civil war and both of whom successively held the viscountcy.

Mansford, ___ Capt. H., 56
Mantell, John Lieut. F., Kent, stray, 164
Manwaring, ___ Capt. H., 32
Manwaring, John Capt. H., Chester, 147
Manwaring, John Capt. F., Southampton, 23
Manwaring, John Cor. H., Nottingham, 125
Manwaring, Peter Capt. H., Stafford, 54
Manwaring, Sir William ___ F. (k. 1644; Chester), stray, 165
Manwaring, William Lieut. H., Lancaster, 153
Maplesden, Edw. Capt. H., Kent, 74
March, Nicholas Quart. H., Devon, 14
Markenfield, Thomas Capt. H., York, 36
Markham, ___ Lieut. Col., 36
Markham, ___ Capt. H., Sir Peregrine Berty, 25
Markham, ___ Capt. H., Lord St. Albans, 121
Markham, Phillip/Philip Capt. H., Lincoln, Sir William Savile, 125
Marks, Robert Lieut. Col. H., 10, 106
Marks, Robert Capt. F., 83
Marks/Markes, Samuel Capt. H., Somerset, 106
Marlay, ___ Capt. F., 128. I.O. does not give Marlay's arm of service, but an ensign claims him as his officer, indicating foot.
Marlay, Sir John Col. H., F. & Dr., (d. 1672), 100. Usually 'Marley'.
Marlay, John Capt. F., 100. Mentioned under Sir John Marlay. Possibly the colonel himself.
Marlborough, [James Ley] 3rd Earl of, Col. H. & F. (d. 1665), 100
Marler, John Quart. H., Somerset, stray, 160
Marrow, John Col. H. (k. 1644; Northwich), 101
Marsh, John Lieut. Col. H., 137
Marsh, William Capt. F., Sussex, 67
Marsh, William Capt. F., stray, 165
Marshal/Marshall, Walter Cor. H., Worcester, 17
Marshall, Anthony Cor. H., York, 117
Marshall, Benjamin Capt. F., York, 67
Marshall, Ingram Capt. F., Durham, 109
Marshall, John Capt. F., Cornwall, 50
Marshall, Richard Lieut. F., Cornwall, 69
Marshall, Robert Ens. F., Durham, 118
Marshall, William Capt. Lieut. H., Leicester, 26
Marten/Martin, Roger Ens. F., Cornwall, 50
Martin, ___ Capt. H., 64
Martin, ___ Capt. F., 138
Martin, Charles Ens. F., L. & W., 25
Martin, Clement Capt. & Quart. Gen. H., L. & W., 119

Martin, James Cor. H., Cornwall, 19
Martin, John Quart. H., Worcester, 124
Martin, Simon 'Muster Master & Commissary of Musters', Stafford, 169
Martin, William Lieut. H., Rutland, 32
Martin, William Ens. F., Cornwall, 24
Martindall, John Capt. F., 58
Martingdall, Percivall Quart. H., Durham, 54
Marwood, William Lieut. H., Devon, 77
Marychurch, ___ Capt. F., 142
Mascal/Mascall, John Ens. H., Worcester, 40
Mascal, Jonas Lieut. F., York, 118
Mascall, Henry Capt. H., Sussex, stray, 157
Mascall, Richard Capt. F., 123
Mascall, Theophilus Commissary, Worcester, 169
Mascall, Thomas Capt. F., 118
Mascall, Thomas Lieut. F., Worcester, 123
Masham, Francis Lieut. H., Lancaster, 143
Mason, Francis Lieut. 'of a Fregat', Salop, 167
Mason, George Cor. H., Hertford, 137
Mason, John Capt. H., Northampton, 108
Mason, John Cor. H., Durham, 148
Mason, Michael Maj. Dr., L. & W., 11, 17
Mason, Richard Capt. Lieut. F., York, 129
Mason, Richard Cor. H., Derby, 75
Mason, Robert Cor. H., Lancaster, 17
Mason, Robert Ens. F., Monmouth, 87
Mason, Solomon Lieut. F., Essex, 97
Mason, Thomas Maj. H., L. & W., 11, 101
Mason, Thomas Capt. F., Hereford, 151
Mason, Thomas Lieut. H., L. & W., 101
Mason, Thomas Ens. F., Somerset, 83
Mason, Sir William Col. H., 101, 148. Mentioned by one officer under Lord Widrington, and several directly.
Mason, William Cor. H., Warwick, 102
Massey, Sir Edward Col. H. (d. 1674), 101. Formerly a Parliamentarian; regiment fought for Charles II at Worcester in 1651.
Massey, Francis Lieut. F., L. & W., 150
Massey, George Cor. H., L. & W., 150
Massey, Hamlet Cor. H., Lancaster, 31
Massey, John Ens. F., Somerset, 28
Massey/Massy, William Regt. Quart. H., L. & W., 109
Massham/Masham, William Capt. H., Wilts, 95
Massy/Massey, Peter Capt. F., York, 86
Massy, William Capt. Lieut. H., Chester, 115
Master, Edw. Capt. H., Gloucester, 145

Master/Masters, Robert Cor. H., Gloucester, 64
Masters, Charles Quart. H., Cornwall, 82
Masters, John Quart. H., Somerset, 78
Masterson, ___ Capt. H., 116
Mateland, James Capt. Dr., 81
Mathar, John Lieut. H., Stafford, 96
Mathews/Matthewes, John Lieut. H., 147
Matthew/Matthewes, Francis Capt. H., Somerset, 71
Matthew/Matthewes, Hopkin Lieut. F., Glamorgan, 152
Matthew/Matthewes, Howell Lieut. F., Glamorgan, 126
Matthew/Matthewes, John Lieut. F., Cornwall, 20
Matthew/Matthewes, Miles Capt. F., Glamorgan, 82
Matthew/Matthews, William Cor. Dr., Wilts, 83
Matthew/Matthewes, William Ens. F., L. & W., 72
Matthewes, ___ Capt. F., 143
Matthews/Matthewes, Edw. Ens. F., Carmarthen, 94
Matthews, Hugh Capt. F., stray, 164
Matthews, Humphry ___ F., 101, 153. Mentioned by one officer under the Marquess of Worcester, and by one directly. Neither give Matthews' rank.
Matthews, John Lieut. H., Flint, stray, 158
Matthews, John Ens. F., Wilts, 132
Matthews/Matthewes, Lewis Lieut. F., Glamorgan, 87
Matthews/Matthewes, Richard Lieut. H., Cornwall, 72
Matthews/Matthewes, Richard Lieut. F., Montgomery, 111
Matthews, Robert Capt. F., 39
Matthews/Matthewes, Thomas Lieut. F., Denbigh, 111
Matthews, William Capt. Lieut. F., Glamorgan, 153
Matthews, William Ens. F., Hereford, 45
Matthews/Matthewes, William Ens. F., Cornwall, 139
Maudsley – *see* Mandsly
Maughan, John Quart. H., Cumberland, 137
Maurice, Prince, Col. H., F. & Dr. (drowned 1652), 101
Mawditt/Mauditt, John Cor. H., Devon, 23
Mawson, Thomas Capt. H., Leicester, 95
Maxfield, William Lieut. Dr., L. & W., 117
Maxton, Ambrose Lieut. Col. F., 58
Maxwell, George ___ F., 102. I.O. gives no arm of service for Maxwell or the ensign who cited him, but the rank of ensign indicates foot.
Maxwell, Thomas Capt. H., L. & W., 95
Maxy, ___ Lieut. Col. H., 97
May, Edmund Capt. F. Northampton, 29
May, John Lieut. H., L. & W., 74
May, Robert Quart. H., Cornwall, 82
May, Thomas Cor. H., L. & W., 82
Maycock, John Cor. H., Lincoln, 91

Mayley, Alpheus Cor. Dr., L. & W., 94
Maylord, Edward Capt. F., L. & W., 88
Maynard, Henry Capt. F., Cornwall, 103
Maynard, Henry Lieut. F., Surrey, 152
Maynard, John Lieut. F., Cornwall, 103
Mayne, Sir John Col. H. & F. (d. c. 1676), 102. Usually 'Mayney'.
Mayo, John Capt. Lieut. H., Somerset, 26
Meacham, ___ Capt. Dr., 45
Meade, ___ Capt. H., 32
Meade, John Ens. F., Somerset, 145
Meadway, Richard Capt. Pioneers, Dorset, 172
Meager, Gilbert Lieut. F., Cornwall, 14
Meakins, Richard Quart. H., L. & W., 147
Meautys, John Lieut. Col. F., Warwick, 10, 93
Medd, Christopher Quart. H., York, 87
Meeke/Meek, William Quart. H., Hereford, 130
Meeres, Anthony Ens. F., L. & W., 28
Mellicheap/Mellicheape, Thomas Ens. F., L. & W., 121
Mennell, ___ Capt. F., 144
Mennell, Anthony Capt. H. (k. 1644; Marston Moor), 97. Buried St Cuthberts York, 4th July 1644 (Young, p.246).
Mennell/Mennel, James Lieut. H., York, 142
Mercer, Thomas Lieut. H., Somerset, 79
Merchant, Hugh Cor. H., L. & W., 129
Meredith, Sir Ames, ___ H., 35, 77. Mentioned by officers under Sir Henry Cary and Sir Thomas Hele.
Merrick, ___ Capt. H., 136
Merrick, ___ Capt. F., 111
Merrick, John Ens. F., Pembroke, 30. I.O. does not give an arm of service, but the rank of ensign indicates foot.
Merrick, Thomas Capt. F., York, 144
Merryfield, John Ens. F., Devon, 139
Merryman, Gerrard Lieut. H., York, 115
Merryman, Michael Lieut. H., L. & W., 39
Merryman, Robert/John Quart. Dr., Durham, 84. Named in the main I.O. text as Robert, and in the index as John.
Merryweather, ___ Capt. H., 76
Merson, Ralph Ens. F., Devon, 35
Merydale/Meridel/Meridall, Richard Lieut. Col. F., L. & W., 10, 25
Messenger, Henry Capt. H., York, 39, 62, 159. Claims in his own right under Sir Robert Clavering; mentioned by three officers under Colonel John Forcer, who took over the regiment after Sir Robert's death. Mentioned also by a stray cornet claiming from York.
Messinger, ___ Capt. H., 142
Metcalf/Metcalfe, Anthony Capt. Lieut. H., York, 61

Metcalf/Metcalfe, Christopher Lieut. H., York, 61
Metcalf/Metcalfe, Edw. Lieut. F., York, 40
Metcalf/Metcalfe, John Capt. H., Durham, 61
Metcalf, Thomas Capt. F., 49
Metcalfe, ___ Lieut. Col. F., 129
Metcalfe, Bryan Cor. H., York, 142
Metcalfe, Charles Capt. H., Newcastle, 100
Metcalfe, Edw. Lieut. H., Warwick, 126
Metcalfe, Henry Lieut. H., York, 41
Metcalfe, Thomas Lieut. Col. H., 129
Metcalfe, Thomas Capt. Lieut. F., York, 149
Metcalfe, William Capt. F., York, 56
Methwold, Thomas Capt. F., L. & W., 33
Meux, Thomas Lieut. F., York, 117
Mew, John Ens. F., Southampton, 23
Meyo, John Ens. F., Dorset, stray, 165
Meysy/Meysey, Francis Lieut. F., Worcester, 113
Michaell/Michell, Robert Cor. H., York, 38
Michell, Andrew Quart. H., Wilts, stray, 160
Michell, Hugh Lieut. Dr., L. & W., 45
Michell, James Ens. F., L. & W., 151
Michell, William Quart. H., York, 27
Middlemore, ___ Capt. F., Sir William Russell, 121
Middlemore, ___ Capt. F., Marquess of Worcester, 154
Middlemore, Edward Col. F., 103. I.O. does not give an arm of service for Middlemore or the ensign who claims under him, but the rank of ensign indicates foot.
Middlemore, Thomas Lieut. H., Worcester, 92
Middleton, ___ Lieut. Col. H., 68
Middleton, Sir Francis Col. H., 103. At least two of Middleton's officers – Captain William Foxcroft/Foxcraft) and Cornet John Thornborough/Thornborow – also claim personally in the strays list, whilst a third stray, Lieutenant Thomas Turver, claims Foxcroft as his officer and therefore must also have been in the regiment. Why none of these men gave their colonel's name is not known, but this may give an insight into how the lists were collated: perhaps one person gathered the regiment's names and submitted them, but neglected to identify the colonel.
Middleton, Sir George Col. H. (d. 1673), 103
Middleton, Hugh Capt. F., Flint, stray, 163
Middleton, Jeffery Cor. H., Lancaster, 103
Middleton, John Lieut. H., York, 55
Middleton, John Quart. H., Durham, 107
Middleton, Robert Capt. H., Lancaster, 104
Middleton, Thomas Capt. Lieut. H., York, 55
Middleton, Thomas Lieut. H., Lancaster, 143
Middleton, Thomas Lieut. F., L. & W., 103

Middleton, William Col. F. (k. 1643; Hopton Heath), 103
Midwinter, Robert, Marshall, Devon, 171
Milburne/Milborn, John Cor. H., Cumberland, 47
Mildmay, ___ Capt. H., 146
Mildmay, Humphry Capt. Lieut. Somerset, 40
Mildmay, Thomas Cor. H., Oxon, 32
Miles, Thomas Lieut. F., Glamorgan, 132
Milford, ___ Maj. F., 88
Mill, Edw. Capt. F., Southampton, 112
Mill, Sir John (junior) Col. H., 103. Not to be confused with his father, Sir John Mill senior, who died in July 1648 (CCC III, p.1831). Mill junior also died at some point before June 1649, when the Committee for Compounding recorded that ⅔ of his estates had been sequestered due to his widow's recusancy (*ibid.*).
Mill, Lewkenor Capt. F., Southampton, 103
Mill, Richard Quart. H., Cornwall, 19
Millborne/Milborne, Henry Capt. Dr., Durham, 149
Miller, Abraham Cor. H., Dorset, 91
Miller, John Capt. H., 91
Miller, Marmaduke Cor. H., York, 105
Miller, Thomas Lieut. Pioneers, Nottingham, 172
Miller, William Quart. H., L. & W., 63
Millet, Robert Lieut. Col. H., 155
Millington, ___ Capt. F., 124
Million, Lewis Lieut. H., L. & W., 18
Mills, Stephen Lieut. H., Durham, 47
Millward, John Col. F. & Dr., 103
Milner, John Lieut. F., York, 22
Milner, John Quart. H., York, 125
Milton, Randolph Quart. H., Flint, stray, 161
Milward, ___ Capt. H., 96
Milward, Thomas Capt. F., 83
Milward/Millward, Thomas Cor. H., Stafford, 96
Mince, William Ens. F., Worcester, 76
Minshall, Peter Lieut. F., L. & W., 82
Minshall, Randall Ens. F., Chester, 64
Mittford/Mitford, Henry Lieut. H., Kent, 100
Mittford, Robert Quart. F., Durham, 149
Mohan, Robert Maj. F., stray, 165
Mohun, Reynold Capt. H., 72
Mohun, Teage Ens. F., Cornwall, 128
Mohun, [Warwick] Lord, Col. F. (d. 1665), 103
Moldsworth, Guy ___ H., 104. Known to have been lieut. col. of Prince Maurice's Horse.
Mole, Thomas Lieut. F., Devon, 62

Molineux, ___ Capt. H., Matthew Eure, 55
Molineux, ___ Capt. H., Ralph Eure, 56
Molineux, Charles Capt. F., L. & W., 153
Molineux, Edmund Cor. H., Nottingham, Ralph Eure, 56
Molineux, Edmund Cor. H., Lancaster, Lord Molineux, 104
Molineux, Francis Lieut. H., Nottingham, 56
Molineux, James Capt. F., Lancaster, 50
Molineux, Prestland Maj. H., L. & W., 11, 77
Molineux, [Richard] Lord, Col. H. & F. (d. 1654), 104
Molineux, Roger Col. H. & F., 104
Molineux, William Lieut. F., Hereford, 94
Monck, Henry Lieut. H., L. & W., 96
Monck, Richard Capt. H., L. & W., 136
Monck, Thomas Col. H., 104. Brother of George Monck, Duke of Albemarle.
Monck, Thomas Capt. F., L. & W., 22
Monckton, ___ Capt. F., 81
Moncton/Monckton, Edmund Capt. Lieut. H., York, 81
Monington, Thomas Capt. F., Radnor, 143
Monk, George Lieut. H., Northampton, 34
Monox, Morley/Morlee Ens. F., Kent, 138. Served in 1648.
Monro, Coll. Capt./Lieut. Col. Dr./F., 117, 147. Mentioned as a captain of dragoons under Sir John Redman; listed as a captain lieutenant when captured at Lincoln, 6th May 1644 (*Perfect Occurrences*, E.47[3]). claims as a lieutenant colonel of foot under Redman's successor, Thomas Wheatly. At Lincoln, captured with the lieutenant who later mentioned him in 1663.
Montfort, Thomas Quart. H., Essex, stray, 160
Montgomery, Ezekiel Lieut. H., L. & W., 98
Montgomery, Robert ___ H., 105
Montgomery, William Quart. H 'to the Lifeguard', L. & W., 120
Moody, Richard Capt. F., Rutland, 32
Moody, William Capt. Dr., Berks, 91
Moon, Alexander Ens. F., Cornwall, 54
Moon, Thomas Lieut. H., L. & W., 142
Moor, Hugh Ens. F., L. & W., 65
Moore, ___ Capt. H., 109
Moore, Alexander Cor. H., Huntingdon, 119. Served in 1651.
Moore, Ames Lieut. H., Devon, 82
Moore, Charles Cor. H., Dorset, 40
Moore, Daniel Maj. F., L. & W., 11, 145
Moore, Francis Capt. Lieut. H., Bucks, 144
Moore, Francis, Chaplain, Devon, 174
Moore, George Capt. H., 82
Moore, Giles Cor. H., L. & W., 137
Moore, Goyen Lieut. F., Cornwall, 43
Moore, John Ens. F., Kent, 40

Moore, John Ens. F., Worcester, 121
Moore, Maurice Cor. H., Cambridge, 46
Moore, Philip Cor. H., Somerset, 45
Moore, Richard Capt. F., Worcester, 120
Moore, Richard Ens. F., L. & W., 106
Moore, Robert Capt. F., Northumberland, 39
Moore, Robert Capt. H. & F., Surrey, Sir John Fitzherbert, 59
Moore, Robert Capt. H., Essex, Sir George Lisle, 94. Must have served under Lisle during the Essex campaign of 1648, as during the first civil war the colonel only commanded foot.
Moore, Robert Lieut. H., L. & W., 109
Moore, Robert Ens. F., Durham, 121
Moore, Thomas Lieut. F., L. & W., 57
Moore, William Lieut. H., Somerset, 151
Moore, William Ens. F., Devon, stray, 165
Moores, Hugh Lieut. F., Cornwall, 139
Mopson, William Quart. H., Worcester, 124
Morall, John Chirurgion, L. & W., 172
Morall, John Chirurgion, Norfolk, 173. Probably the man above.
More, ___ Maj. F., 124
Morey, Simon Quart. H., Devon, 78
Morgan, ___ Col. H., 116
Morgan, ___ Lieut. Col. F., 116
Morgan, ___ Maj. F., 55
Morgan, ___ Capt. F., Richard Donnell, 52
Morgan, ___ Capt. F., Lord Hopton, 83
Morgan, ___ Capt. F., Lord Charles Somerset, 130
Morgan, Alexander Ens. F., Somerset, 132
Morgan, Anthony Col. F., 105. The three Welsh claimants naming Anthony Morgan as their officer could have served under any of three men: Sir Anthony Morgan of Northamptonshire (d. 1668), who served in South Wales under the Earl of Worcester but then changed sides; Sir Anthony Morgan of Tredegar, a Catholic who went abroad after the first civil war; or Colonel Anthony Morgan of Marshfield, Monmouthshire, who also served under Worcester.
Morgan, Arnold Capt. F., 132
Morgan, Charles Ens. F., Monmouth, Richard Donnell, 52
Morgan, Charles Ens. F., Hereford, John Gainsford, 64
Morgan, Edmund Lieut. H., Monmouth, 55
Morgan, Sir Edward Col. F. (d. 1653), 105
Morgan, Edw. Capt. H., stray, 161
Morgan, Edw. Capt. F., Sir Francis Gamul, 64
Morgan, Edward Capt. F., Monmouth, 132. Mentioned by two officers under Sir Edward Stradling; claims in his own right under Thomas Stradling, the regiment's lieutenant colonel.
Morgan, Edw. Ens. F., Carmarthen, 143

Morgan, Ellis Lieut. F., Montgomery, 65
Morgan, James Col. F., 105
Morgan, John Lieut. Col. H., stray, 159
Morgan, John Maj. F., 114
Morgan, John Capt. ___, 28
Morgan, John Capt. F., 55
Morgan, John Capt. F., 45
Morgan, John Capt. F., Glamorgan, 52
Morgan, John Capt. F., Hereford, 64
Morgan, John Capt. F., Brecon, 152
Morgan, John Lieut. F., Carmarthen, 128
Morgan, John Capt. F., Monmouth, 153
Morgan, Lewis Lieut. F., Glamorgan, 153
Morgan, Matthew Capt. F., Brecon, 105
Morgan, Michael Capt. F., James Morgan, 105
Morgan, Michael Capt. F., Marquess of Worcester, 153
Morgan, Rees Capt. F., Monmouth, 101
Morgan, Thomas Col. H. (k. 1643; Newbury), 105
Morgan, Thomas Capt. Lieut. F., Monmouth, 21
Morgan, Thomas Ens. F., Hereford, 64
Morgan, Thomas Ens. F., Monmouth, 132
Morgan, Turbervile Maj. F., 116
Morgan, William Maj. F., 118
Morgan, William Capt. F., 28
Morgan, William Ens. F., Brecon, 152
Morley, ___ Lieut. Col. H., 139
Morley, Bartholomew Cor. H., L. & W., 134
Morley, [Henry Parker] Lord, ___ H. (d. 1655), 105
Morley, Francis Capt. F., 14
Morley, Miles Cor. H., L. & W., 129
Morlye/Morley, John Lieut. F., Durham, 53
Morley, John Quart. H., York, 149
Morley, Richard Lieut. H., Cambridge, stray, 158
Morpaigne/Morpaing, John Cor. H., L. & W., 91
Morpeth, Richard Capt. H., Durham, 136
Morphey, Daniel Cor. H., L. & W., 91
Morphy/Morphey, Cornelius Cor. H., L. & W., 134
Morphy, John Lieut. H., L. & W., 134
Morris, ___ ___ F., 105. Reid believes this to be Colonel John Morris, executed in 1650 for his govenorship of Pontefract in 1648.
Morris, ___ Capt. F., stray, 164
Morris, Anthony Ens. F., Carmarthen, stray, 166
Morris, Charles Capt. F., 53
Morris, Edmund Capt. F., Glamorgan, 87
Morris, Edw. Capt. F., Glamorgan, 87

Morris, Griffith Lieut. F., Carnarvon, stray, 164
Morris, Henry Lieut. F., L. & W., 116
Morris, James Sea Capt., L. & W., 167
Morris, Hugh Capt. H., stray, 158
Morris, Lewis Lieut. F., Monmouth, 143
Morris, Nicholas Capt. Lieut. F., York, 146
Morris, Somerset Capt. F., Gloucester, 63
Morris, Thaddeus/Thadeus Capt. H., L. & W., 106
Morris, Theodore Maj. F., 86
Morris, Walter Capt. F., Monmouth, 130
Morris, Walter Lieut. F., Worcester, 29
Morris, William Capt. F., Carnarvon, stray, 163
Morrison, ___ Maj. Dr., 145
Morse, Adam Capt. F., Devon, 101
Morse, John Capt. F., Norfolk, 67
Morse, John Quart. H., Somerset, 53
Morse, Robert Lieut. H., Gloucester, 102
Mort, George Capt. H., L. & W., 38
Mort, Seth Capt. F., Lancaster, 60
Morton, Barra. Lieut. F., Northumberland, 86
Morton, Henry Capt. H., Northumberland, 29
Morton, Henry Lieut. F., Dorset, 19
Morton, James Quart. H., Durham, 61
Morton, John Capt. F., 105
Morton, Richard Lieut. F., L. & W., 24
Morton, Sir William Lieut. Col. F. (d. 1672), 105. Governor of Sudeley Castle.
Morton, William Quart. H., Durham, 85
Mosely, Charles Capt. H., L. & W., 152. Served in Scotland, 1654.
Moses, John Lieut. F., Worcester, 121
Moses, Richard Capt. Dr., Worcester, 74
Mostyn, Henry Ens. F., Devon, 37
Mostyn, Peter Capt. F., Flint, 106
Mostyn, Sir Roger Col. F. (d. 1690), 105. Knighted 1660.
Mottershed/Mottershead, Thomas Lieut. F., L. & W., 17
Moughly, Thomas Capt. H., York, 57
Moulins/Moulines, Adrian Ens. F., Somerset, 51
Moulins/Moulines, Charles Cor. H., Oxon, 25
Moulins, John Capt. F., 51
Moulton, Adam Quart. H., Somerset, 41
Mountain/Mountaine, James Capt. H., York, 87
Mountayn/Mountaine, Richard Lieut. F., L. & W., 122
Mowbray, William Cor. H., Middlesex, 98
Mowbray, William Quart. H., Lincoln, 104
Mowbrey, John Lieut. F., Rutland, 32
Mowshall, Peter Ens. F., Warwick, 98

Mowsley/Mowsly, Thomas Cor. H., Leicester, 96
Moyser, George Ens. F., Cornwall, 144
Mozey/Morey, John Capt. F., Worcester, 66
Mozin, ___ Capt. H., 108
Mozine, Anthony Capt. H., 75
Mozine/Mozin, Francis Cor. H., Nottingham, 75
Mozyn, John Capt. H., 40
Muckleston, Edw. Quart. H., Wilts, 41
Muckly, Thomas Capt. H., 56
Muddiford, Thomas Col. H. & F., 106
Mudford, Stephen Quart. H., Somerset, 129
Mulbanck, Mulbranke – *see* Malbrank
Muller, ___ Lord, ___ H., 106. In 1645 Rushworth calls him 'Lord Miller'; little about him is traceable, but Muller (Müller) is German for 'Miller', which suggests he was probably a German immigrant or volunteer.
Munday, ___ Capt. F., 122
Munday, John Lieut. F., Cornwall, 122
Munday, John Quart. H., Devon, 133
Munday, William Capt. H., Southampton, 23
Munnes/Munns, John Quart. H., Kent, stray, 159
Murfill, William Lieut. F., Cornwall, 71
Murray, William Cor. H., L. & W., 128
Murrey, William Ens. F., L. & W., 119
Murrin, Edw. Cor. H., Northumberland, 72
Murton, Thomas Quart. H., Northumberland, 88
Muschamp, Edw. Lieut. Col. H., Northumberland, 46
Muschamp, Sir George ___ F., 106
Muschamp, Robert Capt. F., Northumberland, 106
Musgrave, ___ Capt. H., 62
Musgrave, Anthony Cor. H., Cumberland, 107
Musgrave, Sir Edward Col. H. & F. (d. 1673), 106. Both 1648 regiments.
Musgrave, Henry Lieut. Col. H., L. & W., 10, 107
Musgrave, Sir Phillip Col. H. & F. (d. 1678), 107. Both 1648 regiments.
Musgrave, Sir Richard Capt. F., 107
Musgrave, Richard Capt. Lieut. F., Cumberland, 107
Musgrave, Simon Capt. H., 106
Musgrave, William Capt./Col. H., Cumberland, 107. Mentioned as a colonel by several first civil war officers; claims as a captain in Sir Phillip Musgrave's regiment of 1648.
Mussell, Nicholas Lieut. H., L. & W., 75
Musset, David Capt. Dr., 74
Musson, William Cor. H., Leicester, 18
Mustchamp, ___ Capt. F., 135
Mustchamp/Muschamp, Michael Lieut. F., Northumberland, 135
Mylott, Ralph Col. H., 107

Mynne, Nicholas Col. H. & F. (k. 1645; Redmarley D'Abitot), 107
Mynne, Robert ___ F., 108
Mynors, Richard Lieut. F., Hereford, 33
Mynors, Roger Cor. H., Hereford, 74
Nailor/Naylor, Joseph Cor. H., York, 92
Nalson, Robert Lieut. H., York, 109
Nance, William Lieut. F., Cornwall, 15
Nanfan, Giles Capt. F., Worcester, 29
Nanfan, Richard Cor. H., Gloucester, 71
Nanfan, Thomas Maj. F., 71
Nanny, John Capt. Lieut. F., L. & W., 111
Nanny, Robert Capt. Lieut. H., Merioneth, 32
Napier, Robert Capt. F., L. & W., 51
Napier, Thomas Col. F., L. & W., 9, 31. Reid lists Napier as a lieutenant colonel.
Napier, William Lieut. H., L. & W., 68
Napper, ___ Capt. F., 152
Napper/Napier, Andrew Lieut. F., Dorset, 77
Napper, Matthew Quart. H., Sussex, 62
Nash, John Capt. F., 155
Nash, Richard Lieut. F., Salop, 85
Nation, Francis, Chaplain, Devon, 174
Nation, George Quart. H., Cornwall, 102
Naylor, James Ens. F., Lincoln, 57
Naylor, Thomas Capt. H., York, 36
Naylor, Thomas Ens. F., L. & W., 25
Naylor, Walter Capt. Lieut. H., L. & W., 154
Neale, James Sea Capt. *Duke of York*, L. & W., 167
Neale, John Lieut. H., York, 27
Neale, Richard Quart. H., Nottingham, stray, 160
Neale, William Ens. F., Suffolk, 42
Nedham/Needham, Peter Capt. H., Stafford, 96
Needs, Richard Cor. H., Devon, 106
Needs, Thomas Lieut. H., Devon, 106
Nelson, ___ Capt. F., 120
Nelson, Abraham Capt. H., York, 103
Nelson, Robert Lieut. H., York, 46
Nesse, Richard Ens. F., Cumberland, stray, 165
Neve, ___ Capt. F., 112
Nevill, Anthony Maj. H., stray, 158
Nevill, Anthony Capt. H., 100
Nevill, Gervase Capt. H., stray, 159
Nevill, Gervase Cor. H., stray, Nottingham, 159
Nevill, Henry Capt. H., 37
Nevill, Matthias Capt. Lieut. F., L. & W., 133
Nevill, Richard Col./Lieut. Col. H. (d. 1676), 78, 108. Mentioned as lieutenant colonel

by an officer at Newark claiming under garrison governor Sir John Henderson; then as a colonel, by several officers in his own regiment.
Nevill, Roger Capt. H., York, 125
Nevill, Thomas Lieut. H., Somerset, 37
Nevill, William Col. H., 108
Nevinson, Roger Capt. H., Wilts, 47
Newbury/Newberry, James Adjutant General, L. & W., 170
Newbury/Newberry, John Lieut. F., Northampton, 112
Newcastle, [William Cavendish] Marquess of, Col. H., F. & Dr. (d. 1676), 108
Newcourt, ___ Maj. F., 67
Newcourt, Richard Capt. F., Somerset, 131
Newland, Thomas Capt. Dr., L. & W., 17
Newman, John Lieut. F., Dorset, 83
Newman, John Quart. H., Somerset, 40
Newman, Nicholas Capt. F., 35
Newman, Richard Capt. F., 24
Newman, Robert Cor. H., L. & W., 75
Newport, William Cor. H., Hertford, 59
Newsham, Edw. Cor. H., Cornwall, 78
Newsham, Thomas Capt. F., Carmarthen, 132
Newshaw, George Lieut. H., Somerset, 81
Newstead/Newsted, Robert Capt. H., Lincoln, 47
Newton, Bryan Capt. Lieut. F., L. & W., 154
Newton, Christopher Lieut. H., Northumberland, 108
Newton, Edw. Lieut. F., Nottingham, 147
Newton, Gilbert Ens. F., Devon, 86
Newton, Sir Henry, ___ H. (d. 1701), 32. Later assumed the surname Puckering.
Newton, John Quart. H., Chester, 142
Newton, Miles Quart. H., York, 148
Newton, Peter Capt. F., 78
Newton, Thomas Lieut. H., Durham, 29
Newton, William Capt. H., Devon, 77
Newton, William Lieut. H., Northumberland, 34
Newton William Ens. F., Chester, 92
Nicholls, Edw. Capt. H., 63
Nicholls, Edw. Sea Capt. 'of the *Charles* of Jersey', L. & W., 167
Nicholls, John Chirurgion, L. & W., 172
Nicholls, Robert Lieut. H., Chester, 55
Nicholls, Thomas Capt. F., L. & W., 120
Nicholls, Thomas Quart. H., L. & W., 40
Nicholls, Thomas Quart. H., Somerset, 129
Nichollson, Cutbert, Quart. H., Northumberland, 73
Nichollson, Thomas Ens. F., Newcastle, 77
Nicholson/Nichollson, George Lieut. F., Newcastle, 77
Nicholson/Nichollson, John Cor. H., Cumberland, 47

Nicholson/Nichollson, Richard Ens. F., Glamorgan, 132
Nicholson/Nichollson, Richard Quart. H., L. & W., 36
Nicholson/Nichollson, Thomas Capt. F., York, 89
Nicholson/Nichollson, Thomas Capt. F., Cornwall, 140
Nicholson, William Lieut. H., Northumberland, 148
Nodding, John Lieut. F., York, 22
Nokes, Richard Capt. F., L. & W., 13
Norborne, Edw. Capt. Lieut. H., Wilts, 128
Norborne, William Capt. F., Wilts, 85
Norbury, Edw. Lieut. F., York, 94
Norgrove, John Lieut. H., Worcester, 74
Norman, ___ Maj. F., 126
Norman, Edw. Quart. H., Dorset, 44
Norman, John Ens. F., Devon, 139
Norman, Thomas Quart. H., Somerset, 131
Normcott/Normcot, Richard Lieut. F., Salop, 121
Norris, ___ Capt. F., 31
Norris, Sir Edward Col. F., 109
Norris, Edw. Capt. F., Middlesex, 51
Norris, Henry Lieut. H., Cornwall, 54
Norris, William Lieut. H., L. & W., 64
North, Thomas Quart. H., York, 40
Northam/Northan, Francis Lieut. Dr., Lincoln, stray, 166
Northampton, [Spencer Compton] 2nd Earl of, Col. H., F. & Dr. (k. 1643; Hopton Heath), 110
Northampton, [James Compton] 3rd Earl of, Col. H., F. & Dr. (d. 1681), 109
Norton, ___ Lieut. Col. Dr., 99
Norton, ___ Capt. H., 121
Norton, ___ Capt. F., Sir Edward Berkly, 23
Norton, ___ Capt. F., Lord John Byron, 31
Norton, Anthony Capt. F., York, 111, 112. Claims under Sir James Pennyman; also mentioned by an ensign under Sir Richard Page, who took over Pennyman's regiment in 1644.
Norton, William Capt. H., 77
Norwich, [George Goring] 1st Earl of, Col. H. & F. (d. 1663), 110
Norwood, ___ Capt. Dr., 145
Norwood, Charles Maj. F., L. & W., 11, 59
Noy, William Capt. H., Cornwall, 19
Noyse, Richard Capt. Lieut. H., L. & W., stray, 158
Nugent, ___ Capt. Dr., 81
Nunnes, Robert Lieut. H., York, 125
O Brian, Morrough Capt. H., Middlesex, 76
O'Donoghue/Odonoghue, Mortaugh Ens. F., L. & W., 120
Oakes, Edmund Quart. H., L. & W., 144
Oakly, Anthony Lieut. Dr., Salop, 43

Index

Oatley, Sir Francis Col. F. & Dr. (d. 1649), 110. Usually 'Ottley'.
Ockley, William Ens. F., Worcester, 123
Odber, John Capt. Dr., Southampton, 83
Odby, John Cor. Dr., York, 70
Oddy, Edw. Quart. H., Lancaster, 137
Odham, John Quart. H., Sussex, 62
Odling, Richard Quart. H., Lincoln, 25
Offly, ___ Lieut. Col. H., 150
Ogar, Edmund Capt. H., Lincoln, 115
Ogden, Thomas Lieut. F., York, 117
Ogle, Charles Capt. Lieut. H., Northumberland, 152
Ogle, John Capt. F., Northumberland, 129
Ogle, John Cor. H., Durham, 148
Ogle, [Sir William] 1ˢᵗ Viscount, Col. H. & F. (d. 1670), 110
Ogle, William Capt. H., stray, 161
Ogle, William Lieut. H., L. & W., 75
Oglethorpe/Oglethorp, Robert Capt. H., Cumberland, 107
Oglethorpe, Robert Lieut. H., L. & W., 154
Ogstone, William D. D., Chaplain, L. & W., 173
Okelly, Daniel Ens. F., Norfolk, 21
Okelly, Robert Quart. H., Chester, 44
Oker, ___ Capt. H., 115
Oldfield, James Capt. ___, 88
Oldfield, William Lieut. H., Wilts, stray, 158
Oldham, Edw. Lieut. H., Chester, 55
Oldham, William Cor. H., Chester, 89
Oldis, John Capt. H., Dorset, 42
Oliver, George Quart. H., Middlesex, 77
Oliver, John Cor. H., York, 58
Oliver, John Ens. F., Cornwall, 140
Oliver, Thomas Capt. H., Cornwall, 77
Olivers, Robert Lieut. F., Lancaster, stray, 164
Olliver/Oliver, Thomas Capt. F., Cornwall, 140
Olyvy/Olyvie, Richard Quart. F., Cornwall, 20
Oneale, Hugh Capt. F., L. & W., 13
Orbel, ___ Capt. F., 22
Orbell, Nicholas Capt. F., Lancaster, stray, 163
Orchard, William Capt. F., Cornwall, 69
Ord, ___ Lieut. Col. F., 135
Ord, ___ Maj. F., 138
Ord, ___ Capt. H., Lord General King, 87
Ord, ___ Capt. H., Sir William Savile, 125
Ord, Francis Capt. H., Ralph Carnaby, 34
Ord, Francis Capt. H., Sir Robert Clavering, 39
Ord, John Capt. F., Northumberland, 62

Ord, Ralph Cor. H., Northumberland, 93
Ord, Thomas Capt. F., 39
Ord, William Lieut. H., Northumberland, 136
Orrat, Thomas Ens. F., Chester, stray, 165
Orrey, John Lieut. F., York, 22
Osborn, Thomas Quart. H., Worcester, 93
Osborne, Sir Edward ___ H. (d. 1647), 110
Osborne/Osborn, Edw. Capt. F., L. & W., 120
Osborne/Osborn, Thomas Ens. F., Salop, 120
Osgood, Francis Ens. F., Cornwall, 140
Oswold, Richard Ens. F., Durham, 30
Ottley – *see* Oatley
Otway, Thomas, Chaplain, Wilts, 174
Outon, John Cor. H., Salop, 149
Overfield, Christopher Cor. H., L. & W., 36
Overley/Overly, William Ens. F., L. & W., 67
Overton, ___ Lieut. Col. F., 114
Overton, ___ Capt. F., 131
Owen, ___ Capt. F., 122
Owen, Edward Sea Capt. 'of the *Lyon*', Merioneth, 167
Owen, Sir John Col. F. (d. 1666), 111
Owen, Pontsbury Capt. F., 110
Owen, Thomas Quart. F., Somerset, 23
Owen, William Col. F., 111
Owen, William Capt. F., Pembroke, 65
Owens, Edmund Quart. F., Monmouth, 154
Owens, Evan Lieut. F., Worcester, 45
Owston, Christopher Quart. F., York, 154
Oxenbridge, Thomas Quart. F., 27
Oxley/Oxly, John Lieut. F., York, 125
Packington, Sir John Col. ___ (d. 1680), 111. A 1651 regiment. I.O. does not state his arm of service; Reid says it was horse.
Packington, Thomas Cor. H., York, 87
Paddison, James Cor. H., Surrey, 101
Paddon, Robert Capt. H., Middlesex, 52
Paganuzzi, Daniel Capt. H., L. & W., 23
Page, Henry Lieut. F., Leicester, 98
Page, John Regt. Quart. H., Carmarthen, 48
Page, Sir Richard Col. F. (d. before 1659), 111
Page, Richard Quart. H., Gloucester, stray, 160
Page, William Quart. H., Northampton, 109
Pagenham, ___ Capt. F., 53
Painter, John Lieut. F., Cornwall, 69
Palfry/Palfrey, Thomas Lieut. F., Devon, 62
Pallester, Cutbert Quart. H., York, 90

Index 309

Pallester, James Quart. H., Durham, 27
Palmer, ___ Lieut. Col. H., 124
Palmer, ___ Maj. F., 13
Palmer, Henry Lieut. F., Carmarthen, 65
Palmer, John Capt. F., Somerset, 28
Palmer, Peter Maj. F., 73
Palmer, Richard Col. H., 111
Palmer, Richard Ens. F., Devon, 24
Paly, Thomas Quart. F., Bedford, 51
Panton, Edw. Capt. H., L. & W., 150
Panton, Thomas Maj. H., 108
Pardew, Stephen Ens. F., Cornwall, 139
Parfet, Henry Ens. F., Somerset, 131
Parfet/Parfett, Michael Ens. F., Somerset, stray, 165
Parfet/Parfett, Richard Cor. H., Somerset, 131
Parfet/Parfett, William Ens. F., Somerset, 28
Parfett, John Quart. H., Somerset, 106
Parham, William Capt. F., L. & W., 66
Paris, John Lieut. F., L. & W., 110
Paris, John Quart. H., L. & W., 30
Paris, Lewis Quart. H., Somerset, 155
Parker, Alexander Capt. H., L. & W., 30
Parker, Austin Lieut. H., Somerset, 77
Parker, Edmund Capt. F., Warwick, 16
Parker, John Lieut. H., Lancaster, 31
Parker, John Quart. H., York, 90
Parker, Richard Lieut. H., Lincoln, 48
Parker, Robert Sea Capt., Sussex, 167
Parker, Thomas Lieut. F., Kent, 75. Served in 1648.
Parker, Thomas Cor. H., Lancaster, 136
Parkin, Timothy Capt. F., Durham, 53
Parlet, William Lieut. F., Cambridge, 110
Parr, Thomas Lieut. F., Middlesex, 68
Parrock, John Quart. H., Southampton, 82. The main I.O. text spells Parrock's name as 'Farrock'; however, extensive searching of public records suggests that has never been a surname, and is therefore probably a spelling mistake for 'Parrock', as per the I.O. index entry.
Parry, David Ens. F., Anglesey, 29
Parry, James Capt. F., L. & W., 105
Parry, James Ens. F., Hereford, 35
Parry, Owen Lieut. Col. F., L. & W., 10, 35
Parry, William Lieut. F., L. & W., 35
Parsly, Richard Capt. H., 34
Parson, ___ Capt. H., 149
Parsons, George Capt. H., Chester, 118

Parsons, John Capt. H., Wilts, 81
Parsons, Matthew Capt. H., Cornwall, 77
Partridge, ___ Capt. F., 52
Partridge, George Capt. F., Suffolk, 118
Partridge, John Cor. H., Essex, stray, 159
Partridge, Oliver Cor. H., L. & W., 76
Parving, John Cor. H., York, 27
Pasket/Posket, John Lieut. F., York, 144
Paslew, ___ Capt. H., 109
Paslew, Richard Capt. H., L. & W., 108
Paslew, William Quart. H., Oxon, 45
Pasmuch, John Quart. H., Nottingham, 30
Patchcote/Patchcot, William Quart. H., Cornwall, 78
Pate, Edmund Capt. F., 51, 67. Pate was mentioned by two officers under Sir John Digby, then by a third under Sir Anthony Gilby, who later commanded Digby's regiment.
Pate, Sir John Col. H. (d. 1659), 111
Patrickson, Jos. Capt. H., 46
Patrickson, Richard Lieut. F., Cumberland, 47
Patrickson, Thomas Lieut. H., Cumberland, 46
Pattison, Richard Quart. H., L. & W., 90
Pattison, Robert Ens. F., Westmorland, stray, 165. An addition from the errata.
Paty, Andrew Lieut. H., L. & W., 68
Paul, Richard Quart. H., York, 115
Paul, Robert Lieut. F., Kent, 92
Paul, Thomas Capt. H., Durham, 118. Claims as a captain of horse under Sir Thomas Riddell, but two subordinate officers cite him as a captain of foot.
Paulden, Thomas Capt. F., L. & W, stray (d. btwn 1702-1710), 163, 165. Claims from London but noted as 'in Pontefract'. Also mentioned by a stray London ensign. One of the party who captured Parliamentarian Colonel Thomas Rainsborough at his quarters near Pontefract; the colonel was killed while trying to escape.
Paulden, William Capt. H., stray, 160. Probably the William Paulden, brother of Thomas, Paulden above; William died of fever in Pontefract in 1648, shortly after the abortive capture of Colonel Rainsborough.
Paulet, Francis Capt. H., 76
Paulet/Poulett, John 1st Baron Poulet Col. H. & F. (d. 1649), 112. Usually known as 'Lord Paulet'. *Not* John Paulet, 5th Marquess of Winchester.
Paulet, Sir John Col. F. (d. 1665), 112. Son of Baron Paulet, above.
Paulett, Ames Capt. H., stray, 160
Paulett/Paulet, John Capt. H., L. & W., stray, 157
Pawlet/Paulet, John Capt. F., L. & W., 38
Pawle/Paulet, William Quart. H., L. & W., 106
Pawston, Henry Cor. H., Northumberland, 148
Payne, John Waggon Master General, Middlesex, 170

Payne, William Capt. F., L. & W., 150
Payne, William Capt. F., L. & W., 150. An identical entry to above, and in the same regiment; probably a printing error, but is listed twice in the index.
Peachell, Richard Capt. F., L .& W., 92
Peachy, Gregory Capt. H., Southampton, 41
Peachy, Thomas Lieut. H., Southampton, 70
Peak/Peake, Gregory Cor. H., L. & W., 30
Peake, Sir Robert [Lieut. Col.] F. (d. 1667), 150. I.O. does not give a rank, but Peake is known to have been lieutenant colonel to the Marquess of Winchester. Knighted March 1645.
Peaker, ___ Capt. F., 156
Pearce – *see* Pierce
Pearne, John Lieut. F., Durham, 43
Pearson, James Cor. H., Lancaster, 137
Pearson, John Capt. H., 82
Pearson, John Lieut. H., York, Lord Belassis, 21
Pearson, John Lieut. H., Durham, John Forcer, 62
Pearson, Thomas Capt. H., Newcastle, 147
Pearson, Thomas Lieut. F., Durham, 80
Pearsons, William Capt. F., 16
Pease, Stephen Cor. H., Durham, 87
Peele, John Quart. H., L. & W., 90
Peere, Benjamin Capt. F., L. & W., 65
Peirce – *see also* Pierce
Peirce, John Ens. F., Flint, 106
Pelham, ___ Capt. F., 112
Pelham, Charles Capt. F., stray, 165
Pelham, Sir William Col. H. & F. (k. 1644; Montgomery), 112
Pell, Sir Bartholomew Lieut. Col. F., L. & W., 10, 67
Pemberton, John Capt. F., 89
Pemberton, Robert Capt. F., Northumberland, 135
Pen/Penn, Humphry Cor. Dr., Salop, 43
Pen/Penn, Roger Lieut. H., L. & W., 108
Penbertha, John Lieut. F., Cornwall, 139
Pendarvis/Pendarvys, Thomas Capt. F., Cornwall, 107
Penfound, Arthur Capt. Dr., Cornwall, 20
Penhallow, Emmanuel Capt. H., Cornwall, 81
Peniall, Matthew Capt. H., Berks, 43
Penkeath, ___ Capt. F., 119
Penketh, William Capt. Lieut. H., Lancaster, 127
Penlease, William Ens. F., Cornwall, 69
Penn, Edward Lieut. H., Bucks, stray, 158
Penx n, William Capt. H., Worcester, 127. Served in 1651.
Pennington, Sir John, Admiral (d. 1646), 167
Penny, William Lieut. F., Cornwall, 44

Penny, William Lieut. F., L. & W., 144. Claims naval captain Sir Baldwyn Wake as his senior officer.
Pennyman, Sir James Col. F. (d. 1679), 112
Pennyman, Sir William Col. H. & F. (d. 1643), 113
Pennyman, William Capt. F., 19
Penrose/Penvose, William Lieut. Dr., L. & W., 83
Penruddock, Edw. Capt. F., Wilts, 43
Penry, Henry Capt. H., Glamorgan, 29
Penry, Henry Ens. F., Kent, 40
Penser, Henry Lieut. Dr., York, 91
Penwarden, John Ens. F., Cornwall, 43
Penwarne, Anthony Chirurgion, Cornwall, 173
Percivall, Edw. Quart. H., L. & W., 115
Percy (Piercy), Lord Henry Col. H. & F. (d. 1659), 114
Perkins, Isham Col. H., 113. Governor of Ashby-de-la-Zouch.
Perkins/Perkin, John Ens. F., Cornwall, 154
Perkins, Thomas Lieut. H., Kent, 100
Perkinson, William Quart. H., L. & W., 64
Pershall, Thomas Capt. F., Chester, stray, 163
Pert, Thomas Col. H. & F., (k. 1646), 113. No officers from Pert's horse regiment claim in I.O.
Petegrew, Nicholas Lieut. F., Cornwall, 15
Peters, ___ Lieut. Col. H., 17
Peters, William Cor. Dr., L. & W., 146
Pethick, John Ens. F., Cornwall, 20
Petts, ___ Capt. H., 55
Pettus, Sir John Col. H. (d. 1685), 113
Petty, Walter Ens. F., Stafford, 18
Pey, John Cor. H., Salop, 30
Phelps, Giles Quart. H., Somerset, 78
Phelipps/Phelips, Arthur Capt. F., Somerset, 113
Phelips, Edward Col. H. (d. 1680), 113. Reid states that he was killed near Winchester, but this appears to be a mistake.
Phelips, Robert Col. H. & F. (d. 1707), 113. Younger brother of Edward, above.
Philcott/Philcot, Peter, Commissary, Kent, 169
Phillips, ___ Capt. H., 151
Phillips, Arthur Lieut. F., Durham, 136
Phillips, Charles Lieut. F., L. & W., 88
Phillips, Edw. Capt. F., Flint, 31
Phillips, Henry Lieut. H., Lincoln, 56
Phillips, John Capt. H., Chester, 147
Phillips, John Capt. F., Pembroke, 33
Phillips, John Ens. F., Pembroke, 33
Phillips, Owen Capt. F., L. & W., 127
Phillips, Owen Lieut. F., Carmarthen, 96

Phillips, Rice Capt. F., L. & W., 14
Phillips, Richard Capt. F., Salop, Christopher Sayers, 126
Phillips, Richard Capt. F., Salop, Sir Michael Woodhouse, 152
 Phillips, Thomas Capt. F., Carmarthen, 65, 165. Claims under Lord Gerard; also mentioned by a stray Carmarthen ensign.
Phillips, William Capt. F., L. & W., 151
Phillipson, ___ Maj. H., 134. Served in 1648.
Phillipson, ___ Capt. H., 107
Phillpott/Philpot, George Capt. H., Southampton, 44
Philpot, John Capt. F., 83
Phipps, Benjamin Capt. H., Warwick, 93
Phipps, William Quart. Dr., Warwick, 110
Pickering, John Capt. Lieut. H., L. & W., 19
Pickering, John Lieut. F., L. & W., 69
Pickhay, Agmondisham Capt. H., 36
Pierce – *see also* Peirce
Pierce, Sir Edmond Col. H. (d. 1667), 114
Pierce, Gabriel Cor. H., Salop, 92
Pierce, John Capt. F., 78
Pierce, John Lieut. Pioneers, L. & W., 172
Pierce, John Ens. F., Cornwall, 15
Pierce, Richard Ens. F., Cornwall, 15
Pierce, Thomas Capt. F., 19
Pierce, Thomas Ens. F., Devon, 36
Pierce, Thomas Ens. F., Devon, stray, 165
Pierce, Thomas Ens. F., Cornwall, 139
Piercy, Lord Henry, *see* Henry Percy
Piercy, Thomas Capt. F., Lord John Berkly, 24
Piercy, Thomas Lieut. Dr., L. & W., 81
Pierepoint/Pierpoynt, William Lieut. F., Hereford, 153
Pierpoint, Ralph Scoutmaster, Hereford, 172
Pigeon, Ambrose Cor. Dr., Salop, 43
Piggen, Edw. Lieut. H., L. & W., 146
Pigott, ___ Capt. Dr., 43
Pigott, Thomas Col. F., 114
Piggott/Pigget, Thomas Ens. F., Essex, 58
Pike, George Ens. F., Kent, 42
Pikes, Walter Capt. F., Somerset, 132
Pildrim, William Lieut. F., Cambridge, 119
Pile, William Quart. H., Southampton, 26
Pilkington, ___ Capt. F., 117
Pilkington, Henry Lieut. Col. Dr., L. & W., 10, 52
Pilkington, Ralph Cor. H. L. & W., 103
Pilkington, Thomas Lieut. F., Durham, 53
Pilkington, Thomas Lieut. F., Worcester, 66

Pilkington, William Ens. F., L. & W., 146. Claims as foot, but served in Henry Washington's dragoons.
Pinchback, ___ ___ F., 114. Probably Colonel Thomas Pinchbeck, killed at the first battle of Newbury. His regiment was taken over by Sir Henry Bard.
Pinckard/Pinkard, Robert Ens. F., Durham, 118
Pinckney, Christopher Cor. H., Durham, 73
Pinckney, Henry Cor. H., York, 27
Pindar, John Cor. H., L. & W., 101
Pinder, Samuel Capt. H., 37
Pine – *see also* Pyne
Pine, ___ Capt. F., 98. I.O. gives no arm of service for Pine or the ensign who cited him, but the rank of ensign indicates foot.
Pine, Robert Sea Capt. 'of the *Charles* Fregat', L. & W., 167
Pinner, John Capt. F., Somerset, 141
Piper, Arthur Capt. F., 43
Piper, Arthur Ens. F., Cornwall, 43
Piper, John Capt. Pioneers, Cornwall, 171
Pippin, Matthew Quart. H., Leicester, 18
Pistor, William Capt. Dr., stray, 166
Pitchard, William Lieut. F., York, 133
Pitcher, ___ *Capt. F.*, 91
Pitchford, Andrew Cor. Dr., Salop, 75
Pitman, Thomas Capt. F., 16
Pitt/Pitts, Henry Ens. F., Hereford, 45
Pitt/Pitts, John Lieut. H., Devon, 151
Pitt/Pitts, John Lieut. F., L. & W., 83
Pitt, Richard Lieut. H. & Quart. Gen., Worcester, 70
Pittard, Amos Quart. H., Somerset, 155
Pittman, ___ *Capt. F.*, 131
Pittman, William Cor. H., Hereford, 126
Pitts, ___ *Capt. F.*, 110
Pitts, James Capt. H., Glamorgan, 111
Plackledge, ___ *Capt. F.*, 66
Place, Robert Cor. H., York, 79
Platt, William Capt. F./Maj. H., Kent, 86. '[Captain] at Worcester, and formerly Maj. to the Marquess Montrose'. Worcester service implies that he fought in 1651. Although I.O.'s main text does not specify his arm of service while a major, the index states that it was horse.
Plaxton, William Capt. Lieut. ___, York, 40
Play, ___ *Capt. F.*, 135
Playdell, Oliver Lieut. H., Oxon, stray, 158
Playters, Thomas Col. H., 114
Plimpton, John Capt. F., 56
Plinton/Plimpton, Anthony Lieut. H., Somerset, 151
Plucknet, Robert Lieut. F., Somerset, 51

Plucknett, Thomas Capt. H., Dorset, 75
Plumly, Henry Cor. H., Somerset, 112
Plumly, John Capt. F., Cornwall, 20
Plush, Thomas Lieut. F., Somerset, 118
Pocklington, Thomas Capt. F., L. & W., 26
Pole, German/Germain Capt. H., Nottingham, 56
Polewheele, Stephen Capt. F., Cornwall, 139
Polkinhorne, Edw. Capt. Pioneers, Carnarvon, 172
Pollard, ___ Lieut. Col. H., stray, 159
Pollard, Ames Col. H. & F., 114
Pollard, Anthony Capt. H., Oxon, 52
Pollard, Charles Ens. F., L. & W., 65
Pollard, Gowen Cor. H., Kent, 100
Pollard, Sir Hugh Col. F. (d. 1666), 115
Pollard, Lewis Lieut. F., L. & W., 65
Pollatsy, Percivall Lieut. H., Surrey, 81
Pollock, John Capt. F., 22
Polsue, Peter Lieut. F., Cornwall, 15
Polwheele, ___ Maj. H., 19
Pomeroy, ___ Maj. H., 81
Pomeroy, ___ Capt. H., 78
Pomeroy, ___ Lieut. Col. F., 20
Pomeroy, Hugh Capt. F. 'at Sea and Land', Devon, stray, 163
Pool/Poole, Benjamin Capt. H., L. & W., 44
Poole, ___ Capt. H., 41
Poole, Sir Courtney ___ H., 77
Poole, Gervase Capt. H., 63
Poole, Ignatius Lieut. H., Derby, 63
Poole, Robert Ens. F., Nottingham, 51
Poole, William, Marshall, Dorset, 171
Pooly, William Cor. H., L. & W., 21
Poore, Francis Capt. F., L. & W., 122
Poore, Thomas Capt. F., Durham, 135
Pope, ___ Capt. F., 83
Pope, Jeffery Lieut. F., Wilts, 19
Pope, John Ens. F., Cornwall, Sir Pierce Edgecumbe, 54
Pope, John Ens. F. Cornwall, Sir Pierce Edgecumbe, 54. Same regiment and arm as above: probably a duplicate or printing error.
Pope, Mark 'Conductor of the Train', L. & W., 170
Popham, Andrew Capt. H., Stafford, 98
Poppleston, Ferdinando Ens. F., Cornwall, 54
Poppleston, Lyney Lieut. F., Cornwall, 54
Porter, Andrew Capt. F., L. & W., 21
Porter, Anthony Capt. F., Cumberland, 30
Porter, Atwell Lieut. F., Somerset 'in Dunstar', stray, 164

Porter, Benedict Chirurgion, L. & W., 172
Porter, George General H. (d. 1683), 115
Porter, Nicholas Lieut. F., Cumberland, 122
Porter, Ralph Ens. F., Devon, 145
Porter, Richard Capt. F., 71
Porter, William Capt. H., Cumberland, 90
Portington, ___ Lieut. Col. H., 125. Reid suggests this could be Roger Portington (see below).
Portington, ___ Maj. H., 68. Reid states that this is Michael Portington, who was dead before 1650, when his son requests his estate be discharged (CCC IV, p. 2619).
Portington Henry Capt. H., York, 124
Portington, Roger Capt. H., 125
Portworthy, James Lieut. F., L. & W., 147
Posket – *see* Pasket
Pott, Thomas Lieut. F., Derby, 103
Potter, Ralph Ens. F., York, 58
Potter, Samuel Capt. F., Oxon, 44
Potter, William Lieut. F., Durham, 136
Potters, John Capt. F., 66
Potts, ___ Maj. H., 46
Potts, Eleazar Lieut. F., Newcastle, 135
Potts, John Capt. H., Stafford, 93, 161. Claims under Thomas Leveson; also mentioned by a stray quartermaster.
Potts, Reynold Quart. F., Northumberland, 92
Pouch, ___ Capt. H., 91
Poulton, Edw. Capt. F., 83
Poulton, Thomas Capt. H., 82
Poulton, Thomas Lieut. H., Wilts, 95
Poulton, William Capt. F., 83
Pouncy, Roger Quart. Dr., Dorset, 45
Pound, Thomas Capt. F., stray, 163
Powel/Powell, David Cor. H., L. & W., 30
Powel/Powell, Reynold Lieut. F., Monmouth, 153
Powel, William Maj. F., 84
Powell, ___ Lieut. Col. F., 131
Powell, Anthony Cor. H., Somerset, stray, 159
Powell, Daniel Ens. F., Nottingham, stray, 165
Powell, David Capt. F., Devon, 24
Powell, John Lieut. F., Flint, stray, 164
Powell, Peter Capt. F., Brecon, 116
Powell, Richard Lieut. H., L. & W., 32
Powell, Richard Quart. H., Worcester, stray, 160
Powell, Thomas Capt. F., Denbigh, 55
Powell, Thomas Lieut. F., Brecon, 116

Powell, Thomas Lieut. F., Denbigh, 111
Powell, Thomas Ens. F., Flint, 106
Powell, Walter/Water Lieut. F., Brecon, 116. The spelling 'Water' in the I.O. index sis almost certainly a printing error.
Powell, William Capt. F., 87
Powell, William Capt. H., Carmarthen, 91
Powell, William Lieut. F., Denbigh, 31
Powell, William Lieut. F., Lancaster, 66
Powell, William Cor. H., Warwick, 109
Pownall, John Capt. H., Kent, 130
Poyer, John Col. H. (executed 1649), 115. Parliamentarian governor of Pembroke Castle, who rebelled in 1648. Executed in April 1649.
Poyntz, ___ Capt. H., Lord Henry Cavendish, 36
Poyntz, ___ Capt. H., Charles Proger Herbert, 78
Poyntz, Edward Lieut. F., Devon, 14
Prees, William Lieut. F., Brecon, 116
Prescot/Prescott, Richard Quart. H., Oxon, 46
Preston, Anthony Lieut. F., Westmorland, 22
Preston, Sir John Col. H. (k. 1645), 115. Of Furness, Lancashire.
Preston, [George] Lieut. Col. H., 115. I.O. does not give the officer's name, but this would appear to be the George Preston of Holker in Lancashire who was killed serving under Sir John Preston in March 1644 (Newman, *Old Service*, p.233). Reid states that he was killed at Bradford.
Preston, John Cor. H., Durham, 13
Preston, Simon Capt. H., L. & W., 34
Prestwich, Sir Thomas Col. H. & F. (d. 1674), 9, 115, 146. Claims under Thomas, Lord Wentworth; several officers claim under Prestwich directly.
Prestwich, Thomas Maj. H., Middlesex, 11, 115
Pretheretch/Pretherech, William Ens. F., L. & W., 66
Prethero, Philip Ens. F., Pembroke, stray, 165
Pretty, William Col. F., 116
Price, ___ Lieut. Col. H., 64
Price, ___ Capt. F., William Price, 116
Price, ___ Capt. F., Sir Barnaby Scudamore, 126
Price, Bartholomew Capt. H., 116
Price, David Ens. F., Carmarthen, 107
Price, Edw. Lieut. Col. H., 54
Price, Edw. Capt. F., Denbigh, Edward Herbert, Lord Cherbury, 78
Price, Edw. Capt. F., Salop, Lord Richard Herbert, 78
Price, Edw. Cor. H., Hereford, 126
Price, Sir Herbert Col. H. & F. (d. 1678), 116
Price, James Capt. F., Radnor, 116
Price, James Ens. F., L. & W., 153
Price, John Lieut. Col. H., 143
Price, John Capt. H., L. & W., 116

Price, John Capt. F., Glamorgan, 105
Price, John Lieut. F., L. & W., 37
Price, Morgan Maj. F., Monmouth, 11, 153
Price, Richard Maj. F., L. & W., 11, 116
Price, Robert Capt. H., Denbigh, 29
Price, Robert Quart. H., Worcester, 124
Price, Thomas Capt. F., Denbigh, William Salisbury, 123
Price, Thomas Capt. F., Flint, Sir Roger Mostyn, 105
Price, William Col. F., 116
Price, William Capt. F., Glamorgan, 132
Prichard, Phil. Capt. F., 101. I.O. gives no arm of service for Prichard or the ensign who cited him, but the rank of ensign indicates foot.
Prichard/Pritchard, Rice Ens. F., Carmarthen, stray, 165. Listed as a stray, but claims under Captain Thomas Phillips, who claims under Lord Gerard.
Prichard, Robert Lieut. F., L. & W., 16
Prickett, Anker Quart. H., Gloucester, 120
Pride, Thomas Chirurgion, Cornwall, 173
Prideaux, ___ Capt. H., stray, 159
Prideaux, Francis Ens. F., Cornwall, 122
Prideaux, John Maj. F., 139
Prideaux, John Capt. F., Cornwall, 139
Prideaux, William Col. Dr., 117
Prince Charles, Col. H., 37. The Prince did not personally command the regiment.
Prince, George Chirurgion, Devon, 173
Prince, John Quart. H., York, 143
Pris, Ellis Capt. F., Denbigh, 61
Prissoe, Richard Capt. F., Westmorland, 22
Prist, John Quart. H., Middlesex, 93
Pritchard, John Cor. H., Monmouth, 64
Pritchard, Samuel Quart. F., Salop, 152
Pritchard, Thomas Ens. F., L. & W., 28
Pritchard, Thomas Ens. F., Monmouth, 143
Proctor, ___ Capt. F., 118
Profitt, ___ Lieut. Col. H., 74
Proger, Charles Lieut. F., Monmouth, 65
Proger/Progers, Wroth Ens. F., L. & W., 105
Progers, Charles Lieut. Col. F., 117
Progers, James Col. F., 116
Progers, James ___ F., 153. Possibly the Colonel Progers above.
Protherech, ___ Capt. F., 130
Proudlove, Hugh Capt. Lieut. H., L. & W., 140
Prouse, ___ Lieut. Col. F., 35
Prouse/Prowse, Robert Lieut. F., Devon, 35
Pruden, John Chirurgion, L. & W., 172
Pruett, William Quart. H., Wilts, 51

Prust, ___ Lieut. Col. H., 135
Prust, ___ Capt. H., stray, 159
Prym, Thomas Capt. F., Devon, 24
Prythero, ___ Capt. F., 154
Pryor, Michael Ens. F., Monmouth, 105
Pryor, Robert Ens. F., Northumberland, 128. I.O. does not give Pryor's arm of service but the rank of ensign indicates foot.
Pudsay/Pudsey, Peter Maj. H., York, 11, 115
Pudsey, Ralph Lieut. Col. H., 57
Pudsey, Ralph Capt. H., stray, 160
Pugh, John Capt. F., 111
Pugh, Thomas Ens. F., L. & W., 61
Pugh, Robert Capt. H., Montgomery, 153
Pugh, Robert Capt. F., Carnarvon, 123
Pugh, William Capt. F., Hereford, 130
Pugh, William Lieut. F., Merioneth, 111
Pullen, Henry Capt. F., York, 56
Pullen, John Lieut. H., York, 36
Pullen, John Ens. F., Cornwall, 140
Pullen, Robert Ens. F., York, 56
Punchion, John Capt. F., 85
Punchion, William Capt. F., 85
Purday, William Capt. F., York, 57
Purdee/Purday, John Cor. H., Derby, 55
Putham, Walter Capt. H., Somerset, 135
Putham, William Lieut. H., Somerset, 135
Pyard, Godfrey/Godfry Lieut. H., L. & W., 76
Pybus, Christopher Ens. F., York, 49
Pye, James Cor. H., Monmouth, 116
Pye, John Maj. H., 126
Pye, Richard Lieut. F., L. & W., 138
Pye, Sir Walter Col. H. (d. 1659), 117
Pye, Walter Capt. H., Hereford, 107
Pyne – *see also* Pine
Pyne, ___ Capt. F., 120
Pyne, Henry Lieut. H., Southampton, 114
Pyne, Lionell Capt. F., Dorset, 51
Pyne, William Ens. F., Somerset, 120
Pyott, Simon Lieut. F., L. & W., 33
Quadring, Richard Cor. H., Lincoln, 47
Quadring, William Capt. H., Lincoln, 47
Quarles, John Capt. H., L. & W., 146
Queen's Regiment of Horse – *see* Lord St. Albans and Sir John Cansfield
Quinsey, Thomas Quart. H., Lincoln, 29
Quoyle, Patrick Lieut. F., L. & W., 150

Rackett/Racket, William Lieut. H., Durham, 52
Raddall, Thomas Ens. F., Devon, stray, 165. Listed as a stray, but claims under Major John Jacob of Sir Henry Cary's regiment.
Raddon, Robert Capt. H., 79
Radford, Arthur Col. H., 117
Radly, Charles Cor. H., Lincoln, 117. Claims under Sir Henry Radley, below, despite Sir Henry being known as an infantry officer.
Radly, Sir Henry ___ F. (d. 1653), 117. Radley was in the King's Lifeguard of Foot. In 1644 the Royalist Ordnance Papers record an issue of arms to his company (vol. 2, p.346), so he must have ranked at least as a captain.
Raggett/Ragget, John Lieut. H., York, 46
Raines, Edmund Capt. H., stray, 159
Rainsford, Francis Capt. F., L. & W., 21
Rames, Roger Lieut. F., Northumberland, 85
Ramsden, Hugh Ens. F., York, 117
Ramsden, Sir John Col. F. (d. 1646; Newark), 117. Died during the siege of Newark.
Ramsden, Thomas Quart. H., York, 87
Ramsy, Robert Quart. H., Northumberland, 73
Ramsy/Ramsey Simon Quart. H., Surrey, 45
Ranakers, Roger Capt. Dr., Chester, stray, 166
Randal/Randall, Thomas Capt. Lieut. ___, Worcester, 111. Served in 1651. I.O. does not give his arm of service, but Reid states that his Colonel, Sir John Packington, commanded a cavalry regiment.
Randal/Randall, Thomas Lieut. Dr., Newcastle, 100
Randall, ___ Capt. F., 83
Randall, Andrew Cor. H., Northampton, 111
Randall, Richard, Quart. H., L. & W., 64
Ranes, Edward Capt. H., Lincoln, 57
Ranger, Evan Maj. F., Wilts, 53
Ranson, James Capt. H., 52
Rashly, ___ Capt. F., 140
Rask, John Cor. H., Lincoln, 112
Rastall, Henry Capt. H., L. & W., 125
Ratcliffe, Charles Capt. F., stray, 164
Ratcliffe, Molineux Capt. F., stray, 163, 164. Mentioned by two stray lieutenants.
Ratcliffe, Sir William ___ H., 17, 117. Two officers claim under him in Sir Thomas Aston's regiment; three more claim under him directly.
Raven, Miles Chirurgion, Wilts, 173
Raven, Roger Capt. H., Middlesex, 114
Ravenscroft, ___ Capt. H., 147
Rawdon – *see* Roydon
Rawleigh, Joseph Licut. F., Devon, 67
Rawley, Walter Capt. H., Wilts, 77
Rawling, Henry Quart. F., Cumberland, 47
Rawling/Rawlings, John Quart. F., Cornwall, 20

Rawson, Thomas Capt. H., L. & W., 53
Rawson, Thomas Quart. H., York, 125
Rawson, William Cor. H., Lincoln, 97
Rawston, Edward Col. H. & F., 117
Ray, George Quart. H., L. & W., 148
Raymond, Edw. Lieut. F., Somerset, 155
Raymond, Thomas Capt. Lieut. H., Devon, 59
Raynger, Francis Maj. F., 11. Requests inclusion, but no officers claim so his regiment is unknown.
Raynsford, John Lieut. F., Oxon, 65
Read, Francis Capt. H., 13
Read, Francis Lieut. F., L. & W., 100
Read, James Ens. F., Salop, 113
Read, John Lieut. H., York, 68
Read, John Lieut. F., Devon, 24
Read, John Lieut. F., Carmarthen, 132
Read, John Ens. F., Devon, 115
Read, Leonard Ens. F., York, 111. I.O. does not give Read's arm of service, but the rank of ensign indicates foot.
Read, Robert Capt. Dr., L. & W., 80
Read, Roger Cor. H., Durham, 148
Read, Thomas Capt. F., L. & W., 52
Reardan, Aeneas Lieut. F., L. & W., 20
Rearsby, Francis Capt. H., stray, 160. Mentioned by a stray quartermaster from York. Probably the Captain Francis Reesby of Ames Pollard's regiment, who also claims from York.
Reasby, Leonard Cor. H., York, 36
Reddish/Reddich, William Quart. H., York, 125
Redhead, Arthur Col. H., 117
Redhead, Henry Capt. H., 117
Redman, Sir John Col. F. & Dr. (d. 1645), 117. After Redman's death, his regiment was taken over by his lieutenant colonel, Thomas Wheatly.
Redman, Phillip/Philip Lieut. F., Monmouth, 151
Redman, Thomas Capt. F., York, 88
Reed, John Quart. H., York, 107
Reed, Lancelot Ens. F., Northumberland, 39
Reed, Robert Quart. H., York, 38
Reed, Thomas Lieut. H., Northumberland, 84
Reed, Thomas Quart. H., York, 26
Reed, William ___ F., 39
Rees, David Ens. F., Carmarthen, 33
Rees, John Lieut. F., Hereford, 81
Reesby/Reasby, Francis Capt. H., York, 114
Reeve/Reeves, Francis Quart. H., Warwick, 121
Reeveley – *see also* Ryvely

Reeveley/Reevely, Rowland Cor. Dr., Northumberland, 149
Reeves, John Cor. H., Somerset, 79
Reeves, William Capt. F., 13
Reevly/Reevely, William Maj. H., 84
Reghamorter, John Capt. H., L. & W., 101
Remphry, Warne Lieut. F., Cornwall, 139
Renekers, Roger Capt. H., 102
Reniger, Richard Ens. F., Lincoln, 130
Reniger, Samuel Capt. F., Southampton, 52
Renthall, Robert Quart. H., York, 90
Rentham, John Capt. Dr., L. & W., 81
Reresby, Thomas Capt. Lieut. H., Nottingham, 40
Reskilly, Anthony Capt. Lieut. F., Cornwall, 69
Revel/Revell, Robert Lieut. F., Pembroke, 154
Revell/Revell, Edw. Capt. H., Salop, 92
Rey, Arthur Capt. H., L. & W., 74
Reymes, Bullen Col. F. (d. 1672), 118
Reynell, Nicholas Capt. H., Devon, 81
Reynell, William Capt. F., Devon, 62
Reynolds, Peter Ens. F., Somerset, 23
Reynolds, Samuel Capt. F., Salop, 152
Reynolds, Thomas Lieut. F., Cambridge, stray, 164. Listed as a stray, but claims under Lieutenant Colonel William Blakeston.
Rice, Morgan Ens. F., Carmarthen, 132
Rich, Thomas Capt. H., 77
Richards, Sir Edw. Capt. F., Southampton, 112
Richards, John Ens. F., Cornwall, 115
Richards, John Quart. H., Carmarthen, 54
Richards, Pierce Ens. F., Cornwall, 139
Richards, Richard Capt. F., Devon, 14
Richards, Robert Cor. H., Cornwall, 19
Richardson, ___ Capt. F., 77
Richardson, Bryan Lieut. H., Durham, 119
Richardson, Henry Ens. F., Durham, 18
Richardson, James Capt. H., Northumberland, 87
Richardson, John Capt. H., 119
Richardson, John Capt. F., L. & W., William Ashburnham, 15
Richardson, John Capt. F., Philip Champernon, 37
Richardson, John Capt. F., Durham, John Hilton, 80
Richardson, John Cor. H., Westmorland, 97
Richardson, John Ens. F., York, 56
Richardson, John Quart. H., Durham, Anthony Eyre, 57
Richardson, John Quart. H., Lord Langdale, York, 90
Richardson, Richard Lieut. F., Durham, 89
Richardson, Thomas Lieut. H., L. & W., 75

Richardson, Thomas Cor. Dr., York, 99
Richardson, Thomas Ens. F., Northumberland, 134
Richardson, Thomas Quart. H., Northumberland, 73
Richardson, William Capt. H., L. & W., 68
Richardson, William Lieut. H., Northumberland, 73
Riches, John Cor. H., L. & W., 31
Richmond, Peter Cor. H., Monmouth, 84
Richmond, William Quart. H., 142
Rickaby, George Ens. F., Newcastle, 100
Rickaby, James Lieut. H., Durham, 61
Rickitt/Ricket, George Lieut. H., Lincoln, 20
Riddell, Sir Thomas Col. H., F. & Dr. (d. 1652), 118. Governor of Tynemouth Castle; surrendered it 27th October 1644, a week after the surrender of Newcastle. Thereafter listed as a prisoner (*Perfect Occurrences*, E.258[35]), although in fact he escaped to the continent in a fishing boat (ODNB). Not to be confused with his father, also Sir Thomas Riddell, who had been a mayor and MP of Newcastle and was also captured when the city surrendered.
Riddling/Ridding, John Providor General, Stafford, 169
Ridly/Ridley, Thomas Quart. Dr., Somerset, 74
Ridpeth, John Maj. H., Col. James Hamilton, 74
Ridpith, John Capt. H., Earl of Crawford, 45. Reid states this is the man above.
Rigby, Thomas Capt. F., 38
Rimbron, Herbert Capt. F., Glamorgan, 152
Rimmington, James Quart. F., York, 154
Ripley, John Ens. F., Northumberland, 109
Risbrooke, Rivers Chirurgion, L. & W., 172
Rishton, Ralph Cor. H., Southampton, 104
Rishton, Richard Ens. F., Sussex, 127
Rivers [John Savage] 2nd Earl, Col. H. (d. 1654), 118
Rivers, Marcellus Capt. H., L. & W. 146
Rixon, John Lieut. F., Worcester, 53
Rixon, John Lieut. F., Kent, stray, 164
Roade, John Lieut. H., Derby, 18
Roan/Roane, Humphry, Cor. H., Worcester, 128. Served in 1651.
Roane/Roane, John Capt. Lieut. H., L. & W., 62
Robbins/Robins, Herbert Lieut. F., Carnarvon, stray, 164
Robbins/Robins, Thomas Capt. F., Gloucester, 37
Robbins/Robins, Thomas Capt. F., L. & W., 37. Listed adjacent to the man above; possibly the same individual.
Roberts, ___ Maj. H., Fitzwilliam Coningsby, 42
Roberts, ___ Maj. H., Roger Whittly, 147
Roberts, Henry Ens. F., Cornwall, 71
Roberts, Hugh Lieut. F., Somerset, 132
Roberts, Hugh Ens. F., Glamorgan, 113
Roberts, James Scoutmaster, Radnor, 172

Roberts, John Capt. F., Somerset, 155
Roberts, John Lieut. F., Cornwall, 13
Roberts, John Lieut. F., Monmouth, 116
Roberts, John Lieut. F., Monmouth, 116. Same regiment as man above. Possibly the same man.
Roberts, John Lieut. F., Salop, 111
Roberts, John Ens. F., Anglesey, 111
Roberts, John Sea Capt., *Phoenix*, Lord Hopton, Somerset, 167
Roberts, Leonard Lieut. F., Dorset, stray, 164
Roberts, Lewis Ens. F., Montgomery, 86
Roberts, Peter Lieut. F., Denbigh, 155
Roberts, Thomas Capt. H., Lord Hopton, 81
Roberts, Thomas Capt. H., L. & W., Prince Maurice, 101
Roberts, Thomas Quart. H., L. & W., 150
Roberts, Wolston Cor. H., Leicester, 96
Robins, Robert Capt. Lieut. F., Cornwall, 139
Robins, William Cor. H., Cornwall, 19
Robinson, ___ Lieut. Col. F., 15
Robinson, ___ Capt. H., 52
Robinson, ___ Capt. F., 146. Mentioned by an officer in Henry Washington's dragoons.
Robinson, ___ Capt. F., 96. Possibly the Captain George Robinson mentioned in the same regiment, although that captain was a horse officer.
Robinson, Daniel Lieut. Col. F., Stafford, 10, 28
Robinson, Daniel Ens. F., Leicester, 96
Robinson, Edw. Quart. H., Salop, 44
Robinson, Francis Capt. F., Cornwall, 69
Robinson, Francis Capt. F., L. & W., 143
Robinson, George Capt. H., Nottingham, 95
Robinson, Henry Lieut. F., Bedford, 108
Robinson, James Lieut. F., L. & W., 94
Robinson, John Col. F. (d. 1681), 118
Robinson, John Lieut. F., York, 49
Robinson, John Ens. F., Durham, 135
Robinson, Matthew Lieut. F., Westmorland, 107
Robinson, Michael Capt. F., L. & W., 84
Robinson, Michael Capt. F., Cumberland, 107
Robinson, Nicholas Capt. F., Devon, 24
Robinson, Richard Lieut. H., York, stray, 158
Robinson, Richard Lieut. F., L. & W., 122
Robinson, Stephen Quart. H., L. & W., 73
Robinson, Thomas Quart. F., York, 86
Robinson, William Lieut. F., Newcastle, 100
Robinson, Sir William Col. F. (d. 1658), 118
Roche, Adam Maj. F., Somerset, 11, 114
Roche, Adam Capt. H., L. & W., 134

Roche, James Capt. F., L. & W., 156
Roche, Pollidore Master of the Ordnance, Devon, 170
Rock, James Cor. H., Montgomery, 110
Rockly, Toby Cor. H., L. & W., 22
Rodd, Humphry Lieut. F., Hereford, 126
Roddam, ___ Lieut. Col. F., 77
Roddam, Edmund Lieut. Dr., Northumberland, 73
Rode, Thomas Capt. H., L. & W., 130
Rodes, Clifton Cor. H., Derby, 63
Rodney, Sir Edward Col. F. (d. 1657), 118
Rodney, George Capt. H., 103
Rodney, William Capt. F., Somerset, 118
Roe – *see also* Row, Rowe
Roe, Clinton Quart. H., York, 101
Roe, Francis Lieut. Col. F., L. & W., 10. 71
Roe, John Capt. H., York, 136
Roe/Rowe, John Lieut. F., L. & W., 110
Rogers, ___ Capt. F., 91
Rogers, Edmund Capt. F., 78
Rogers, Elkanah Cor. H., Somerset, 131
Rogers, Francis ___ H., 118
Rogers, George Maj. F., 57
Rogers, John Capt. F., Hereford, 126
Rogers, John Lieut. F., Somerset, 83
Rogers, Thomas Capt. F., 83
Rogers, Thomas Quart. H., Northampton, 98
Rogers, William Lieut. F., Dorset, 51
Rogerson, Edw. Quart. H., Lancaster, 137
Rolleston, William Lieut. Col. H., 56, 118. Mentioned by a quartermaster in Sir Ralph Eure's horse, and directly by a captain-lieutenant.
Rooksby, ___ Capt. H., Lord Loughborough, 96
Rooksby, ___ Capt. ___, ___ Parry, 111. I.O. does not give Rooksby's arm of service, but the fact than an ensign claims under him indicates foot.
Rooksby, ___ Capt. H., Ralph Snead, 130
Rooksby, John Cor. H., York, 47
Roper, Christopher ___ F., 119. Possibly the Christopher Roper, brother of Lord Baltinglass, who was killed at Marston Moor (Young, p.245).
Roscruge/Roskruge, Henry Ens. F., Cornwall, 63
Rose, Gerard Ens. F., Westmorland, 22
Rose, John Lieut. F., L. & W., 114
Rose, Richard Lieut. Dr., L. & W., 145
Rose, Thomas Cor. H., Durham, 62
Rose, William Chirurgion, Sussex, 173
Rosecarrock, ___ Lieut. Col. F., 20
Rosecarrock, ___ Capt. F., 97

Rosecarrock, Edward Maj. H., 72, 75, 119. Mentioned by officers under Sir Richard Greenvile and Edward Hammond; also directly by a captain.
Rosecarrock, Humphry Lieut. H., L. & W., 72
Ross, William Lieut. Col. F., Hereford, 10, 64
Rossant, Francis Cor. H., Pembroke, 19
Rosse, ___ Capt. H., 113
Rossiter, John Maj. F., L. & W., 11, 20
Rossiter, William Lieut. F., L. & W., 20
Rosthorne, ___ ___ F., 119. I.O. does not gives Rosthorne's arm of service, but as two ensigns claim under him, he must have been a foot officer.
Rothes [John Leslie] 7th Earl, Col. H. (d. 1681), 119. Taken at Worcester in 1651.
Rottenbury, John Lieut. F., Somerset, 13
Rountree, Thomas Lieut. F., Durham, Sir William Carleton, 33
Rountree, Thomas Lieut. F., Durham, Sir Robert Clavering, 39. Almost certainly the same man as above. Rountree and his captain, John Carre, appear together in both Carleton's regiment and that of Sir Robert Clavering.
Rous, Walter Capt. F., Devon, 139
Routledge, John Capt. H., Westmorland, 48
Row, Rowe – *see also* Roe
Row/Rowe, Henry Ens. F., Cornwall, 71
Rowcliffe, Roger Capt. F., Devon, 14
Rowden, Edmund Quart. H., Huntingdon, 37
Rowe, Francis Ens. F., Devon, 139
Rowe, Nicholas Ens. F., Cornwall, 140
Rowel/Rowell, Robert Lieut. H., York, 47
Rowes, ___ Capt. H., 113
Rowland, John, Chaplain, L. & W., 173
Rowles, Giles Lieut. H., Worcester, 124
Rowlett, Isaac Capt. F., 119
Rowlinson/Rawlingson, Richard Cor. Dr., Somerset, stray, 166
Rowly, George Capt. H., 109
Rowly, Thomas Quart. H., Lincoln, stray, 160
Roydon, Sir Marmaduke Col. H. & F. (d. 1646), 119. Usually 'Rawdon'.
Royston, Ralph Lieut. F., Nottingham, 67
Royston, Ralph Cor. H., Derby, 87
Royston, Thomas Capt. F., Nottingham, 60
Ruckly, Richard Cor. H., Gloucester, 154
Rudd, Thomas Ens. F., York, 69
Rudd, Thomas Ens. F., Cumberland, stray, 165
Rudde, Thomas Capt. H., 55
Ruddell, Christopher Cor. H., L. & W., 106
Ruddings, William Capt. H., Essex, 95
Ruddock, Christopher Provost Marshall, York, 171
Rudds, ___ Capt. F., 113
Rudsby, Philip Cor. H., Southampton, 44

Rudston, John Lieut. F., L. & W., 153
Rudyer, ___ Capt. F., 119
Rudyer, John Capt. Lieut. H., Stafford, 127
Rugely, ___ Capt. H., 18
Rules, Robert Ens. F., Essex, 17
Rumball, William Lieut. Col. H., Sir Horatio Cary, 36
Rumball, William Capt. H., Sir Richard Crane, 44
Rumny, Thomas Ens. F., Cumberland, Sir William Carleton, 33
Rumny, Thomas Ens. F., L. & W., Thomas Leveson, 93
Rumsey, ___ Capt. F., 149
Rupert, Prince (d. 1682), 119. Besides a great many horse and foot officers, also mentioned by two naval officers.
Rush, James Lieut. H., Somerset, 113
Russel, ___ Lieut. Col. H., 64
Russel/Russell, Thomas Quart. H., L. & W., 48
Russell, ___ Capt. H., 64
Russell, Francis Lieut. H., Worcester, 42
Russell, George Lieut. F., Middlesex, 97
Russell, John Lieut. Col. F., 120
Russell, Robert Lieut. F., Hereford, 126
Russell, Sir William Col. H. & F. (d. 1669), 120. Of Strensham, Worcs. Governor of Worcester.
Russell, William Ens. F., Salop, 126
Rustat, Robert Maj. F., L. & W., 11, 152
Ruthen, [Patrick] Lord General, Col. H. & F., (d. 1651), 121. Properly, 'Ruthven'.
Rutherford, John, Commissary, L. & W., 169
Rutherford, Ralph Lieut. H., Northumberland, 46
Rutherford, Thomas Lieut. F., Northumberland, 27
Rutter, John Capt. F., 109
Rutter, Reynold Capt. F., Denbigh, 123
Rutter, Robert Ens. F., Newcastle, 100
Rutter, Thomas Quart. H., Wilts, 134
Rychaut, ___ Maj. F., 63
Rychaut, Andrew Capt. H., Kent, 102
Rychaut, James Capt. H., L. & W., Earl of Crawford, 44
Rychaut, James Capt. H., Col. James Hamilton, 74
Rycroft, Thomas Ens. F., L. & W., 93
Ryder, Roger Ens. F., L. & W., 37
Rydley/Ridley, Musgrave Lieut. H., Northumberland, 72
Ryly, Edmund Lieut. F., L. & W., 88
Rymer/Rimer, Simon Lieut. H., York, 61
Rysleye, ___ Lieut. Col. H., 28
Rythe/Ryth, James Lieut. F., L. & W., 67
Ryvely – *see also* Reeveley
Ryvely/Rively, Edw. Quart. H., L. & W., 116

Ryves, Cosme Quart. H., Southampton, 103
Sadler, Henry Lieut. H., Wilts, stray, 158
Sadler, William Quart. H., Durham, 136
Sadlington, [Dimod] Maj. F., 133. His first name is known from *Mercurius Civicus*, which lists him as a prisoner at Selby in 1644 (TT E.43[10]).
St. Albans, [Henry Jermyn] 1ˢᵗ Earl of, Col. H. & F. (d. 1684), 121. Horse regiment usually known as the Queen's Regiment.
St. Aubyn, Thomas Col. F., 122
St. Clare, William Lieut. Col. F. & Adj. Gen., L. & W., 10, 121
St. George, ___ Lieut. H., L. & W., 64
St. George, William Col. F. (k. May 1645; storming of Leicester), 122
St. Leger, ___ Maj. H., 14
St. Leger, Maj. ___ F., 116. Reid names him as John St. Leger of Lenham, Kent.
St. Leger, Sir Anthony Col. H., Kent, 9, 32, 74, 81, 122. Mentioned by a quartermaster under Lord Capel and a cornet under James Hamilton, and directly by a lieutenant. Claims in his own right as a colonel of horse under Lord Hopton.
St. Leger, Sir William Col. F. (k. 1644; Newbury), 122
St. Michael, ___ Capt. F., 122
St. Paul, ___ Col. H., 122. Usually 'St. Pol'. Reid notes that the regiment was a mixture of Irish and Lorrainer mercenaries, and that it fought at Marston Moor; therefore possibly St. Paul is the 'Monsieur St. Paul' listed k. there by Young (p.247).
Sale, John Quart. F., Derby, 31
Salisbury, John Capt. H., Denbigh, 101
Salisbury, Thomas Capt. H., Flint, 104
Salisbury, Sir Thomas Col. F. (d. 1643), 123. The circumstances of Salisbury's death are uncertain, but he died mid-1643 and the regiment was taken over by Sir Charles Lloyd.
Salisbury, William Col. F. (d. 1659/1660), 123
Salkield, Edw. Capt. F., L. & W., 132
Salkield, George Lieut. Col. F., L. & W., 10, 88
Salkield/Salkeild, Henry Lieut. H., Northumberland, 73
Salkield/Salkeild, John Lieut. Col. H., 73
Salkield, John Quart. H., Northumberland, 79
Salmon, John Lieut. F., Worcester, 124
Salter, George Capt. F., Somerset, 82
Salter, John Capt. H., L. & W., 129
Salter, Thomas Ens. F., Devon, 24
Saltmarsh, ___ Capt. H., 112
Saltmarsh, Philip Quart. H., York, 70
Salvin, [Francis] Maj. H. & F. (k. 1644; Marston Moor), 136. Mentioned by two officers, one as a major of horse and the other as a major of foot. Served under Sir Richard Tempest, who appears to have had a dragoon unit: possibly Salvin was a dragoon officer, which would explain his being

mentioned under both arms. Young gives his first name as Francis (p.245).
Salvin, John Capt. H., Durham, 112
Salvin, John Quart. H., Durham, 108
Salvin, Thorp Quart. H., York, 90
Salway, Thomas Maj. F., L. & W., 11, 51
Salway, Thomas Capt. Dr., 17
Sampson, Jeffery Lieut. H., L. & W., 135
Sampson, John Capt. H., L. & W., 34
Samwayes, Andrew Lieut. H., Dorset, 133
Sanders, Bernard Ens. F., Devon, 145
Sanders, Christopher Quart. H., L. & W., 156
Sanders, John Lieut. F., Cornwall, 83
Sanders, William Capt. F., Carmarthen, 65
Sanderson, John Cor. H., Cumberland, 47
Sanderson, Thomas Quart. H., Derby, 59
Sandford, Arthur Cor. Dr., Salop, 43
Sandford, Edmund Lieut. H., Westmorland, 13
Sandford, Robert Capt. F., Sir Francis Fane, 57
Sandford, Robert Capt. Dr., Sir Vincent Corbett, 43
Sandford, Sir Thomas Col. F. (d. 1659), 123
Sandford, Thomas Capt. H., 107
Sandford, Walter Ens. F., Stafford, 93
Sandford, William Capt. H., 155
Sands/Sandys, Richard Ens. F., Cornwall, 15
Sandys, ___ Capt. F., 124
Sandys, Dudly Lieut. Col. H., 10. Requests inclusion, but no officers claim so his regiment is unknown.
Sandys, Edwin Capt. H., L. & W., 41
Sandys, Henry [Col.] H. (k. 1644; Alresford), 123
Sandys, Sir Martyn Col. F., 123
Sandys, Martin Capt. H., Carmarthen, 123
Sandys, Robert ___ H., 123
Sandys, Samuel Col. H. & F., 123
Sandys, Sir Thomas Col. H., 124
Sargison, George Capt. Lieut. H., Westmorland, 73
Sarraway, ___ Capt. F., 61
Sartan, Allen Lieut. F., 113
Satterthwaite, Richard Ens. F., Northumberland, 39
Saul, ___ Capt. F., stray, 165
Saul, Francis Capt. F., Cornwall, 140
Saul, John Col. H. & F., 125. I.O. does not give Saul's rank, but as both horse and foot officers claim under him, presumably he was a colonel of both.
Saul, Richard Cor. H., Cornwall, 19
Saul, Thomas Capt. H., 79
Saul, Lambert Capt. F., 45

Savage, ___ Capt. H., Samuel Sandys, 124
Savage, Henry Capt. H., Lord Rivers, 118
Savage, John Lieut. F., Worcester, 92
Savill, John Capt. H., York, stray, 157
Savile, Thomas Capt. H., stray, 160
Savile, Sir William Col. H., F. & Dr. (d. January 1644 at York; unspecified illness), 124. Governor of York.
Sawkins, Richard Ens. F., Essex, 22
Sawyer, ___ Lieut. Col. H., 37
Sawyer, ___ Capt. H., 37
Sawyer, Stephen Ens. F., Kent, stray, 165
Saxby, John Quart. H., Monmouth, 153
Saye, John Capt. H., 30
Sayer, George Lieut. H., L. & W., 41
Sayer, John Lieut. Col. H., 61
Sayer, John Capt. H., 39
Sayer, Laurence Capt. H., 56, 160. Mentioned by three officers under Sir William Eure, and by a stray quartermaster.
Sayer, Robert Quart. H., Southampton, 119
Sayer, Thomas Cor. H., 56
Sayers, Christopher Col. H. & F., 125. I.O. does not give Sayers' rank, but as both horse and foot officers claim under him, presumably he was a colonel of both.
Sayes, Edw. Capt. F., Glamorgan, 87
Sayes, Richard Ens. F., Hereford, 83
Scafe, Peter Quart. H., York, 22
Scarborow, Robert Quart. H., Leicester, 74
Scargill, Robert Lieut. H., L. & W., 123
Scarlet, Edw. Engineer, L. & W., 170
Scarlett/Scarlet, Silvanus Cor. H., Montgomery, 28
Scawen, John Capt. F., Cornwall, 54
Scawen, Thomas Capt. F., Cornwall, 54
Scawen, William Lieut. Col. F., stray, 164
Sclater, William Capt. H., Warwick, 125
Sclater, William Quart. H., York, 90
Scorer, Hugh Quart. H., Derby, 63
Scot, ___ Capt. F., 16
Scot, Henry Cor. H., Huntingdon, 26
Scot, Thomas Quart. H., L. & W., 30
Scot, Sir W__ Lieut. Col. H., 119. Served in 1651.
Scott, ___ Lieut. Col. H. (k. 1644; Cheriton), 100
Scott/Scot, Andrew Cor. Dr., Middlesex, 45
Scott, John Maj. H., 69
Scott/Scot, John Capt. F., Northumberland, 39
Scott/Scot, John Cor. H., L. & W., 69
Scott, Leonard Maj. H., 128

Index

Scott/Scot, Richard Ens. F., Salop, 110
Scott, Thomas Capt. F., 24
Scott/Scot, Walter Capt. H., L. & W., 134
Screven/Scriven, William Ens. F., Salop, 126
Scriven, Andrew Lieut. H., Derby, 75
Scroop, ___ Maj. H., 112
Scroop, Sir Adrian Lieut. Col. H. (d. 1667), 126. Not to be confused with his distant relative Adrian Scrope, the Regicide.
Scroop/Scroope, Adrian Cor. H., Middlesex, 126. Ditto above: not the regicide.
Scroop, Thomas Capt. F., York, 93
Scroope, John Col. H. & F., 126. I.O. does not give Scroope's rank, but as both horse and foot officers claim under him, presumably he was a colonel of both.
Scruggs, ___ Maj. H., 128
Scudamore, Sir Barnaby Col. H. & F. (d. 1651/1652), 126
Scudamore, George Ens. F., Dorset, 46
Scudamore, Henry Ens. F., York, 118
Scudamore, James Capt. F., Monmouth, 153
Scudamore, Rowland Capt. H., Hereford, 87
Scudamore, Thomas Capt. F., York, 118
Scudamore, Vincent Cor. H., L. & W., 18
Seabish, Charles Frederick Capt. Dr., 45
Seaborn, Benedict Cor. H., Hereford, stray, 159
Seaborn/Seaborne, Richard Lieut. F., L. & W., 154
Seaborne, Edw. Lieut. F., Hereford, 94
Seagar/Seager, William Cor. H., Devon, 72
Seager, Hugh Cor. H., Devon, 72
Seahouse/Senhouse, Joseph Lieut. Dr., Cumberland, 84
Searell, Thomas Lieut. F., Devon, stray, 164
Searles, William Quart. H., Lincoln, 25
Seaton, Ralph Quart. H., York, 142
Seavyer/Seavier, Thomas Lieut. F., Somerset, 83
Sedgewick, Lancelot Quart. H., Durham, 121
Sedgwick/Sedgewick, John Cor. H., Durham, 97
Segor/Seager, Thomas Capt. F., Middlesex, 113
Seile, Thomas Chirurgion, L. & W., 173
Selby, Alexander Cor. H., Northumberland, 73
Selby, Ralph Capt. F., Northumberland, 19, 109. Mentioned by a Durham ensign under Sir Arthur Basset; claims in his own right under the Marquess of Newcastle.
Selby, Thomas Capt. H., Durham, 47
Sell, Daniel Regt. Quart. F., Kent, 102. I.O. does not give an arm of service for Sell or the ensign listed with him, but the rank of ensign indicates foot.
Sellwyn, Sir Nicholas Col. F., 127. A foot regiment raised from within Oxford as a garrison unit, mid to late 1643. Sellwyn was one of the King's gentlemen pensioners. The regiment was taken over by Colonel William Legge when

he became governor of the city early in 1645.
Semple, William Lieut. H., Cumberland, 46
Senhouse, Anthony Capt. H., Cumberland, 148
Sergeant, Humphry Lieut. F., Essex, 57
Sergeant, John Lieut. H., Lincoln, 112
Sergeant, William Capt. F., Bucks, 121
Sergeant, William Quart. H., Lancaster, 121
Serry, Mark Quart. H., Somerset, 23
Settle, William Quart. H., York, 125
Sevidall, ___ Capt. Dr., 94
Sewell, George Ens. F., L. & W., 156
Sewell/Seywell, Richard Ens. F., Stafford, 109
Seymore, Sir Edward Col. F. (d. 1659), 127
Seymore, John Capt. H., Devon, 32
Seymore, Richard Lieut. F., Dorset, 132
Shadforth, George Quart. H., Durham, 26
Shafto, Ninian Capt. F., 100
Shafto/Shaftoe, Thomas Cor. H., Newcastle, 148
Shaftoe, John Capt. H., 47
Shaftoe, Robert Cor. H., Newcastle, 47
Shaftoe, William Lieut. F., Durham, 77
Shakerly, Sir Jeffery [Lieut. Col.] H., (d. 1696), stray, 159. Mentioned by a stray cornet. Richard Symonds notes that Shakerly was lieutenant colonel under Robert Werden, who took over John Marrow's Horse after Marrow's death in 1644 (Symonds, ed. Long, p.259).
Shales, William Capt. F., Cardigan, 91
Shallcrosse, John Col. H., 127
Shapcote, Phil. Capt. F., Devon, 24
Shapcote Philip Ens. F., Devon, 14
Sharp/Sharpe, John Ens. F., Stafford, 22
Sharpe, ___ Capt. Dr., 83
Sharpe, Isaac Quart. H., York, 101
Sharpe/Sharp, Thomas Ens. F., Lincoln, 112
Sharpe, William Lieut. H., Lancaster, 137
Sharper, Thomas Capt. F., 109
Sharsell, Philip Ens. F., Cornwall, 71
Shatford, William Quart. H., Cornwall, 79
Shaw, ___ Capt. H., 121
Shaw, Alexander Quart. H., York, 62
Shaw, Edmund Lieut. H., Monmouth, 153
Shaw, John Capt. H., Lancaster, 143
Shaw, William Lieut. F., York, 57
Sheafe, ___ Capt. F., York, 38
Sheales, William Capt. F., 29
Sheen, Thomas Cor. H., L. & W., 51

Sheere/Sheeres, Isaac Cor. H., Devon, 78
Sheere/Sheeres, Joseph Cor. H., Devon, 72
Sheere/Sheeres, William Ens. F., Devon, 72
Sheeres, George Capt. F., Cornwall, 14
Sheeres, George Ens. F., Durham, 135
Sheeres, William Gentleman of the Ordnance, L. & W., 170
Sheffield, George Capt. H., Rutland, 32
Sheffield, Thomas Capt. F., 32
Sheldon, Edw. Ens. F., York, 86
Sheldon, John Cor. H., Worcester, 102
Sheldon, Richard Lieut. F., Salop, stray, 164
Sheldon, Thomas Maj. H., Warwick, 94
Sheldon, Thomas Capt. F., Worcester, 120
Sheldon, William Capt. F., 92
Sheldon, William Capt. H., 102
Shelley, Henry Col. F., 127
Shelley, John Capt. F., Sussex, 127
Shelly, Thomas Ens. F., Sussex, 127
Shelly/Shelley, William Lieut. H., Surrey, 41
Shelton, Alexander Quart. H., L. & W., 142
Shenton, Richard Quart. H., Stafford, 93
Shepheard, David Ens. F., Somerset, 82
Shepheard, John Capt. F., Somerset, 82
Shepheard, Nicholas, Chaplain, Norfolk, 174
Shepheard, Peter Capt. F., 22
Shepheard, Sylvester Lieut. F., L. & W., 63
Shepheard, Thomas Quart. H., Devon, 78
Shepheard, Vincent Capt. F., Salop, 46
Shepheard, Walter Ens. F., Hereford, 126
Sheraton, William Capt. F., Durham, 43
Sherborn, Thomas Capt. H., Lancaster, 104
Sherborne/Sherborn, Alexander Lieut. H., Lincoln, 68
Sherborne/Sherborn, John Capt. F., Stafford, 60
Sherborne, Richard Maj. H., 52
Sherborne, Robert Lieut. H., York, 34
Sherborne, Robert Cor. H., Lincoln, 47
Sherborne, Thomas Capt. F., Lancaster, 145
Sherburn/Sherborne, Richard Lieut. H., Nottingham, 125
Sherle, Richard Capt. F., Gloucester, 152
Sherley, Sir Thomas [Lieut. Col.] F., 51. Knighted January 1646, Oxford.
Sherly, Scanderdine Lieut. F., Surrey, 131
Sherman, Francis Lieut. F., Worcester, 123
Sherman, John Capt. H., Suffolk, 113
Sherman, John Quart. H., Lincoln, stray, 160
Sherwood, Henry Cor. H., Oxon, stray, 159

Sherwood, Laurence Capt. H., L. & W., 153
Sherwood, Thomas Cor. H., Somerset, 142
Sherwood, William Cor. H., Somerset, 141
Shevyll, David Chirurgion, Newcastle, 173
Shield, Francis Lieut. H., Northumberland, 58
Shield, Ralph Quart. H., Northumberland, 58
Shipman, John Capt. H., L. & W., 126
Shipman, Robert Lieut. H., Lincoln, 141
Shippy, George Lieut. H., Somerset, 155
Shirly, James 'Quart. Gen. in Newark', Nottingham, stray, 166
Shobrooke/Showbrooke, John Lieut. F., Devon, 13
Short, Thomas Lieut. H., Kent, 17
Shrewsbury, [John Talbot] 10th Earl of Col. H. (d. 1654), 127. A 1651 regiment.
Shuckborough, ___ Capt. H., 72
Shuter, Thomas Chirurgion, Somerset, 173
Shuttlewood, George Capt. H., Leicester 'in Ashby', stray, 157
Sibbett, ___ ___ H., 128. I.O. does not give Sibbett's rank.
Sibsey, John Quart. H., Lincoln, 48
Sibson, Anthony Ens. F., Cumberland, 47
Sill, Wellsborne/Welsborn Cor. H., L. & W., 102
Sillyard, ___ Lieut. Col. H., 153
Sillyard, ___ Maj. H., 153
Silson, John Capt. H., Kent, 68
Silver, John Lieut. F., Southampton, 110
Simcocks/Simcockes, Thomas Capt. F., Somerset, 131
Simons/Simmons – *see also* Symonds and variants
Simmons, John Quart. H., L. & W., 109
Simmons, Thomas Maj. F., 16
Simms/Simmes, John Ens. F., Dorset, 83
Simms/Simmes, Ralph Quart. H., Southampton, 95
Simons/Simmons, Thomas Capt. H., L. & W., 134
Simons, Thomas Lieut. F., Cornwall, 15
Simons/Symonds, William Lieut. F., Somerset, 155
Simpson – *see also* Sympson
Simpson, Edmund Quart. H., Bucks, 67
Sinclare, ___ Maj. Dr., 81
Singe, Richard Capt. F., 88
Singleton, Thomas Cor. H., York, 129
Singleton, Thomas Quart. H., Lancaster, 115
Skantlebury, Thomas Ens. F., Cornwall, 139
Skeldain, John Capt. F., L. & W., 86
Skelden, Thomas 'Master Cooper to the Train', L. & W., 170
Skelton, ___ Capt. F., 91
Skelton, George Capt. H., Cumberland, 47
Skelton, Henry Cor. H., York, 69

Index

Skelton/Skelten, Robert Lieut. H., L. & W., 56
Skelton, Thomas Cor. H., Cumberland, 46
Skelton, Thomas Ens. F., Cornwall, 54
Skingsly, John Ens. F., Oxon, 27
Skinner, Anthony Maj. H., 36
Skipton, Nicholas Cor. H., York, 38
Skipwith, ___ ___ H., 128
Skipwith, ___ Lieut. Col. H., 25
Skipwith, John Lieut. H., Lincoln, 112
Skipwith, John Lieut. F., York, 133
Skipwith, William Capt. H., 29
Skirrow, Robert Maj. F., L. & W., 11, 17, 94, Mentioned by a first civil war lieutenant under George Lisle; claims in his own right under William Ayliffe in 1648.
Skottow, Robert Lieut. F., Norfolk, 24
Skrimshaw, ___ Lieut. Col., 36
Skurray, John Quart. H., York, 113
Slade, Henry Ens. F., Somerset, 118
Slaney, ___ Capt. H., 109
Slanning, Sir Nicholas Col. F. (k. 1643; Bristol), 128
Slape, Thomas Lieut. F., Somerset, 44
Slape, Tristram Capt. Pioneers, Somerset, 171
Slater, ___ Lieut. Col. H., 142
Slater, ___ Lieut. Col. F., stray, 164
Slater, ___ Lieut. Col. Dr., stray, 166. Name sometimes 'Slaughter'.
Slater, Stephen Quart. F., York, 133
Slaughter, ___ ___ F., 128. I.O. does not give a rank. Reid believes this is Colonel William Slaughter of Carmarthenshire.
Slaughter, ___ Maj. F., 116
Slee, George Lieut. F., Devon, 140
Sleepe, John Ens. F., Cornwall, 103
Sleigh, John Quart. H., Westmorland, 107
Slemming, Roger Capt. F., Cornwall, 139
Slingsby, ___ Col. H., 129. Reid believes this is Sir Charles Slingsby.
Slingsby, ___ Lieut. Col. H., 114
Slingsby, ___ Maj. H., 45
Slingsby, Sir Arthur Col. H. & Dr. (d. 1665), 128
Slingsby, Sir Charles Col. F. (k. 1644; Marston Moor), 128. Peter Young states that he was lieutenant colonel to either William Lambton or Guilford Slingsby (*Marston Moor 1644*, p.245). The latter is not possible, however, as Guilford was killed in January 1643 and the regiment taken over by his cousin Thomas Slingsby, who led the regiment at Marston Moor.
Slingsby, Sir Henry Col. F. (executed 1658), 129
Slingsby, Thomas Col. F., 129. Took over Guilford Slingsby's regiment in January 1643, after Guilford mortally wounded at Guisborough.
Slocombe, Richard Quart. H., Somerset, 151

Sluer, Edw. Ens. F., Norfolk, 65
Smallwood, John Lieut. H., L. & W., 64
Smally, John Capt. Lieut. F., Cornwall, 43
Smart, Collet Capt. H., Surrey, 29
Smart, William, Marshall, Somerset, 171
Smart, William Scoutmaster, Stafford, 172
Smith, ___ Lieut. Col. F., 92, 127. Mentioned by an ensign under Sir Nicholas Sellwyn, and a lieutenant under Col. William Legge, who took over Sellwyn's regiment early in 1645.
Smith, ___ Maj. H., 152. Served in Scotland, 1654.
Smith, ___ Capt. H., Lord Loughborough, 96
Smith, ___ Capt. H., Prince Rupert, 119
Smith, ___ Capt. H., Sir William Smith, 129
Smith, ___ Capt. H., Sir Richard Tempest, 136
Smith, ___ Capt. F., 142
Smith, Anthony Lieut. H., Lincoln, 47
Smith, Benjamin Quart. H., Sussex, 70
Smith, Charles Capt. Lieut. F., Salop, 119
Smith, Christopher Lieut. H., Warwick, 109
Smith, Christopher Lieut. F., Durham, 43
Smith, Edw. Lieut. H., Northumberland, 152. Served in Scotland, 1654.
Smith, Erasmus Capt. H., L. & W., 102
Smith, Francis Lieut. H., L. & W., 64
Smith, Francis Quart. H., York, 90
Smith, Francis Quart. H., Oxon, 109
Smith, George Cor. H., Hereford, 126
Smith, George Ens. F., Durham, 135
Smith, Hezekias/Ezekias Quart. H., L. & W., 104
Smith, Sir James Col. H., 129
Smith, James Capt. H., stray, 159
Smith, James Quart. H., York, 56
Smith, James Chirurgion, L. & W., 172
Smith, John Capt. H., stray, 158
Smith, John Capt. F., Suffolk, 150
Smith, John Col. H., 129
Smith, John Capt. F., L. & W., 49
Smith, John Capt. F., Suffolk, 151
Smith, John Capt. Pioneers, Carnarvon, 172
Smith, John Lieut. H., L. & W., 27
Smith, John Cor. H., Hereford, 42
Smith, John Cor. H., Surrey, 62
Smith, John Cor. H., York, 126
Smith, John Ens. F., Somerset, 28
Smith, John Ens. F., Northumberland, 74
Smith, John Ens. F., Westmorland, 107

Smith, John Quart. H., Worcester, 74
Smith, John Quart. H., Southampton, stray, 160
Smith, Malcomb Capt. H., L. & W., 72
Smith, Miles Capt. F., L. & W., 116
Smith, Nicholas Capt. Lieut. F., Cornwall, 50
Smith, Paul Lieut. Col. H., L. & W., 10, 150
Smith, Richard Cor. H., York, 59
Smith, Richard Cor. Dr., L. & W., 81
Smith, Robert Ens. F., Northumberland, 77
Smith, Stephen Lieut. Col. F., 58
Smith, Stephen Cor. H., York, 90
Smith, Stephen Cor. H., L. & W., 102
Smith, Sir Thomas, ___ H., 32, 121. Queen's Regiment of Horse. Mentioned by one quartermaster under Lieut. Col. Sir John Cansfield, and a second directly under 'Lord St. Albans' (Henry Jermyn, the regiment's colonel).
Smith, Thomas Lieut. Col. H., stray, 158
Smith, Thomas Capt. F., 94
Smith, Sir William Col. H., 129
Smith, William Maj. H., 70
Smith, William Capt. F., L. & W., Earl of Derby, 50
Smith, William Capt. F., York, James King (Lord Eythin), 88
Smith, William Lieut. H., L. & W., William Eure, 56
Smith, William Lieut. H., Lincoln, Duke of Gloucester, 69
Smith, William Lieut. H., Sussex, Lord Charles Goring, 70
Smith, William Lieut. H., Derby, Sir John Harpur, 75
Smith, William Lieut. H., Kent, Lord Hopton, 81
Smith, William Lieut. H., Somerset, Sir James Long, 95
Smith, William Cor. H., Wilts, 40
Smith, William Ens. F., L. & W., 21
Smith, William Quart. H., Cornwall, Sir Thomas Basset, 20
Smith, William Quart. H., Nottingham, Charles Cavendish, 36
Smith, William Quart. H., Derby, Sir John Harpur, 75
Smith, William Quart. Dr., Bucks, 146
Smith, William Provost Marshall General, L. & W., 171
Smithson, Robert Cor. H., York, 148
Smithwick, Francis Capt. F., L. & W., 82
Smyth/Smith, Henry Quart. H., York, 52
Smyth/Smith, Robert Capt. F., Cornwall, 43
Snary, William Lieut. F., Durham, 109
Snawden/Snawdon, Gowen Lieut. H., Northumberland, 148
Snead, John Cor. H., Hereford, 94
Snead, Ralph Col. H. (k. 1650; Isle of Man), 130
Snead, Robert Capt. H., 102
Snell, George Cor. H., Devon, 135
Snellgrove, ___ Capt. F., 42

Snelling, John Capt. F., Suffolk, 25
Snow, John Capt. H., Hertford, 150
Snowsdale, Henry Lieut. F., York, 117
Soames, ___ Capt. F., 65
Sober, Edmund Lieut. H., Durham, 136
Sollet, Francis Lieut. F., York, 27
Solley, ___ Lieut. Col. F., 123
Somerset, [William Seymour] 2nd Duke of, Col. H. (d. 1660), 130
Somerset, Lord Charles Col. H. & F. 130, 153. The 6th son of Henry Somerset, 1st Marquess of Worcester. Newman states that he drowned in 1647 (*The Old Service*, p.98). Mentioned also by an officer in his father's regiment.
Somerset, Henry Lieut. Col. F., 153
Somerset, Lord John Lieut. Col. F., 62, 130. The 2nd son of Henry Somerset, 1st Marquess of Worcester. Newman notes that he was lieutenant colonel to Edmund Fortescue's Foot (*The Old Service*, p.98). Mentioned by an ensign under Fortescue, and directly by a quartermaster.
Somerset, John Cor. H., Devon, 78
Somerton, Thomas Capt. Pioneers, Devon, 171
Soper, Francis Cor. H., Berks, stray, 159
Soulby, Christopher Quart. H., Northumberland, 58
Soule, John Quart. H., Worcester, stray, 160
South, Edw. Capt. F., Southampton, 23
South, Francis Quart. H., Bucks, 141
Southcot, Henry Capt. F., 14
Southcote/Southcott, Henry Capt. F. 'and Frega[t]', Essex, stray, 163. 'Fregat' was 'Frigate', meaning that Southcote also served at sea.
Southcott, Sir Popham Col. F. (d. 1643), 130. Buried at Bovey Tracey 23rd April 1643 (Crisp, p.161)
Southern/Southerne, William Quart. H., Lincoln, 48
Southgate, Edw. Lieut. F., Cumberland, 47
Sowter, Humphry Quart. H., Derby, stray, 160
Sowtrell/Soutrell, Isaac Quart. F., Somerset, 24
Sparrey/Sparry, John Lieut. F., Worcester, 120
Sparrow, George Cor. H., Lincoln, stray, 159.
Speccot, Thomas Capt. F., L. & W., 139
Speed, Walter Capt. F., Dorset, 51
Spencer, John ___ H., 130
Spencer, John Capt. H., L. & W., 17
Spencer, Thomas Quart. F., Lincoln, 57
Spicer, ___ Capt. H., 130
Spicer, Thomas, Commissary, Somerset, 169
Spink, John Lieut. H., York, 70
Spooner, William Lieut. H., Lincoln, 24
Spoore, Anthony Quart. H., Northumberland, 13
Spour, Henry Ens. F., Cornwall, 71

Index

Sprecklow, William Quart. H., L. & W., 25
Spry, John Maj. F., 15
Spry, John Lieut. F., Cornwall, 15
Spry, Richard Quart. H., Cornwall, 20
Spurgen, Thomas Lieut. H., York, 125
Spyer, Henry Quart. H., Wilts, 114
Squire, Robert Capt. F., York, 90
Squire, William Capt. H., Leicester, 95
Stacy, Henry Capt. Lieut. F., Glamorgan, 87
Stacy, Montagu Quart. H., Lincoln, 99
Stacy, Ralph Ens. F., Worcester, 42
Stacy, Reignold Ens. F., Cornwall, 50
Stafford, Edward Cor. H., York, 87
Stafford, Humphry Cor. H., Berks, 114
Staining, Nicholas Ens. F., York, 86
Stainsby, Thomas Capt. F., Southampton, 110
Stamford, Edward Lieut. Col. H., 130. I.O. does not give Stamford's rank, but Reid notes that he was lieutenant colonel of Lord Digby's Horse.
Stamford, James Capt. H., L. & W., 103
Stamp, John Capt. F., Berks, 16
Stamp, Simon Ens. F., L. & W., 65
Stanbury, John Lieut. F., Cornwall, 115
Standelo, ___ Capt. H., 134
Standen, Griffith Capt. H., L. & W., 21
Standen, Nicholas Lieut. H., Devon, 35
Standford, ___ Lieut. Col. H., 96
Standish, ___ Col. H., Earl of Derby, 50
Standish, ___ Lieut. Col. H., Earl of Carnarvon, 34. Reid states that his first name was Alexander.
Standish, Edw. Capt. H., 104
Standish, Laurence Quart. H., Lancaster, 34
Standish, Ralph Cor. H., Middlesex, 128. Served in 1651.
Standish, William Lieut. H., Lincoln, 56
Stanhop, Phillip Capt. H., 96. Reid states that this is the lieutenant colonel below.
Stanhop, George Capt. H., Lord Mansfield, 100
Stanhop, Miles Capt. H., 102
Stanhope/Stanhoppe, George Capt. H., Lord Henry Cavendish, 36. Possibly the man above, as Cavendish was Lord Mansfield's younger brother and both fought within the orbit of their father, the Marquess of Newcastle.
Stanhope, Phillip Lieut. Col. H. (k. 1645; Shelford House), 69, 130. Commanded the Duke of Gloucester's regiment (the Duke was only three or four years old). Mentioned by a lieutenant under Gloucester, and directly by three other officers. Two of these say they are foot officers.
Stanly, George Capt. H., 96
Stanly, Thomas Lieut. H., Salop, 84

Stanly, William Capt. F., Middlesex, 66
Stanton, Edw. Capt. F., Lancaster, 88
Stanton, John Cor. H., L. & W., 52
Stanton, Robert Sea Capt. 'of the *Swallow*', Kent, 167
Stanton, William Col. H. & F., 130
Staples, ___ Capt. H., stray, 159. Mentioned by a Wiltshire cornet. Possibly the man below, as James Long's regiment was Wiltshire based.
Staples, Richard Capt. H., James Long, 95
Starky/Starkey, Edw. Lieut. H., L. & W., 17
Starky/Starkey, Thomas Capt. Dr., Chester, 17
Startin, Timothy Capt. Lieut. F., Stafford, 17
Statham, Henry Quart. F., Nottingham, 104
Statham, John Lieut. H., Derby, 60
Stavely, Edw. Capt. F., Hereford, 130
Stavely, John Ens. F., Cumberland, 60
Stavely, Thomas Capt. Lieut. F., York, 99. Also mentioned by an officer of dragoons in the same regiment.
Stawell, ___ Capt. F., 131
Stawell, Sir Edward Col. H., 131
Stawell, George ___ H., 131
Stawell, Sir John Col. H., F. & Dr. (d. 1662), 130
Stawell, Humphrey Quart. H., Devon, 35
Steadman, William Lieut. F., Wilts, 114
Steele, Francis Capt. H., York, 47
Steele, Francis Quart. F., York, 103
Steele, John Ens. F., York, 40
Steele, Michael 'Physitian and Chirurgion', Westmorland, 173
Steele, Thomas Quart. H., York, 56
Steele, William Cor. Dr., York, 99
Steeple, John Quart. H., Derby, 57
Steevens/Stephens, John Capt. F., Lincoln, 98
Steevenson/Stephenson, Humphry Ens. F., Durham, 39
Steevenson, John Capt. F., 53
Steevenson, Nicholas Capt. F., Lancaster, 50
Steley, John Lieut. F., L. & W., 114
Stephens, ___ Capt. F., 127
Stephens, John Lieut. F., Cornwall, 154
Stepney, Sir John ___ F. (d. 1676), 132
Stepney/Stepny, Thomas Capt. F., Pembroke, 132
Steude, James Quart. H., York, 142
Stevens – *see also* Steevens, Stephens
Stevens, Ezekiel Ens. F., Cornwall, 37
Stevens, Matthew Capt. F., Essex, 57
Stevens, Matthew Ens. F., Monmouth, 149
Stevens, Nicholas Lieut. F., Cornwall, 37

Stevens, Robert Ens. F., Surrey, 16
Stevens, William Ens. F., Cornwall, 139
Stevenson – *see also* Steevenson, Stephenson
Stevenson, Charles Capt. F., L. & W., 98
Stevenson, John Capt. F., Cumberland, 33
Stevenson, William Capt. H., Middlesex, 56
Stevenson, William Ens. F., Oxon, 127
Stobbart, John Ens. F., Durham, 80
Stobbs/Stubbs, Thomas Quart. H., Durham, 41
Stockdale, Thomas Ens. F., York, 70
Stocker, John Col. H. & F., 132
Stocker, John Capt. H., 82
Stocko, Francis Cor. H., Northumberland, 35
Stocko, John Cor. Dr., Durham, 136
Stoke, ___ Capt. H., stray, 159
Stokeld, William Capt. F., Northumberland, 68
Stokes, John Capt. F., Kent, 75. Served in 1648.
Stone, John Capt. F., L. & W., 151
Stone/Stoner, William Capt. Dr., Wilts, 83
Stoner, William Quart. H., York, 125
Stones/Stone, Richard Quart. H., Durham, 62
Storkey/Starkey, Henry Capt. F., L. & W., 144
Storre, James Lieut. F., York, 113
Storzaker, John Lieut. Dr., York, 99
Stow, Joseph Cor. H., Lincoln, stray, 159
Stradling, Sir Edward Col. F. (d. 1644; Oxford), 132. Captured at Edgehill; regiment commanded meanwhile by his younger brother John. Exchanged May 1644, died of fever on 20th June.
Stradling, Sir Henry Col. F. (d. 1649? Cork?), 132
Stradling, John Col. H. & F. (d. 1649; imprisoned at Windsor), 132. Commanded elder brother Edward's regiment after Edward's capture at Edgehill.
Stradling, Thomas Lieut. Col. F., 10, 132. Lieutenant colonel to his elder brother John.
Strangewayes, ___ Maj. H., 133
Strangewayes, Giles Col. H., 133
Strangewayes, James Col. H. & F., 133
Stratford, Anthony Capt. H., Worcester, 123
Streat, ___ Capt. H., 94
Street, Thomas Ens. F., L. & W., 88. I.O. does not give an arm of service, but the rank of ensign indicates foot.
Strickland, ___ Capt. F., 133
Strickland, Sir Robert Col. F. (d. 1671), 133
Strickland, Sir Thomas Capt./Col. H. (d. 1694), L. & W., 22, 133. Claims as a captain of horse under Sir John Bellasis; three officers claim in his 1648 regiment. Knighted on the field at Edgehill.
Strickland, Thomas Capt. H., L. & W., 22

Striker, Nicholas Lieut. F., Wilts, 101
Stringer, Anthony Cor. H., Gloucester, 150
Stringer, Peter Quart. H., Chester, 101
Stripling, John Lieut. H., Devon, 77
Strode, George Capt. H., Dorset, 133
Strode, John Capt. F., Dorset, 62
Strode, Richard Capt. F., Somerset, 101
Strong, John Capt. H., L. & W., 52
Strother, Arthur Quart. H., Northumberland, 39
Strother, Edw. Capt. F., Northumberland, 134
Strother, William Col. F., 134
Strut, Anthony Capt. F., 37
Stuart, ___ Capt. F., 98
Stuart, Alexander Capt. Lieut. F., Durham, 20
Stuart, Lord Bernard Col. H. (k. 1645; Rowton Heath), 134. Regiment usually known as the King's Lifeguard of Horse.
Stuart, Francis Col. H. (k. 1644; Marston Moor), 134
Stuart, Lord John Lieut. Col. H. (k. 1644; Cheriton), 134. Commanded the Earl of Cleveland's horse.
Stuart, William Col. Dr., L. & W., 9, 109, 134. Claims under the Marquess of Newcastle as a colonel of dragoons; his lieutenant colonel claims under him directly.
Stubbing, William Lieut. H., Essex, stray, 158
Stubbs, Thomas Capt. F., Monmouth, 105
Stuckey, Thomas Capt. H., Devon, 32
Studdurt/Studdart, Richard Capt. F., Cumberland, 85
Stukely, Hugh Lieut. H., Middlesex, 104
Stukely John Ens. F., Devon, 14
Stukely, Sir Thomas Col. H. (d. 1663), 135
Stump, Thomas Capt. F., Norfolk, stray, 163
Sturdy, Peter Cor. H., L. & W., 36
Sturges, ___ Capt. H., 82
Sturges, Tristram Scoutmaster General, stray, 160
Sturton, Philip Capt. H., Dorset, 43
Sturton, Robert Cor. H., Oxon, 59
Sturton, Thomas Capt. F., L. & W., 72
Styles, ___ Capt. H., 135
Styles, Edw. Capt. F., 21
Styles, Thomas Capt. H., Northampton, stray, 157
Styles, William Col. H. & F., 135
Styles, William Capt. F., Nottingham, 51
Sugar, William Lieut. H., Salop, 142
Summers, John Lieut. F., Devon, 115
Summers, William Capt. Dr., Dorset, 102
Sunderland, Abraham Lieut. H., York, 68

Surdevile, George Cor. H., York, 102
Surtys, Edw. Lieut. F., Durham, 100
Surtys, William Cor. H., Northumberland, 34
Sutherland, Langdale Capt. H., 90
Suttle, William Quart. H., York, 47
Sutton, Ellis Capt. F., Denbigh, 31
Sutton, Richard Lieut. H., Lincoln, 48
Swain/Swayne, George Quart. H., Salop, 71
Swale, James Capt. H., Lincoln, 70
Swale, Thomas Ens. F., L. & W., 22
Swan/Swanne, John Capt. H., Essex, 32
Swanton, William Capt. F., 83
Swarland, Thomas Quart. H., L. & W., 111
Sweat, John Quart. H., Cambridge, 26
Sweatman, William Quart. H., Wiltshire, 82
Sweet, John Quart. H., Cornwall, 82
Sweet, Nathaniel Quart. H., Devon, 23
Swillivant, Anthony Lieut. H., York, 92
Swinburn, William Capt. Dr., stray, 166
Swinburne, ___ Capt. H., 148
Swinburne, John Cor. H., Durham, 56
Swinburne, Thomas Capt. F., Northumberland, Sir Thomas Glenham, 68
Swinburne, Thomas Capt. F., Sir John Marlay, 100
Swinburne, Thomas Cor. H., Durham, 56
Swinglehurst, ___ Capt. H., 137
Swinglehurst, ___ Capt. F., 138. Young says k. Marston Moor (p.246).
Swinhoe, Gilbert Col. F., 135
Swinhoe, James Capt./Col. F., 39, 109, 135. Took over Sir Robert Clavering's Foot after the colonel's death in 1644. Mentioned as a captain by one officer under Clavering, and one under the Marquess of Newcastle; and directly by a third, although Swinhoe's rank not given.
Swinhoe, William Lieut. F., Northumberland, 39
Sydenham, Humphry Maj. H., 155
Sydenham, William Capt. F., Somerset, 67
Syke, ___ Capt. H., 75
Syley, Robert Lieut. H., York, 21
Symonds/Symmonds – *see also* Simmons and variants
Symmonds/Symonds, Caleb Lieut. F., Kent, 41
Symonds, Edw. Cor. H., Bucks, stray, 159
Symonds, Nicholas Lieut. F., Worcester, 123
Symonds, Thomas Capt. H., Worcester, 128. Served in 1651.
Sympson – *see also* Simpson
Sympson/Simpson, Christopher Quart. H., York, 36
Sympson/Simpson, Henry Capt. Lieut. H., Northumberland, 154
Sympson/Simpson, John Capt. F., York, 112

Sympson, John Quart. F., York, 70
Sympson, Stephen Quart. H., York, stray, 160. Claims under Captain Laurence Sayer, who is mentioned by several claimants in William Eure's regiment.
Tainton, Edmund Cor. H., Hereford, 126
Talbot, George Capt. H., 31
Talbot, John Col. F., 135. Of Thorton-le-Street, Yorkshire. Not to be confused with the Colonel John Talbot in the Oxford Army, whose men were reputedly Irish yellowcoats.
Talbot, William Quart. H., Somerset, 50
Tallant, Roger Capt. F., Devon, 43
Tallowcarne, John Capt. F., 66
Tampian, William Quart. H., Northampton, 32
Tankard, Sir Richard Maj. F. (d. 1668), 86
Taprell, John Lieut. F., Cornwall, 72
Tarrant, Hercules Cor. H., Southampton, stray, 159
Tart, Christopher Lieut. F., L. & W., 15
Tasborough, Peregrine Capt. F., L. & W., 150
Tassell/Tassel, John Quart. H., Cambridge, 57
Tatham, Anthony Lieut. F., L. & W., 113
Tatham, Edmund Capt. H., York, 99
Tattershall, ___ Capt. F., 150
Tattershall, John Capt. Lieut. H., Devon, 104
Tattershall, John Cor. H., Wilts, Charles Finch, 59
Tattershall, John, Cor. H., Dorset, Thomas Monck, 104
Taunton, Robert Ens. F., Somerset, 28
Taverner, John Capt. F., 71
Tayler/Taylor, Bryan Lieut. F., Westmorland, 22
Tayler/Taylor, Christopher Lieut. F., Durham, 23
Tayler/Taylor, Edward Lieut. H., Surrey, stray, 158
Tayler, Henry Capt. H., L. & W., 84
Tayler/Taylor, Henry Ens. F., Hereford, 25
Tayler/Taylor, James Lieut. H., York, 58
Tayler/Taylor, John Capt. H., Durham, Sir Francis Anderson, 13
Tayler, John Capt. H., James Hamilton, 74
Tayler,/Taylor John Capt. H., Hertford, stray, 157
Tayler, John Capt. F., York, Henry Hillyard, 80
Tayler, John Capt. F., Sir George Lisle, 94
Tayler/Taylor, John Cor. H., York, 124
Tayler/Taylor, John Quart. H., Durham, 152
Tayler/Taylor, Michael Quart. H., York, 55
Tayler/Taylor, Ralph Lieut. H., Durham, 13
Tayler/Taylor, Ralph Lieut. F., Northumberland, 149
Tayler, Richard Ens. F., York, 109
Tayler/Taylor, Robert Cor. H., L. & W., 44
Tayler/Taylor, Robert Cor. H., York, 97

Tayler/Taylor, Robert Quart. H., Chester, 147
Tayler/Taylor, William Capt. H., Kent, 68
Tayler/Taylor, William Capt. Lieut. H., York, 22
Tayler/Taylor, William Lieut. F., Hereford, 45
Tayler/Taylor, William Cor. H., Stafford, 74
Taylor, ___ Col. F., 135. Reid believes this is John Taylor, and the regiment a Bristol trained band unit.
Taylor, ___ Capt. F., 135
Taylor, Anthony Capt. F., Kent, 147
Taylor, Francis Lieut. Dr., L. & W., stray, 166
Taylor, John Capt. Lieut. F., York, 118
Taylor, John Quart. H., L. & W., 51
Taylor, Robert Ens. F., Durham, 69
Taylor, Thomas Capt. H., Suffolk, 56
Taylor, Thomas Capt. F., 131
Teadman, Giles Ens. F., L. & W., 119
Teasdale, Anthony Ens. F., York, 144
Teasdel/Teasdale, Robert Quart. H., Durham, 13
Teige, Cornelius Lieut. F., L. & W., 69
Tempest, ___ Capt. H., Sir Richard Tempest, 136
Tempest, ___ Capt. Dr., Sir Richard Tempest, 135. Possibly the man above.
Tempest, Charles Cor. H., Durham, 148
Tempest, John Col. F. (d. 1697), 135
Tempest, Sir Richard Col. H., F. & Dr. (d. 1662), 135
Tempest, Richard Lieut. H., York, 137
Tempest, Richard Quart. H., York, 143
Temple, Thomas ___ H., 136
Tenham, John Quart. H., Wilts, 95
Terrick, Samuel Capt. H., L. & W., stray, 157
Terwhyt, ___ Lieut. Col. F., 106
Tettershall, George Capt. F., 16
Thacham, Robert Quart. H., Wilts, 119
Theaker, William Lieut. F., L. & W., 27
Theckston/Theckson, Thomas Quart. H., Worcester, 128. Served in 1651.
Thelwell, Anthony Col. F. (k. 1644; Newbury II). Sometimes 'Thelwall'.
Theobald/Theobalds, Thomas Lieut. F., Suffolk, 114
Theobalds, William Capt. F., Durham, 100
Thick, John Quart. H., Somerset, 155
Thimbleby, George Capt. Lieut. H., York, 138
Thody, Henry Capt. Lieut. H., Hertford, 125
Thomas, ___ Col. H., 136
Thomas, ___ Capt. H., 148
Thomas, Edmund of the Captain's Magazine, Cornwall, 171
Thomas, Gabriel Capt. F., Glamorgan, 87
Thomas, Gabriel Provost Marshall, Surrey, 171

Thomas, George 'Quart. to the Train', Glamorgan, 170
Thomas, Gilbert Capt. F., 69
Thomas, Henry Cor. H., Glamorgan, 70
Thomas, Humphry Capt. H., Surrey, 118
Thomas, John Capt. F., Glamorgan, Sir Charles Kemys, 87
Thomas, John Capt. F., Glamorgan, Thomas Pert, 113
Thomas, John Lieut. F., Hertford, 16
Thomas, John Ens. F., Cornwall, 140
Thomas, John Quart. H., Montgomery, 17
Thomas, John, Chaplain, Cornwall, 174
Thomas, Peter Capt. F., Cornwall, 72
Thomas, Philip/Phillip Lieut. F., Carmarthen, 66
Thomas, Rice Lieut. Col. F. (k. 1645; Naseby), 136
Thomas, Robert Capt. H., 38
Thomas, Thomas Lieut. F., Glamorgan, 132
Thomas, William Cor. H., Carmarthen, 19
Thompson, ___ Capt. H., 90
Thompson, ___ Capt. F., 106
Thompson, John Chirurgion, Essex, 173
Thompson, Joseph Capt. F., Nottingham, 51
Thompson, Luke Ens. F., York, 49
Thompson, Michael Capt. H., York, 21
Thompson, Patrick Cor. H., L. & W., 87
Thompson, Robert Cor. Dr., York, 52
Thompson, Thomas Lieut. F., Northumberland, 73
Thomson/Thompson, James Lieut. F., L. & W., 13
Thomson/Thompson, Peter Quart. H., York, 143
Thomson/Thompson, Robert Ens. F., Northumberland, 109
Thomson/Thompson, William Lieut. H., Monmouth, 153
Thornborough, John Cor. H., Lancaster, Sir Francis Middleton, 103
Thornborow/Thornborough, John Cor. H., L. & W., stray, 159
Thornborow/Thornborough, Benjamin Cor. H., L. & W., 113
Thornborrow/Thornborough, Henry Ens. F., Leicester, 91
Thorne, Martin Cor. H., Cornwall, 82
Thornes, Francis Ens. F., Salop, stray, 165
Thornhill, Richard Col. H., 137
Thornly, Richard, Cor. H., L. & W., 22
Thornton, ___ Lieut. Col. H., Sir William Blakeston, 26
Thornton, John Lieut. Col. H., Lord Widrington, 148
Thornton, Hamm Lieut. H., Nottingham, 48
Thornton, Jacob Ens. F., Dorset, 77
Thornton, James Capt. H., 101
Thornton, Samuel Ens. F., Dorset, 77
Thornton, William Capt. F., York, 68
Thornton, William Lieut. H., York, 22

Thornton, William Lieut. H., Dorset, 77
Thorold, John Ens. F., L. & W., 61
Thorold, Robert Capt. H., L. & W., 69
Thorp/Thorpe, Henry Capt. H., Oxon, stray, 157
Thorpe, ___ Capt. H., 142
Thorpe, George Capt. H., Wilts, 139
Thorpe, John Capt. H., York, 85
Thorpe, Lancelot Capt. F., L. & W., 110
Thorpe, Robert Lieut. H., Durham, 73
Thorpe, Roger Chirurgion, Wilts, 173
Thorpe, Thomas Lieut. H., Lincoln, 48. An addition from the errata.
Threlkeild/Threlkieid, John Lieut. H., Westmorland, 133. Served in 1648.
Throckmorton, Sir Baynham, ___ H. (d. 1680), 137. Commanded Lord Capel's horse in 1643. Reid lists him as a lieutenant colonel.
Throckmorton, Sir Nicholas ___ H., 126
Throckmorton, Sir William Col. F., 137
Throwly, John, Commissary General, L. & W., 169
Thurloe, Simon Capt. F., L. & W., 154
Thurnham, Thomas Cor. H., L. & W., 52
Thursby, ___ Capt. H., 128
Thursby, John Lieut. H., Durham, 128
Thurscrosse, Toby Capt. F., stray, 165
Thurston, Hamon/Hammand Capt. F., Norfolk, 22
Thurston, John Lieut. H., L. & W., 134
Thurston, Ralph Cor. H., Kent, 123
Thwaytes/Thwayts, Thomas Quart. H., Suffolk, 119
Thwing, ___ Capt. H., 142
Thwing, Alphonso Capt. F., 22. Usually 'Thwenge'.
Tichborne, John Capt. F., 94
Tickell/Ticklell, Thomas Capt. F., Cumberland, 47
Tickle, Robert Quart. H., Lancaster, 31
Tidmarsh, John Lieut. H., Gloucester, 133
Tilden, John Capt. F., Monmouth, 120
Tildesly, Sir Thomas Col. H. & F. (k. 1651; Wigan Lane), 137
Tildsly, Edw. Capt. H., Lancaster, 27
Tilford, William Capt. F., Essex, 57
Till, James Col. F., 138. A 1648 regiment.
Tillyard/Tyllier, William Lieut. H., Oxon, stray, 158
Tillyer, Henry Col. F., 138. Usually 'Tillier'.
Tilson, Samuel Cor. H., Lincoln, 45
Tirry, Christopher Lieut. H., L. & W., 82
Tirry, Roger Regt. Quart. H., L. & W., 63
Tirwhyt, ___ Capt. F., Earl of Northampton, 110
Tirwhytt, ___ Capt. F., Marquess of Newcastle, 109
Tirwhytt, John Capt. F., L. & W., Sir Matthew Appleyard, 13

Titchburne, ___ *Capt. F.*, 110
Todd, James Lieut. F., Surrey, 145
Todd, John Capt. Dr., Lincoln, 103
Todd, Thomas Ens. F., Durham, 80
Tolley/Tolly, Stephen Quart. H., Cornwall, 59
Tomkins, ___ *Capt. H.*, stray, 160
Tomkins, Edw. Lieut. F., Cornwall, 69
Tomkins, John Quart. Gen. F., Devon, 70
Tomkins, Thomas 'Quart. &c.', Stafford, stray, 165
Tomlin, Thomas Cor. H., York, 90
Tomlinson, John Capt. H., Lord Langdale, 90
Tomlinson, John Capt. H., Lord Mansfield, York, 100. P. R. Newman recounts how Tomlinson was wounded at Marston Moor and left for dead; a lady passing in her coach rescued him from the side of the road, and he recovered after treatment (*Marston Moor*, p. 126). Newman does not give his source for the story. Possibly the same John Tomlinson mentioned by an officer under Lord Langdale, above. Young states that he died in 1650 (p.247).
Tomlinson, Thomas Lieut. F., Somerset, 83
Tomlinson, William Quart. H., York, 27
Tommes, Richard Lieut. F., Dorset, 101
Tomms/Tommes, John Cor. H., York, stray, 159
Tompson, ___ *Capt. F.*, 27
Tong, William Cor. H., Nottingham, 100
Tonge, George Lieut. Col. H., 13, 79. Mentioned by one officer under George Heron, and two under Sir Francis Anderson, who took over the regiment after Heron's death. Of Denton, Northumberland.
Tonney/Tonny, Barnard Cor. H., Kent, 71
Tonstall, Thomas Ens. F., Lincoln, 150
Tonstall, William Capt. H., 27
Toogood, ___ *Capt. F.*, 112
Toogood, Edw. Quart. H., Somerset, 51
Tooly, Robert Cor. H., L. & W., 27
Tooly, Thomas Cor. H., L. & W., 27
Tootall, Oliver Lieut. F., Lancaster, 138
Topples, Ralph Quart. H., Derby, 59
Torack, William Ens. F., Cornwall, 70
Tottle, Jeffery Lieut. H., Berkshire, 106
Tourney, ___ *Col. F.*, 138. Reid names him as Edward Tourney.
Towerson, Erasmus Capt. H., Cumberland, 46
Towne, ___ *Capt. H.*, 108
Townesend/Townsend, Robert Lieut. F., L. & W., 51
Townsend, Ralph Capt. H., Wilts, 95
Townsend, Robert Quart. H., Norfolk, 144
Tozer, William Quart. F., Cornwall, 154
Trafford, Francis Col. H., L. & W., 9, 108, 138. A number of officers claim under

Trafford directly; he claims under the Marquess of Newcastle.
Traherne, ___ Lieut. Col. F., 143
Traherne/Trahern, James Ens. F., Hereford, 126
Traherne, Phil. Ens. F., Hereford, 143
Trant, Edward Ens. F., L. & W., 114
Trapps, Edward Cor. H., L. & W., 97
Trapps/Trappes, Henry Capt. F., L. & W., 32
Traughton/Troughton, Robert Cor. H., Northampton, 135
Trees, George Cor. H., Nottingham, 113
Tregascus, John Quart. H., Cornwall, 77
Tregellas, Abell Quart. H., Cornwall, 129
Treglawne, Matthew Ens. F., Cornwall, 15
Tregone, Reignald Capt. F., Cornwall, 20
Tregonnell, Thomas Col. H., 139
Tregonner, Andrew Ens. F., Cornwall, 140
Trelawny, Jonathan Col. F., 139
Tremayne, ___ Lieut. Col. F., 140
Tremayne, Degory Maj. F., 71
Tremayne, Lewis Col. F., 139
Tremayne, Phillip Capt. F., Cornwall, 139
Trenhale, George Ens. F., Cornwall, 122
Trenhick, Michael Ens. F., Cornwall, 70
Trenwith, Thomas Lieut. F., Cornwall, 69
Tresahar, Henry Cor. H., Cornwall, 72
Tresahar, James Comptroller, Cornwall, 170
Tresahar, Thomas Marshall General, L. & W., 171
Treswell, ___ Capt. H., 41
Treswell, ___ Capt. F., 145
Trevanion, Sir Charles Col. F., 140
Trevanion, John Col. H. (k. 1643; Bristol), 140
Trevillian/Trevillyan/Trevyllyan, Peter Maj. F., L. & W., 11, 102
Trevillyan, ___ Capt. F., Lord Gerard, 65
Trevillyan, ___ Capt. F., Thomas Walker, 145
Trevillyan, George Col. F., 140
Trevor, ___ Maj. H., 108
Trevor, Mark Col. H. (d. 1679) 140. Took over Lord Capel's first regiment of horse in 1643. Often 'Marcus Trevor'.
Trimme, George Secretary at War, Somerset, 172
Trimnell, William Capt. H., Leicester, 95
Trollop, Michael Lieut. Col. H., 29
Trollop, William Cor. H., Durham, 13
Trott, Robert, Chaplain, Kent, 174
Troutbeck, William Lieut. F., Cumberland, 47
Trowbridge, John Capt. F., Somerset, 140
Trowe, Gilbert Quart. H., Oxon, 124

Trueman, William Capt. F., York, 226
Trussell, John Lieut. H., Middlesex, 149
Trym/Trymm, John Cor. Dr., Cambridge, 146
Tucker, Charles Col. H., 140
Tucker, Mark Lieut. F., Cornwall, 20
Tucker, Joseph Ens. F., Cornwall, 15
Tudor, Thomas Lieut. H., L. & W., 109
Tudor, William Lieut. H., Cornwall, 23
Tuer, John Cor. H., L. & W., 128
Tufnell, Edw. Capt. H., Hertford, 97
Tuke, Samuel Maj. H.; later Col. H. (d. 1674), 36, 141, 156. Originally in Colonel Charles Cavendish's regiment (known as the Duke of York's horse). Tuke took over when Cavendish was killed at Gainsborough in 1643. One man claims Tuke as his officer under Cavendish, and another as his officer under the Duke of York; three more claim under Tuke directly.
Tuke, William Capt. Dr., Essex, 145
Tunstead, James Capt. Dr., Derby, 57
Turbervile, Francis Cor. H., Glamorgan, 91
Turbervile/Turbevile, Thomas Cor. H., Dorset, 133
Turges, Thomas Cor. H., Devon, 78
Turges, Tristram Capt. F., 83
Turner, ___ Maj. F., 127
Turner, ___ Capt. H., 108
Turner, Christopher Sea Capt., *Mary* fregat, Prince Rupert, L. & W., 167
Turner, Edward Quart. F., York, 60
Turner, John Lieut. H., York, 47
Turner, John Cor. H., L. & W., 104
Turner, Robert Marshall General, Devon, 171
Turner, Thomas Capt. H., 55
Turner, Thomas Lieut. H., L. & W., 45
Turner, William Capt. H., Berks, stray, 157
Turner, William Ens. F., Lancaster, 104
Turnpenny, Zach. Capt. F., 18
Turver, Thomas Lieut. H., Lancaster, stray, 158. Claims under a Capt. William Foxcraft, probably he of Sir Francis Middleton's regiment, which was raised in Lancashire.
Twaddell, Edmund Capt. H., Lancaster, 137
Twiggs/Twigges, Francis Lieut. F., Cornwall, 15
Twining/Twinning, William Lieut. H., Surrey, 150
Twisleton/Twissleton, John Capt. F., L. & W., 68
Twisse, Laurence Quart. F., Lancaster, 38
Twittey, Thomas Ens. F., Worcester, 121
Twydall, Arthur Quart. H., L. & W., 55
Tyack, Wilden Lieut. F., Cornwall, 20
Tye, John Capt. Lieut. F., Nottingham, 67

Tye, John Quart. H., Derby, 67
Tyler, John Cor. H., Monmouth, 149
Tyler, William Lieut. F., Hereford, 45
Tynt, Edw. Capt. H., 141
Tynt, Hugh ___ H., 141
Tynt, John Col. H. & F., 141
Typper, Nicholas Ens. F., Cornwall, 104
Tyre, William Capt. F., Southampton, 110
Tyrer, Humphry Capt. F., Worcester, 123
Tyrrell, Anthony Quart. H., L. & W., 114
Tyrrell, Sir Timothy ___ H. (d. 1701), 64, 141. Mentioned by one officer under Lord Gerard, and by one directly.
Tyrringham, Francis Capt. F., L. & W., 69
Tyrringham, Oliver Ens. F., Bucks, 16
Tyrringham, Sir William Col. H. (d. 1685), 141. Tyrringham is listed twice in the main list: one of these mentions may be an error for men claiming under his elder brother Sir John, who was also a colonel and died at Oxford in 1645.
Tyrwhyt, Edw. Lieut. Col. F., 61
Uffington, John Quart. H., Middlesex, 32
Ullathornes, Thomas Cor. H., Durham, 107
Ulting, Thomas Capt. F., Essex, 58
Underhill, John Ens. F., L. & W., 110
Underhill, Samuel Adjutant, L. & W., 170
Underhill, Thomas Lieut. H., L. & W., 18
Underwood, Thorp Quart. H., Kent, 100
Unthank, John Quart. H., Durham, 13
Unthank, William Capt. H., Durham, 44, 108; mentioned by a quartermaster under the Marquess of Newcastle; claims in his own right under the Earl of Crawford.
Upton, Arthur Capt. H., 50
Upton, John Ens. F., Cornwall, 115
Upton, John Quart. F., Devon, 13
Uriall, ___ Capt. F., 88. Young says k. Marston Moor (p.246).
Ursgat/Ursgate, John Quart. F., Salop, 110
Urwin, Robert Cor. H., Northumberland, 87
Urwin, Edw. Regt. Quart. Dr., Durham, 118
Usher, James Col. Dr. (k. 1643; Lichfield), 141
Uvedale, Edmund Maj. F., 73. I.O. prints as 'Vuedall'.
Valence/Vallence, Luke Quart. H., Derby, 75
Vampere, ___ ___ F., 141. Reid names as Henry Vampere.
Vangarish, John Capt. H., 44
Varley, William Ens. F., Devon, 24
Vasey, Thomas Lieut. H., Durham, 87
Vashmond, John Lieut. F., Cornwall, 104
Vaughan, ___ Lieut. Col. F., 105
Vaughan, ___ Capt. F., 132

Vaughan, Alban Quart. H., Merioneth, 147
Vaughan, Bithell Capt. F., Flint, 116
Vaughan, Evan Lieut. F., Denbigh, 155
Vaughan, Sir George Col. H., 141
Vaughan, Sir Henry Col. F. (d. 1660/1661), 142
Vaughan, Henry Lieut. H., Brecon, 116
Vaughan, Herbert Capt. H., 82
Vaughan, John Capt. F., Denbigh, 60
Vaughan, John Lieut. F., Denbigh, 61
Vaughan, Morgan Lieut. H., Radnor, 142
Vaughan, Richard Capt. F., Denbigh, 65
Vaughan, Robert Lieut. F., Denbigh, 152
Vaughan, Roger Capt. F., Monmouth, 33
Vaughan, Roger Capt. F., Middlesex, 153
Vaughan, Roger Quart. H., Chester, 140
Vaughan, Thomas Capt. F., 116
Vaughan, Sir William Col. H. & F. (k. 1649; Ireland), 142
Vaux, Gilbert Quart. H., Denbigh, 61
Vavasor, ___ Capt. H., 142
Vavasor, John Lieut. Col. H., 85
Vavasor, Robert Capt. F., York, 97
Vavasor, Thomas Maj. H., 27. Young says k. Marston Moor (p.245).
Vavasor, Thomas Cor. H., York, 129
Vavasor, Sir Walter Col. H., 142. Usually 'Vavasour'. Badly wounded at Selby in 1644 and subsequently went abroad. In December 1644 he wrote to Sir William Vavasor from abroad, explaining his predicament (*CSP Domestic, 1644-1645*, pp.197-198).
Vavasor, Sir William Col. H. & F. (k. 1659; Copenhagen), 143. Usually 'Vavasour'.
Vavasor, William Maj. H., 142
Veale, Thomas Col. F. (d. 1663/1664), 143
Veale, ___ Maj. F., 143
Venman, Thomas Lieut. F., Cornwall, 139
Venner, Roger Ens. F., Devon, 67
Vennor/Venner, John Lieut. H., Devon, 63
Ventris, ___ Maj. F., 142
Vere, Edward Col. H., 143
Vernatt, Abraham Capt. H., 125
Vernon, ___ Capt. H., 40
Vernon, Walter Capt. ___, 94
Verny/Verney, Francis Lieut. H., Lincoln, 112
Verrall/Verrell, Christopher Capt. F., Kent, stray, 163
Vicary, John Lieut. F., Somerset, 151
Vigors, Stephen Lieut. F., Cornwall, 24
Vigors, John Lieut. F., Cornwall, Sir Peter Courtenay, 43
Viguers/Vigors, John Lieut. F., L. & W., Lord John Berkly, 24

Vile, John Lieut. F., Devon, 24
Villequier, Isaac Lieut. F., L. & W., 88
Villiers, ___ Maj. F., 143. Reid identifies this officer as George Villiers.
Villiers, Edward Col. F. (d. 1689), 144. Younger brother of William, Lord Grandison.
Villiers, Robert Col. F., 144
Vincent, John Lieut. F., Cornwall, 101
Vincent, Richard Capt. H., York, 52
Vincent, Richard Lieut. F., Hereford, 126
Vine, Thomas Providor General, Durham, 169
Visack, William Deputy Quart., Cornwall, 172
Vivian, John Lieut. F., Cornwall, 140
Vivian, Sir Richard Col. F. (d. 1665), 144. Sometimes 'Vyvyan'.
Vivian, Richard Capt. H., Devon, 71.
Vokes, John Quart. H., Lincoln, stray, 160
Vokliere, ___ Capt. F., 76
Vosper, Thomas Ens. F., Cornwall, 104
Waad, John Cor. H., Warwick, 18
Waad, Samuel Lieut. Dr., Lincoln, 99
Waddam/Wadham, George Capt. F., L. & W., 102
Wade, James Capt. F., Glamorgan, 132
Wade, Thomas Lieut. H., York, 87
Wadeson, Thomas Lieut. F., L. & W., 17
Wadhall/Waddall, Peter Capt. Lieut. F., Northumberland, 152
Wadley/Wadly, John 'Comptroller and Master Gunner', Gloucester, 170
Waggstaffe, Sir Joseph Col. F. (d. 1666/1667), 144
Wainehouse/Wainhouse, John Lieut. H., Lancaster, 64
Wainwright, Francis Quart. H., L. & W., 124
Wainwright, John Lieut. F., Derby, 57
Waite, Henry Col. F., 144
Wake, Sir Baldwyn ___ ___, 144. A naval officer. Parliament summoned him for delinquency on 4th July 1642, and declared him unworthy of command (JHC, 2, 1640-1643, p.650). Accompanied Prince Charles to Jersey in 1646 (captained the royal frigate) and was knighted there (Manwaring, pp.311, 314).
Wake, Christopher Lieut. H., L. & W., 87
Wake, Sir John Col. H. (d. 1663), 144
Wake, Thomas Ens. F., Somerset, 151
Wake, Thomas Quart. H., York, 87
Wake, William Cor. H., Dorset, 155
Wakefield, ___ Capt. F., 145
Wakefield, Bold Ens. F., Southampton, 150
Wakefield, Giles Ens. F., Essex, 58
Wakefield, John Ens. F., Nottingham, 96
Wakeman, ___ Capt. H., 153
Walbanck/Walbank, Thomas Provost Marshall, York, 171
Waldron, Gideon Capt. F., 36

Waldron, Henry Cor. H., Leicester, 96
Waldron, John Capt. F., Somerset, Lord Hopton, 82
Waldron, John Capt. F., William Hopton, 84. Possibly the man above.
Waldron, Thomas Lieut. F., Somerset, 84
Waldron, William Lieut. F., L. & W., 66
Wales, Prince of – *see* Prince Charles
Walgrave, Sir Edward Col. H. (d. 1644; Oxford), 144. Usually 'Waldegrave'.
Walker, ___ Capt. F., 81
Walker, Francis Capt. F., 45
Walker, Henry Capt. H., Middlesex, 69
Walker, James Quart. H., York, 90
Walker, John Lieut. F., York, 126
Walker, John Quart. H., Worcester, 120
Walker, Lancelot Capt. F., Cumberland, Sir William Carleton, 33
Walker, Lancelot Capt. F., Cumberland, Henry Cheator, 38
Walker, Laurence Capt. F., 49
Walker, Marmion Capt. F., L. & W., 43
Walker, Phillip Col. F., 145
Walker, Richard Cor. Dr., Nottingham, 117
Walker, Steward Capt. H., L. & W., 124
Walker, Thomas Col. F., 145. Took over Lord Paulet's Foot after the death of its commander Sir Richard Cholmondly in 1644.
Walker, Thomas Capt. F., L. & W., 13
Wall, Bartholomew Lieut. F., Hereford, 45
Wall, Gregory Capt. F., 45
Wall, James Ens. F., L. & W., 16
Wall, John Ens. F., Cornwall, 128
Wallcot/Wallcott, Edward Capt. Lieut. H., Dorset, 50
Wallcot, William Capt. H., 72
Wallis, Richard Quart. H., Cornwall, 54
Walls, Edw. Quart. H., Cambridge, 115
Wallys/Willis, Richard Capt. Dr., Cornwall, 83
Walmsly, John Quart. H., Lancaster, 27
Walmsly, Richard Lieut. F., Stafford, 18
Walmsly, Thomas Ens. F., Lancaster, 138
Walmsly, William Capt. H., L. & W., 153
Walrond, George Lieut. F., L. & W., 110
Walsh – *see also* Welch
Walsh, ___ Capt. H., 74, 120. Mentioned by a lieutenant under Sir James Hamilton, and by a quartermaster under Sir William Russell, who took over Hamilton's regiment.
Walsh, ___ Capt. F., 143
Walsh, Edmund Cor. H., Somerset, 151
Walsh, Edw. Cor. H., L. & W., 145
Walsh, Henry Lieut. F., Somerset, 131

Index 355

Walsh, Sir Robert Col. H., L. & W., 9, 119, 141, 145. One man in Sir George Vaughan's horse claims Walsh as his officer; three give his name directly; Walsh himself claims as a colonel under Prince Rupert.
Walsh, Robert 'Commissary Train', L. & W., 169
Walsh, Stephen Quart. H., York, 99
Walsh, Thomas Capt. F., Somerset, 18
Walsh, Walter Lieut. H., L. & W., 145
Walter, ___ Capt. H., Sir Herbert Price, 116
Walter, ___ Capt. H., Sir Barnaby Scudamore, 126
Walter, David Col./Maj. Gen. H., 64, 145. Mentioned as a major general by one officer under Lord Gerard; and as a colonel by two other officers.
Walter, John Capt. H., 86
Walter, John Capt. F., stray, 164
Walter, John Quart. H., Oxon, 74
Walter, Peter Lieut. H., Somerset, 155
Walter, Robert Quart. F., Wilts, 85
Walter, Thomas Capt. H., Kent, Sir Barnaby Scudamore, 126
Walter, Thomas Capt. H., Kent, stray, 157. Possibly the man above.
Walter, Thomas Capt. F., 87
Walter, Thomas Lieut. F., Somerset, 83
Walter, Thomas Cor. H., York, 119
Walter, William Lieut. H., Monmouth, 86
Walters, ___ Maj. F., Sir Henry Cary, 36
Walters/Walter, Edmund Maj. F., Glamorgan, ___ Gamage, 11, 63
Walthal, ___ Capt. F., 149
Walthall, ___ Capt. H., 101
Walthall, Alexander Capt. H., Derby, stray, 157
Walthall, Peter Capt. F., 59
Waltham, John Capt. F., 36
Walton, George Quart. H., Durham, 26
Walton, William Lieut. Col. H. & F. (k. 1645; Naseby), 30, 31, 145, 161. Commanded Robert Byron's horse. Mentioned by men in both Lord John Byron's, and Col. Robert Byron's forces; by two officers directly; and a stray quartermaster.
Walwyn, ___ Capt. F., 120
Walwyn, Richard Ens. F., Hereford, 120
Walwyn, Thomas Capt. H., Huntingdon, 66
Wandsford, Francis Cor. H., Southampton, 40
Wanklen, ___ Maj. F., 127
Warberton, William Capt. F., Nottingham, 66
Warcopp/Warcoppe, Gervase Regt. Quart., Somerset, 51
Warcoppe, Samuel Capt. F., Middlesex, 92
Ward, Arthur Capt. F., Chester, 67
Ward, Christopher Ens. F., Durham, 53
Ward, Christopher Quart. H., Devon, 35
Ward, Francis, Commissary General, Derby, 169

Ward, Henry Capt. F., Westmorland, 123
Ward, John Capt. H., L. & W., 143
Ward, John Lieut. F., L. & W., 31
Ward, John Ens. F., Hereford, 94
Ward, Joseph Capt. F. (in York), Durham, 46
Ward, Marmaduke Capt. H., Durham, 81
Ward, Richard Capt. F., L. & W., 76
Ward, Robert Quart. H., Derby, stray, 161
Ward, Thomas Cor. H., Dorset, 50
Wardell, Richard Cor. H., York, 55
Warder, Edw. Capt. H., 113
Wardropper, John Lieut. Dr., York, 91
Warham, John Quart. Dr., Somerset, 83
Warham, Thomas Ens. F., Somerset, 131
Warham, William Capt. H., Somerset, 129
Waring, Edw. Quart. H., Middlesex, 137
Waring, Richard Lieut. H., Lancaster, 137
Warner, ___ Capt. H., Thomas Playters, 114
Warner, ___ Capt. H., Prince Rupert, 120
Warner, Henry Capt. H., Bedford, 92
Warner, Peter Ens. F., L. & W., 94. I.O. does not give an arm of service, but the rank of ensign indicates foot.
Warner, William Maj. H., 18
Warnock, Patrick 'Conductor of the Train', L. & W., 170
Warren, Henry Col. F., 145
Warren, Robert Maj. F., 37
Warren, Thomas ___ F., 145
Warren, Thomas Chirurgion, Chester, 173
Warren, Thomas Capt. F., 37
Warton – *see also* Wharton
Warton, Michael Capt. H., L. & W., stray, 157
Warwick, ___ Lieut. Col. H., 48
Warwick, Guy Cor. H., Cumberland, 48
Washburne, ___ ___ F., 145. Reid identifies him as Colonel John Washburne of Wichenford, Worcestershire.
Washington, Henry Col. Dr., 145. Several officers claim under him as horse or foot, but he only commanded dragoons; as dragoons were a combination of both, it was not uncommon that no distinction was made from the major arms.
Washington, John Regt. Quart. Dr., Warwick, 146
Wastnesse, John Lieut. F., York, 51
Waterhouse, Matthew Ens. F., York, 125
Waters, Thomas Cor. H., Lincoln, 112
Waterton, ___ Capt. F., 129
Watkin, Hopkin Ens. F., Glamorgan, 52
Watkins, ___ Capt. H., 120

Watkins, Thomas Cor. H., L. & W., stray, 159
Watmough, Laurence Cor. H., Lancaster, stray, 159
Wats/Watts, Robert Lieut. F., Dorset, 97
Watson, George Cor. H., L. & W., 120
Watson, John Maj. H., Sir John Girlington, 68
Watson, John Capt. H., Northumberland, Sir Francis Liddel, 93
Watson, John Lieut. H., Kent, 146
Watson, John Lieut. F., Durham, 89
Watson, Nicholas Lieut. Dr., L. & W., 145
Watson, Robert Maj. H., 92
Watson, Robert Lieut. Dr., Newcastle, 58
Watson, Robert Cor. H., York, 100
Watson, Robert Quart. H., L. & W., 85
Watts, Edw. Capt. H., 53
Watts, Sir John Col. F., 146. Commanded Chirk Castle garrison. Still in arms in 1648, at Colchester.
Watts, John Quart. H. 'to the Lifeguard', L. & W., 102
Watts, Richard Lieut. F., Leicester, 33
Wattson, John Cor. H., Lincoln, 20
Wawfer, William Lieut. H., L. & W., 77
Way, Richard Quart. H., Devon, 133
Wayes, Richard Capt. Lieut. H., Devon, 106
Wayte, John Lieut. F., Cornwall, 72
Weaver, Hatton Cor. H., Chester, 101
Weaver, James Cor. Dr., Hereford, 154
Weaver, Thomas Capt. ___, Hereford, 154. Weaver does not specify his arm of service.
Webb, ___ Capt. F., 31
Webb/Webbe, Benedict Quart. H., Somerset, stray, 160
Webb, Edward Cor. H., L. & W., 100
Webb, George Lieut. F., L. & W., 144
Webb, John Capt. H., 84
Webb, John Capt. H., Wilts, stray, 157
Webb, William Col. H., 146. German. Commanded the Lord Treasurer's horse, an Oxford garrison regiment.
Webb, William Capt. F., 24
Webb/Webbe, William Cor. H., Westmorland, 37
Webbe, ___ Maj. H., 59
Webbe/Webb, Francis Lieut. F., L. & W., 84
Webber, John Ens. F., L. & W., stray, 165
Webber, Matthew Lieut. F., Berks, stray, 164
Webber, Robert Capt. F., Devon, 24
Webber, Samuel Quart. H., Devon, 78
Webster, Robert Regt. Quart. F., Cumberland, 106
Wedgegood/Wedgewood, Giles Quart. H., L. & W., 150
Weekes, Simon Capt. F., 13

Weeks, ___ Capt. H., stray, 159
Weeks, John Chirurgion, Devon, 173
Weeks, Richard Capt. H., 110
Weeks, Richard Capt. F., 72
Weeks, Richard Lieut. F., Cornwall, 140
Weeks, William Lieut. F., Cornwall, 72
Weightman, Cutbert Quart. H., Northumberland, 148
Welborne, Robert Lieut. H., York, 38
Welby, Phillip Col. Dr., 146
Welch – *see also* Walsh
Welch/Walsh, Thomas Quart. H., Kent, 41
Weld, Alexander Lieut. H., Chester, 101
Welham/Wellham, John Lieut. F., Suffolk, 25
Wellfoot, ___ Capt. H., 56
Wells, Henry Capt. H., 44
Wells, John, Commissary, Somerset, 169
Wells, Samuel Cor. H., Bedford, 40
Wells, Thomas Lieut. F., Oxon, 127
Wells, Thomas 'Bridge Master', Surrey, 170
Wellstead, George Cor. H., L. & W., 108
Wels/Wells, Swithen Lieut. H., Southampton, stray, 158
Wentworth, [Matthew] Maj. H., 125
Wentworth, Sir George Col. F. (d. 1660), 146
Wentworth, Michael Lieut. H., York, 125
Wentworth, [Thomas] Lord, Col. H. & Dr. (d. 1665), 146
Werden, [Robert] Maj./Lt. Col. H. (d. 1690), 101, 147. Werden's first name is known from other sources. Mentioned as a major in John Marrow's regiment; later lieutenant colonel, took over the regiment after Marrow's death in 1644. A number of men claim under him directly.
Werden, William Lieut. F., Lancaster, 138
Wesled, ___ Capt. H., 112
Wesled, Thomas Cor. H., Lincoln, 112
West, Charles Maj. F., 58
West, Cromwell Capt. F., Berks, 25
West, Henry Cor. H., Cumberland, 84
West, John Lieut. H., York, 108
West, John Quart. H., Nottingham, 55
West, Marmaduke Quart. H., York, 88
West, William Lieut. F., L. & W., 21
Westbrook, John Cor. H., Southampton, 62
Westby, Charles Capt. H., Lancaster, 137
Westby, George Capt. H., L. & W., 137, 161. Claims under Sir Thomas Tildesly; also mentioned by a stray Lancaster quartermaster.
Westby, Robert Capt. H., Lancaster, 138
Westby, William Maj. H., 40

Westcot/Wescott, Robert Lieut. F., Devon 24
Westcott/Wescott, John Ens. F., Devon, 130. I.O. does not give an arm of service, but the rank of ensign indicates foot.
Westgarth, Anthony Cor. H., Newcastle, 61
Westly, Thomas Capt. H., 89
Weston, Cornelius Lieut. F., Somerset, 16
Weston, Humphry Quart. H., Surrey, 145
Weston, Ralph Capt. H., Stafford, 41
Weston, Ralph Ens. F., Carmarthen, 130
Weston, Richard Lieut. F., Chester, 31
Westwood, Edw. Quart. H., Essex, stray, 160
Westwood, Jonas Capt. H., 77
Wettinghall, Christopher Capt. F., York, 60
Whaley/Whalley, William Ens. F., L. & W., stray, 165
Whare, John Capt. H., Cornwall, 19
Whare, Samuel Lieut. F., Cornwall, 14
Wharton – *see also* Warton
Wharton, ___ Capt. F., Thomas Blague, 25
Wharton, ___ Capt. H., Sir Hugh Cholmly, 38
Wharton, ___ Capt. H., Thomas Slingsby, 129
Wharton, Abraham Capt. F., Lincoln, 67
Wharton, Christopher Capt. H., Nottingham, 149
Wharton, John Capt. H., L. & W., 95
Wharton, Richard Lieut. F., L. & W., stray, 164. Claims from London but noted as 'in Jersey'.
Wharton, Richard Cor. H., York, 155
Wharton, Robert Capt. Lieut. H., Oxon, 46
Wharton, William Capt. H., Lord Langdale, Westmorland, 90
Wharton, William Capt. F., Henry Cheator, L. & W., 38
Wheat, John Quart. H., Lincoln, 25
Wheatly, Daniel Quart. H., Southampton, 128
Wheatly, Drew Quart. F., Wilts, 127
Wheatly, Edw. Capt. F., York, 147
Wheatly, Francis Capt. F., York, 147
Wheatly, John Quart. H., Bucks, stray, 160
Wheatly, Thomas Col. F., 146. Lieutenant colonel to Sir John Redman's Foot; took over the regiment after Redman's death in 1645.
Wheatly, Thomas Capt. F., York, 147
Wheeler, ___ ___ F., 147
Wheeler, Thomas Lieut. F., Kent, 138. Served in 1648.
Whelland, ___ Capt. H., 36
Whelpdale, John Capt. F., 47
Whelpdale, Thomas ___ F., 33
Whichalls, Robert Cor. H., Devon, 50
Whinyates, John Capt. Lieut. H., Derby, 75

Whinyates, Richard Cor. H., Derby, 75
Whistler, John Cor. H., Southampton, 23
Whitchcote, ___ Lieut. Col. H., stray, 160
Whitchcote, ___ Capt. H., 56
Whitchcott, Edw. Capt. H., 25
White, ___ Capt. H., 100
White, Edw. Ens. F., Dorset, 62
White, Edward Quart. Gen. H., L. & W., stray, 160. *Mercurius Civicus* lists him as a prisoner at Arundel in January 1644, as 'Quarter-master-generall of Col. Bamfields Regiment' (TT E.81[22]).
White, George Lieut. Dr., L. & W., Sir Thomas Aston, 17
White, George Lieut. H., Somerset, Sir Lewis Dives, 51
White, George Cor. H., L. & W., stray, 159
White, George Cor. Dr., Salop, 73
White, Gerard Capt. F., L. & W., 120
White, Henry Capt. Lieut. F., L. & W., 88
White, James Lieut. F., Essex, 57. An addition from the errata.
White, John Capt. H., Wilts, 43
White, Jonathan Cor. H., York, 38
White, Richard Ens. F., Cornwall, 140
White, Robert Capt. F., 100
White, Robert Lieut. H., Nottingham, 95
White, Robert Lieut. F., Oxon, 127
White, Thomas Lieut. H., Sussex, 13
White, Thomas Cor. H., Dorset, 82
White, William 'Commissary Train', L. & W., 169
Whitechurch/Whitchurch, William Lieut. H., Devon, 50
Whitehead, Francis Capt. H., Berks, 16
Whitehead, William Quart. H., York, 80
Whitehead, William, Commissary General, Southampton, 169
Whiteside, John Lieut. F., Lancaster, 138
Whitfield, Arthur Quart. H., Durham, 73
Whitfield, David Quart. F., Devon, 19
Whitfield, John Capt. F., Westmorland, 39
Whitfield, Richard Quart. H., Northumberland, stray, 160. Claims under Sir Edward Charleton, who is also mentioned by officers under Sir Edward Widrington.
Whitfield, Robert Capt. H., Cumberland, 137
Whitford, David Capt. F., L. & W. (d. 1674), 114
Whitgrave, Humphrey Capt. F., Essex, 94
Whitehead, William Quart. H., York, 80
Whitley, John Capt. H., Flint, stray, 157
Whitly/Whitley, William Quart. H., L. & W., 46
Whitney, William Lieut. H., Essex, 109
Whitny/Whitney, Courteen Capt. H., 133
Whittingham, Henry Lieut. F., Wilts, 66

Whittingham, Thomas Ens. F., Lancaster, 138
Whittington, Luke Capt. H., L. & W., 68
Whittington, Mark Capt. H., 68
Whittly, Roger Col. H. & F., 147
Whittly, Thomas ___ F., 147
Whittmore, Sir Thomas ___ H. (d. 1653), stray, 160
Whittorn, Christopher Capt. Lieut. F., Pembroke, 81
Whittorn, George Capt. Lieut. H., Gloucester, 53
Whittorne/Whittorn, Conway Capt. F., Gloucester, 121
Wickham, John Cor. H., L. & W., 134
Wickham, Thomas Cor. H., Somerset, 28
Wicks/Wickes, Thomas Lieut. H., L. & W., 45
Wickstead, Charles Quart. H., Chester, 101
Widrington [Sir William] Lord, Col. H., F. & Dr. (k. 1651; Wigan Lane), 148. Usually 'Widdrington'.
Widrington, Sir Edward Col. H. (d. 1671), 147, 148. Usually 'Widdrington'. Commanded a brigade. Besides his own officers, is mentioned by a quartermaster under Lord (William) Widrington, presumably serving in a brigade capacity.
Widrington/Widdington, Oswald Lieut. H., Hereford, 126
Widdrington, ___ Lieut. Col. F., stray, 164
Widdrington, ___ Capt. H., 35
Widdrington/Widdington, Francis Lieut. H., Nottingham, 69
Widdrington, Francis Cor. H., Northumberland, 35
Widdrington, Henry Capt. Lieut. H., Northumberland, 147
Widdrington, Michael Capt. Dr., Northumberland, 146
Widdrington, William Cor. H., Northumberland, 148
Wiggemore/Wiggmore, Daniel Cor. H., Lincoln, 97
Wiggemore/Wiggmore, John Lieut. H., Hereford, 153
Wiggly, Edw. Lieut. H., Leicester, stray, 158
Wigmore/Wiggmore, Richard Lieut. Col. F., L. & W., 10, 42
Wigmore/Wiggmore, Robert Lieut. Col. H., L. & W., 10, 71
Wilcocks/Wilcox, William Lieut. H., Wilts, 81
Willcocks/Wilcox, William Cor. H., Rutland, 75
Wilcox, Robert Quart. H., Stafford, 18
Wild – *see also* Wyld
Wild, ___ Maj. H., Samuel Sandys, 124
Wild, John Ens. F., Oxon, 127
Wild, Thomas Maj. F., stray, 165
Wilde, John Maj. H., Edward Dyer, 53
Wilkins, John Quart. H., L. & W., 130
Wilkinson, ___ Capt. H., 62
Wilkinson, ___ Capt. Dr., 40
Wilkinson, Anthony Capt. H., L. & W., 104
Wilkinson, Edw. Lieut. H., York, 90
Wilkinson, George Lieut. H., Cumberland, 107

Wilkinson, John Cor. H., Lincoln, 104
Wilkinson, John Ens. F., Derby, 51
Wilkinson, Oswald Cor. H., Northumberland, 73
Wilkinson, Ralph Cor. H., Durham, 68
Wilkinson, William Lieut. H., Durham, 136
Wilkinson, William Quart. H., Lancaster, 121
Wilks/Wilkes, John Quart. F., Stafford, 17
Wilks/Wilkes, Roger, Marshall, Stafford, 171
Wilks/Wilkes, William Lieut. F., Stafford, stray, 164
Willford, Thomas Lieut. H., L. & W., 149
William/Williams, David Ens. F., Brecon, 116
William/Williams, Meredith Lieut. F., Brecon, 116
Williams, ___ Lieut. Col. F., 142
Williams, ___ Maj. H., 141
Williams, ___ Maj. F., 152
Williams, Andrew Ens. F., L. & W., 152
Williams, Arnold Ens. F., Glamorgan, 97
Williams, Edmund Ens. F., Carnarvon, stray, 165
Williams, Edw. Maj. H., 44
Williams, Edw. Lieut. F., Flint, 106
Williams, Edw. Ens. F., Pembroke, 87
Williams, Edw. Cor. Dr., Montgomery, 26
Williams, Francis Capt. F., L. & W., 61
Williams, George Lieut. H., Pembroke, 91
Williams, George Ens. F., Cornwall, 15
Williams, Griffith Capt. F., Carmarthen, 65
Williams, Henry Capt. F., Dorset, 19
Williams, Henry Lieut. F., Northampton, 83
Williams, Henry Quart. H., Monmouth, 149
Williams, James Lieut. H., York, 143
Williams, John Capt. F., Denbigh, 155
Williams, John Lieut. H., Somerset, 79
Williams, Peter Capt. F., Flint, stray, 163
Williams, Richard Lieut. F., Pembroke, 65
Williams, Richard Lieut. F., Worcester, 121
Williams, Richard Cor. H., Somerset, 131
Williams, Richard Ens. F., Denbigh, 65
Williams, Richard Quart. H., Carmarthen, 64
Williams, Roger Capt. F., Salop, 61
Williams, Roger Quart. H., Bucks, 151
Williams, Roger Lieut. H., Glamorgan, 114
Williams, Stradling Ens. F., Glamorgan, 116
Williams, Thomas Lieut. F., Monmouth, 78
Williams, Thomas Lieut. F., Carmarthen, 96
Williams, Thomas Cor. H., Brecon, 44

Williams, Thomas Cor. H., L. & W., 134
Williams, Thomas Ens. F., Carmarthen, Thomas Floyd, 61. I.O. does not give an arm of service, but the rank of ensign indicates foot.
Williams, Thomas Ens. F., Carmarthen, Sir Henry Vaughan, 142
Williams, Sir Trevor Col. H. & F. (d. 1692), 149. Reid notes that Williams switched to the Parliament's side in 1645; he switched back in 1648.
Williams, Walter Lieut. H., Monmouth, 82
Williams, Walter Cor. H., Hereford, 150
Williams, William Capt. F., Cornwall, 140
Williams, William Capt. F., stray, 164, 165. Mentioned by two stray Pembroke officers.
Williams, William Lieut. F., Monmouth, Richard Donnell, 52
Williams, William Lieut. F., Monmouth, Sir Charles Kemys, 87
Williams, William Cor. H., Cornwall, 50
Williams, William Ens. F., Glamorgan, 99. I.O. does not give an arm of service, but Williams' rank of ensign indicates foot.
Williams, William Quart. H., Dorset, 133
Williams, William 'Muster Master', Northampton, 169
Williamson, ___ Capt. F., 89
Williamson, Thomas Ens. F., Durham, 89
Williscot/Willyscott, Edw. Lieut. H., Hereford, 126
Willmot, John Lieut. F., L. & W., 31
Willoughby, [   ] Lord, ___ F., 149. This man is probably Montagu Bertie, Lord Willoughy d'Eresby (and 2nd Earl of Lindsey). There is a chance he is Francis Willoughby, Lord Willoughby of Parham, a Parliamentarian who defected to the King and fought for him thereafter; however, once with the King he became a naval man and is not known to have commanded any foot troops.
Willoughby, Andrew Quart. F., Cornwall, 86
Willoughby, Christopher Capt. Lieut. H., Dorset, 51
Willoughby, Richard Cor. H., Somerset, 113
Wills, ___ Col. H., 150
Wills, John Capt. H., 24
Wills/Willys, John Lieut. H., Cornwall, 23
Wills, John Quart. F., Monmouth, 87
Willy, ___ Maj. H., 71
Willy, Theophilus Cor. H., Cornwall, 45
Willy, Ralph Capt. F., Durham, 38
Willys, George Ens. F., York, stray, 165
Willys, Henry Lieut. F., Somerset, 117
Willys, John Ens. F., Somerset, 131
Willys, Sir Richard Col. H. (d. 1690), 149. I.O. does not give an arm of service for Sir Richard or his men, but he is known to have been a cavalry officer.
Willys, William Lieut. Col. H., 149. Brother of Sir Richard Willys and deputy of his regiment of horse.
Wilmot, [Henry] Viscount, Col. H. (d. 1658), 150
Wilsford, Edward ___ H., 150

Wilson, ___ Capt. H., 143
Wilson, ___ Capt. F., 107
Wilson, Abraham Ens. F., Wilts, 73
Wilson, Charles Maj. H., 69
Wilson, Christopher Capt. H., 25
Wilson, James Lieut. F., York, 68
Wilson, Jeremy Cor. H., York, 34
Wilson, John Lieut. Dr., Gloucester, 81
Wilson, Richard Cor. H., York, 36
Wilson, Robert Lieut. F., Nottingham, 88
Wilson, Thomas Capt. H., York, 142
Wilson, Thomas Lieut. F., Cumberland, 48
Wilson, William Cor. H., Lincoln, 128
Wilson, William Quart. H., Durham, 41
Wilson, William Quart. H., Wilts, 95
Wilston, Henry Lieut. F., Devon, 37
Wiltsheere/Wiltshire, John Lieut. F., Somerset, 82
Wiltshire, ___ Capt. H., 17
Wiltshire, Richard Lieut. Col. H., 116
Wincheppe, Roger Capt. F., L. & W., 17
Winchester, [John Paulet] 5th Marquess of, Col. H. & F. (d. 1675), 150
Winckly, Thomas Capt. H., 137
Wind, Robert Capt. F., L. & W., 112
Wind, Robert Capt. F., L. & W., 112. Two identical individuals listed side by side in this regiment; the second is almost certainly a duplicate.
Windebank, Francis Col. H. (executed 1644), 151. Shot at Oxford for the surrender of Bletchingdon House garrison.
Winder, Peter Cor. H., Cumberland, 47
Windham – *see also* Wyndham
Windham, Francis Col. F., 151
Windham, Sir Hugh Col. H. (d. 1684), 151
Windle, Jasper Lieut. H., Gloucester, 81
Windsor, [Thomas Hickman-Windsor] Lord, [Capt.] H. (d. 1687), 151. Hickman-Windsor served in Shropshire and was captured at Naseby. I.O. does not offer a rank, but he is known to have been cavalry captain in 1642, aged fifteen, and according to Symonds (ed. Long, p.12) was later lieutenant colonel to Colonel Samuel Sandys. Created 7th Baron Windsor in 1660, and Earl of Plymouth in 1682.
Windsor, ___ Capt. H., 64
Wine, ___ Lieut. Col. F., 88. Reid believes this to be Thomas Wynne.
Wingfield, ___ Capt. F., 113
Wingfield, John Cor. H., Rutland, 24
Winnington, ___ Maj. F., 84
Winnington, Francis Capt. H., Salop, 37
Winslade, James Lieut. F., Cornwall, 20

Winter, Francis Quart. H., Somerset, 151
Winter, George Cor. H., Durham, 148
Winter, Henry Capt. F., Somerset, 131
Winter, John Quart. H., Somerset, 131
Winter, Thomas Cor. H., L. & W., 79
Winter, William Capt. H., Dorset, 41
Winterscale, Michael Lieut. F., York, 135
Wintle, Samuel Lieut. F., 79
Wintour, Sir John Col. F. (d. 1676 or later), 152
Wintour, William Col. F., 9, 151. Requests inclusion but no location given.
Winwood, ___ Capt. H., 93
Winwood, Arthur Lieut. H., 93
Winwood, Ralph Quart. H., 93
Wisdom/Wisedome, William Quart. H., Northampton, 109
Wise, Edw. Lieut. F., Oxon, 21
Wise, John Lieut. Dr., York, 99
Wise, Matthew Col. F., 152
Wise, Metcalf/Metcalfe Capt. H., York, 21
Wise, William Ens. F., Cornwall, stray, 165
Wiseman, Samuel Ens. F., L. & W., 109
Withes, John Lieut. F., York, 100
Wivall/Wyvall, Duke Capt. F., Sussex, 16
Wolsley, Devereux ___ H. & F. (d. 1648), 152. Several genealogical sources give his date of death as 1648, aged 31, but none state the cause.
Wombwell, ___ Capt. F., 67. I.O. spells as 'Womtwell', almost certainly a misprint.
Womersly, John Quart. H., York, 97
Wood, Basil Capt. H., Oxon, 30
Wood, Bowyer Lieut. H., Essex, 115
Wood, Henry Cor. H., Salop, 119
Wood, John Cor. H., Oxon, 134
Wood, John Quart. H., Surrey, 134
Wood, Phineas Quart. H. (Brigade), York, 84
Wood, Robert Capt. Dr., L. & W., 75
Wood, Robert Lieut. H., Nottingham, 69
Wood, Thomas Capt. H., York, 47
Wood, Thomas Cor. H., York, 86
Wood, Thomas Quart. H., Durham, 61
Wood, Tobias Capt. H., Essex, 34
Woodcock, Thomas Capt. H., 82
Woodfield, David Lieut. H., Oxon, stray, 158
Woodhall, ___ Capt. Dr., 73
Woodhall, Thomas ___ H., 152
Woodhall/Woodall, Thomas Cor. H., L. & W., 109
Woodhouse, John Capt. F., Durham, 42
Woodhouse, Sir Michael Col. F., 152. Regiment known as Prince Charles's Foot.

Woodington, Henry Capt. H., Berks, 59
Woodman, Charles Lieut. H., Surrey, 100
Woodman, Thomas Cor. H., Surrey, 134
Woodrow, ___ Capt. F., 125
Woodrow/Woodrowe, Joseph Ens. F., York, 125
Woodward, ___ Capt. H., 108
Woodward, John Lieut. H., L. & W., 109
Woodward, Richard Maj. F., L. & W., 11, 156
Woogan, Edward Col. H., 152. Usually 'Wogan'. English Royalist regiment in Scotland in 1654.
Woogan, Thomas Ens. F., Worcester, 120
Woolland, Robert Cor. H., Leicester, 111
Woolgrove, John Quart. H., L. & W., 136
Woolrich, Henry Capt. F., York, 146
Woolrick, Sir Thomas Col. F. (d. 1668), 153. Usually 'Woolrych'.
Woolscot/Woollscott, Thomas Cor. H., L. & W., 36
Woolverston/Wolverston, John Capt. F., L. & W., 22
Wootton, William Quart. H., Warwick, 109
Worcester, [Henry Somerset] 1ˢᵗ Marquess of, Col. H. & F. (d. 1646), 153
Worker, William Quart. H., York, 90
Worly/Worley, Thomas Capt. F., L. & W., 76
Worly/Worley, Thomas Lieut. F., L. & W., 76
Worrall, George Lieut. F., L. & W., 65
Worsdall/Worsdale, Richard Ens. F., Nottingham, 51
Worsley, Jeroboam Lieut. H., Salop, 121
Worsly, John Cor. H., York, 102
Worsopp/Worsop, Walter Maj. F., L. & W., 11, 97
Worthington, Thomas Quart. H., Lancaster, 34
Wortley, Sir Francis Col. H., F. & Dr. (d. 1652), 154
Wraughton, James Col. Dr., 154. Commanded a second arm, but the claiming officer does not specify whether it was foot or horse.
Wray, Sir Chichester Col. F. (d. 1668), 154. Also, 'Wrey'.
Wray, George Col. F., 154
Wray, Jonathan Lieut. F., Nottingham/York, 51, 67. Wray claims under Sir John Digby, and also Anthony Gilby, who later commanded Digby's regiment.
Wray, William Capt. F., Cornwall, 154
Wren/Wrenn, Henry Capt. F., Durham, 136
Wren, Lyndly Lieut. Col. F., 80
Wrench, William Lieut. F., Gloucester, 143
Wrentmore, John Lieut. F., Somerset, 83
Wright, ___ Capt. H., 96
Wright, Alexander Cor. H., York, 73
Wright, Anthony Lieut. H., York, 98
Wright, Anthony Cor. H., Lincoln, 112
Wright, Cholmly Capt. F., Durham, 38

Wright, Christopher Ens. F., L. & W., 89
Wright, Edw. Capt. F., Lincoln, 99
Wright, George Lieut. H., Leicester, stray, 158
Wright, Henry Lieut. H., York, 73
Wright, Henry Quart. F., York, 129
Wright, Hustthwayte/Husthwaite Maj. H., L. & W., 46, 112. Mentioned at the rank of captain by a Lincoln cornet under Sir William Pelham; claims himself as a major under James Cromwell, who had taken over Sir Richard Willys's regiment in November 1645.
Wright, John Capt. F., L. & W., 42
Wright, John Ens. F., York, 49
Wright, John Sea Capt., L. & W., 167
Wright, John Chirurgion, L. & W., 173
Wright, Richard Lieut. F., Chester, 64
Wright, Richard Lieut. F., York, 91
Wright, Robert Lieut. H., Chester, Sir Thomas Aston, 17
Wright, Robert Lieut. H., York, Sir Thomas Aston, 17
Wright, Robert Quart. F., York, 117
Wright, Thomas ___ H., Newcastle, 70. Wright's rank appears as '&c.' under Kenelm Digby, a general of ordnance. Possibly '&c.' indicated that Wright held a similar role.
Wright, Thomas Capt. H., 112
Wright, Thomas Capt. F., 100
Wright, Thomas Lieut. F., Newcastle, 100
Wright, Thomas Cor. H., Nottingham, 75
Wright, Thomas Cor. H., Durham, 142
Wright, William Lieut. F., L. & W., 145
Wyat, Thomas Lieut. F., Cornwall, 15
Wyatt/Wyat, Benjamin Capt. H., Somerset, 151. Mentioned by an officer under Sir Hugh Windham; claims for himself under Sir Francis Windham.
Wyber, Thomas Cor. H., Cumberland, 89
Wyborn, John Ens. F., Kent, 133
Wyche, Richard Cor. H., Lincoln, 135
Wyche, Robert Ens. F., Lincoln, 135
Wyld/Wild, Richard Cor. H., Nottingham, 60
Wyndham – *see also* Windham
Wyndham, Edmond Col. H., F. & Dr., 155
Wyndly, Robert Quart. H., Surrey, 118
Wynne, Cadwallader Lieut. F., Denbigh, 28
Wynne, Ellis Quart. H., Denbigh, 156
Wynne, Francis Cor. H., L. & W., 70
Wynne, Hugh Col. F., 155
Wynne, Hugh Lieut. F., Anglesey, 118
Wynne, Humphry Lieut. F., Anglesey, 111
Wynne, John Lieut. F., Denbigh, 156

Wynne, Matthew Capt. F., Denbigh, 155
Wynne, Owen Ens. F., Denbigh, 156
Wynne, Robert Lieut. Col. F., 155
Wynne, Robert Capt. F., 111
Wynne, Robert Lieut. F., Denbigh, 123
Wynne, Robert Ens. F., Carnarvon, 156
Wynne, Thomas Lieut. Col. F., stray, 164
Wynne, Thomas Lieut. F., Carmarthen, 111
Wynne, William Col. H. & F., 156
Wynne, William Capt. F., John Robinson, 118
Wynne, William Capt. F., Carmarthen, Edward Gerard, 66
Wynne, William Capt. F., Flint, Sir Roger Mostyn, 105
Wynne, William Capt. F., Carnarvon, stray, 163
Wyvall, Edw. Capt. H., Cumberland, 138
Yale, Thomas Capt. F., Denbigh, 60
Yarborow, ___ Capt. H., 79
Yarmouth, Edmund Ens. F., Middlesex, 21
Yate/Yale, Robert, Commissary, Flint, 169
Yates, Thomas Ens. F., Lancaster, 138
Yeabsley/Yeabsly, John Lieut. H., Devon, 77
Yeo, Humphry Capt. H., Cornwall, 36
Yeo, Robert Capt. F., L. & W., 24
Yeomans, Richard Capt. F., 83
Yeord, ___ Capt. H., 90
Yngs, Richard Cor. H., Somerset, 43
York, Duke of, Col. H., 156. York did not personally command the regiment.
York, Edw. Quart. H., L. & W., 70
Young, ___ Capt. F., 153
Young, Evan Lieut. F., Monmouth, 83
Young, Gabriel Capt. F., Surrey, 66
Young, John Capt. H., Salop, 43
Young, John Capt. F., L. & W., 65
Young, Richard Capt. Lieut. F., Berks, stray, 164
Young, Richard Sea Capt. 'of the *Greyhound*', L. &. W., 167
Young, Robert Ens. F., Hereford, 154
Young, Robert Quart. H., Dorset, 82
Young, William Capt. F., 66
Young, William Lieut. H., Berks, 23
Young, William Cor. H., York, 38
Young, William Quart. H., Durham, 120
Zacherly, Sampson Capt. F., Cornwall, 14
Zouch, ___ Capt. F., 156
Zouch, Edw. Capt. H., 36
Zouch, James ___ H., 156
Zouch, James Capt. F., Lancaster, 50